THE NEARLY PERFECT STORM

An American Financial and Social Failure

UYLESS BLACK

THE NEARLY PERFECT STORM
An American Financial and Social Failure
BY
UYLESS BLACK

2013 Lightning Source Edition

Available at on-line booksellers and local bookstores

Communicate with the author at:
www.UylessBlack.com, Blog.UylessBlack.com
or BlacksStreets@gmail.com

Additional works by Uyless Black are available at:
www.UylessBlack.com

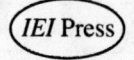

IEI Press

Information and Entertainment Institute
9323 N. Government Way, #301
Hayden, Idaho 83835

Library of Congress Control Number: 2012911460
ISBN 13: 978-0-9800107-5-6
ISBN 10: 0-9800107-5-6

Copyright © 2012 Uyless Black
All rights reserved

Cover & Book Design by
Arrow Graphics, Inc.
info@arrow1.com
Printed in the United States of America

Dedication

To the small business owners of the world. In spite of the odds stacked against them, they continue to practice the best aspects of capitalism.

Recent and upcoming books by Uyless Black
See pages 441–442 for essays and other books

Lea County Museum Press
The Light Side of Little Texas

SAMS
Teach Yourself Networking in 24 Hours

IEI Press
A Swimmer's Odyssey: From the Plains to the Pacific
The Nearly Perfect Storm: An American Financial and Social Failure
The Deadly Trinity (revision available mid 2013)
Networking 101: An Introduction to the Internet and Social Networking (revision available 2013)
My Capital, My America (available 2014)
Cold Wars, Hot Wars and America's Warm War (available 2014)

Contents

Preface		vii
Forewarned		ix
Notes About the Text		xv
Acknowledgments		xix

Part I: Reports

1	Setting the Stage	3
2	Rules of Life and Finance	22
3	Risk and Debt	36
4	Eight Nails in the Meltdown Coffin	60
5	Modeling the Meltdown	73
6	Looping Along to Financial Disaster: A Review	84
7	Uncle Sam: Asleep at the Wheel or Driving too Fast?	90
8	Financial Weapons of Mass Destruction	119
9	Greed, Stupidity, and the Herd Rule	154
10	Alice in Mortgage Land	168
11	Media Distortions	183
12	Surveying the Landscape: What's Next?	194
13	Sobering Statistics for Financial Rock Stars	202
14	The Mortgage Market and Regulation	216
15	Give Me Liberty and Give Me Bailouts: No Creative Destruction Please!	221
16	Other Pieces to the Meltdown Puzzle	228
17	Investment Banks, Underwriting, and Goldman Sachs	237
18	Financial Reform: Putting the Wrappings around Legislation	254
19	Synthetic Capitalism	269
20	Financial Cabals	278
21	Wrapping Up the Reports	285

Part II: Reflections

22	The Storm's Aftermath	299
23	Income Disparity and Freedom of Speech	312
24	Corrupting Influences	330
25	The Rule of Law, Its Misrule, and Resultant Loss of Faith	346
26	Debt and Responsibility	365
27	A Broken System	384
28	Fixing a Broken System	394
29	The Invisible Hand and the Visible Mind	401

Readers' Comments on Part I	408
Banking Experience of Uyless Black	419
Bibliography	423
Index	429

PREFACE

In *The Nearly Perfect Storm: An American Financial and Social Failure*, I do not offer new revelations about financial theory or disclosures about dreamlike computer models of Wall Street's operations. I offer a look at aspects of human behavior in relation to this financial debacle and the broader scope of America's social and political ills. For this book, we take a short step away from Darwin in barefoot to Darwin in Guccis. In many instances, it will not make for pleasant reading.

* * *

An objection several online readers expressed about Part I of this book is my taking issue with the federal government using borrowings and taxpayer money to rescue insurance companies, car companies, and banks. They claim Uncle Sam will get this money back. I agree that these companies will likely find ways to gain credit and recapitalize, and I also agree with these readers who said the bailout—however noxious—was essential. The U.S. government might break even or make a profit from its rescues.

I remain steadfast in my criticism because these bailouts distort the roles that government and commerce should play in a free market society. In many circumstances, partnerships between Uncle Sam and business make sense. But scores of government/business relationships that have emerged over the past few decades are counter-productive and dangerous to our society. In Part I, and especially Part II of this book, I set forth this assertion with examples I hope will raise your ire and lead you to action.

I remain an advocate of the notion that government and private enterprise are natural enemies. Nonetheless, the economic strength of a nation rests on its public and private leaders accepting that mutual assertion *and* restraint—applicable to both parties—are essential to a vibrant democracy.

I am aware this sentiment is not entirely realistic. Government and private enterprise are foreordained to lock into combat with one another, often without giving or granting quarter.

Nonetheless, where one loses, the other prevails, often to the disadvantage of our Republic and its citizens. Therein lies the challenge to America: to achieve a balance between these two adversaries.

Forewarned

I am not a practicing professional in the fields of banking and finance. Like most citizens, I have been affected by America's big recession. Being curious by nature and wondering why my bank accounts were not paying enough interest to compensate for inflation; why buying real estate had become a dead end deal; why investing in seemingly sound investments had come to resemble shooting dice in Las Vegas—I delved into the matter.

I had done nothing to America's economy to warrant America's economy turning on me. During my professional life of owning privately held computer network companies, I had toiled away. I had paid my taxes. I had been both smart and imprudent with my investments, but overall, I was okay.

Okay in the sense that I did not write this book from the view of a financially ravaged investor. I wrote it from the perspective of a citizen who—reasonably versed in history, politics, social science, and human behavior—was perplexed about how the failure of a single sector in America's economy (the financial sector) could have led to a crisis for millions of Americans, as well as millions of other world citizens.

As thoughts and ideas crystallized, it became clear to me that many of Wall Street's vaunted operations are not only smoke-and-mirrors, many Wall Street hawkers are little more than financial snake oil salesmen.

But Wall Street is not the sole culprit in this book. Others include consumers, several government agencies, many members of Congress, numerous commercial and investment banks, real-estate firms, the ratings agencies; as well scores of mortgage brokers, big businesses, and lobbyists. If some of these institutions were not already viewed as tainted institutions, they have now been recognized as corrupt, or at least inept. As well, Joe and Josephine Citizen are not innocent actors in this cast. Often, their shortsightedness, greed, and stupidity provided fuel to stoke the engines of their more sophisticated predators.

Yet the vast majority of citizens as well as the people who populate these institutions are not at fault or to blame for the havoc wreaked on America. *Unfortunately, a relatively few did a lot of damage to many.* Therein lies both the tragedy of the meltdown and the frightening aspect of its occurrence: A few thousand people—acting in greed or ignorance—did great harm to millions.

In this book, you will also learn about a system that creates a culture for a meltdown to occur, then rescues the creators of that meltdown—only to allow yet another (greater) meltdown to occur in the future.

Left to its own, America's financial arrangement and the few people who arrange it can do us in. Yet our government, supposedly tasked with protecting us from such disasters, had a heavy hand in creating an environment that greatly abetted this storm. It is not reassuring to learn that private enterprise and Uncle Sam jointly created this devastating tragedy; one that damaged the lives of millions of innocent citizens.

It is also less than reassuring to learn that neither government nor business is willing or capable of righting America's financial ship. It is even less reassuring to learn that the crisis was not part of a regular business cycle downturn but came about because of the failure of America's leaders (both government and private industry) to do their jobs correctly and prudently.

* * *

Regarding this floundering ship, I was one among millions of people who trusted the honesty of a balance sheet; of the accuracy of an income statement; of the evaluation of a bond by Moody's; of the assurances of a mortgage broker that my contract was for a fixed income payment; of the claims of Wall Street salesmen; of the stalwart nature of Fannie Mae. I wish I could report otherwise, but you and I—ordinary citizens—have not only been duped, we have been treated as fools. And not just recently, the game has been rigged for quite a while.

I have had difficulty coming to grips with these thoughts because I am a (retired) businessman and an ardent supporter of free markets. The trouble is—and as we will witness, the nearly perfect financial storm was laden with government largesse spooned out to supposedly capitalistic enterprises.

I have reluctantly come to this conclusion: Small business generally operates on a free market basis. In contrast, Wall Street and big business often feast at Uncle Sam's quasi-welfare trough. I do not overstate the weird, surreal world I found during my study of the nearly perfect financial storm.

Other than talking with my stockbrokers on occasion, I had little knowledge of this world. I was astounded by how often the United States Government gets in bed with Wall Street, and once there, they do more than cuddle. If you are doubtful, I ask you to read to the end of this book. Then judge for yourself.

I recognize these last statements may be considered extreme, perhaps inflammatory. I rarely resort to hyperbole in my serious writings. I believe I have not done so with these statements but passages later in the book may not be so benevolent. After you have read this book, if you think I have exaggerated these claims, send me an e-mail at BlacksStreets@gmail.com and let me know your thoughts.

Also, before you react to some of the admittedly radically stated prose in this book, consider this statement from a Wall Street investment banker. He described the meltdown as "a speed bump."[1] Yes, for Wall Street, but not for Main Street.[2] Anyway, if that quote does not get your dander up, then close this book and turn on your TV.

* * *

Most of the books about this recession concentrate on the technical aspects that contributed to the meltdown. In an incremental and tutorial way, this book takes this approach. But upon reviewing the literature on the subject, when looking at the damage done, I came to the conclusion that something was missing from these otherwise fine discourses: The human element; the role it played in fueling the fires of the meltdown.

None of the books, articles, and newscasts I have come across is presented by anyone wearing a blue collar. I don't wear one now (actually I prefer collarless), but I grew up so clothed. My approach in this book is to write from the standpoint—not as an economist, banking executive, or financial guru, but as an American citizen trying to come to grips with why much of my financial security, while I sit at my home in Idaho, is dictated by the actions of complete strangers working on a street in New York City.

* * *

On yet another plane, most of the current literature has little to say about this debacle in relation to capitalism and socialism. In the latter reports of Part I and all of Part II of this book, I offer thoughts on this subject.

You will read about my criticism of America's practice of so-called capitalism, especially the way capitalism is handled by Uncle Sam *vis-à-vis* large banks and other large institutions, such as car manufacturers and insurance companies.

That stated, do not interpret these negative views as those of a writer who does not treasure his country. Because I am a patriot, it is my belief that my comments in this book address problems that need fixing. A vibrant republic will keep itself tuned to the will of the people, but only if the people speak out.

As poorly as some sectors (and people) in America's economy behave, we should be thankful the United States has not become a southern Europe-like nanny state. Many of my critiques in this book are attempts to caution about the dangers of both corporate and personal welfare; as well as national welfare, such as that found in several countries in Europe.

* * *

By humans moving to the specialization of trades many years ago, we have become interconnected and dependent on one another; a positive aspect of life leading to our wealth. My point about interconnectedness in this book is not about its positive qualities, which are many. My concern is quite simple: America's financial infrastructure is so deeply interconnected that the failure of a single financial institution can threaten America's economy. Because of the interconnectedness of America to other nations, their economies are also affected, often dangerously so.

* * *

I often cite examples of the differences between Main Street (small businesses) and Wall Street (large companies, especially large financial institutions). *The Wall Street Journal* informs me the term "Wall Street vs. Main Street" is a cliché.[3] In turn, I inform *The Wall Street Journal* this phrase is far from a cliché. It represents a stark reality in how our government treats a relatively few large institutions versus how the government treats millions of small businesses. I respect this journal. The Journal is one of the best newspapers in the world. But on this issue, it is dead wrong.

* * *

Lobbying is an effective way to educate and influence lawmakers, other politicians, and the public. I wish to be clear that I support this practice, even though you may not think so after reading this book. My negative points about lobbying pertain to the influence big money has in creating asymmetrical lobbying: The ability to overwhelm an opponent's viewpoints with massive advertising, huge campaign contributions, and substantial lobbying staffs that spread their clients' views into the nooks and crannies of congress halls and public malls.

I will explain how the Supreme Court decision on granting the right of free speech to nonpersons is leading to fantastic lobbying (with associated campaign) efforts and the erosion of parts of America's republican foundations.

* * *

Sections of the book, especially Part I, go into details about the machinations of finance. I compiled them carefully, as they were sometimes new to me. I have tried to make these descriptions understandable to a general reader. (Also, this book was reviewed for accuracy by several industry experts. Any errors are mine, not theirs. One can read only so many facts.) Nonetheless, if you consider skipping a section with these details, I ask you to keep reading. It is an examination of an important story about America.

Finally, in spite of the subject matter, I hope you get a few laughs along the way. Levity might help the pill of failure go down easier.

---

[1] George Packer, "A Dirty Business," *The New Yorker*, June 27, 2011, p. 55.

[2] Unless otherwise noted, the term Main Street refers to small businesses.

[3] "What's Occupying Wall Street?" *The Wall Street Journal*, October 14, 2011, p. A14.

Notes About the Text

This book began as a series of reports and essays that were sent to a private list of readers. Later, some of the material was posted on Blog.UylessBlack.com. I began writing the material in March, 2009 and concluded at the end of 2011.

I then decided to expand the book into Part II, which I wrote into the summer of 2012, but not as a series of topical reports. Thus, Part I is divided into "reports" and Part II is divided into "chapters."

During the time I wrote Part I, I received comments from many people, both old-hands as well as novices in the subjects of finance and banking. Some readers offered suggestions to make changes to words or phrases. Others, who were better versed in this subject than I, offered corrections or contrary opinions to my views. This input, gratefully acknowledged, is reflected in this book.

That stated, I have kept the original up-to-this-minute format on each report in Part I because the material is reflective of the time it was written, such as reports on congressional hearings, laws that have been passed, press conferences, editorials, and interviews. I have added material to fill in gaps in the story and to add items that were pointed out to me by readers. Thus, some footnotes in the book have dates later than the date in which the report was written.

I have also expanded the original reports because of the release of the 2011 U.S. Senate investigation of the meltdown, the 2011 Financial Crisis Inquiry Report, the 2010 National Commission on Fiscal Responsibility and Reform, and several articles by Gretchen Morgenson; as well as a recent book written by Morgenson and Joshua Rosner. I believe this information is too important to exclude from this book.

For Part I, I have not altered my opinions and views, although I have supplemented them with the information cited above. Consequently, any beliefs, judgments, or outlooks I have written in these initial filings—correct or misguided—remain intact.

Because of the topical nature of the reports in Part I, and later, my second thoughts about some original opinions, several entries in Part II explain my more recent conclusions about several of my earlier opinions. As one example, I now have reservations about the effectiveness of the massive bailout. But I have kept my original thoughts intact to preserve the contemporaneous nature of each report.

Part II takes us on another course. It is related to Part I but expands beyond the specific subject of the financial meltdown into the social and political issues facing America. Granted, I make comments about these two issues in Part I, but I focus on them in Part II.

* * *

Because I was writing each report in Part I as a separate and current piece which spanned almost three years—with the associated need for a review of certain concepts for new readers—some redundancy exists in the material. Financial instruments, the subject of "too big to fail", investment banks, executive compensation, and government regulation are covered more than once, but I have edited these topics to meld them more gracefully into this book.

* * *

I have created a number of illustrations to aid you in following certain passages. My initial readers commented they found these graphics to be helpful in grasping the material. Based on these comments, I added more illustrations to this final manuscript.

While writing the first reports for Part I, I used the term Main Street to refer to private businesses in America. In these first downloads to my readers, I did not explain that this term excluded large companies, such as General Motors. I have made changes to reflect this definition. As mentioned in an earlier footnote, Main Street does not refer to Fortune 500 companies or other large corporations. It refers to the hundreds of thousands of (often) mom-and-pop enterprises that keep America's wheels of commerce spinning.

While cleaning up these reports for Part I of this book, I added references to both previous reports and those found later. Obviously, when I first wrote a report, I had no way of referencing reports that were not yet written. This addition will give you an idea of what follows, and where more details about a specific subject can be found.

* * *

The footnotes follow a consistent, but somewhat unorthodox pattern. My editor suggested many changes to them. Some I accepted. Others I did not. For example, I use "p." and "pp." for page numbers. She said this practice was obsolete. If I cite e-books I provide location number (loc.) and not a page number.

In the endnotes, two of my editors also took me to task for placing the name of a publisher before the city of the publisher. My editors of some forty earlier books took no offense with this ordering, For consistency, I use it in many other works.

I trust you will not be upset at my bending the footnotes rules a bit. One of my editors at McGraw-Hill had this to say about these sorts of minutiae, "Uyless, if you make an error in doing footnotes, make the error consistent in all of them." Enough said.

Acknowledgments

Several of my colleagues and friends read all or parts of this book, and offered comments and suggestions. Some are experts in banking, finance, and the mortgage market. Their time and contributions are much appreciated. Any errors in this book are mine, not theirs. Thank you Pat Fitzpatrick, Ray Morgan, Paul Kositzka, Greg Venit, Phil Dietz, Max Faller, Barbara Blackmon Skeen, Bill Ellefloot, Gail Power, Holly Waters, Al Hughes, Luke Wild, Ken Hanley, Harvey Borkin, Joe and Hilda Mitchell, and Miles Kasik.

Two people, who are well known and highly respected for their investigations of and reporting on Wall Street activities, deserve special mention. They are Michael Lewis (author of *Liar's Poker* and *The Big Short*), and Gretchen Morgenson (correspondent for *The New York Times*, and coauthor (with Josha Rosner) of *Reckless Endangerment*). Their work represents significant contributions to America's banking and mortgage industries. I relied heavily on their books and Ms. Morgenson's newspaper columns for my research.

I read some twenty books to prepare for writing *The Nearly Perfect Storm*. I also relied extensively on *The Wall Street Journal*, *The Economist*, *Foreign Affairs*, and scores of Internet postings. These sources are too numerous to cite here, but evidence of their contributions can be seen in the footnotes.

I offer a modest acknowledgement to my admittedly limited experience in banking and finance. A tongue-in-cheek resume is included at the back of this book.

My wife Holly read the complete manuscript for this book three times, as well as each essay in Part I at least once. With each read, she has encouraged me to tighten up the prose and to reduce the number of times I utter the phrase, "too big to fail." On the third read, her look of resignation made me silently vow not to ask for a fourth.

I am pleased to announce I have assembled an outstanding team to help me in my writing and publishing efforts. Alvart Badalian of Arrow Graphics did the formatting of the book as well as the design of the cover. (One of my friends has informed me the book warrants publication, if for no other reason than its striking cover.) Dawn Hall, my editor, repaired scores of grammar and composition deficiencies. Jerry McClain and Tommy Black are my video experts, and are preparing trailers for this book for YouTube and Facebook. My agent, Sylvia Gann Mahoney of Design4Writers, has been a great supporter in making my work known to the public. The GoDaddy.com staff has done a first rate job in supporting my web and blog sites. Bill Ellefloot of Allegra Marketing Print and Mail in Coeur d'Alene, Idaho, has taken over special printing jobs with wonderful results. I make reference to these people and organizations as my team, but of course all are independent contractors; ones I highly recommend to you.

Part I

Reports

Report 1

Setting the Stage

If you cannot let firms fail in a bust, then you must contain them in the boom.
—*The Economist*, July 19, 2008

March 1, 2009

This is Your On the Street Reporter, who is off the streets for a while. The reason for reclining in my chair, away from streets and other byways, is that I have decided to come to a better understanding of why the financial meltdown—a nearly perfect financial storm—has occurred. Its effects are affecting my pocketbook. Likely, they are affecting yours as well.

To any but the experts, the news on the subject is almost bewildering. And I am coming around to the notion that it may be bewildering to many of the experts as well. Even the once esteemed Alan Greenspan, former chairman of the Federal Reserve Board, now confesses he was clueless about a system he was supposedly managing.

Many of my colleagues, friends, and relatives have been damaged by this financial crisis. Some have lost their jobs. Some who are owners of companies have laid people off.

Although I have been fortunate enough to have avoided severe damage, I have not gone unscathed. I had nothing to do with this mess, yet its invisible hand has affected my visible wallet. Many innocent bystanders have been blindsided. Some are financially ruined and psychologically distraught.

I have a friend who is a retired physician. After being idle for a while, he decided to open a clinic devoted to the regeneration of damaged facial skin. Until 2008, he was doing well (and doing fine things for his patients). The meltdown forced him to near insolvency. Who is going to fix their facial skins when their wallets are as thin as skin? Much of this respected doctor's wealth is gone, and gone for keeps. He is another casualty of the meltdown—one among millions.

This calamity did not affect just fancy face fixers. It affected millions of other people. Estimates vary, but several government studies state roughly four million American families have lost their homes to foreclosure and another four and a half million are several months behind in their mortgage payments.

Another acquaintance with whom I once played tennis washes trucks for a living. He and his employees clean 16-wheelers. He owns three washing machine vans that he and his men drive to customers' locations. There, they prepare trucks for the road.

It is a physically demanding job; heavy hoses and heavy lifting. He is not old but he is no spring chicken. Prior to the meltdown, he had managed to place himself into a position of overseeing his company's operations. Now, after laying off employees and mothballing a third truck, he is back to hauling around big hoses and soaping-up cabs…and playing no more tennis. Returning to the washing and rinsing operation is the only factor keeping him from going belly up. His saving grace is that he has no debt on his trucks, equipment, or the trucks' garage. He was hoping for an easier time at this stage of his life. So were many other people.

Empty Stores, Empty Dreams

Let me take you on a virtual walk around the business neighborhoods near my home, as seen in figure 1-1. Many empty business buildings dot the landscape down the way from my place. Many vacant residential dwellings can also be found.

Figure 1-1. Stripped-down strip malls.

Two years ago, each if these empty buildings was filled with the wares of small business merchants, plying their trades on Main Street America. Now, my neighborhood and thousands of other neighborhoods across America offer the same desolate views.

I took bike rides or drove a car from my winter home in Palm Springs, California where I encountered the views seen in figure 1-1. I did not select certain parts of a mall. I cycled or drove by and randomly snapped these photos. In a shopping center near my home on East Canyon Drive, fifteen of twenty-six stores were empty. Starbucks, Target, a mattress store, Subway, Pollo Loco, an optometrist shop, a walk-in clinic and some other enterprises were still doing business. "Space Available" was the sign in front of the other spaces.

Your nearby strip mall is likely stripped as bare as those around my winter home in Southern California. If it is not, I would wager it is an exception, because I see the same sorts of landscapes around America.

One of my friends makes his living dealing with, and collecting money from troubled business owners. After relating to him the story of these empty stores, he countered by telling me most of these former businesses likely went bust because they had outdated "business models" and had gotten behind the times. Fifteen of twenty-six businesses, formerly profitable, went broke—all at about the same time? Because their products were out of kilter with the marketplace? Or succumbing to online order purchases and big box stores? As well as thousands of others across the USA? I doubt it.

Why Me?

As just recounted, all of us can tell stories about friends, relatives, and colleagues who have been taken down—or at least, taken down a notch—by this fiasco. They ask, "What happened? I did nothing to warrant my losing my nest egg."

The meltdown is imbued with so many factors it defies a single answer. On the surface, the road leading to the debacle is easy to understand. But the underpinnings of this road are not so simple to explain. As I labored in attempts to understand what happened, which included trying to grasp the behavior of Wall Street, I came back to the idea of: Focus on human behavior. Other aspects are important, but they are ancillary to the story.

My approach will likely not be lauded by many people who are experts in the field of finance. One such person says any legislation to correct the problems will likely be "designed to solve a largely imaginary set of problems having to do with the mental and moral limitations of bankers (deemed greedy and reckless) and consumers (deemed greedy and reckless) rather than the fundamental problem, which is inept regulation."[1]

I agree with his assertion that inept regulation was a big—maybe the biggest—part of the reason for the 2008 meltdown. But this expert misses the point that greed and recklessness (and I add ignorance and sloth) were imaginary problems. They were instrumental to the debacle. Nonetheless, his point is valid in that regulators set the framework for this disgrace by not doing their jobs.

The tack I will take is: Human behavior first, Wall Street and other big business behavior next, with the idea that the first dictates the second. It is an idea that seems to have been overlooked by the experts of finance, the psychological gurus of capitalism, and the software geeks of computer models. That is understandable. They are experts. I am not. With this approach in mind, here we go.

Fault Line

One major fault line in the meltdown was the inability of many smart people to understand the complexity of the financial system that had evolved on Wall Street over the past few decades. I recognize this statement may come across as far-fetched, because these people themselves created the system. Yet they did not recognize—nor in many instances, care—that the instruments of wealth they were creating for their immediate benefit would be deeply counterproductive to society's long-term well being.

It must also be said that other factors played a major role. In addition to this ignorance, we will come across bizarre examples of stupidity, greed, unethical practice, and fraud.

We will take it one step at a time. The unraveling of this story will take some effort. I will be careful to build up our information base gradually. Parts of this story might entail heavy lifting but stick with me. It will be worth your time.

The Basics

I begin with a simple explanation, and devote the remainder of the book to expanding it. Referring to figure 1-2, a lending institution, such as a mortgage company or a local bank (called a commercial bank in this book), originates a mortgage with a home buyer. Later, this lender hires and pays a Wall Street bank (a bank acting as a middleman and explained in more detail later) to package it and other mortgage loans into a security. The security and its contained mortgages are sold to an investor. The investor now owns the mortgages and reaps the benefits of the mortgage payments.

In this book, the term *security* is used in the same context as a *bond*. The process of aggregating the mortgage assets into a pool that becomes the security is called *securitization*.

A mortgage bond (called a mortgage backed security) is different from a conventional corporate or government bond. Corporate and government bonds are typically a single loan for a fixed time for a single investment. But a mortgage bond consists of thousands of individual home loans. Each loan has a different profile—such as the interest rate and the down payment—which means the mortgage bond that contains these loans is more complex than a conventional bond.

Commercial Bank	Wall Street Bank	Investor
Originates mortgages by lending money to home buyers	Packages mortgages into a security and sells it to investor	Buys security to make money on the mortgages

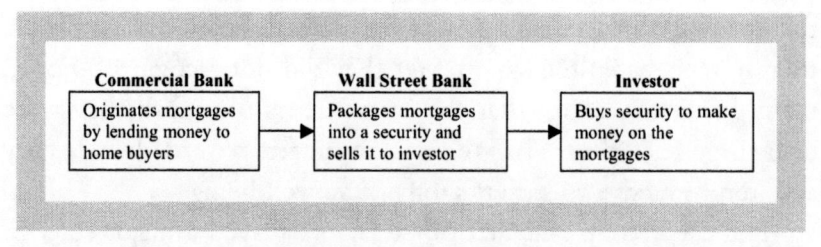

Figure 1-2. Relationship of home mortgages to a mortgage backed security.

Thus, a mortgage backed security is single in name, but plural in content. Consequently, it is more difficult to analyze and assess because of its diversity.

Anyway, a security is a piece of paper representing an asset—something real and of substance. In the situation with real estate, the asset contains mortgages. As seen in figure 1-2, the Wall Street bank sells this security to investors who intend to make money on the mortgages in the security.

Mortgage Bonds: Birth and Growth

In the late 1970s, the demand for housing in the Sun Belt was outpacing the ability of the mortgage companies (banks, finance companies, and Savings and Loan (S&L) institutions) to find money for the loans. In 1977, a Wall Street bank named Salomon Brothers came up with the idea of persuading the Bank of America to sell its home loans packaged into a bond.[2] An investor would pay Bank of America for these loans and take possession of the risks and rewards associated with the mortgages contained in the bond.

Home owners continued to make their loan payments to Bank of America each month but the bank passed this money to the purchaser of the bond. The key aspect of this setup was that the bank received *immediate* cash from the security sale. It could then use this money to make more home loans. In addition, the Wall Street bank received a fee for acting as a middleman.

A Shift in America's Culture. There was another significant consequence of this arrangement. It affected America's traditions and culture. Home mortgages no longer stayed at the local banks and S&Ls that originated them. Home loans lost their ties to a small local bank as they crossed over to a remote Wall Street bank and an even more remote investor. No longer did it matter if you or I knew Mr. Jones, the loan officer at our local bank, or if he knew us and our families. The era of relationship lending began to come to an end. Mr. Jones came to know, as did we, that our once mutual obligations toward one another were no longer mutual; that at the bottom line, they no longer mattered.

But the question remains, if the lender no longer had a neighborly knowledge of the character of the borrower, how could the lender know if the loan would be repaid? Answer: If the lender sold the loan to an investor, the originator of this loan might not care, as he no longer had any significant skin in the game.

Accounting rules did (and do) require the seller (originator) of loans to factor in the possibility that some loans might go sour and would need to be repurchased. Thus, prudent loan originators were careful about the quality of the loans and set aside reserves in case of problems. But in the booming industry of the 1990s and early 2000s, this situation was considered highly unlikely and many banks did not worry about it. They set aside only what the law required. As told later, as a run-up to the meltdown, the laws for setting aside capital for a rainy day were loosened to dangerous levels.

Complexity. What about the Wall Street banks (and other institutions, explained later) who took the loans off the loan originators' books? Their approach was to assemble thousands of these loans into a package to hold or sell. In addition, they often placed multiple security packages into a larger security package. Thus, many mortgage backed securities were often packaged together to create yet another aggregate of the original loans—which further complicated these financial instruments. These complex security instruments became significant factors in the nearly perfect financial storm.

Don't forget, the packager of these loans was largely not responsible for their ultimate worth—or worthlessness. He bought them from a bank or another loan originator, set them up in a security and looked for ways to sell them. The bottom line: he was looking for any way to make a profit.

Sour Statistics. Statistically, if a few loans went sour, the concept relied on the theory that a whole package or package of packages would still be profitable enough to make it worth the time to do all this sorting and packaging. In addition, the entire system—the American mortgage market—was judged as much too diverse for, say, large numbers of mortgage failures in one region of the country to affect another region. Yet, it was discovered—too late—that the number of failed loans in a security could be rather small to render the security being considered of very poor quality.

Besides, all parties could use almost faultless computer models and play statistical games to create "value-at-risk" models on the various packages of mortgages. (Keep the word *almost* in mind.)

Even more, if these computer models revealed an overall package, on average, was solid, the national credit rating agencies would give the entire package of mortgages a high rating, which would make the package even more attractive. Thus, a second party could make a healthy profit by selling the package to a third party. The third party could then sell to the fourth party; the fourth to the fifth, and so on.

Meanwhile, let's return to the desk of the mortgage lender (the originator): He was motivated to approve even more loans and make more money by selling them—*especially if loan defaults were low and he did not have to make good on many defaults*. The process began to feed upon itself.

Uncle Sam Alters the Stakes

Two years after the embryonic mortgage bond market was born, in 1979 Federal Reserve Board Chairman Paul Volcker informed the public that America's financial underpinnings would no longer be set up around the practice of fixed interest rates. Interest rates could float.

Forgive this lapse into monetary policy. The concept is not simple as it also has to do with the policy of managing the money supply of the country. But for this analysis, the effect *was* simple.[3] With this radical change in policy, heretofore conservative bonds, which were affected by interest rates, became slaves to *fluctuating* interest rates. They went from rather staid financial instruments of fixed income to instruments of speculation, subject to gambling bets on changing interest rates.[4] If interest rates changed, so would the value of bonds. The former conservative bond trader became a trader operating in a new casino of uncertainty, and he began to get rich.

Without going into too much detail in this introduction, it will be helpful to understand why these bonds—a key player in the 2008 financial meltdown—became the main chips at Wall Street's gaming tables. It will also be helpful to understand how the people on Wall Street could generate so much income from bonds (any bonds for that matter). Figure 1-3 is used during the discussion.

Company ABC would like to raise capital to build some factories. It issues (sells) $100 million worth of new bonds. A bond trader (versed in financial technicalities) and his salesman (versed in selling techniques) act as middlemen for this sell and its eventual purchase. Their job is to off-load these bonds onto an investor, say pension fund XYZ. This organization is looking for a safe investment with attractive yields. Based on the sales pitch of the bond salesman and the fact that ABC's bonds have been rated high by credit rating agencies, XYZ buys them. The middleman (the bond trader) takes a tiny cut off the top, say 1/8 of a percentage point, which amounts to $125,000.

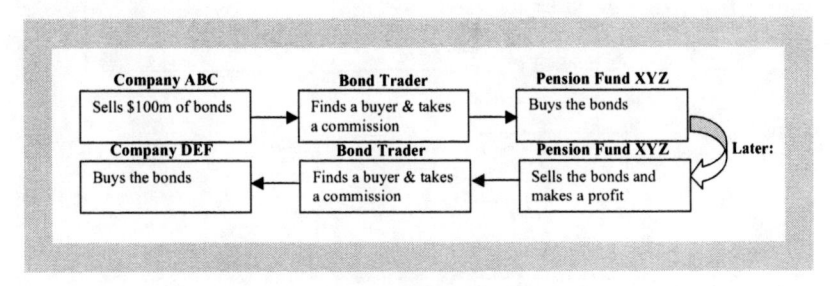

Company ABC	Bond Trader	Pension Fund XYZ	
Sells $100m of bonds	Finds a buyer & takes a commission	Buys the bonds	
Company DEF	Bond Trader	Pension Fund XYZ	Later:
Buys the bonds	Finds a buyer & takes a commission	Sells the bonds and makes a profit	

Figure 1-3. Making money.

The bond trader and his salesman may then (and often do) look to churn these bonds—to find another buyer. They convince company DEF the bonds are worth more than what XYZ paid for them (as they have been highly rated). They also convince XYZ to sell the bonds to make a profit and/or gain liquidity. The Wall Street intermediary also takes a commission from this sale. A little bit here, a little bit there. Before long, those small morsels become feasts.

That is what happened during the early days leading to the nearly perfect financial storm. We return to the story shortly. For now, the bond trader and his salesman are thought of as Wall Street people, also referred to in this book as the "Street." With some exceptions, a mortgage broker is considered closer to home—on Main Street.

Mortgage Broker

Shortly, the difference between a commercial bank and a Wall Street bank is explained in more detail. For now, to continue the introduction of terms, figure 1-4 introduces another participant in the meltdown: the mortgage broker.

Before explaining the role of this actor in the financial storm story, a brief diversion. In the 1980s I was a partner in a mortgage brokerage firm. It had a catchy name, The Mortgage Market. Three people formed the company. My two partners (and friends of mine) ran the day-to day-operations. I sat on the sidelines learning about its operations and the business of home mortgages.

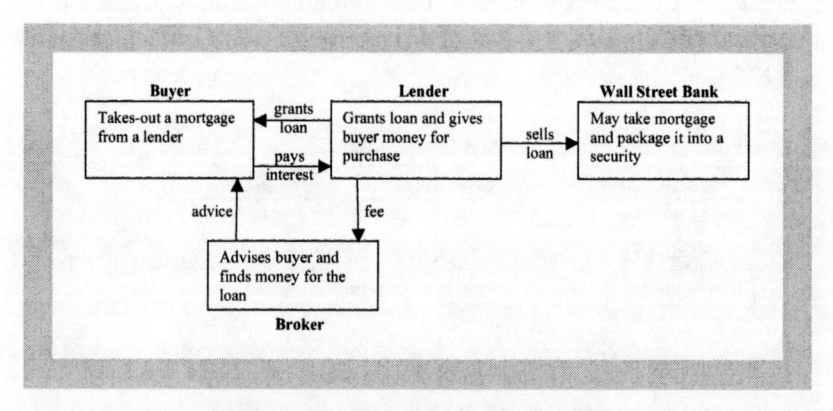

Figure 1-4. The mortgage broker.

A mortgage broker acts as an agent to obtain a loan for a customer. The broker's job is to find the funds (from a bank or some other lender) for an individual or company who needs a loan for a home or commercial property. A fee is charged by the broker for these services. The process is shown in figure 1-4, with a Wall Street bank also in the picture.

There are thousands of mortgage brokerages in the United States and hundreds of thousands of mortgage brokers. Since the meltdown, their numbers have dwindled, but they will make a comeback as investors begin to realize the attractive values awaiting them after the wake of the storm has passed. Presently, they originate close to 70 percent of all residential loans in America. The remainder is handled directly by a lender or a lender's subsidiary.

As the financial meltdown drama unfolds, the mortgage broker will enter and leave the stage several times.

Investment Banks and Proprietary Trading

An investment bank (called a Wall Street bank thus far in this book) is a financial institution that raises capital for its clients (corporations, etc.), trades securities on behalf of its clients, and manages mergers and acquisitions. Investment banks derive income from fees they charge to help raise money for companies and government through issuing and selling securities and providing advice.

Until 1999, the United States maintained a strict separation of investment banks and commercial banks, a topic covered in this book under the Glass-Steagall Act.

In addition, in the past investment banks acted only *on behalf of their customers* (using their customers' assets) in trading stocks, bonds, and such. Nowadays, these banks engage heavily in proprietary trading, where they use their own money (their proprietary holdings) for the trades *on behalf of themselves*. One of the major factors contributing to the nearly perfect financial storm was the huge portfolios of poor-quality mortgage backed securities that the banks themselves held when the marketplace first froze up, then melted.

How large? The Deutsche Bank's mortgage backed security department in New York held $102 billion of mortgage related bonds.

Even small firms were in this market, often taking on over $10 billion worth of these bonds into their holdings.[5]

The idea was that the investment bank could make fine profits—especially with the booming real estate market. But at the same time, proprietary trading meant the firm entered into a riskier world because it was gambling with its own money.

Whose Money? Its own money? Yes, if an investment bank is privately owned, in the event of problems, the owners stand to lose their own money. That was the case in the past. As discussed in more detail later, these banks, previously privately owned, went public.

Thereafter, they were not gambling with their own money, they were gambling with the money of the stockholders.

Granted, many top level managers received parts of their compensation in stock. Nonetheless, company losses did not come directly out of their pocketbooks. We will also see that the investment banks paid such huge salaries and year-end bonuses that many of the employees were millionaires by the time of the 2008 crash. They had already stored away their wealth. The typical stockholder was left holding a bag of severely degraded stock.

For the present discussion, thousands of stores in strip malls around the country are closed. The owners are broke. The investment bankers remain immensely wealthy while millions of Americans suffer from the bankers' actions, many of which were unethical; some illegal. Yet as of this writing, not one red cent from these Wall Street people has been given up. No one has been sent to jail.

Sidebar 1-1. Two Terms.

Buying a stock or bond because the buyer thinks it is a sound investment is called *going long*. The buyer is betting on that financial instrument. It is also possible (and a common practice) to bet against a financial instrument. This practice is called *shorting, short,* or *going short*. I will have much to say about these two forms of betting.

Hedging the Bet, Changing the Fleece, and Fleecing the Taxpayer

To gain a sense of the unhealthy nature that proprietary trading took on, the vaunted investment bank Goldman Sachs bet against (shorted) the very securities it sold to its customers:[6]

> One investment bank, Goldman Sachs, built a large number of proprietary positions to short [bet against] the mortgage market. …In 2006, Goldman Sachs decided to reverse course [from betting on the mortgage market], using a variety of means to bet against the mortgage market. In some cases Goldman Sachs took proprietary positions that paid off only when some of its clients lost money on the very securities that Goldman Sachs had sold to them and then [bet against].

In 2007, Goldman made $1.1 billion from these activities. Later, this firm was given a $10 billion taxpayer bailout under the auspices of a government program, as well as tens of billions of dollars in support through accessing a Federal Reserve facility to assist (only) large financial institutions. "Goldman and other investment banks received billions more in indirect support to ensure their continued existence."[7]

The programs cited in the previous paragraph represent the first time in the history of our country that Uncle Sam has lent to so-called investment banks. I say so-called, because the term *investment bank* is losing its meaning with the demise of Glass-Stegall (discussed in more detail later).

In addition to these programs, Goldman and other institutions were granted an amendment to their charter. In one swift move, they were changed from an *investment bank* to that of a *bank holding company*. This latter category describes a non-commercial banking company that owns a bank or banks. This extraordinary grant from Uncle Sam's beneficence allowed these companies to gain access to the Federal Reserve's deep pockets and obtain loans at interest rates that you and I—and Main Street companies—could realize only in our dreams.[8]

Meantime, Back on Main Street

In the meantime, my next door neighbors are losing jobs and/or income. My tennis buddy dropped his membership at the gym. My doctor friend, recently retired, has unretired. An acquaintance is one missed payment away from dispossession of his home. The strip malls are aptly named: In every city I visit they have been stripped clean.

None is privy to the programs just cited, as these people are too small to qualify. For that matter, few are privy to any credit at all. They still have sterling credit ratings, but the banks are hoarding the very cash for which they were created to distribute. Solution? We need to become banks and especially bank holding companies to obtain dirt-cheap loans from our government.

In the meantime, the Wall Street executives are lying low, taking in only a few millions of dollars a year of wages and bonuses. In a few short years, these folks will be once again raking in tens of millions of dollars *each* for their contributions to themselves.

I hope I will be mistaken and the immense profits of Wall Street will be apportioned to the actual owners of these firms: the stockholders. We'll see. Stay tuned.

By the way, while reading this book, pour yourself a drink. Don't worry about how much liquid you are taking on. You've already been soaked. And it is not going to get any drier.

The Chinese Wall

In theory, the investment bank must keep what it does on behalf of its customers separate and secret from what it does on behalf of itself (it is called a Chinese Wall). This separation is required to prevent the bank from buying or selling on its own account before filling orders from the customer. The potential exists for the bank to manipulate prices by the first action that could be to the detriment of the customer.

The Chinese Wall is also supposed to prevent one side of an investment bank from selling a security to a customer while knowing the other side is buying insurance on the same security.[9] As mentioned, the buying or selling of a security is a bet about its quality.

Taking out insurance is a bit more involved. If the bank thinks the security is solid, but wants to play it safe—to hedge its bet—it makes sense to also buy insurance to protect against the possibility of the security losing value.

However, if the bank is not confident of the security, yet sells it to a customer (bets on it), then takes out insurance on it (bets against it), the bank has breached not only the Chinese Wall, but a wall of integrity and honesty. As weird as it may appear—and unethical as it is—that is exactly what some of the investment banks did.

Factors in the Meltdown

Given these basic ideas, a few additional, general comments can be made about the problems associated with the meltdown. These thoughts set the stage for later reports:

- The federal government is the main culprit, including Congress and several presidential administrations. Under the outlandish goal of giving practically every adult citizen in America their own home, Uncle Sam initiated scores of programs to encourage the granting of mortgage loans to people *who could not afford them*. These policies found their way into government agencies, banks, brokers…almost every place that dealt with commercial and residential real estate. In only thirty years or so, Uncle Sam created a dysfunctional system for the largest marketplace in America: real estate.

- Many people who took out home mortgages during the run-up to the 2008 meltdown did not understand the terms of their loans. The loans were interspersed with so much legal and technical jargon that an average home buyer could not hope to understand all the nuances in a mortgage contract. But as described later, these nuances were very important. One factor, called the adjustable rate mortgage (ARM) led to monthly mortgages increasing beyond the homeowner's ability to meet the obligation.

- In spite of the complex contract, a prospective home owner was eager to take on a mortgage because interest rates were very low for many years—another gift from Uncle Sam. The prolonged low interest rates were helping to feed an expanding residential market, which became known as the "housing bubble." The market was booming, resulting in huge increases in the value of homes.

- The people at a commercial bank or a mortgage company who were making the loans relied on a Wall Street bank to package the mortgage loans into securities. They often organized these securities in such a way that their contents became complex and difficult to evaluate. These (mortgage backed) securities were then sold in the marketplace, with the proceeds of the individual mortgage payments providing income to the buyer (investor) of the security. One reason they were popular was because interest rates paid on other investments were low. For example, the mortgage security paid the investor more than the yield on a bank deposit or a U.S. Treasury bond.

- Yet as implausible as it may appear, many people who bought these securities did not fully understand what they were purchasing. They had unrealistic views of their profitability. They did not know that many of the underlying mortgages in the security were of *very* poor quality. One key reason for this nonchalance stemmed from these investors relying on the credit rating agencies, who as implausible as it may appear, were rating this junk as if it were jewels.

- The financial industry wrote computer programs to simulate these activities and print out a "risk factor" for dealing in mortgage backed securities. These models did not account for something as serious as a housing market downturn, or for the simple fact that the securities contained poor-quality loans. Meanwhile, as the meltdown began, these models continued to be used—with few exceptions—with blind confidence.

- So blind, it bordered on stupidity, because the models had little (almost nothing) to offer about the possibility of the housing market taking a dive; that an expanding bubble might burst. But how could anyone back off from making so much money from the growing housing industry and its expanding bubble? Few people could, as greed clouded their vision.

- Then how could so many people be stupid enough to enter into the purchase of the most expensive investment (a house) in their lives when they had little understanding of the contract that bound them to this investment? Naiveté? Stupidity? Greed? Yes. Make no mistake, much of the blame for the meltdown belongs to the average citizen, who was either irresponsible or clueless (sometimes both) in making decisions about buying a house.

- And to help along the illusions of home buyers, the originators of the mortgages and the people who were packaging their mortgages into securities (usually, Wall Street banks and government-sponsored enterprises) entered into schemes of fantasy to make money with these instruments. As we will see, clouds of artificiality permeated not only the mortgage lenders, but also the Wall Street banks that owned or sold the securities containing the mortgages.

Taking Out Insurance and Hedging Bets: Foundation for the Nearly Perfect Financial Storm

Before closing, in tracing the roots of these problems, another financial condiment is added to the meltdown soup. They are called *credit default swaps*. They played a major role in the unraveling of Wall Street. I introduce them here. Later (see Report 8), they are examined in more detail.

To begin, the mortgage originators began to grant loans to home buyers who were marginally qualified (or unqualified) to make their monthly payments. Later discussions explain why this weird situation came to be. For now, these *subprime*[10] loans (which some analysts call toxic loans) were packaged and sold to investors in the form of mortgage backed securities, introduced earlier. The values of these securities were then *guaranteed* by some companies with an insurance policy called the credit default swap. The result was the issuance of billions of dollars of insurance covering toxic securities.

The effects of this practice were abetted by banks, investors, and government-backed organizations *exponentially* increasing their portfolio of mortgage backed securities—which led to a huge market in associated credit default swaps' insurance on securities containing junk mortgages. Just consider:[11]

- In three years (2000-2003) financial institutions increased their holdings of mortgage backed securities by 325 percent.
- In the same period, Fannie Mae, a government sponsored institution and discussed later, increased its holdings of mortgage backed securities by 439 percent.
- These instruments were protected by credit default swaps.

What is wrong with taking out a little insurance on these securities? Nothing. It is a prudent way to do business. As discussed in detail later, the problem came about because one of the largest insurance companies in the world sold billions of dollars of insurance on mortgage loans that were *worthless*!

Later, as massive loan defaults came into play, this company could not cover its bets. Yet its insured customers, those who had hedged their bets, demanded compensation. It became a standoff. So Uncle Sam came along and bailed everyone out to keep America from going south.

---

[1] Richard A. Posner, *The Crisis of Capitalistic Democracy*, Harvard University Press, Cambridge, 2010, p. 77.

[2] Michael Lewis, *Liar's Poker*, W.W. Norton & Company, New York, 1989, p. 111.

[3] Lewis, *Liar's Poker*, p. 43. In more detailed terms: Money supply would no longer "fluctuate with the business cycle; money supply would be fixed,

and interest rates would float." Also, the following explanation on Wall Street commissions is also taken from this part of Lewis' book.

[4] Speculation, as I will say more than once, is not necessarily "bad." It depends on the nature of the speculation.

[5] "Wall Street and the Financial Crisis," U.S. Senate, Permanent Subcommittee on Investigations, April 13, 2011, p. 35.

[6] Ibid., p. 36.

[7] Ibid.

[8] The U.S. government allowed large investment banks to become bank holding companies, thus privy to the Fed's Discount Window's very cheap loans.

[9] This last statement will likely raise objections from some Wall Street experts, who contend it is the responsibility of the customer to do due diligence on anything the investment bank might be peddling.

[10] One of my e-mail readers took me to task for this use of the term "subprime." I responded that the term is used in this report (and now this book) as the definition cited by "FDIC-Guidance for Subprime Lending". Fdic.gov. http://www.fdic.gov/news/news/press/2001/pr0901a.html. "The term subprime refers to the credit quality of particular borrowers, who have weakened credit histories and a greater risk of loan default than prime borrowers." For convenience I group subprime and Alt-A loans together, and usually just use the term subprime. Alt-A loans are considered of slightly higher quality than subprime, but this distinction is not important for this general treatise of the subject.

[11] Charles Duhigg, "Pressured to Take More Risk, Fannie Reached the Tipping Point," *The New York Times*, October 5, 2008, p. 30.

Report 2

Rules of Life and Finance

March 2, 2009

Hello. Your reporter is once again on the streets of America, meandering into and out of partially closed strip malls. I am told these businesses are hapless victims of big-box stores, Internet web sites, and overseas vendors. Could be. And I agree with these basic premises. But I remain convinced that thousands of small businesses did just not disappear because of these competitive alternatives.

Anyway, in this report, we amplify our outlook on America's finances by examining several aspects of human behavior that played key roles in the story of the nearly perfect financial storm. Understanding these characteristics of our makeup will be helpful in understanding the meltdown. The technical aspects of the financial crisis are complex. The psychological underpinnings are starkly simple; a page out of *Homo sapiens*' mind-set.

I have used these ideas in other writings because I think they are fundamental traits of human behavior. They represent entries in my dictionary titled "The Rules of Life."[1] This chapter will get us started on several traits of humans. Others are introduced in later reports.

The Autocatalytic Process (AKA the Feeding Frenzy)

The Autocatalytic Process describes a feedback cycle wherein a process reinforces another process, which in turn, reinforces the first process, which then reinforces the second process, and so on.

REPORT 2: RULES OF LIFE AND FINANCE   23

An example of this cycle is shown in figure 2-1. Initially, process A has an effect on process B, which in turn, affects A. This change to A has another effect on B, which again, affects A. The smaller circles in the figure show that the feedback loop goes faster and faster with each occurrence of a process in the cycle. The process is catalytic because the interactions of the events cause an increase in the rate, frequency, and intensity of their overall effect.

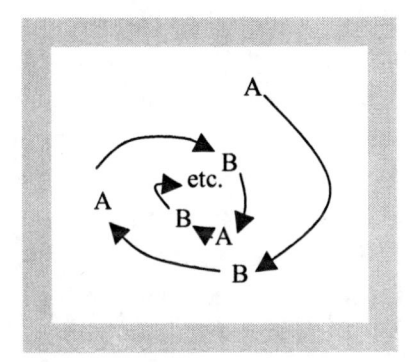

Figure 2-1. The Autocatalytic Process.

An example of this process occurring in the meltdown was the increasing use of low-quality loans (subprime mortgages), that were packaged into securities and sold to investors. As we learned, the lending institution (say, a bank) received cash for the security, which immediately gave it money to make additional subprime loans.

As quickly as possible, the bank made additional loans, had them packaged into securities and sold more of them. Thus, many bank executives pressured their loan departments to bring more loan applications in the door. The approved loans were then sent out the door (sold) as parts of a security.

The faster the better; the more loans a bank made, the more money it made. As one loan officer said, "There is no profit in denying a loan."[2]

The Autocatalytic Process found its way into many nooks and crannies of America's financial netherworld. Netherworld, in that many nooks and crannies were unregulated and opaque to external eyes—including the public and Uncle Sam. This setup was (and is) exactly the way Wall Street wanted it. As a businessman, so would I, but I am not saying my selfish self-interest is healthy for others.

As another example, the government-sponsored agencies, Fannie Mae and Freddie Mac—to whom I apply a skewer later—increased their commitment to these poor quality loans as quickly as they could. Between 2005 and 2007 Fannie Mae had purchased (from loan originators) 62 percent of their *total* portfolio in subprime loans. During this brief time, it acquired 84 percent of interest-only loans: those in which a home buyer only paid interest on the loan.[3]

Let's pause for a moment and consider the concept of an interest-only loan. By paying only interest on a loan, how can a loan be paid-off? Obviously, it cannot be paid-off. A home owner is left with a mortgage that never decreases, conceivably accompanying the home owner to his grave. The home owner never gains any value or any equity in the most expensive undertaking in his life.

Ah, but he does if the Autocatalytic Process is in effect. Each day, the value of his home is increasing. Not each week, or month; each day. Why should he expend any money to reduce his debt when he can flip (sell) this house in a year or so; a month or so; a week or so. Even a day or so, and make a huge profit. In a later report (Alice in Mortgage Land), I document surreal instances of this aspect of the Autocatalytic Process in action.

Regarding this situation, I am reminded of the old saying, "Where ignorance is bliss, 'tis folly to be wise." For now, we return to Uncle Sam's bastions of capitalism.

But why did Fannie and Freddie make such disastrous decisions? Because Congress passed several laws—under the euphemism "affordable housing"—that *forced* these agencies to buy loans from mortgage lenders that were given to people *who could not afford the mortgage in the first place*.

Of course, the mortgage lenders were quite willing to grant these loans to low-income home buyers, because the loans were taken off their books and backs by Fannie and Freddie, who were under orders from Congress to (essentially) undermine the merit-based underpinnings of America's largest industry.

Capitalism in Action? For America's 2008 financial meltdown, the Autocatalytic Process can be characterized as a feeding frenzy. The "capitalists" dined at any trough they could find; anything for the money; anything to increase market share.

Your writer has no problem with the concept of increasing market share. I am now retired from fighting in the trenches of competition for market share, but I still understand the efficacy of free markets. And after all, capitalism in its pure form is white-collar survival of the fittest. As I mentioned in the Preface of this book, in its most basic form, capitalism has no ethics. It's Darwin in Guccis.

And with Guccis, in contrast to bare feet and solitary trekking, comes white-collar networking. However subtle, the Autocatalytic Process of mutual benefits kicked in:[4]

> When borrowers took out larger loans, the mortgage broker typically profited from higher fees and commissions; the lender profited from higher fees and a better price for the loan on the secondary market; and the Wall Street firms profited from a larger revenue stream to support bigger pools of mortgage backed securities.

In a rare moment of clarity, humans invented government to rein in our otherwise nasty behavior toward one another. However, as this saga unfolds, it will become evident that government was as much a part of the problem as it was the solution.

As well, it will become evident that Wall Street "capitalists" are no more free market oriented than an ordinary welfare recipient in a Detroit ghetto. Any risks the investment banker takes are taken with someone else's money.

The white collar handout recipients take more money per person from Uncle Sam than the downtrodden folks do. But that is the only difference between them. The Wall Street people and other big businesses rely on Uncle Sam's doles, K-Street formulated regulations, bailouts, and exclusionary loan rates to support their elevated living as much as the Medicaid souls look to government for food stamps to eke out their survival.

The Threshold Lowering Syndrome

Many events cited in this book take place in the context of the Threshold Lowering Syndrome. This syndrome describes an act by a human or an organization, who by committing the act, makes it easier for this person or company to repeat the act, or to commit another act that is based on the success of the first act. The act might be beneficial or detrimental to the parties involved. But regardless of its merit, the party who commits the act receives positive reinforcement from carrying it out, such as applause, perhaps self-satisfaction—maybe a lot of money.

Figure 2-2 illustrates the Threshold Lowering Syndrome in relation to its dangerous relationship to the meltdown. The horizontal lines are the thresholds between "Acceptable" and "Not Acceptable" behavior. The acceptable notation means an action is beneficial (such as making a home loan for a well-maintained house to a working person with a good credit rating). The not acceptable notation means the behavior is not beneficial (such as making a home loan for a vacant lot to an unemployed person with no credit credentials). This figure is read left to right to show: Leading up to the financial meltdown, as the threshold barrier lowered, it became easier (increasingly acceptable) for a person or an organization to engage in more nonbeneficial acts (nonbeneficial to society).

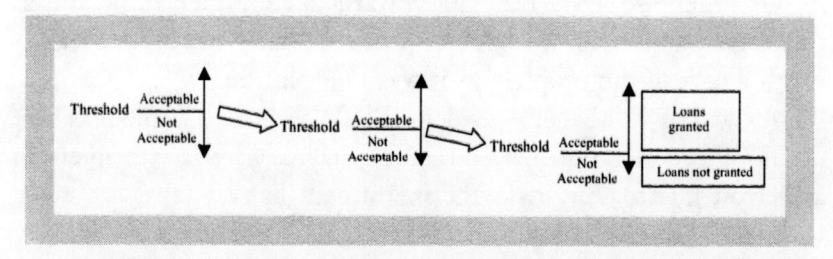

Figure 2-2. The Threshold Lowering Syndrome.

In relation to the 2008 storm, the Threshold Lowering Syndrome was found in the lowering of standards for granting loans because the U.S. government established laws to this effect, or because Uncle Sam ignored its own laws that forbade granting poor-quality loans. In the past, a home mortgage loan was not easy to obtain. At the least, documented records were required about the loan applicant's employment, income and credit history. The events leading to the meltdown turned this situation around to the extreme. As more loans were granted; as the banks received income from selling them; as the housing market kept expanding, the threshold for approving loans continued to be lowered. The threshold sunk to the point where an unemployed person could walk off the street and get a loan from many banks and other financial institutions around the country.

In California, a strawberry picker was lent the *entire* amount to buy a house of $724,000. His income was $14,000. His down payment should have been more than his entire yearly salary. Loans on houses were granted for lots that had no houses on them. They were granted by beefing up a loan application with the incomes of dead spouses.

This Rule of Life and finance was applicable to many other situations in the real estate mortgage industry. One of the most noxious was the behavior of Congress in its credit-loosening decrees to Fannie Mae and Freddie Mac—again, quasi-government bodies and explained in detail later. After opening up their books to the public, it became evident they lowered or even destroyed decades-old standards for banks and other institutions for granting loans to home buyers. They ignored the warnings of their risk assessment departments; even cut the budgets of these departments. They saw the emerging weak mortgage market, yet took on "more mortgage market risk."[5] As these very powerful institutions lowered their standards, they sent signals to others: *Congress tells us we must lower our standards for buying home loans. You can do the same; just lower your standards for granting loans. We'll take them off your hands.*

By the way, during the year of 2007, when Fannie Mae showed a net loss of $2.1 billion, its chief executive's compensation package was $11.6 million—from a quasi-governmental agency.

A Sick Symbiosis. Two Rules of Life fed one another. The Threshold Lowering Syndrome coupled with the Autocatalytic Process to create a financial tornado. Risking excessive metaphor (admittedly, often and again), the trail of this storm will leave scars for many years, seared into those who did not have the storm cellar of an Uncle Sam bailout. The Wall Street folks are once again making innuendos to revive their millions of dollars of bonuses. Down the block from Wall Street, there are near-empty corridors of past commerce.

The Law of Unintended (and Exponential) Consequences

Given the facts cited above, I venture to guess you cannot fathom how (a) so many unqualified people were given loans with (b) adjustable (and increasing) interest rates. Even before the meltdown, while watching the news and listening to commentators discuss this market, your writer thought the lending institutions had lost their collective minds.[6]

However, taking a deep breath, and trying to cut some slack to all concerned, I say to myself, "Maybe no one saw that the combination of credit-deprived buyers and profit-depraved lenders—which resulted in millions of toxic loans—would lead to disaster." The situation reminds me of another Rule of Life and finance.

The Law of Unintended (and Exponential) Consequences is defined as: The consequences of an action or actions in which the consequences are far greater than anyone can predict. This law can be illustrated with a curve, as seen in figure 2-3.

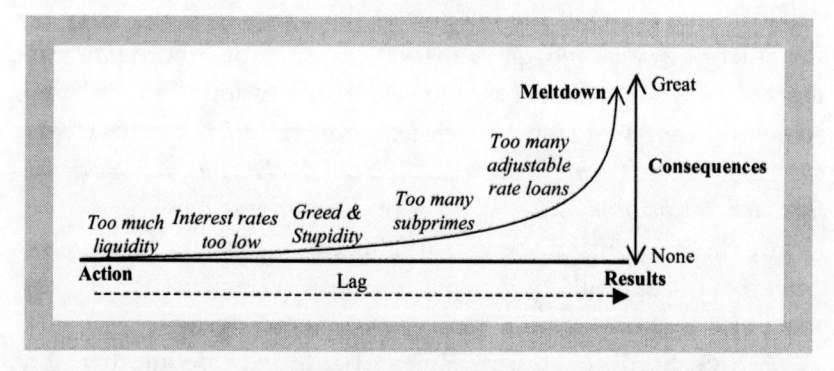

Figure 2-3. The Unintended Exponential Consequences curve.

I have placed several notations along the curve, which I view as the principal causes of the meltdown. With the exception, of "Too much liquidity," they were introduced earlier and are examined in considerable detail later. For now, we can generalize that for many years, other countries funneled a lot of money into the United States in the form of savings, loans (buying U.S. Treasuries), and of course real estate purchases. For a while, America was awash in liquidity. (Its effect is explained in detail in Report 4.)

What to do with all this money? Forget bank deposits and conventional bonds; they did not pay enough. Look for higher yields. What was booming? Because Congress and the Clinton/Bush administrations pushed the financial industry to grant loans to a larger segment of the population, the mortgage market and associated mortgage bonds had become more attractive investments. So, put the money in mortgage backed securities and obtain money from the higher interest rates of the loans packaged inside them.

The idea of *exponential* consequences is shown with the curve rising sharply toward the meltdown. The meltdown's consequences have been exponential in that the downturn has increasingly affected almost everyone in the industrialized world.[7] The term exponential is also apt due to its effects being so suddenly severe that hardly anyone thought a meltdown was possible. Report 5 of this series examines the mathematical models that played a role in the meltdown. They too, did not foresee a financial crisis of the magnitude America is now facing.

Giving the benefit of the doubt to America's financial industry, perhaps the financiers did not realize the consequences of their actions. Perhaps the time lag between the actions and their consequences was so far out on the horizon that no one could see what would happen. Or, as the curve also suggests, perhaps greed or stupidity also contributed to the meltdown, a claim made earlier. In later reports, I will make the case for all those factors (and more).

The Disproportionate Ratio Effect

The next Rule of Life in relation to finance and pertinent to the nearly perfect financial storm is the Disproportionate Ratio Effect, defined as: n:m, where the value of n is small and the value of m is large. This ratio came into play many times and will be used in this book to provide examples of the amazingly small number of people (n) who wrecked the economy to the number of people (m) who were wrecked by the economy.

To be fair, many financial institutions did not get into the subprime mess. They kept their operations focused on traditional ways of doing business. The USAA, a firm with whom I do business, weathered the storm well. So did the Wall Street firm JPMorgan Chase, who through the conservative guidance of CEO Jamie Dimon, kept this bank profitable. Nonetheless, as explained in later reports, a few rotten apples spoiled a very big barrel of fruit.

To Summarize

To this point: (a) The financial industry began processing subprime/adjustable rate mortgages at an increasingly faster pace to bring in yet more income (the Autocatalytic Process). (b) The financial industry increasingly lowered standards for the approval of already low-quality loans (the Threshold Lowering Syndrome). (c) This approach translated into a dangerous environment, one that could (and did) spiral out of control, one that few people predicted (The Law of Unintended and Exponential Consequences). (d) A relatively few individuals created the contagion, but it affected millions of people (The Disproportionate Ratio Effect.)

For the remainder of this chapter, I will introduce two more Rules of Life as they pertain to the nearly perfect financial storm. I have others to share with you, which are discussed later. For now:

The Graveyard Shift Law

Not to be confused with a work schedule. Rather, this law describes the shifting of priorities to implement a long-known solution to a problem, but *only* after the problem has shown itself, resulting in unnecessary loss of life or avoidable loss of financial security. Some well-known examples of this law are (a) the installation of wind shear detection radar at wind-blown airports *after* planes have crashed because of wind shear; (b) refusing to maintain the bridges on America's Interstate highway system, even *after* inspectors cited 70,000 bridges as having poor structures; (c) making sure the patients in America's emergency rooms are periodically checked for their vital signs *after* patients have died while waiting for their vital signs to be checked.

For this story, an example of the law is the actions of the credit rating agencies leading to the crisis of 2008. (For readers who are not familiar with these organizations, refer to Sidebar 2-1.)

> **Sidebar 2-1. Rating Agencies.**
>
> I will have more to say about rating agencies later. For now, a rating agency (Standard and Poor's, Moody's, and Fitch) is a company sanctioned by the U.S. government to analyze and rate the financial soundness of financial instruments and thus the soundness of the institutions that issue these instruments.
>
> These agencies police the American business industry for credit worthiness. Consequently, they have immense influence in America's markets. They can make or break a company.

For many years these firms—through both sloth and greed described in Report 9—incorrectly rated thousands of mortgage backed securities and associated financial instruments.[8] Many of these bonds were owned or were being sold by investment banks. The majority of these instruments were given the highest rating: AAA. We will learn that some of mortgages contained in these bonds were little more than junk, yet the rating agencies awarded them an AAA rating.

Only *after* it became obvious to many Wall Street-savvy people that the ratings were bogus did the rating agencies downgrade them. For starters, they never should have been rated AAA in the first place. We will learn why these securities, overloaded with subprime mortgages, were marked up to high quality. For now, the Law of the Graveyard Effect came into place:

Beginning in July, 2007 these agencies corrected their mistakes. They downgraded thousands of mortgage backed securities and related bonds. "By 2010, analysts estimate that 90 percent of the AAA ratings issued on mortgage backed securities that were originated in 2006 and 2007 had been downgraded to junk status."[9]

The Straw that Broke the Back of an Already Broken Camel. The effect of these sudden downgrades was to create chaos in the financial securities marketplace. Investors of mortgage related bonds were left holding a bag containing trash when they thought the bag was holding a horn of plenty. After all, the vaunted rating agencies had deemed them AAA.

Many investors were required by their charters to sell a security that lost its AAA rating. Because of this sudden about-face by the rating agencies, a school district, or a retirement plan for a company's employees suddenly had to off-load these "assets." They took great losses, which affected the security of many fixed-income citizens.

Because of these downgrades, the Law of the Graveyard Shift came into the picture and put a lot of people into an early grave. Suddenly, widow Mary's pension fund was broke. What to do? At the risk of coming across as maudlin, stories are documented of innocent victims of the meltdown travesty taking their own route to the graveyard.

Financial firms and Mary's pension fund collapsed because the mortgage backed securities market had collapsed. All were left with billions of dollars of suddenly unmarketable investments.

I can only conclude that the behavior of these supposedly treasured American credit rating institutions represented ineptitude, sloth, and greed. Their performance also represented (represents?) a sad and dangerous commentary on America's financial infrastructure. I place "represents?" in quotes because I see no move by government to either eviscerate or at least invigorate their behavior.

Monks Do Not Dissolve Monasteries

Throughout our history, we humans have demonstrated our reluctance, often inability, to eliminate tools of our creativity that are no longer creative. It is a rare occurrence when we witness one of our kind proclaim, "My company is getting too big. I need to scale-down and close some branches." Rather, the more common approach is to expand in order to increase one's wealth and one's pecking order position in life. (For this analogy, I know of no church and its monks closing a "branch" of its own accord.)

But this Rule of Life law goes beyond humans' inclination not to dismantle our monasteries. It also describes our inclination to expand them.

I suspect many people who ascend to being CEOs of a company have a DNA marker that drives them to acquire another company; and yet another. Such is globalization. Such is bigness.[10]

During the run-up to the 2008 run-down, mortgage companies, previously located in a city, branched out across the nation as they expanded into the subprime market. The same situation occurred with Fannie Mae as it grew to support the subprime lenders. Later, I will cite several examples of the Monks Do Not Dissolve Monasteries Law, such as Countrywide Finance, and provide examples of how their greed for growth and unprincipled conduct did much damage to America's economy and its individual citizens.

Examples are also provided of the expansion of the nation's largest banks into becoming even-larger banks; as well as these big banks lobbying Congress to get into Fannie Mae's *government-protected* business. It came down to "seize from Uncle Sam's right hand what I can" capitalism, coupled with "accept from Uncle Sam's left hand anything he will give me" socialism.

Risk and Debt

You are still reading, so I can assume we are off to a good start. But the subjects introduced thus far do not constitute the whole story. To continue our analysis, I introduce another significant component in the meltdown equation: risk and associated debt. I have selected risk as the starting point for a more detailed analysis because it is easier to understand than, say, credit default swaps. Other subjects pertaining to the meltdown will follow in subsequent reports.

The third report will examine how taking on risk—as well as finding ways to avoid it—contributed to the meltdown. To set the stage, we close with these thoughts:[11]

> In the booming American housing market mortgage originators were happy to accept no security at all [from buyers who had no credit rating], lending 100% of the value of the house—partly because they thought house prices would continue to rise, and partly because they assumed the market would be liquid enough for them to palm the mortgages off on other investors. As it happened, the mortgage originators were wrong and the loans that were stuck on their books helped destroy their businesses.

The concept is staggering: No security at all, no credit rating, house prices would continue to rise, palming off mortgages to other investors. No question, greed and stupidity were parts of the mix.

---

[1] Excerpts of "The Rules of Life" are included as a glossary in *The Deadly Trinity*, which is slated for republication in mid 2013. Look for it at Amazon, Barnes and Noble, and such.

[2] *60 Minutes*, CBS, February 15, 2009.

[3] "Wall Street and the Financial Crisis," U.S. Senate, Permanent Subcommittee of Investigations, April 13, 2011, p. 42.

[4] Ibid., p. 20.

[5] Financial Crisis Inquiry Report, p. 182.

[6] I wrote a few paragraphs about this matter in unrelated essays in 2005. But I did not pay enough attention. I was preoccupied with the Traveling America series. Had I an ounce of knowledge about shorting (betting against) securities, I would have been tempted. For my thoughts about this matter, go to Blog.UylessBlack.com and click on Native American cities. Read the last section of this essay.

[7] The so-called third world countries, whose citizens have never been inside a bank, did not escape the meltdown. Some foreign aid programs to nearly starving people have been curtailed.

[8] "Wall Street and the Financial Crisis," p. 30.

[9] Ibid., p. 31.

[10] Besides, if a company cannot innovate, it buys out a company that does. It's an accepted aspect of doing business: "My business can't do the business of that business down the street. Somehow, it got ahead of me. But I have more money than it does, so I will buy-out that business, and its business will become my business." Creative capitalism! If you can't innovate, don't try. Take over someone who can. It's too much trouble to start from scratch. As such, bigness begets more bigness.

[11] "Wild Animal Spirits: Why is Finance so Unstable?" *The Economist*, January 24, 2009, p.8.

Report 3

Risk and Debt

Honey, I can't wait 'till tomorrow, 'cause I'm getting richer every day!
—A store owner to his wife...just before the meltdown.

Honey, I can't wait 'till tomorrow, 'cause I'm getting richer every day!
—A home owner to his wife...just before the meltdown.

Honey, I can't wait 'till tomorrow, 'cause I'm getting richer every day!
—A Wall Street banker...just before and after the meltdown.

March 5, 2009

There is a lot of bad news in the press today. Stocks are down. Unemployment is up. One of my tennis partners, the owner of a company that builds doors and stairs for new homes, recently cut his working force by one-third. He may be back on the line doing manual labor while his former carpenters line up at the unemployment office.

Continuing the analysis of why my doctor friend is in bankruptcy and my truck washing friend has mothballed some of his equipment, this report examines how risk (and associated debt) became a factor in the current financial crisis. The discussion is organized as follows:

(1) Risks taken on by banks and other mortgage lending institutions
   (a) Backing loans with customer deposits
   (b) Backing loans with money from investors and borrowings

(c) Changing the net capital rules
   (d) Selling loans and off-loading risks
   (e) Increasing risks on mortgage backed securities, courtesy of Uncle Sam and Aunt Basel
   (f) Leveraging upon more leveraging
(2) Risks taken on by officials of financial companies
(3) Risks taken on by individuals who purchased homes

Before examining the list above, a few words about debt:

A Debt by Any Other Name Is Still a Debt

In the never ending quest for Americans to own more electronic devices than the nearby Best Buy store:[1]

- American households carry about $8,000 in credit card debt, an increase of close to 200 percent since 1990. At an 18 percent interest it will take more than 25 years to repay (at minimum payment rate).
- About 43 percent of American families spend more than they earn.
- Personal bankruptcies have doubled over the past ten years.
- With wages mostly stagnant, from 2001 to 2007, mortgage debt rose by roughly 63 percent.[2]

In the recent past, this was a hopeless situation for millions of Americans, but along came the second mortgage market to the rescue. Banks and other financial institutions were waving the flags of generosity and concern by consolidating consumers' high interest credit card debt into lower interest home mortgage debt. With this stringer: the new debt was often set up around a variable interest rate, adjusted upward as time went on. Way upward, sometimes to the point of the mortgage payment being unpayable. Later, I offer more information and statistics about this problem.

(1) Risks taken on by banks and other mortgage lending institutions[3]

(a) Backing Loans with Customer Deposits

In the past, when a bank made a loan, it was responsible for the integrity of the loan. The bank assumed the risk for making the loan and giving the money to the party taking out the loan. Why? Because it kept the loan on its books. That is, it owned the loan.

In addition, prior to the 1970s, a bank used customer deposits for 90 percent of its loans.[4] The other 10 percent came from its earnings, stock shares, and borrowings. It was an attractive arrangement: A bank paid, say, 3 percent on a savings account, and charged, say, 6 percent on a loan.[5] It pocketed the 3 percent difference; one reason why so many people wanted to get into banking. If a bank offered high quality services and it was careful to whom it granted loans, it had a lock on making money.

If a potential borrower did not have a good enough credit rating to purchase a home, the bank simply refused the loan or upped the down payment requirement. This latter approach gave the bank leverage on the borrower, who did not want to lose the equity in the home.

The money for the source of the loan was as solid as it gets: customers' deposits. The bank had little concern about depositors making a run on the bank. Their accounts were guaranteed by the FDIC.

(b) Backing Loans with Money from Investors and Borrowings

In the early 1970s, banks began to reduce the financing of their loans from customers' deposits. They began using more funds from wholesale funding sources, such as the Federal Home Loan Bank,[6] or went to the national CD (certificate of deposit) marketplace. Today, only 60 percent of banks' loans are backed by deposits.[7] Why the change? Because a bank pays out hard cash for interest on customer deposits, and loans from the Federal Home Loan Bank are usually of low interest and for a long time. In addition, for safety, the Federal Reserve requires its member banks to hold funds in reserve; funds that cannot be lent. The amount is about 10 percent of a bank's checking account deposits, depending on the size of the bank.

Why should this shift in the source of funds for a bank's loans be a problem? First, loans may be callable. Or a bank may be required to come up with more reserves, but this is generally not a problem. If the bank is sound, the Federal Home Loan Bank will leave the bank alone.

Of more importance, the use of CDs might appear to be safe to a bank. If it pays high rates on CDs, it can attract a lot of buyers. However, big CD investors tend to pull out their deposits more often and faster than the mom and pop depositors. Thus, if a bank has made a lot of loans based on keeping those CDs, and it loses them, it may not be able to continue with the loans and honoring lines of credit. If lines of credit go away, a lot of businesses follow. They cannot operate without lines of credit.

Banks have to answer to the people who own their stock. Not only are most stockholders looking for a large return, they are also looking for a quick ROI (return on investment). Their behavior is a common human trait and another Rule of Life example. It is called the Immediacy Syndrome: the craving and need for immediate fulfillment, even to the detriment of long-term well-being.

Banks must pay their depositors and creditors. As well, they hope to offer a return on shareholders' equity. If a bank makes money, it can keep this money in retained earnings or pay out dividends to shareholders. However, if the bank suffers loan losses, and accumulated losses are larger than its income, it must take money from its assets (retained earnings) to pay for the losses.[8]

A lot of bad loans will deplete these funds, cast a bad light on the bank, and result in the degrading of the shareholders' stock. After all, potential investors know that if shareholders' equity is headed down, so is the bank's stock. This explains why bank stock has plummeted the past year. They are losing their shareholders' money.

This stockholder situation puts pressure on banks to make a profit every quarter, even though tactical profits are sometimes not in the long-term interests of the bank. No better example can be provided of this situation than the pressure exerted on the banks by their shareholders to get into the subprime market. *That's where the money is! You dummies! The bank across the street is making money hand over fist. Get going, or we'll move our money across the street.*

Thus, the bank is no longer granting as many loans with money from its traditional customers. It is granting loans with money from loans it takes from the Federal Home Loan Bank, by issuing CDs, investing in securities, and of course, from the funds it obtained from issuing stock. The volatility of CD deposits and the fickleness of shareholders with short-term tempers bring more pressure to make an immediate big killing. Not to mention that a big killing will provide the bank officers with bonuses, a topic covered later.

(c) Changing the Net Capital Rules

In addition, banks have been engaged in activities that have increased their risk of doing business. They have been making more loans but with less capital to back those loans.

But why? Bankers are supposedly smart people, and risk assessment is (or should be) embedded into their being. It should be part of every decision they make. We can also ask this question to the bank regulators. Why were they asleep at the wheel when they reduced banks' net capital holding requirements?

It comes down to banks and the regulators of banks lulling themselves into the notion that the future would be the same as the present and the recent past: Years of growth; years of moderate recessions; years of insignificant loan defaults; years of profit; years of almost no risk.

As one example, the Financial Services Regulatory Relief Act of 2006 was passed by a 417-15 vote in the House of Representatives and signed into law by President Bush. It allowed banks to lower their capital reserve requirements. Here is an excerpt of this law as it pertains to capital requirements:[9]

"SEC. 5143. REDUCTION OF CAPITAL.

"(a) IN GENERAL.—Subject to the approval of the Comptroller of the Currency, a national banking association may, by a vote of shareholders owning, in the aggregate, two-thirds of its capital stock, reduce its capital.

"(b) SHAREHOLDER DISTRIBUTIONS AUTHORIZED —As part of its capital reduction plan approved in accordance with subsection (a), and with the affirmative vote of shareholders owning at least two thirds of the shares of each class of its stock outstanding (each voting as a class), a national banking association may distribute cash or other assets to its shareholders."

As stipulated in clause (b), this law allowed banks to reduce their capital requirements and distribute the resulting booty to their shareholders! It was not to make more loans, which is the principal function of a bank, but to distribute more money to stockholders. As discussed later, the lowering of capital requirements became a significant reason for the need to bail out many banks.[10]

Another earlier example: In 2004, the Securities and Exchange Commission (SEC) removed rules that limited the 15 to 1 ratio (loans to money in the vault) for investment banking firms, but kept a more restricted limit on commercial banks.[11] As just mentioned, in 2006, Congress passed a law that encouraged commercial banks to become riskier institutions.

The regulators said, *We are philosophically opposed to intervening in the free market. It will regulate itself.* The banks' board, officers, and stockholders said, *So, let's keep it going! More loans. More profits. More money for us.*

Commercial Banks, Investment Banks, and Glass-Steagall: And More Examples of Increasing Risk of Losing Capital

A brief overview: Commercial banks take in deposits and lend money. Investment banks raise capital, issue securities, and manage corporate mergers and acquisitions.

In the past, these two types of banks were kept separate, but in 1999, Congress passed legislation (the repeal of the Glass-Steagall Act) that allowed these two kinds of institutions to commingle much more than before.

Some people believe conflicts of interest must arise for the granting of credit (making loans) and the use of this credit (making investments) by the same organization. ("Hey, you give me a loan, and I'll use part of the money to buy your securities.")

By removing these rules, investment banks (such as Goldman Sachs) began to expand their lending amounts without having to raise any more capital. Because repeal of Glass-Steagall had greatly lessened the separation of commercial and investment banks, what would be a logical strategy? Move more of the lending operations from the commercial bank side to the investment bank side.

By the end of 2007, many banks had altered their debt-to-capital ratio from 15:1 to 30:1. It was accomplished without putting one red cent into their vaults for a rainy day, for a day when the bubble might burst. Rainy day? Bubble burst? Very doubtful. The bank execs opined, "But if it does happen, it's not my money. We've already gone public, and a golden parachute is strapped to my back."

A typical example is Lehman Brothers. The company borrowed huge sums of money and invested heavily in real estate securities. Its debts were about 35 times its capital.[12] During an upturn, if Lehman's investments made only 1 percent, the firm had a return of 35 percent on its own money.

But what about a downturn? Eventually, it is going to happen and Lehman's executives are going to be pilloried (and maybe lose their huge bonuses and parachutes). I can only surmise that the executives at places such as Lehman were thinking (a) business cycles no longer occur, or (b) I'll be out of here with millions of dollars before the cycle turns and the company sinks.[13]

The rainbow for Lehman and others came to an end with the downturn. With a heavily leveraged company, such as Lehman, a small drop (say 1 percent) in the value of its investments changes the ratio. And the drop in mortgage backed securities was not just 1 percent. For example, as the bubble began to burst, Merrill Lynch sold a set of mortgage securities at the distressed price of 22 cents on the dollar. In hindsight, the old saw about leaving money under our mattress for safekeeping seemed wise in the 2008 market.

Some banks, such as Citigroup, set up contracts with the buyers of their securities (which had mortgage backed securities in them) in which the buyers could give them back to Citigroup at the original price if the market for them collapsed.[14] And collapse it did. $25 billion of these instruments came back to Citigroup; one reason the bank is in trouble.

(d) Selling Loans and Off-Loading Risks

Risk. In the financial world, the word means taking a chance on the probability of a loss on an investment versus the probability of a profit. Balanced with this idea is the amount of the potential loss versus the amount of the potential gain. It deals with speculation, which is not a negative word. Each waking moment of our lives we speculate about which actions we might take that will possibly reap the best results.

In the past, banks lent money (mostly) based on how much money they had on hand (deposits). As mentioned, they were *directly* responsible for the integrity of the loan. If a loan defaulted, the banks owned the loan and the associated property. Consequently, they ate the loss and balanced it against their profits. Keeping a firm hand on the loan portfolio was one of the most important jobs of bank management.[15]

But consider this: What if you could make a loan to a home buyer and then sell this loan to someone else? What's the point of such an exercise? First, you (somewhat) check the credit worthiness of the loan applicant. Second, you give the person the money. Third, you sell this loan to a third party for the loan amount plus a markup. Fourth, as long as your paperwork on the loan passes a low quality examination, you *relinquish responsibility* for the person paying off the loan.

Granted, if the loan goes bad, the buyer can come back to you for redress, but you can play the odds: If a few loans go sour, you don't care. Statistically, you've covered your rear end and you don't have to wait twenty to thirty years to gain back the principal and interest on the loan to make more loans. You're mostly whole and can make more loans.

Moral Hazard

In such an environment, why should a bank care if a loan here or there goes bad? With the loss of risk—and with the loss of an affiliation with the borrower—goes the loss of responsibility. This idea is called a moral hazard: *If an actor is not responsible for his actions, the actor will not act responsibly.*

The idea became so prevalent in practice that it became known as "originate and sell."[16] Companies were formed for the sole purpose of originating a mortgage and selling it as soon as possible. The time-honored concept of "originate and hold" was becoming passé.

Yes, but the fact remains that an originator was still ultimately responsible for the loan. But in a booming market, who's going to worry about loan defaults? Everyone, including banks and homeowners, were making a lot of money riding the expanding bubble.

In addition, what if the loan itself was broken up into different parts? What if these parts were then packaged in different mortgage backed securities? What if these securities were later broken up into yet other securities? What if a different type of security was invented to gamble on the worthiness or unworthiness of the mortgage backed securities, some containing only a portion of a loan? What if bookkeeping departments lost track of these increasingly indecipherable financial instruments? All these events formed a Dickens tragic comedy, which is recounted in later reports.

In the meantime, with the lowering of standards and subprime loans becoming common, the Threshold Lowering Syndrome kicked-in. Adjustable rate mortgages' high interest rates came into place and the situation took a turn for the worse. The turn was aided by a surreal accounting maneuver called book as profit.

Book as Profit

Banks did not off-load all their loans. The number varied, depending on the bank management's philosophy about the matter. However, for those loans held, banks were allowed to "book as profit the *expected future value* of those loans. [Italics are mine]. The accounting rules allowed them to assume the loans would be completely repaid. And not prematurely; the assumption was that the borrower would hold his mortgage until all the interest and principal were paid."[17]

This idea is staggering in relation to how the real estate market evolved. In the old days of prime/fixed rates, this assumption was close to the mark. With the new days of subprime/adjustable rate mortgages (ARM), it wasn't even on the dart board. Adjustable rate mortgages usually had the adjusted and higher interest rate kick-in after two years. When it did, the mortgage payment often went up several hundred dollars. A supposedly solid mortgage—solid for two years—quickly became almost worthless as defaults mounted. Yet the book as profit arrangement ignored this reality.

As said by Michael Lewis, "This assumption was the engine of doom."[18] It led to false conclusions about a supposedly valid set of accounting books.

(e) Increasing Risks on Mortgage Backed Securities, Courtesy of Uncle Sam and Aunt Basel

In the past, banks have been held to high standards for setting aside reserves on their assets as a cushion during down times and associated loss of income. Additionally, regulators require banks to hold more capital for riskier assets. The "Tier 1" bank capital is the most conservative and least risky of a bank's financial holdings. In the past, Tier 1 consisted of cash and the proceeds from the stock it had issued. No debt was allowed in Tier 1. The lower tiers, such as certain securities that carry debt as part of their contracts, are more risky and the Feds required more capital to back them up.

In the 1990s an international bankers' consortium called the Basel Committee of Bank Supervision established rules that reduced the capital requirements on riskier assets. In addition, the Federal Reserve followed by allowing banks to include some riskier securities in the banks' calculation of Tier 1 capital [notably trust preferred securities (TRUPS)] that a bank could issue to raise funds.[19] The effect was the relaxation of a heretofore conservative measure of a bank's financial health.

This seemingly innocuous change to a bank's capital requirements was another example of the Law of Unintended Consequences. The banks prized TRUPS and began issuing them with thousands of offerings. Uncle Sam made them even more attractive: The issuer of this security could deduct the interest on its tax return that it paid to an investor.

A bank executive would ask himself, "Why worry about the hassle and expense to raise money by issuing yet more stock?" And he would answer, "I'll just issue more TRUPS."

This situation did not end with a bank issuing these debt instruments to someone else. Banks bought other banks' TRUPS. After all, they were now given Tier 1 capital preference. By 2005, the TRUPS market stood at $85 billion, with more than 800 banks issuing them and an untold number of investors and other banks buying them.

These events led to an even more interconnected, interdependent world. When the 2008 unraveling began, the owners of TRUPS raced to the gates to unload them. But to whom? No one, because no one wanted them.

Other Securities. There were other proposals to further reduce bank capital requirements that did not take effect. However, in January, 2001 the Basel Committee of Bank Supervision said the guidelines for the risk weightings regulators would apply to mortgage backed securities. These instruments were issued by institutions such as banks and mortgage lending companies (one example is defunct Countrywide Financial). In addition, most banks (with the exception of a few global banks) *were allowed to use their own internal ratings* "by tying risk weightings on securitizations to the ratings the rating agencies assigned to them."[20] (See Sidebar 3-2 for a quick look at Basel's risk weightings.)

Sidebar 3-2. A Quick Look at Basel's Risk Ratings.[21]

There are four categories of Basel risk weightings. The best rating is for the safest securities, such as U.S. Treasuries (with a requirement of a 0 percent set-aside of capital). The worst rating is for unsecured lines of credit such as credit cards (and 100 percent capital set-asides). The securities in between these two categories carry risk weightings of 20 percent or 50 percent.

In later reports, I will explain how inaccurate these ratings were and how the banks paid rating agencies to rate the very securities the banks were holding or issuing. We will also learn the rating agencies were supremely incompetent. (Just one example for now: Moody's mortgage analysis did not take into account a borrower's debt-to-income ratio! That is akin to your mortgage company not assessing how much income you have in relation to your debt.)[22]

Keep in mind that many of these mortgage backed securities were loaded with worthless mortgage loans, yet regulators lowered the capital that banks had to set aside for them. This action encouraged banks to increase their holdings of these securities. The procedure also gave more credence and authority to the rating agencies.

In the past, privately issued securities were assigned a 50 percent risk weighting. Those securities issued by Fannie Mae were given a 20 percent risk weighting, because of the implicit understanding that the U.S. government would back them up. This practice irked banks because they (rightly) believed this preference for Fannie Mae put them at a disadvantage.

It seems to this writer, having now been exposed in a general way to Fannie, that this company's very existence is a contradiction to free market principles. I'll hold my final judgment, ask for your comments about the matter, and maybe write more later about this notion. Anyway:

Disaster Looms

In 2001 the Basel Committee proposed that any asset-backed security—such as a security that contained mortgages (a mortgage backed security)—that had a credit rating of AAA (highest) or AA (next highest) would be assigned a 20 percent risk weighting. It did not matter who issued the security. It could be respected JP Morgan or a shady loan shark company. As long as the credit rating agencies, which erroneously rated thousands of securities, tagged a security as AAA or AA, the banks could reduce their capital set-asides from 50 percent to 20 percent. I can only say again: Fantastic.

In November, 2001, Uncle Sam followed Basel's proposals. Thereafter, a huge herd of financial lemmings headed for the cliffs:

(a) Wall Street entered into closer relationships with the rating agencies—often manipulating the firms to their own ends—to develop methodologies to falsely rate subprime mortgages to the higher-yielding AAA or AA grades.

(b) Mortgage lenders began to become more aggressive in finding ways to increase residential mortgage loans that could be off-loaded at a healthy profit to naive investors.

(c) Wall Street increased its involvement in this highly lucrative field of securities—which were filled with high-interest-yielding junk.

(d) Banks and other mortgage lenders jumped into the feeding trough. They did not have to worry about worthless loans that had been securitized and were no longer on their books. The subprime market for mortgage originators exploded.

(e) The subprime market for Wall Street mortgage securitizers also exploded. Lending fees, consulting revenue, loan purchase proceeds, and underwriting income[23] led to huge profits and huge payouts to employees.

(f) Not to be left off the bandwagon, investors—such as a credit union funds and our mother-in-law's pension plans—

purchased securities that contained mortgages (and related instruments, explained later) for their investment portfolios. After all, Uncle Sam and Aunt Basel had anointed them as AAA or AA.

Leveraging Upon Leveraging

In this section the term leverage refers to using borrowed money to make investments. Banks and other financial institutions rely on leverage. We are told they cannot do business without it. Most individuals are in the same boat. For example, how many people can buy a home (or a boat) with cash only?

When we buy a home, we take on debt. The mortgage represents debt; it creates leverage. We learned that a mortgage is often packaged with other mortgages into a security (a mortgage backed security [MBS]) and sold to an investor. Because mortgages contain much more debt than equity, this MBS is little more than debt, which represents further leverage. In addition, the investor often uses borrowed money to purchase the MBS, which creates more leverage. The MBS is often packaged into another security (called a collateralized debt obligation [Report 8]) and sold to an investor. Thus, the CDO also represents debt and is purchased by an investor who uses borrowed money to buy the CDO. More leverage.

If you are following me, regardless of what the specific names of what these securitites may be, and however they may be "packaged," everything mentioned thus far contains far more debt than equity. Everything is highly leveraged. And there is more leveraging to come.

In case these investments go bad, most are insured, just as we insure our homes against fire. Again, in Report 8, we will learn a prevalent form of insurance in the finance industry is the credit default swap (CDS), which was briefly mentioned earlier. A CDS is usually purchased with borrowed money to hedge against an investment. More leverage.

The situation is more complex than the situation just cited. We will also learn in Chapter 8 that many CDSs can be packaged into another security, which creates yet more leverage as it is purchased with borrowed money.

The ongoing purchases and borrowings just described create huge flows of money and immense potential wealth for the participants. They also create gigantic piles of debt, resulting in byzantine networks of interdependence among the sellers and borrowers of these complex sets of financial instruments.

Pride in Fostering a Ponzi Scheme? We can be proud of ourselves. With the simple act of purchasing our home and taking out a mortgage, we help start the huge engines of the financial industry's wealth, debt, and leverage. From this outsider (and a businessman who operated with little of no debt for over twenty five years), it seems reasonable to say piles of debt purchased by more piles of debt could be construed as a Ponzi scheme. But I cannot make such a claim, as this debt hierarchy is considered to be a sound business practice. And I suppose it is, until a financial storm passes by.

Anyway, competent regulators and prudent business people keep a wary eye on how much debt is held in relation to the capital to back up the debt. Later reports will likely lead you to a state of disbelief. Examples are provided of institutions that purchased billions of dollars of securities that contained debt *with very little or no capital to back up the debt.* (Of course, so did a lot of home owners, recounted in Report 10).

In some instances, financial institutions created securities[24] that did not contain mortgages but commercial paper (unsecured debt to finance short-term money needs). Unsecured means unsecured, except by the company's good name. It's an accepted way to do business, and Uncle Sam says, "OK."

As one example, regulators did not require Citigroup to hold any capital against the possibility that these securities might tank. However, Citigroup was permitted to use its own computer-based models (Report 5) to assess the risk of these highly volatile instruments. When the meltdown began, and as the paper matured, Citigroup had to buy back $25 billion of commercial paper. The bank had to buy the paper because there were no other buyers.

Should the regulators have put a brake on these actions? If they affected others (you and me), the answer is yes. Did they do their job? The answer is no. Should the financial industry have put a brake on itself? Yes. Did it? With rare exceptions, the answer is no.

The Multiplier Effect. When the housing industry collapsed, the leveraging upon leveraging created a multiplier effect. Borrowers defaulted on their mortgages and investors in the mortgage backed securities that contained these mortgages lost money. So did investors in the securities that contained mortgage backed securities themselves (another form of packaging and leverage). So did investors who put money into yet more (and different) securities who were betting on the mortgage industry to succeed. "As a result, the losses from the housing collapse were multiplied exponentially."[25]

Not everyone lost. Those who bet against the housing industry by purchasing credit default swaps made a lot of money. These people became billionaires. Their winnings put a Las Vegas tycoon to shame. No speed bump for these savvy investors.

(2) Risks taken on by officials of financial companies

For every loan you (say, as a commercial banker) approve, execute, and off-load to someone else, the more money you and your bank make. If the loan defaults, you have sold enough of them to repurchase a few bad apples. Even more, the initial loan money— before the loan was sold—did not come from your pocketbook or from your depositors. It came from an outside investor. No big deal.

As a bank officer, you personally have no financial stake in this loan. Well, with this caveat. If you are privately owned, you and your partners are personally responsible for these kinds of transactions. Then be careful. But if you are publicly traded, then it is not your money. The shareholders take a bath, but by then, you have reaped millions in bonuses and golden parachuted into your new retirement home in the Caribbean.

Leverage again. For many years, investment banks were owned by their bank's management who were directly responsible for covering any losses that might occur. By going public, these people became financially blameless if the company went into the red.

To gain a sense of the absurdity of the situation, let's use a 35:1 debt-to-assets ratio, such as that taken on by Lehman, an example cited earlier.[26] Further, let's relate these ideas to personal circumstances:

Say Uyless Black owns a home, two cars, and assorted consumer items. Assuming the home is not underwater (worth less than the mortgage), and the two cars are paid for, Uyless has, say, $300,000 worth of stuff. Uyless owes money to credit card companies but pays it off each month. He has an IRA worth, say, another $300,000. So, Uyless has net assets of roughly $600,000. If Uyless chooses to take the same fiscal and financial management mentality that some of the financial institutions took and leverages himself to a 35:1 debt-to-assets ratio, his debt would be $21,000,000.[27]

Where am I going to get the money to service this debt? Where was Lehman going to get the money to service its debt? I head to Las Vegas to gamble on Texas Hold'em and hope to keep myself above water. Lehman heads to Wall Street to gamble on subprime mortgage bonds to do the same. If all goes well, I win several million dollars to stave off bankruptcy. Trouble is, I don't know all that much about Texas Hold'em. Lehman hoped the mortgage bond market bubble will never burst. Trouble was, Lehman did not know all that much about subprime mortgage bonds.

Here is a summary of this situation:[28]

> The argument is that managers in recent times took excessive risks because they did not own their own firms. Moreover, their pay gave them huge incentives to gamble with the business. In *Liars Poker*, his tale of Salomon Brothers in the 1980s, Michael Lewis records the words of a senior trader who worked for Lew Ranieri, the creator of mortgage backed securities: "At other places management says, 'Well, gee, fellas, do we really want to bet the ranch on this deal?' Lewie was not only willing to bet the ranch, he was willing

REPORT 3: RISK AND DEBT 53

to hire people and let them bet on the ranch too. His attitude was: 'Sure, what the fuck, it's only a ranch.' "

Just make certain you have that golden parachute clause in your contract. Make sure you start the Autocatalytic Process humming to more rapidly increase the bank's revenue stream. Turn those loans out the door; sell them; loans beget more loans; use the income and profit to make more loans. Ignore the long-term consequences to the stockholders; you are a short-term guy.

Running out of loan applicants? Can't have that! Your competitors across the street have them lined up at the door. If you can sell the loan, you get instant cash, so just lower your requirements for granting a loan. After all, that is what everyone else is doing. Don't forget to include the dead husband's income in the balance sheet. See figure 3-1.

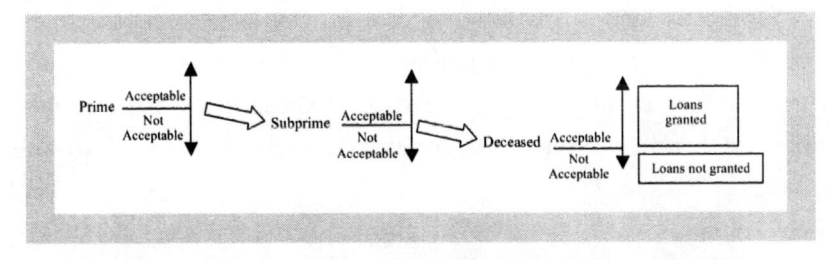

Figure 3-1. Can the loan applicant fog a mirror?

Betting with a Bank's Own Money. Increasingly, investment banks have been making speculative investments using their own money. What's wrong with that? If a bank loses money on the bet, it's the bank's money. Furthermore, if a large loss does not disrupt the highly interconnected financial industry, there is nothing iniquitous about this practice. However, if it does affect and endanger the financial system, and the bank goes about this business secretly, it's akin to asking for big trouble. Just ask Lehman Brothers and those millions of people affected by the meltdown.

This situation represents a pervasive practice on Wall Street. As discussed in more detail later, it involves the *nonregulated* trades of financial instruments called *derivatives* (a *secret* contract between two parties, often dealing with the granting of *credit* or simply an opportunistic bet on, say, stock.)

Please stick with me on this topic. I've introduced it here and will explain: (a) why it is opaque to the public and to regulators, (b) why Wall Street wants to keep it this way, and (c) why unregulated derivatives are dangerous to America's financial system, and thus to America.

(3) Risks Taken on by Individuals Who Purchased Homes

Three factors contribute to home owners staying in a home: (1) They have equity in the home. (2) They can afford to make the monthly mortgage payment. (3) The house is worth more than the mortgage on the house. As mentioned, if the mortgage is larger than the value of the house, the property is said to be underwater.

Home owners are willing to take on the largest debt in their lives (a home mortgage) for twenty to thirty years as long as these three factors come into play. If one of these criteria no longer holds, a home owner loses incentive to keep his end of the mortgage bargain.

Coupled with the factors cited above, during the years just before the meltdown, banks increasingly lowered or even removed equity (down payment) requirements for a buyer. Adjustable interest rate clauses in mortgage contracts kicked in, suddenly making the loan payment unpayable. The financial industry coined a nickname for this practice, the NINJA loan, given to people with no income, no job, and no assets.

If I have no stake in the house, and my loan payment has increased beyond my ability to pay it, what else can I do but default on my contract and abandon the property? That is exactly what happened, leading to many companies holding worthless paper, which led to vacant houses, and to the collapse of home values. Increasingly, one fed on the other. Homes underwater no longer referred only to residences flooded by Katrina.

Personal Responsibility

Nonetheless, at the end of the day—and on the signature line of a mortgage contract—the individual is responsible for his or her actions. It is the mortgage buyer who signs the contract, no one else. Because this book's themes are oriented toward America's macrofinances, it does not contain as much text about this country's huge problem with its microfinances; namely, the irresponsibility of individual citizens. To somewhat balance this discussion:

Debt Consolidation. This report began with a brief summary of consumer debt in America. Let's expand on the subject with a more detailed discussion. The idea of debt consolidation into a second mortgage sounds enticing: *Pay off all those credit cards, your car loan from GM, your honeymoon loan from Screw You Finance, your amphitheater TV screen loan from Best Buy! We'll pay off all of them, and give you one simple monthly payment. At a low rate!*

That is, until the teaser rate for the second mortgage no longer teases. Then other rates come into effect. Thousands of Americans, already up to their necks in debt, consolidated their debt into their adjustable rate mortgage contracts; or if not these contracts, then in contracts with rates higher than their former rates.

Consider a poor, uninformed family of struggling parents and their kids. They were wannabe consumers. They were told by the advertising world—marketers, salespeople—that they were entitled to the American Dream. So, they went to the shopping center and hocked themselves to the hilt to realize that dream. Now they were real consumers. They had all the trappings of affluence. Except for one salient fact: They were not affluent. They were close to insolvency.

No need to worry, they could use the equity in their home to obtain yet another loan; one they could not pay for. But the loan company did not care. They just sold the junk to someone else. The age-old human solution to a problem: Out of sight, out of mind.

Where Does the Fault Lie? To be clear—and to repeat this important point—many home buyers are to blame for their financial situation with their mortgage contracts. They overextended. But on the other side of the coin, many home buyers, having done due diligence (prosaically known as homework) on their finances and their home mortgage, were deceived—often outright lied to—by their mortgage lenders. Should they have read the contract? Sure. But I've read such contracts and they are not user friendly, especially for people who fall into the subprime market to begin with. These people are not noted for their textual and verbal skills.

The mortgage lending predators knew their quarry. They cast their bait in the form of falsehoods and incomprehensible contracts. They reeled in their prey, constructed phony and usurious mortgages, packaged them up, and off-loaded them to other victims. These victims were often unwary custodians of retirement funds, amateur stewards of bonds for a township, and other guiltless but naive targets. They trusted their investment banker who sold them worthless wares. They trusted the rating agencies who certified the wares as not only worthy, but stellar.

For certain, much of the fault of this meltdown lies with the home buyer. But as told in this book, there are several other parties who share the blame.

Human Nature

The elements of the meltdown described thus far are principally related to taking on risk or not taking it on. The assessment of risk versus reward is part of human nature. We make risk versus reward decisions almost constantly. We speculate.

Most humans take a balanced approach to taking on risk. Typically, we mitigate our behavior if we think the risks are too great. However, if a person stands to gain by committing a specific action and this action is perceived to carry little or no risk, this person will be more willing to commit the act.

I do not mean to overly simplify the meltdown, but from my perspective, the removal of risk on the part of lending institutions (and associated bonuses for short-term gains)—with its commensurate removal of long-term responsibility—was one of the most important factors contributing to the crisis. It allowed the moral hazard specter to raise its head.

The instruments that we hear were the villains—toxic loans packaged into securities, and so on—were certainly part of the equation. But they were just that: They were instruments supposedly devised to reduce risk and maximize profits. Were they effective? That depended on who was holding them at the time of the meltdown.

To close this report, here is an apt summary of risk and its relation to this meltdown:[29]

> Here's how it goes. You bet big with someone else's money. If you win, you get a huge bonus, based on the profits. If you lose, you lose someone else's money rather than your own, and you move on to the next job. ...If you're especially smart...you take a lot of money off the table.

Subsequent reports will analyze the instruments used during the bubble, such as credit default swaps, which have been touched on. As well, we will examine other psychological aspects of the meltdown, including greed, ethics, stupidity, and sociopathy.

I will keep it simple because I do not know enough to make it complex. I will leave that task to the people who created the meltdown in the first place.

---

[1] http://moneycentral.msn.com/content/savinganddebt/p70581.asp.

[2] Financial Crisis Inquiry Report, p. xx.

[3] Unless noted, institutions that deal in home mortgages are sometimes called banks in these reports. I recognize I am taking leave with the term and my banking friends might take issue with this shortcut.

[4] Stephen Gandel, "Why Your Bank Is Broke," *Time*, February 9, 2009, no page.

[5] In the 1980s, after several laws were passed to deregulate aspects of banking, banks were allowed to pay interest on checking accounts.

[6] Local lending institutions can borrow funds from the twelve Federal Home Loan Banks, a system established in the early 1930s to encourage home

financing. According to the Atlanta FHLB, about 80 percent of U.S. lending institutions rely on these banks. Their low costs are passed on to their borrowers.

[7] Gandel, "Why Your Bank is Broke," no page.

[8] Ibid.

[9] Public Law 109–351, 109th Congress.

[10] Some high level government officials have stated the term "bailout" is not accurate because Uncle Sam's infusion of money into failing institutions will be paid back with interest. They think of it as a forced loan. They miss the point. The money was placed into the financial system to save the system from itself. Loan or gift, it has the effect of shoring up a so-called capitalistic system that is supposed to self-correct (with the invisible hand of *laissez-faire*), or self-destruct (by destructive creation).

[11] There are a number of ways of calculating leverage. The simplest is called the loans to deposits ratio. It includes actual deposits and not other instruments. In 2008, the FDIC reports that the national average for FDIC insured institutions was 85 percent: banks carried 85 cents in loans for every dollar in deposits. Some of the troubled banks exceeded this ratio. A failed bank in Colorado carried a 95 percent to 105 percent ratio. Stephanie Simon, *The Wall Street Journal*, June 16, 2009.

[12] Andy Serwer and Allan Sloan, "The Price of Greed," *Time*, September 29, 2008, pp. 35-36.

[13] Lehman's Richard S. Fuld Jr. was awarded $255.9 million from 1998 to 2007. *The New York Times*, February 22, 2009, p. 7.

[14] "How to Play Chicken and Lose: Finance Suffers from Reverse Natural Selection," *The Economist*, January 24, 2009, p. 17.

[15] In my days at the Stonier Graduate School of Banking (where I was sent to learn the rudiments of a trade for which I wrote software), we students spent about 50 percent of our time learning to analyze and dissect financial statements and balance sheets. I was a lost computer waif in a population of accountants. Somehow, I survived and made my way back to the Federal Reserve Board, thankful my profession was writing code to help bean counters count beans, but not counting them myself.

[16] Michael Lewis, *The Big Short*, W. W. Norton & Company, New York, 2010, p. 24.

[17] Ibid., pp. 13-14.

[18] Ibid., p. 14.

[19] Gretchen Morgenson and Joshua Rosner, *Reckless Endangerment*, Henry Holt and Company, New York, 2011, pp. 111-114.

[20] Ibid., p. 134.

[21] Ibid., pp. 134-135.

[22] Ibid., p. 134.

[23] Accessing risks of taking on ownership of, say, securities versus potential income from the securities.

[24] In this case, CDOs (collateralized debt obligations).

[25] Financial Crisis Inquiry Report, p. 145.

[26] Serwer and Sloan, "The Price of Greed," pp. 35-36.

[27] Several approaches and terms are used to define and calculate debt and assets, such as capital and equity. In the financial industry, the term "assets" can include instruments of debt, such as mortgages. They are called assets because they (supposedly) have value and can be sold. Thus, the term debt-to-assets could mean. "How much debt do I have in relation to how much debt I am holding?" For this book, it does not matter. What matters are: What is my debt? How can I service it?

[28] "How to Play Chicken and Lose: Finance Suffers from Reverse Natural Selection," *The Economist*, p. 16.

[29] Serwer and Sloan, ibid., p. 37.

Report 4

Eight Nails in the Meltdown Coffin

March 6, 2009

This is Your On the Street Reporter, once again trying to come to grips with how the meltdown occurred. As mentioned, so many factors came into play it is difficult to put a handle on all of them and to understand how they are related. This report will continue the theme of keeping it simple, and make an attempt to frame the major components and culprits in the home mortgage fiasco part of the meltdown.

Yes, fiasco. The more we learn about the meltdown, the more it becomes obvious it was not foreordained; that it was not a consequence of capitalism's cyclic ups and downs, or a natural occurrence. It was a consequence of:

- Investors, financiers, and home owners shoving risk and responsibility aside, and letting greed and fear (and often fraud) take their place.
- Incompetence on the part of the regulators.
- The blind belief in a never ending housing market bubble.
- The creation of financial instruments that became so complex, few people understood them.

REPORT 4: EIGHT NAILS IN THE MELTDOWN COFFIN 61

- The acceptance of flawed computer models.
- The assumption that markets are self-regulating.

Which came first? Greed, then fraud? Ignorance, then irresponsibility? Fear, then folly? Prolonged low interest rates? Did the subprime market start it off? How about predatory lending from unsavory loan officers, abetted by dishonest mortgage brokers? Was the oblivious naivete of clueless home buyers the problem? I could list other possibilities. To put a loop around something that might be somewhat comprehensible, consider the Autocatalytic Process in figure 4-1.

This report examines the events (processes) in this spiral. For clarification, a point about figure 4-1: The events are depicted as happening in a domino fashion; in lock-step order, one after the other. In some situations they did occur as shown in the figure. But some events occurred in parallel, or nearly parallel with other events. In addition, some events had an effect on multiple events and vice versa.

The figure shows two factors that permeated most aspects of the nearly perfect financial storm: *The insistence with related legislation of the Bush and Clinton administrations—abetted by Congress—to increase home ownership for citizens in the lower economic classes; coupled with the failure of government to regulate these mortgages and their associated securities.*

Given these fundamentals, the figure shows an event in roughly the order in which it occurred, as well as its primary relationship to other events:

1. Liquidity
2. Interest rates
3. Subprime mortgages
4. Adjustable rate interest loans
5. Loan defaults
6. Foreclosures
7. Home prices
8. Mortgage backed securities (and other securities, which are explained in more detail later)

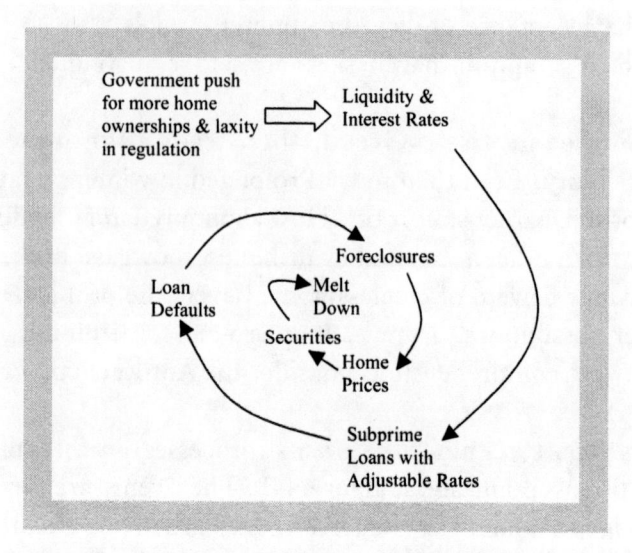

Figure 4-1. The Autocatalytic Process and the mortgage meltdown.

Liquidity

We begin our analysis with the subject of liquidity. For the past few years the countries of China, Singapore, India and most of the oil-producing states have had a lot of money on their hands. The money came from selling goods to America as well as loaning money to the United States. Billions of dollars found their way to America. The money was cycled back in the form of investments: stocks, corporate bonds, government bonds, and of course, real estate.

Bonds and U.S. Treasuries are safe, but their yields are low. Thus, "Facing low yields, this mountain of liquidity sought higher yields. One basic law of finance is: the stronger the borrower, the lower the yield, and vice versa."[1]

Consequently, many of these funds flowed to financial instruments dealing with high yield but weak borrowers. Who might that be? The weak, high yield borrowers in the subprime mortgage marketplace.

The long period of low return on U.S. Treasuries (because of Federal Reserve Board Chairman Greenspan's emphasis on low interest rates) had investors looking for other instruments with a higher return.

Interest Rates

As just mentioned, going hand in hand with the liquidity glut were low interest rates. The U.S. Federal Reserve kept interest rates very low from the end of December of 2001 to June of 2004.[2] As a consequence, for several years mortgage interest rates were also very low.

A potential homeowner might not be able to qualify for a loan with a 5.5 percent interest rate, but he might qualify for a loan at, say, 4.5 percent. The long period of low interest rates began to attract marginally qualified home buyers. A difference of a percentage point could represent the ability or inability to make the loan payment.

Liquidity x Low Interest Rates = A Flood of Money and a Flood of Borrowers. The combination of liquidity and low interest rates over a prolonged time is characterized by some experts as a "lethal combination."[3] Especially if the liquidity seeks high yields, which is what happened in the meltdown. High yields were obtained by picking the low-hanging fruit from the lending tree: the subprime market.

So, which came first? I am not qualified to give an authoritative answer (and experts are divided on this issue). But the case can be made that a long period of huge liquidity and low interest rates provided the fuel to ignite the fires that led to the meltdown. My bias is reflected in the first two elements of the Autocatalytic Process shown in figure 4-1. (Abetted first, by Uncle Sam's heavy hand in the ongoing process; second, by Uncle Same doing nothing.)

Subprime Mortgages

If a person does not have an acceptable credit rating, he might be eligible for a subprime home loan. Generally, this idea translates into charging the borrower more interest for the loan. The logic is that the loan is riskier, so the bank should make a larger profit on it. Again, one rule of finance is, "The stronger the borrower, the lower the yield, and vice versa."

But the logic also holds that an unemployed musician who is taking out a loan will have even more trouble paying off the loan because of the higher interest, which was levied on the borrower because he was marginal in the first place. Even more, a subprime borrower has little cash to make a down payment. Thus, many subprime loans were approved with the borrower having little or no equity in the house.

There's a troubling aspect to this logic because its success rests on an idea called financial leverage, introduced in the previous chapter. A subprime borrower has little or no financial leverage. He is living check to check, deferring the paying of one bill to paying another. He cannot afford any downward turn in his income; none whatsoever. He has no financial leverage. As one person put it, "He's one broken refrigerator away from insolvency." It is a sad and sorry way to live one's life.

A slight change in the borrower's income means he cannot make the loan payment. But he will give it a go if his home is appreciating because he can use the value of the house to take on a home equity loan and, yes! Go deeper into debt. Are there other options for a home owner who has no financial leverage? I know of none.

The truth of the matter is that he should have never been given the loan in the first place. But he was. And so were hundreds of thousands of other folks who had little or no financial leverage.[4]

The result was the huge growth in subprime loans. Take a look at figure 4-2. It shows the percentage of subprime loans as a share of all mortgages that were issued in the United States from 2001 to 2006.[5]

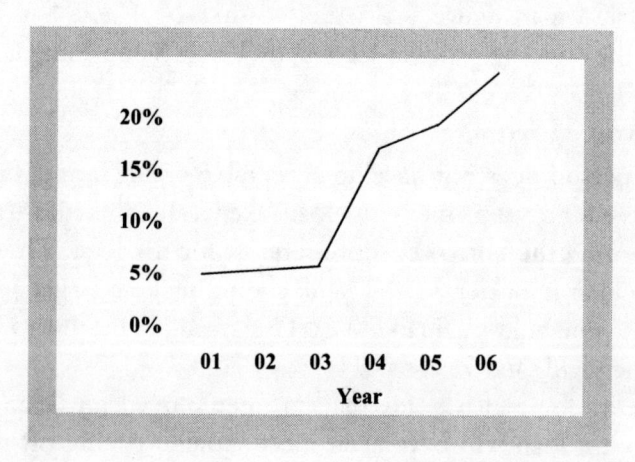

Figure 4-2. Subprime loans as a share of all loans.

Far-fetched? Not really; human nature and the Immediacy Syndrome in action. Consider the following scenario:

Adjustable Rate Interest Loans

- Mortgage salesman, "Have I got a deal for you! We're going to offer you a variable interest rate on your home loan. We'll start you off at a very low rate. The rate may go up but that won't happen for a while. You'll be able to make those low payments into the next two years...or so. Even if the interest rate goes up, it won't go up by very much. Chances are, your loan will stay at the current rate or even go down."

- Mortgage applicant, "I'll barely be able to make the payment now, so...."

- "Don't worry! The value of the property will increase. You can borrow against it or sell it at any time. Besides, why worry about the future?"

- "Yeah, out of sight, out of mind. And I'd really like to sleep in that house as soon as possible."

We begin the analysis of the fourth process of the Autocatalytic Process in the home mortgage meltdown that led to the global wide financial market meltdown, which was introduced in Report 1. It is called an adjustable interest rate (also adjustable rate mortgage or ARM). I have related it to the Immediacy Syndrome, which is another Rule of Life embedded into the human genome. Let's expand this definition: a genetically controlled desire for the immediate fulfillment of a wish, in which any delay toward satiation creates an acute breakdown of the hedonistic areas in the brain.

I make light. But I do not make light. I suspect millions of potential homeowners never considered the long-term consequences of taking out a loan with an adjustable interest rate attached to it. As slaves to the Immediacy Syndrome, they had a short-range view. They had just taken a second tour of their potential home; they wanted to be sleeping in that home as soon as possible.

Did they do the math? Some may have; many did not. Did the mortgage salesman help them with the math? *There is no profit in denying a loan.*

Let's do some math. First: "To avoid high initial mortgage payments, many subprime borrowers took out adjustable rate mortgages (ARMs) that give them a lower initial interest rate. But with potential annual adjustments of 2 percent or more per year, these loans can end up costing much more."[6]

Payment shock may occur if a mortgage payment rises sharply at a rate adjustment. Figure 4-3 shows what happens in the second year if the rate on a discounted 4 percent ARM were to rise to a 6 percent or 7 percent rate.[7]

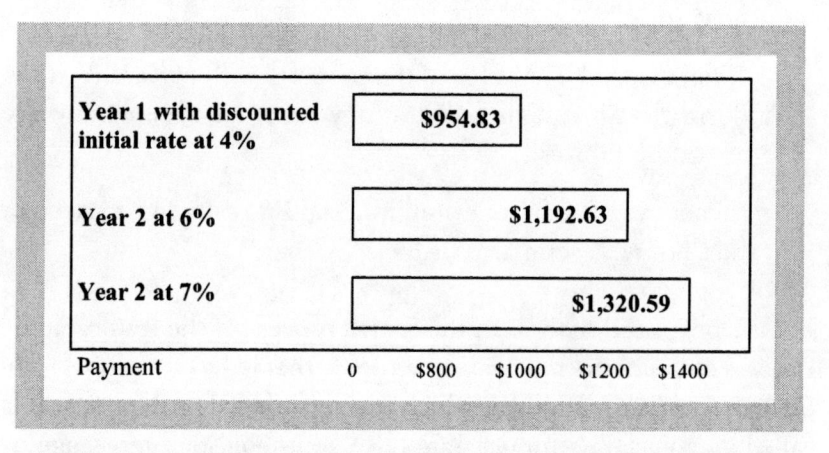

Year 1 with discounted initial rate at 4%	$954.83
Year 2 at 6%	$1,192.63
Year 2 at 7%	$1,320.59

Figure 4-3. Increase of adjustable rate mortgage payment.

As the example shows, a monthly payment goes up from $954.83 to $1,192.63 in the second year. Suppose that the ARM rate rises to 7 percent. A payment in the second year would be $1,320.59. That's an increase of $365.76 in the monthly payment—far beyond the ability of many homeowners to meet this obligation.

One key factor in the meltdown was that so many home owners opted for adjustable rate mortgages. They were on the edge anyway. They had little or no financial leverage on life. How could they come up with the money for that increased monthly payment? They couldn't.

To gain a sense of the magnitude of the problem, consider these quotes from Michael Lewis:[8]

> In 2000 there had been $130 billion in subprime lending, and 55 billion dollars' worth of those loans had been repackaged as mortgage bonds (mortgage backed securities). In 2005, there would be $625 billion in subprime mortgage loans, $507 billion of which found its way into mortgage bonds.
>
> Back in 1996, 65 percent of subprime loans had been fixed-rate, meaning that typical subprime borrowers might be getting screwed, but at least they knew for sure how much they owed each month until they paid off the loan. By 2005, 75 percent of subprime loans were some form of floating-rate, usually fixed for the first two years.

Wall Street Traders and the Immediacy Syndrome

It was not just the lure of the ARM that disarmed the home buyer. It was the lure of immediate profit for the broker, the mortgage lender, and of course, the Wall Street people who were peddling junk. They may have had notions that the mortgage securities were junk, but with immediate payoffs of millions of dollars in commissions and year-end bonuses, they did not care. One of the savvy men who bet against this market posed a question to a trader working at Bear Sterns: "...after [he] asked (the Bear Sterns employee) what was likely to happen to these [mortgage securities] in seven years, he said, 'Seven years? I don't care about seven years. I just need it to last for another two.' "[9]

Will Rogers put it well, "It's not politics that is worrying this country; it's the second payment."[10] Or the third, or fourth. Succumbing to the Immediacy Syndrome, people focused on today. Tomorrow was not immediate; tomorrow was called tomorrow for a good reason.

Loan Defaults

The home mortgage cloth began to unravel when the subprime, adjustable interest rate kicked in. Homeowners came to the conclusion that tomorrow had become today; that they could not make their mortgage payments. As shown in figure 4-4, from 2001 to 2006 the defaults on mortgages in America stayed under 1 million annually.[11] As the variable interest rates came into play, loan defaults skyrocketed to 2.7 million, increasing by almost 500 percent in two years. (The computer models (Report 5) were not programmed to capture this possibility.

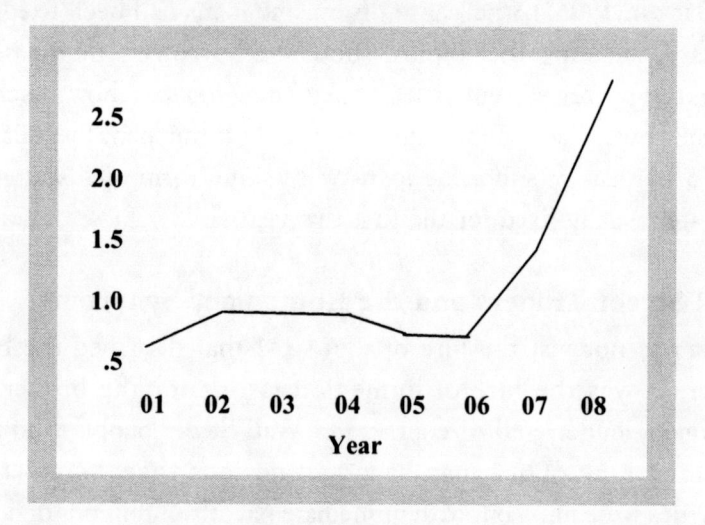

Figure 4-4. Mortgage defaults in America (in millions).

The effect of these defaults began to boomerang throughout the financial world—the Autocatalytic Process in action. The mortgage backed securities, which were laden with subprime loans, dropped precipitously in value. These securities were usually insured and the insurers of the mortgage backed securities had to post collateral to the insured if the mortgages in these securities defaulted. The quality of the mortgage backed securities deteriorated, which led to a decrease in the insuring companies' position on Wall Street, the erosion of their liquidity, and a decline in their stock. Other firms, leery of these holders of poor quality investments, became reluctant to deal with them and to exchange ongoing short-term loans. Credit began to freeze up, a death knell for a society that lives on credit and dies without it.

Foreclosures

As loan defaults mounted, so did associated foreclosures. From 2004 to 2008 foreclosure sales on residences went from 0.3 million to 1.4 million, an astounding 460 percent increase. As said, the computer models were not programmed to capture this possibility.

Home Prices

The coup de grace? From December 2007 to December 2008, the median home price fell from $207,000 to $175,000. But the majority of financial experts, mortgage salesmen, buyers of mortgage backed securities, and homeowners had assumed home prices would *never* decrease, so why factor this improbability into risk assessments? Why worry about the mortgage balance exceeding the value of the house?[12]

As a consequence of this mortgage debt-to-home-value imbalance, many homeowners could not refinance their loans. By the end of 2008, 26.4 percent of all homeowners in the United States had a negative equity in their homes; a sobering statistic, leading to many less-than-sober homeowners.

Mortgage Securities and the Meltdown

Remember mortgage backed securities (MBS)? Let's dance around them a bit, but let's keep our distance, because many are now "toxic." Recall that a mortgage backed security is a bundle of mortgages packaged and sold as a bond. They make money if the mortgages in them are sound. They became the rage during this bubble because their yield was higher than U.S. Treasury securities.

According to the Bond Market Association, the total market value of all outstanding mortgage backed securities at the end of the first quarter of 2006 was approximately $6.1 trillion. The MBS market in America was larger than the total market value of outstanding asset-backed securities (securities based on, say, credit card payments, car loans, movie revenues, and so on). The MBS market overtook the market for U.S. Treasury notes and bonds. Given the value of these financial instruments, the meltdown of the MBS market has had a catastrophic effect on the financial market in general.

Who Put Pressure on Whom?

Several Wall Street experts have offered opinions on who exerted pressure on whom to create this nearly perfect financial storm. Some have this view, as seen below: Investors pressured investment firms to issue more mortgage securities; who pressured banks to make more home loans; who pressured brokers to find more borrowers.

Investors —pressured→ Investment Firms —pressured→ Banks —pressured→ Brokers —pressured→ Borrowers

I do not hold this view. Mine is a two-way arrow, as shown below. Everyone put pressure on everyone else. With so much money to be made, all parties joined in a mutually beneficial feeding frenzy. Their fear was missing out on the action.

Investors ←pressured→ Investment Firms ←pressured→ Banks ←pressured→ Brokers ←pressured→ Borrowers

Bandwagon Effect

We have heard about the bandwagon effect and of the herd instinct, where people tend to behave in accordance with how others behave. Often the behavior is known to be wrongheaded, inefficient, even disastrous. Various studies have verified this type of behavior and it is known that we often make choices we know to be incorrect, but we are persuaded to do so because those around us apply peer pressure. This aspect of human behavior partially explains the feeding frenzy just described.

But herding does not paint the full picture. Many speculators knew the subprime market stank. They just wanted to ride the bubble while the bubble was growing and then get out before it burst. It is

REPORT 4: EIGHT NAILS IN THE MELTDOWN COFFIN 71

said that fear and greed have the largest eyes of all. And all had their eyes on the subprime pie. Some speculators made billions of dollars.

Meanwhile, Joe Citizen trying to run, say, a cattle-growing business, could not manage the wildly unstable fluctuations of feed prices. One man I met (and recounted later) had to sell his farm in Minnesota because he could not deal with the instability. He was one among thousands of innocents who were bushwhacked by the system.

I cannot let these thoughts go without bringing in another group of people who put pressure on banks, investment firms, and government agencies to toss their dice into this gluttonous crap game. That would be Congress and especially the esteemed Barney Frank. He paints himself as a hero in the meltdown fiasco. Quite the contrary. As explained in a later report, Frank played a role in this debacle. He is still in self-serving self-denial.

There you have it. I hope this discussion made some sense. You might want to refer to figure 4-1 to review the major factors contributing to the meltdown. There are others. I have discussed risk in segment 3 of this report. In the next segment, we examine the role software simulation and computer models played. In this next report, another Rule of Life is examined. It's called The Law of the Instrument.

---

[1] Roger C. Altman, "The Great Crash, 2008," *Foreign Affairs*, January/February, 2009, p. 4.

[2] http://www.federalreserve.gov/fomc/fundsrate.htm.

[3] Altman, "The Great Crash, 2008," p. 4.

[4] Any mortgage originating company worth its salt will not ignore the subprime market. After all, there's money to be made and it's the American apple pie notion (no matter how ill conceived) that low income people should be given a chance at the American dream. But if the company is wise, it will require a subprime loan holder to make a big down payment. The company USAA did subprime loans, but it required 30 percent down. Result? Default rates on USAA-originated loans are almost one-half the industry average.

[5] Stephanie Armour, "Millions Could Get Help, but Is the Plan Fair?" *USA Today*, February 19, 2009, p. 2A.

[6] Wikipedia, key in "adjustable rate interest."

[7] http://www.federalreserve.gov/pubs/arms/arms_english.htm#paymentshock.

[8] Lewis, *The Big Short* p. 23.

[9] Lewis, *The Big Short*, p. 147.

[10] Donald Day, ed., *The Autobiography of Will Rogers*, 1949. Secondary source: Leonard Roy Frank, *Quotationary*, Random House, New York, 2001, p. 188.

[11] Armour, "Millions Could Get Help," p. 2A.

[12] A few prudent and smart mortgage originators took the time to look at the rising bubble and rein in their risks; as they say in the financial world "to get closer to home." For example, USAA reduced the amount of money a home owner could borrow on his home equity. It was not a popular decision with some of USAA's customers, but it was a wise one.

REPORT 5

MODELING THE MELTDOWN

*The model used before the financial meltdown
was like an air bag that works all the time,
except when you have a car accident.*
—Nassim Nichloas Taleb, a critic of mathematical models

*The greatest risks are not those you can see and measure,
they are the ones you can't see, and therefore can never measure.*
—Other critics of mathematical models

*The data put into the risk-management models generally covered
only the past two decades, a period of euphoria.*
—Alan Greenspan, in a rare *mea culpa*

March 8, 2009

This is Your On the Street Reporter. In this segment, the focus is on the role computer-based mathematical models played in the financial meltdown.

Software programs simulating the real world and extrapolating conclusions from the simulations have been around since software was invented. When I was writing computer software for a living, I worked at the Federal Reserve Board. There, I coded programs that modeled the nation's money supply. My model was the first of its kind. It was simple, working with only a few money supply variables (such as checking and savings accounts). Nonetheless, each week its millisecond executions saved the Fed's economists and clerks hundreds of hours spent laboring over their calculators. I mention this experience to bolster my ego and impress you with my banking background, but I will also use the story to make some points about computer-based modeling.

Models use mathematics to provide information about causality and correlation. An event will be associated with a cause in relation to how/why the event happened. For example, a model could make an assessment that an altered investment portfolio has become more risky (an event), and that the cause was overloading the portfolio with flaky securities instead of solid U.S. Treasuries.

The goal of modeling is to increase humans' understanding of an event (or events). In so doing, one goal of simulation is to ensure that a model fits our experience and observations and not just our theories. Fine, but if increased understanding of what we already know is the limit of the model, then why bother modeling at all?

Because modeling goes further than what is already known. By using tools such as probability theory, differential equations, random number generators, and Gaussian theory, a model should be able to extrapolate beyond our empirical world to provide information we do not ordinarily know.

For the meltdown, models were supposed to have alerted the experts to the emerging dangers forming in the marketplace that led to so many debacles: the collapse of Bear Sterns, the federal government takeover of Freddie Mac, the bailouts of the banks and the insurance company AIG, the demise of Lehman Brothers, the loss of home ownership, and other calamities.

The Law of the Instrument

What happened? How could the financial industry get it so wrong? In hindsight, the answer to this question is an easy one: Wall Street succumbed to the Law of the Instrument. This law is best defined by an example: A child, who picks up a hammer, looks for something to pound. The law reflects humans' propensity for using tools, often without forethought.

For the financial industry, the hammer is exemplified by the mathematical models. The child is exemplified by the people who relied almost solely on the models to make risk assessments of their investment portfolios at the expense of judgment and common sense.

Prudent Hammering

In contrast, and to demonstrate how computer models should be used, the economists at the Federal Reserve Board frequently examined and questioned my money supply model. Often, I was asked to come in on weekends or evenings to make alterations to the code. Its logic was not in error. It was bug free, but its output might not be "jiving" with the practical knowledge of the Fed economists: *Uyless, this doesn't look right...Uyless, let's try this...No, that doesn't fit with the other reports; make these changes and let's see what comes out...Yep, it seems to fit with our other data...We'll use these three runs of the model for the FOMC (Federal Open Market Committee) meeting.*

Just because a computer spewed forth output did not mean the output was taken as monetary gospel. In fact, *because* it was a computer doing the spewing, the savvy Fed guys took a more skeptical view of the process. That's the way to use computer-based models. That is not the way they were used by the financial industry prior to the meltdown.

The Power of Modeling

The most widely used risk assessment model in the financial industry is called Value at Risk, or VaR. It is very complex but its output is as simple as it can be. It expresses risk as a single number and as a dollar figure. But behind this simplicity is a sophisticated software system. It models portfolios consisting of bonds and other financial instruments. It also takes into account volatility and diversification.

The VaR model is based on the works of David X. Li who developed ideas about how to determine correlation between various financial instruments. That is, the degree (if any) to which these instruments were related to one another. Li's ideas on correlation were set up in a software model to determine if seemingly disparate financial events were related.[1]

Because of its flexibility and seeming accuracy, banks and other financial institutions used VAR to decide what to place in their portfolios, as well as to set their capital requirements. It became such a common tool that a report was handed out to finance personnel every day, just after the stock market closed. They used it to determine a trading desk's estimated profit and loss in comparison to the risks taken, and how each desk tallied-up for the firm.

Buyer Beware

Some people in the industry knew the limitations of VaR and used it accordingly. A well-known example is Goldman Sachs, one of the few firms that did not take a huge loss in 2007/8 from the suddenly devalued mortgage backed securities.[2] In December 2006, VaR and other models were producing output indicating that something was amiss in the housing market. Nothing of major consequence, but the company had lost money ten days in a row on mortgage business. The officers concluded the situation was worthy of more analysis. The risk managers at Goldman Sachs spent the better part of an afternoon going over the firm's trading positions. They concluded the mortgage backed securities market did not "feel" right. So they took actions to rein in their risk.[3] Granted, a small group of traders came to this conclusion, but it led Goldman as a company to offset its own mortgage-related losses by making bets that mortgage securities would fail.

This tale is recounted here because it shows how models should be used: prudently and with intelligent reservations. In a later report, we learn that Harry Markopolos used models to help dissect Bernard Madoff's Ponzi scheme.

The Model and Probability

Let's pose a question to ourselves. Suppose a model could predict 99 percent of the time if we would lose or make money on a day's

REPORT 5: MODELING THE MELTDOWN 77

activities of selling and buying certain financial instruments? This idea sounds attractive and VaR did just that. It measured risk along a normal distribution curve (the bell-shaped curve), as seen in figure 5-1.[4]

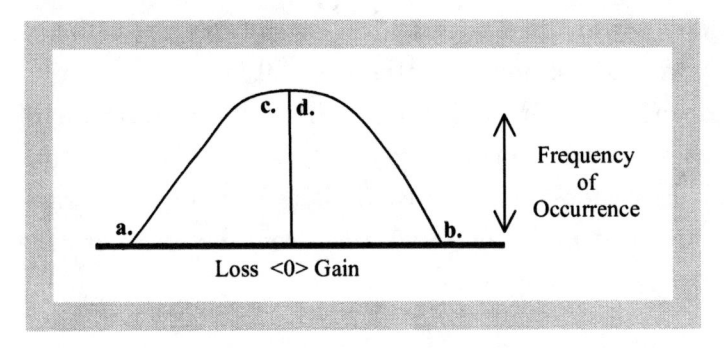

Figure 5-1. Modeling with a distribution curve.

Where:
a. Low probability of a big loss.
b. Low probability of a big gain.
c. High probability of a small loss.
d. High probability of a small gain.

The curve is a statistical measure first identified by Carl Gauss (it is also called the Gaussian distribution). Its rise in the center signifies that the closer an event takes place toward the middle of the curve, (1) the smaller the change of this event will be and (2) the more frequently the change is likely to occur. For example, a set of stocks is more likely to gain or lose a few points in a day than many points. Thus, the smaller changes are bunched up in the middle of the curve (c. and d.). The less frequent events tail-out at the ends of the curve (a. and b.). *They are less frequent but they entail very large gains or losses.*

Prior to the use of models, the pricing of complex financial instruments was not much more than an educated guess. In contrast, these models showed how to "work out a price." Then, "Confidence in pricing gave buyers and sellers the courage to pile into [complicated financial packages]."[5]

The models showed how to use real prices of stock shares and bonds to correlate to a formerly vague or unknown price for a complex security. It was a godsend for financial traders and their companies. Its value was aptly described by a modeling expert, "In a thirsty world filled with hydrogen and oxygen, someone had finally worked out how to synthesize H_2O."[6]

Financial nirvana! The almost unbelievable complexities of Wall Street's toys were rendered into a simplistic correlation of the price behavior of stocks and bonds. "It is as if you had a formula for working out the price of a fruit salad from the prices of the apples and oranges that went into it."[7]

The Black Swan

We pause for a moment to examine this mentality. First, it relies on mathematics to gauge and predict the behavior of humans, and therefore, the stock market. Second, many financial whizzes believed (and still believe) the market is self-correcting; that Wall Street's fortunes are guided by Adam Smith's *invisible* hand. Thus, government should stay away from Wall Street and let Wall Street model what is largely *invisible*.[8]

My sarcasm may seem out of place, but I think not. A later segment of this series explains that contrary to the supposition of the models, the disciplines of behavioral economics and neuroeconomics state that humans (and financial institutions) make mistakes, behave ambiguously, do not always correct themselves, and often fall prey to herding (deciding based on others' decisions). Therefore, stock and bond markets cannot be modeled accurately with variables and algebraic symbols.

These thoughts relate to the use of an interesting term: the *black swan*: a metaphor for an event that lies outside conventional expectations but carries extreme impacts. These impacts are only explainable after the dust has settled, the casualties counted, and the black swan has swum past the wreckage.[9]

No Black Swan Here. In 2005, the gurus of Wall Street "said the same thing...They'd go back to historical real estate prices over sixty years and say they had never fallen nationally, all at once."[10]

This mentality was reflected in the computer models. It was also reflected in how many of the mortgage securities were packaged. Sure, a few mortgages contained in a mortgage backed security might default, but not enough of them to affect the overall value of the security.

But what if *many* of the mortgages failed? What if the securities containing them failed? Then the models also failed. Which meant the black swan was moving away from the pond bank and headed downstream.

The combinations of these events were considered to be so improbable that the black swan's presence was ignored. The swan was considered an unlikely visitor, much too remote and far too complicated to be considered.

AAA rating for D Day Minus One. Failure on D Day.

In addition to this delusion about the ability to predict the market, and/or the arrogance of ignoring the black swan (take your pick), most everyone in the financial industry felt secure trading in mortgage backed securities that contained "highly rated" mortgages. As strange as it may appear, these mortgages were rated by the rating agencies as sound investments. Not just sound, but supersound.

Besides, no one believed thousands of homeowners would default on their loans at the same time. A few poor souls might fall by the wayside, but thousands? Not likely, especially with all those AAA ratings.

Life was good. Everyone was making money. The model was modeling life. Therefore, the model was good. Except for one minor point: the model, like life itself, was flawed. Black swans come by on occasion; always have, always will. But the models and their programmers chose to ignore them.

Chinks in the Theory

Correlations of the sort Li postulated and programmed into the VaR was, to put it mildly, venturing into dangerous waters:[11]

The damage was foreseeable and, in fact, foreseen. In 1998, Paul Wilmott wrote that "the correlations between financial quantities are notoriously unstable." Wilmott, a quantitative-finance consultant and lecturer, argued that no theory should be built on such unpredictable parameters. And he wasn't alone. During the boom years, everybody could reel off reasons why the (Li idea) wasn't perfect. Li's approach made no allowance for unpredictability. It assumed that correlation was a constant rather than something mercurial.

To complicate matters, Li did not attempt to account for the many relationships among the various loans that made up a pool. How could he? After all, as stated earlier, there was a wide array of relationships involved. As examples, what happens when the number of pool members decrease? When a loan is paid off? When a loan defaults? When a loan is refinanced? When the negative correlations of all these possibilities are melded with positive ones? It was too complex. It bordered on the extreme. So, it was ignored.

The Software was so Soft, It Melted

At the risk of oversimplifying this analysis, I think it fair to say the meltdown could have been avoided if the so-called experts had not become so dependent on modeling. Of course, my claim rests on the assumption that the industry could have changed its course, even if it knew it was headed for a huge meltdown (which would undermine the idea of herding). I suppose it is all academic now. So, we continue this report with a summary of the flaws of VaR and the mistakes the users of VaR made.

Measuring Short-Term Statistics. VaR was a short-term measure of risk. It used current data for its computations and measured risk no more than two years out. Thus, "it assumes tomorrow will be more or less like today."[12] Nothing could be further from reality in relation to the meltdown. If the model had measured past periods of stress "capital requirements would have been much higher and the financial world would be in far better shape."[13]

Murphy's Law was not Taken into Account: *Black Swans*

VaR did not take into account Murphy's Law: "Anything that can go wrong, will." The VaR designers' approach to Murphy's Law was, "Anything is impossible to program. After all, it's nearly infinite! We'll focus on the more probable things that might go wrong—the middle of the normal distribution curve. The chances of an event happening on the tails of the curve are so remote, we won't bother with it."

VaR measured what might happen, say, 99.99999 percent of the time. It did not take into account what might happen for that remaining .00001 percent. Take another look at the curve in figure 5-1. The tail ends of the curve are not covered in VaR. They are known as black swans, introduced earlier. They may occur only once in one's lifetime or even beyond, but when they do occur, they could be catastrophic.

You read me correctly, VaR, an institutionalized model for assessing risk, did not measure or report on "the biggest financial risk of all, the possibility of a financial meltdown."[14] Perhaps as big a black swan as can be imagined.

As one example, some mortgage-related products had generated frequent yet small gains, but very rarely did they show large losses. However, with the meltdown, their losses were huge. VaR ignored this possibility because it was outside an expected probability.

Double Down for Risks That Are Not Risky?

The Securities and Exchange Commission (SEC) required financial firms to use VaR to estimate the risks of their portfolios. If the VaR indicated a problem, did the SEC mandate the firms to take corrective measures? No. The SEC *only* required these firms to disclose this information. Disclose it to whom? To their stockholders, who did not know a VaR from a Viagra. The SEC abandoned its vital role of oversight.

SEC was not the only "asleep at the wheel" driver. As just mentioned, investors read VaR values in annual reports and ignored them. (As I would have done. How could a lay investor hope to understand something as arcane as the VaR?)

But others should have been more attuned. Financial firm board members, officers, and CEOs seemed to forget the model did not cover all bases. Unlike the pragmatists at Goldman Sachs, others wrapped themselves up in a cocoon of ignorance and doubled down their bets on questionable investments.

This doubling down also took place at Fannie Mae, the institution that bought mortgages, pooled them into mortgage backed securities, and sold them to investors. Fannie Mae also promised to pay off the mortgage if the borrower defaulted. It used models to assess the risks involved. A later report will detail the results of Fannie's operations, which will not make you, as a taxpayer, happy.

The Only Game in Town Is Gamed

Before long, VaR was gamed. As banks began to rely on VaR, their managers rewarded their trading desks for making big money, but also for making smaller profits on low risks. As mentioned, certain securities (described in more detail shortly) generated frequent yet small gains, and very rarely did they show large losses. But it turns out that issuing these securities became very big risks, because they were often based on insuring soon-to-be toxic mortgage backed securities. Uh oh.

Pound That Hammer Children!

It was not the math in the mathematical models that caused the problems. Goldman Sachs looked at the math, and then made sound, subjective judgments. The problem came from the blind acceptance of the math. Judgment was cast aside.

In the end, many financial institutions and their financial experts forgot the figures appearing on the screens of their computers did not emanate from an unerring Hal. The output was the function of software code written by erring humans. "As Li said of his own model, 'The most dangerous part is when people believe everything coming out of it.' "[15] Nonetheless, for the bankers, the model's output became an end unto itself. The Law of the Instrument in action.

In Report 7, I focus on the role government played in the meltdown. I have already criticized the SEC, and I will continue to do so. For the next serving, I skewer Fannie Mae, Alan Greenspan, and that witty fellow who has refused to make any apology for his role in bullying Fannie Mae into dire straits, Barney Frank.

Later, I also return to the folly of trying to model Adam Smith's invisible hand; of the futility of modeling human behavior—at least to the extent of ignoring herding and the making of irrational decisions.

Before examining Uncle Sam's behavior, Report 6 provides a pause in these discussions to briefly review several key subjects covered in the first five reports. If you feel confident about the material thus far, go on to Report 7.

---

[1] http://www.wired.com/techbiz/it/magazine/17-03/wp_quant?currentPage=all.

[2] Joe Nocera, "Risk Mismanagement," *The New York Times Magazine*, January 4, 2009, p. 27.

[3] But according to later revelations, they did not bother to rein in the risk of their customers, who they say should have known what Goldman knew! The function of a service organization is to take care of the customer and not to assume the customer knows the ropes. More later on Goldman Sachs.

[4] *The Economist*, January 24, 2009, p. 12.

[5] Ibid.

[6] Ibid.

[7] Ibid.

[8] If not invisible, then not fully subject to mathematical modeling.

[9] Mr. Taleb states in his book *The Black Swan* (Random House, New York, 2010, p. 321) that this crisis was "not a Black Swan." It might not have been a black swan for him, but it was a black swan for less erudite humans.

[10] Lewis, *The Big Short*, p. 89.

[11] http://www.wired.com/techbiz/it/magazine/17-03/wp_quant?currentPage=all.

[12] Nocera, p. 29.

[13] Ibid.

[14] Nocera, p. 28.

[15] http://www.wired.com/techbiz/it/magazine/17-03/wp_quant?currentPage=all.

Report 6

Looping Along to Financial Disaster: A Review

March 10, 2009

Hello from Your On the Street Reporter. The explanation thus far of the meltdown is contained in five reports. I decided to write a shorter and simpler explanation—a summary—with the use of a flow chart. The material has been covered in previous reports, but I present it here in a different format. However, as I stated at the end of Report 5, if you are comfortable with the material, turn the pages to Report 7.

Using five cycles (or loops), I title this report appropriately, "Looping Along to Financial Disaster." Please use the flow chart on page 88 as you read the following explanations.

Subprime/ARM mortgage is taken out: During the turn of this century, mortgage lending institutions made extensive use of two mechanisms for processing their loans: (a) subprime mortgage contracts with (b) adjustable rate mortgages (ARM). A subprime borrower was someone who, in the past, could not obtain a loan to purchase a home. He (or she) was a poor credit risk, perhaps with a limited income. Some lenders approved loans to people who had almost no income.

Recall that an ARM was a contract in which the home buyer was initially given a "teaser" loan, one with a modest interest rate

REPORT 6: LOOPING ALONG TO FINANCIAL DISASTER...   85

and monthly payment. But after, say two years, the adjustable rate came into place, resulting in a higher interest rate and a higher monthly payment.

A lending firm, such as a bank, would arrange the loan in which the down payment on a house was small and the initial interest rate modest. This practice translated into the borrower not having to come up with much up-front money. In some situations, he also did not have to make large monthly payments.

But the home owner was often unable or unwilling to make even the first or second payment. That's why the mortgage was called "subprime." He found himself in a pickle. He was financially marginal to begin with. Now, he might have trouble meeting his monthly payment.

House value appreciates: No need to worry. The bank knew house prices were going up. Thus, the homeowner was gaining more equity in the property.

Mortgage refinanced: Consequently, the mortgage firm (say, a bank) would refinance the mortgage, based on the increasing value of the house. Often the home owner was given a large amount of cash for the refinancing. He usually paid nothing for the new financing and any interest that had accumulated was rolled into a higher balance. The result was a larger loan and a larger monthly mortgage payment. It was called by a long name: the interest-only, negative-amortizing, adjustable-rate subprime mortgage...AKA, "Adios former home owner. There's a rental unit down the street."

Loop 1: Thus, a loop (cycle) came into effect: The appreciating house value allowed the homeowner to refinance, leading to a larger loan and larger house payments. On and on, one fed on the other.

ARM now in effect: After, say, two years, the ARM kicked in. The homeowner now had to refinance. He had no choice because the increased mortgage payment left him without any money. Still no problem, as his house was appreciating in value. He could use this equity to offset the increased rates. Thus, **Loop 2** came into effect, and in many instances, interplayed with **Loop 1**.

Homeowner defaults: This insanity could not continue. The homeowner was a short step away from insolvency. One reason is that even if home prices did not fall, if they merely leveled out, the ARM homeowner could not pay his mortgage. Eventually, both loops were exited as the homeowner exited his house. He also exited the mortgage contract. He could not meet his obligations (if he had even made an initial attempt). So he walked away.

But why would a bank enter into a self-destructive flow of events and these two illogical loops?

Mortgage packaged into MBS (mortgage backed securities): Because the bank was not responsible for the integrity of the loan. With the aid of an investment bank (Goldman Sachs, for example), the lending bank could off-load this subprime mortgage (as well as others) onto someone else. They were packaged into a mortgage backed security and:

(The) MBS (was) sold to an investor: say, the city of Cedar Rapids. This city gained the income from the security. Goldman Sachs took a fee from the bank for packaging and marketing the security. In turn, the bank removed the loan from its books. It also used the money from the sale to make more subprime/ARM loans.

The MBS was toxic. It contained loads of worthless mortgages. But Cedar Rapids did not know this fact. Why? Because the salesman at Goldman Sachs touted the MBS as being solid, principally because the rating agencies (Moody's, for example) evaluated the contents of the security and rated it high (AAA). Guess who was assisting the rating agencies in the ratings? Goldman Sachs. Guess who was paying Goldman for the rating? Moody's. (A dysfunctional loop unto itself.)

Investor: buys a CDS (credit default swap) on MBS (from insurer): Here it became even dicier. An investor, say a speculator, did his homework. He examined the contents of the MBS and discovered many of its loans would likely default, especially when the ARM interest rate kicked in. Plus, he knew that only a small percentage of the loans needed to go bad for the MBS to fail (only 7 percent).

This investor might have been you or me; anyone who had simply taken the time to look at the mortgages inside this MBS. It could also have been (and often was) a firm such as Goldman Sachs. Yep. Goldman peddled the MBS to Cedar Rapids as a fine AAA bond.

Goldman then turned around and bought a CDS on this very security, hoping it was *not* very fine.

In the parlance of Wall Street, the hawking and selling of a security to an investing customer (and the customer buying) is called "going long." It's betting on the security to succeed. On the other hand, the taking out of insurance; that is, buying the CDS on the security, is called "going short." It's betting on the security to fail.

But how did Goldman know the MBS was dangerous? Because it had also done its homework. It looked at the mortgages inside the MBS and surmised many were going to default.

Then who was this stupid insurer, the party that issued insurance policies against the failure of something that was destined to fail? It was AIG, the largest insurance company on earth. (And others as well.) AIG was insuring toxic real estate mortgage bonds (securities) like there was no tomorrow.

But why? If AIG had just looked at the contents of the security, it would have been obvious it contained many (dangerously) poor quality mortgages. Then again, why? Because the rating agencies declared the security to be AAA (its highest rating). That made AIG happy and secure. AIG led itself to believe it was issuing insurance on something that would never suffer a decline in value: the real estate industry in America.[1]

And besides, all the computer models informed AIG and other insurers that the chances of massive mortgage defaults were next to none. (Not none, just next to none.)

MBS devalued: When the homeowner defaulted, the MBS containing the mortgage decreased in value. This resulted in the downgrading of the MBS and the insurer of the MBS. One or a few mortgage defaults didn't have much of an effect, but the subprime/ARM was huge.

Insurer: posts collateral to investor: Part of the agreement between the CDS holder/investor (say, Goldman Sachs) and the insurance company (say, AIG) is called a "trigger." If the fair market position of the securities that AIG insures goes down—if the market moves against AIG—then AIG must post collateral to Goldman.

88 THE NEARLY PERFECT STORM

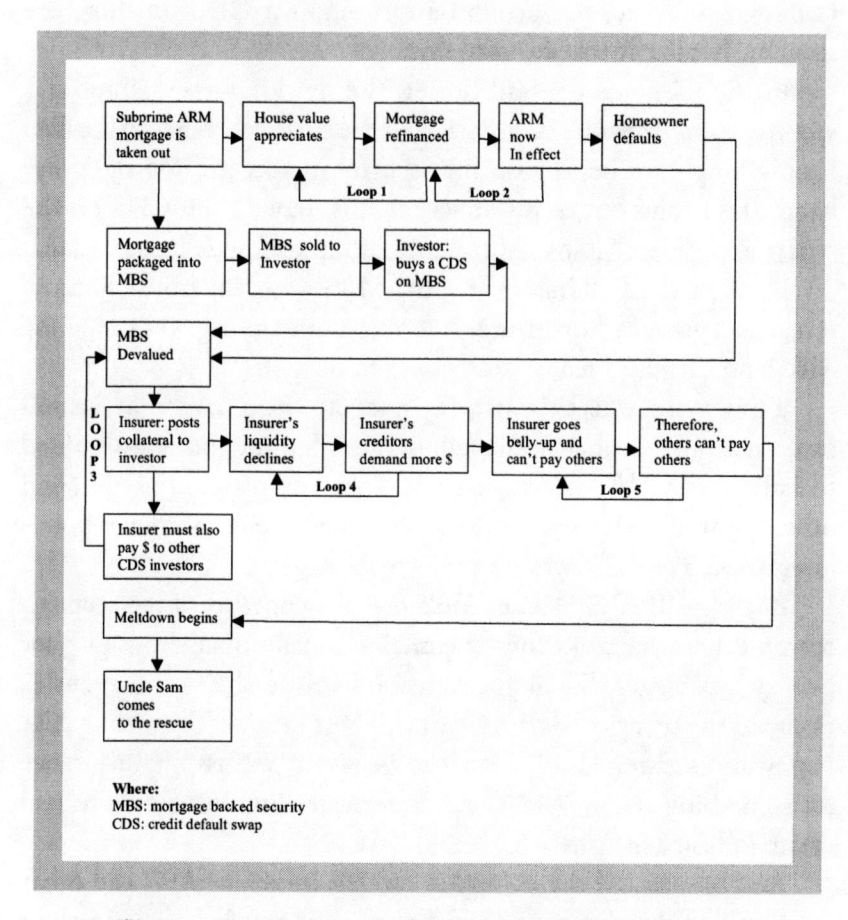

Figure 6-1. Looping along to financial disaster.

Of course, **Insurer (AIG) must also pay $ to other CDS investors** of CDS insurance, who bought insurance on the MBS (or other securities). This led to further deterioration of the MBS, which continued to deteriorate anyway, because more homeowners of mortgages in the MBS were defaulting, thus leading to **Loop 3**. This loop could be occurring in consonance with **Loop 2**.

Before long, the **Insurer's liquidity declines**, which leads **Insurer's creditors to demand more $ (collateral)** as safety margins against the increasingly precarious standing of the insurer. Thus, **Loop 4** is entered.

Before long, the **Insurer goes belly-up and can't pay others** as well. In this example, AIG can't pay Goldman and other firms holding credit default swaps issued by AIG. **Therefore, others can't pay others.** Thus, **Loop 5** is entered; the bubble bursts and the **Meltdown begins**.

The good news about these dismal loops is that all five of them are stopped (exited) when **Uncle Sam comes to the rescue.**

And you thought this story might not have a happy ending.

---

[1] Maybe this statement is true; maybe not. We will likely never know. It could be that AIG's executives knew they were playing with an expanding bubble, but as long as they got their millions before the bubble burst, it did not matter. Michael Lewis, an expert on the subject (see his *The Big Short*), thinks most of it was a matter of stupidity; of believing the housing market would never turn down.

Report 7

Uncle Sam: Asleep at the Wheel or Driving too Fast?

*Almost no one expected what was coming.
It's not fair to blame us for not predicting the unthinkable.*
—Daniel H. Mudd, former chief executive, Fannie Mae

March 11, 2009

Hello from your reporter. In this segment, the focus is on the role the U.S. government played in the financial meltdown. The focus is also on the role our government should have played (but did not), as well as the role it frequently overplayed. The Law of Unintended Consequences will be at the forefront in this report.

We will see that laws were passed in the 1990s to allow the Federal Reserve to oversee and regulate what became the subprime market and that Fed Chairman Alan Greenspan ignored the laws. We will see that Congress also passed a law making it impossible for a government agency to monitor what Warren Buffett called *financial weapons of mass destruction*. We begin with the mortgage giant Fannie Mae, and a sketch of its former chief executive, James A. Johnson.

The Federal National Mortgage Association (FNMA or Fannie Mae)

Fannie Mae is a publicly traded company chartered by the U.S. government to buy mortgages, pool them, and sell them to investors as mortgage backed securities (MBS). It is called a government-sponsored enterprise (GSE), though it has been publicly traded since 1968. It has long been a venue for implementing politicians' social programs:[1]

- In 1992, President George H.W. Bush signed the Housing and Community Development Act which stated GSEs "have an affirmative obligation to facilitate the financing of affordable housing for low-income and moderate-income families."

- The Clinton administration put pressure on Fannie Mae to expand mortgage loans to the people living in distressed inner city areas. In 1994, Fannie's chief executive Johnson created "William Jefferson Clinton's National Partners in Homeownership," which was dedicated to eliminate "redlining" (discussed shortly). Consequently, lending institutions also pressed Fannie Mae to lower its standards for evaluating loans, which eventually led to the growth of the subprime market.

- Beginning in 1993, the Department of Housing and Urban Development (HUD)—the overseer of Fannie Mae—mandated that Fannie's operations had to support home ownership for citizens who could not afford to own a home in the past (because of previously high lending standards). Fannie was directed to lower its standards for assessing the soundness of a home mortgage.

To be clear, Fannie Mae, under the helm of James A. Johnson, was a willing participant in many government-mandated programs. For example, Clinton's National Partners in Homeownership was used by Johnson to create the Fannie Neighbors program that encouraged granting loans to home owners who previously could not qualify for a mortgage loan.[2] These initiatives were early driving forces for subprime mortgages and the eventual 2008 breakdown of America's financial machine.

Redlining and the Boston Fed Paper

A significant contributor to these programs was a paper released by the Boston Federal Reserve Bank. The paper dealt with a practice called "redlining."[3] The term describes the denial of services to residents in certain areas of a city, typically in black inner city neighborhoods (or neighborhoods of other minorities). Its name is based on the marking of a red line on a map to delineate the area where banks will not grant loans and if it grants them, requires large down payments.

The Boston Fed study was widely publicized and distributed. In some circles, it was hailed as a landmark exposure of lending bigotry. Here is the first paragraph of the study:[4]

> The results of this study indicate that minority applicants, on average, do have greater debt burdens, higher loan-to-value ratios, and weaker credit histories and they are less likely to buy single-family homes than white applicants, and that these disadvantages do account for a large portion of the difference in denial rates. Including the additional information on applicant and property characteristics reduces the disparity between minority and white denials from the originally reported ratio of 2.7 to 1 to roughly 1.6 to 1. But these factors do not wholly eliminate the disparity, since the adjusted ratio implies that even after controlling for financial, employment, and neighborhood characteristics, black and Hispanic mortgage applicants in the Boston metropolitan area are roughly 60 percent more likely to be turned down than whites. This discrepancy means that minority applicants with the same economic and property characteristics as white applicants would experience a denial rate of 17 percent rather

than the actual white denial rate of 11 percent. Thus, in the end, a statistically significant gap remains, which is associated with race.

The rejection ratio of minorities to whites of 2.7 to 1 or even 1.6 to 1 was sufficiently alarming to spur government and private industry to assemble a herd and stampede toward subprime mortgages. This mad dash was accompanied by a bizarre yet planned deterioration of traditional lending practices:[5]

- Credit history was downplayed. Lack of this history was no longer a significant impediment to obtaining a mortgage loan.
- High expenses relative to income would not (as in the past) result in the denial of a loan.
- Gifts from others could now be used as part of a down payment. (Later, no down payment was required.)

Perhaps the most significant result of the policies of government and the Boston Fed paper was the Federal Reserve's statement that lending institutions should understand that Fannie and Freddie had modified their approval standards for borrowers in low income areas who did not have credit histories.

That did it! Mortgage lenders were now certain risky loans could be made and then taken off their books; that they could dole out homes to the houseless masses. Uncle Sam would take on the loans and not return them to the loan originators if they proved faulty.

Fannie Mae was the top gun in house mortgages and finance. It was the leader that often blazed the trail for America's home mortgage commerce. As Fannie extended its risk, so did the industry.

The United States, the bastion of rugged capitalism, was taking on the patina of those socialistic European nations. However, these countries had nothing closely resembling America's model of nanny-state behavior toward home ownership.

About the famous Boston Fed paper? It was found to have major flaws. The most serious deficiency was the finding that there was no relationship between race and default rates. If discrimination were indeed at work, default rates among blacks would have been lower than whites because blacks would have already been taken through the bigotry filter. *Mea culpa.* But it was too late.

Besides, the Boston Fed paper was not the only match that ignited the financial meltdown. The housing market was booming. Buyers and brokers—subject to the Autocatalytic Process and the Threshold Lowering Syndrome—were increasingly caught up in a vortex of exploiting the worthless home mortgage market. Fannie and Johnson, abetted by Congress and America's presidents, were adding their own matches.

From the Past to the Present

In the past, Fannie Mae had the reputation of helping ordinary Americans own a home. With this caveat: If these citizens demonstrated they could pay-down the mortgage. Fannie (and Freddie) was well liked by mortgage loan companies because Fannie purchased thousands of banks' loans, thus permitting banks to make even more loans.

The setup seemed safe enough for Fannie and the banks. If a property owner defaulted on a loan, the property remained as collateral. The idea behind this practice was that the property would *never* depreciate significantly from the loan value. *Never* is a very long five letter word.

Fannie's portfolios were prime specimens for inputting into a computer model. That is exactly what Fannie Mae did. It used models to assess its risks, and with this information, plunged into low quality mortgages and risky loans (the subprime market). To be fair to these simulations, the models cautioned Fannie that home buyers were not putting enough money into the loans. But parts of the organization's charter mandated serving low-income home buyers. So, Fannie ignored the models' advice. After all, it had orders from Congress and the White House. Thus, it expanded its purchase and support of low-income and moderate-income mortgages

By August, 2008, Fannie Mae's mortgage portfolio was in excess of $700 billion. The initial annual goal for low-income and moderate-income mortgage purchases for each GSE was 30 percent of the total number of dwelling units. By 2007, that figure had increased to 55 percent.[6] (I would use another exclamation point here, but my editors have advised me they should not be used in a serious book. I'll use one anyway: By 2007, that figure had increased to 55 percent! There, I feel better.)

As they say, the rest is history. So was America's booming housing industry and America's booming Main Street. Oh yes, Wall Street took a big hit, too. But as of this writing, I'll wager Wall Street makes a comeback well before Main Street does. I'll offer reasons for this bet in later reports.

Clouds on the Horizon

As noted, in the early 2000s Fannie Mae came under pressure from Congress and our presidents to steer more loans to low-income citizens. Congress also increased Fannie's funds for buying more subprime loans. Roughly $40 billion of newly minted (and borrowed) money was allotted for this program. What should Fannie do to placate Congress, George, and Bill? Buy more subprime mortgages.

The companies issuing home loans put pressure on Fannie to buy more of their loans. If not, these firms threatened they would sell directly to Wall Street or package the loans into their own privately issued securities. By 2003, Fannie Mae had lost 56 percent of its loan-reselling business to Wall Street firms, such as Bear Sterns, and Lehman Brothers (remember them? They are now defunct or owned by another bank). What to do to placate lending firms? Buy more subprime mortgages.

Figure 7-1 shows how extensively Fannie Mae got into the mortgage backed securities market.[7] Figure 7-1 also shows the extent the financial industry committed to holding mortgage backed securities. In three years, the MBS market increased by over 300 percent. On the bandwagon everyone, the train is leaving the station. All aboard! As Chuck Prince, the former CEO of Citigroup, said, "As long as the music is playing, you've got to get up and dance." Then, he added, "We're still dancing."[8] Note the word "former" in Chuck's title.

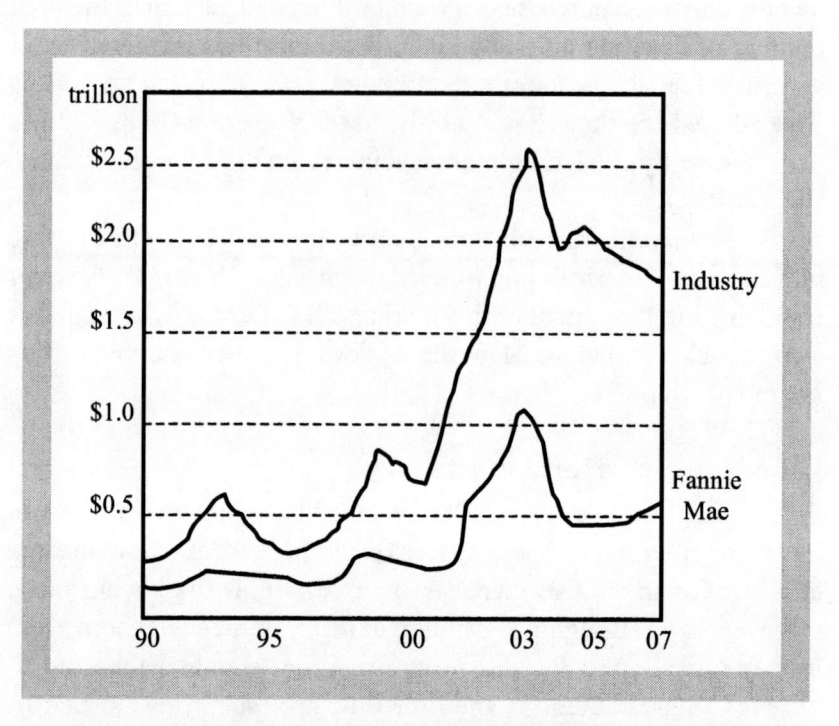

Figure 7-1. Market for mortgage backed securities.

Fannie was being pressured from all sides. Investors told the institution it was not taking on enough risk. One investor called a Fannie officer and said, "Are you blind or stupid? Your job is to make me money!"[9] What to do to placate investors? Buy more faulty mortgages.

These purchases translated into more money for everyone (at least for the short-term) as the situation was seemingly a win-win arrangement. Congress had happier constituents who made more campaign contributions. Mortgage companies were making more money to distribute to their executives. Investors were taking in more money than they could obtain from conventional low-interest yields. Fannie's stockholders were happy, because Fannie's stock price accelerated.

Even Fannie Mae was happy, especially its chief executives. The two CEOs who preceded Mr. Mudd (between 1998 and 2004) received $120.8 million for their time.[10] Poor Mr. Mudd, before his demise, he received only $10 million for his four-year stewardship.

Revisiting Two of the Rules of Life

I am not sure any CEO could have withstood the pressure Mr. Mudd had to endure regarding massive commitment to the subprime market. He has become the fall guy at Fannie Mae but on the other hand, I do not feel sorry for the man. His failure left him a multimillionaire. Still, when consulting two of the Rules of Life, it is easy to understand how Fannie Mae got into so much trouble, and why we Americans are once again saddled with paying for the vacuous stupidity and greed of others.

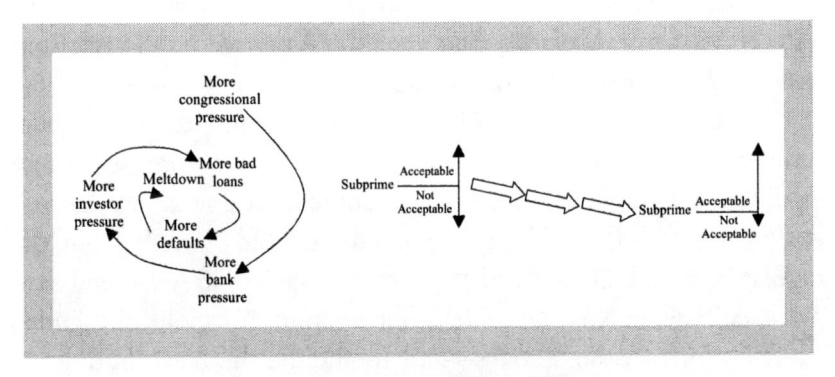

Figure 7-2. Parallel processing.

The left illustration in figure 7-2 shows the Autocatalytic Process in action at Fannie Mae during the run-up to the run-down. The right illustration shows the effect of the Threshold Lowering Syndrome. The figure illustrates the power of parallel processing; their combined effects led to big problems, especially with the influence Fannie Mae had in the mortgage industry:[11]

> Fannie Mae led the way in relaxing loan underwriting standards…a shift that was quickly followed by private lenders. Johnson's company also automated the lending process so that loan decisions could be made in minutes and were based heavily on a borrower's credit history, rather

than on a more comprehensive financial profile as had been the case in the past.

Conflict of Roles and Distortion of the Process

Because of the Federal Housing Enterprises Financial Safety and Soundness Act of 1992, HUD's Office of Federal Housing Enterprise Oversight (OFHEO) became the watchdog of Fannie Mae. Nonetheless, Johnson persuaded Congress that it should review any OFHEO regulation affecting Fannie Mae. This action took away a relatively nonpolitical overseer and placed Fannie Mae into the hands of legislators that Fannie Mae could manipulate with pork barrel and campaign contributions.

Government agency? Hardly, spearheaded by Johnson, Fannie Mae created organizations that resembled private public relations and lobbying firms. One example was its Partnership Offices (POs).[12]

These storefront offices were placed in communities throughout America. They helped foster Fannie's close ties to Congress because a politician could take advantage of Fannie's housing efforts in their voting areas. This strategy further distanced Fannie from the regulators at HUD. In Georgia, Newt Gingrich; in Massachusetts, Ted Kennedy; in Missouri, Christopher Bond. All spoke of Fannie's contributions to these states—and implicitly, the contributions of these politicians as well.

The POs and their local operations had an enormous impact on Congress. When this body was deliberating potential legislation to place more control over Fannie, Fannie and its POs would muster huge responses from local citizens with massive write-ins to Congress. Time and again, efforts to rein in Fannie's behavior were defeated.

I do not mean to imply that Fannie Mae's effort to foster more home ownership with the POs was a bad idea. It led to more ownership; it led to the creation of many jobs. But as the POs inculcated themselves into their communities, the influence of fifty-five offices on citizens, home builders, lenders, real estate firms, and nonprofit housing advocacy groups compromised the political process.

Eventually, HUD went public about its concern (and likely, its loss of turf), stating the partnership offices "were not confined to affordable housing initiatives, rather a central purpose ...was to engage in activities that were primarily designed to obtain access to or influence members of Congress."

The actions of Fannie were not just about gaining access to or lobbying of Congress. It was influence peddling, pure and simple, and by an agency chaperoned by Uncle Sam no less:

- Fannie Mae created a nonprofit foundation. Each year, the foundation gave out millions of dollars for its peddling. Examples: Congressional Hispanic Caucus Institute and the Congressional Black Caucus. (One could ask why a government-sponsored organization had created a charitable foundation in the first place?)

- "During one trip to the Senate Caucus Room in 1998, Johnson handed out envelopes containing $2.5 million for Washington, D.C.-based advocacy groups." During this display of open bribes in a congressional building, local senators and representatives "sang Johnson's praises."

- A bank lobbyist attempted to find academics to perform research and offer unbiased critiques of Fannie Mae. He could find none of any consequence as most experts had been paid by Fannie to write favorably about the organization. He summed it up, "I had people say to me are you going to give me stipends for the next twenty years like Fannie will?"

Johnson, in essence a ward of Uncle Sam, received $5.1 million in compensation for 1995. That same year, it was revealed that for every $3 Fannie received in savings to America's borrowers and passed to them, it kept $1 for itself and its shareholders.

The story of Fannie Mae (and Freddie Mac) in relation to America's public and private sectors presents a sobering reality: America's government has created privately held and publicly traded enterprises that regardless of their facades, are guaranteed not only success, but their very existence. All is courtesy of the American taxpayer. Their executives are paid wages and bonuses that place them orders of magnitude above a civil servant's pay grade. Yet that is what they are: civil servants. It is not my intent to demean the role of civil servants in our society, but I take issue with the salaries some of them make.

The Distortion of America's Free Enterprise System

This distortion of our country's political process of free markets by breaching the wall between (quasi) private enterprise and government oversight does not confine itself to government-sponsored enterprises (GSEs). It extends to Wall Street and many other avenues of America populated with "too big to fail" institutions. The welfare doles were not confined to the financial sector. The bailout rescued insurance firms and car companies. They were made safe from capitalism's creative destruction.

Who knows? Perhaps WalMart is next in line to be fed by Uncle Sam (you and me). But rest assured the companies who formerly occupied those now empty stores in our local shopping mall were small enough to be placed on capitalism's chopping block.

How can we have faith in a system that routinely discriminates against ordinary citizens and these citizens' ordinary businesses? Especially when banks and other large companies are given a free pass? Especially when Wall Street states the nearly perfect financial storm was a "speed bump," and is now lobbying to curtail legislation to rein in the Street's excesses?

While doing research for these reports and this book, I've come across many explanations to justify this system's existence. They will be discussed and critiqued in subsequent reports.

Barney Frank Is Not Frank

I have been watching news about the meltdown saga on TV, and on occasion have come across Congressman Barney Frank's comments about the affair. Previously, I had paid little attention to the man, other than observing he was often dismissive of others, and mistook his own sarcasm for wit. But my casual observations led me to believe he was a beacon of restraint in the meltdown fiasco, a facade I am certain he wanted to project to the public.

My attention span lengthened when I chanced upon his appearance on the Bill O'Reilly show. I tuned into the program at the time the two men were yelling at each other. O'Reilly was shouting to Frank that he was phony, incompetent, a major factor in the financial crisis, and should not be in Congress. Logically enough, Frank did not agree and said he regretted showing up for the roast.

Who was correct? It turns out Mr. O'Reilly was. Congressman Frank was part of the congressional mortgage mafia that put pressure on Fannie Mae to enter into the surreal world of subprime mortgages. One that led to predatory lending, falsified loan applications, mortgages on vacant lots, escalating usurious loan payments, and the Alice in Wonderland vision of a bubble that would never burst. Here is a quote from Frank's philosophy on the issue:[13]

> I'm not worried about Fannie and Freddie's health. I'm worried that they won't do enough to help out the economy. That's why I've supported them all these years—so they can help at a time like this.

"At a time like this." A time when Congress *mandated* Fannie Mae begin to buy bad loans; a time when Congress later required Fannie Mae to buy *another* $40 billion of bad loans. How do we Americans reward hubristic incompetent citizens? We continue to elect them to Congress.

During the time leading to the meltdown, Frank was the chairman of the House Financial Services Committee, which has oversight responsibility of the nation's housing sector. When the public, regulators, and Congress itself were becoming concerned about the financial soundness of Fannie and Freddie, Frank stated there was an unwarranted concern about safety and soundness in relation to "our ability to do housing."[14]

His statement essentially informed his listeners that "doing housing" through the sponsorship of an unsound organization—one whose health was vital to the entire nation's health—was more important than America's overall soundness.

His narrow and arrogant stand might have been encouraged by: (a) his partner being hired by Fannie, (b) an organization founded by his mother (!) being awarded the "Fannie Mae Maxwell Award of Excellence", (c) the granting of $50,000 to his mom's organization. You slap my back, I'll slap yours.

I have been watching Frank's caustic evasions and acerbic retorts on the talk shows and congressional panels these past few weeks. Just own up Congressman. Why can't you show a bit of humility for being a big part of the Fannie Mae and national meltdown tragedy? Maybe saying that you are sorry for being so misguided would be a start. Mr. O'Reilly has you pegged. So do Gretchen Morgenson and Joshua Rosner, the source I used in this section.

Credit Rating Agencies

I have included the credit rating agencies in this part of the book because I believe they take on the responsibilities of what Uncle Sam should be doing: assessing the worth of financial instruments and associated financial institutions. The SEC should be the organization that oversees the credit worthiness of bonds, securities, and financial institutions, but the SEC stands by the sidelines. To gain a sense of the absurdity of this situation, consider the following.

Like many people, I had assumed a high credit rating of a company's bond by Moody's or Standard and Poor's meant just that: the company's bond was sound. My assumption was incorrect. An example is Enron. Four days before the company went bankrupt, its securities were rated at "investment grade (AAA, or triple-A)," the highest rating.[15]

These agencies (and Fitch) are sanctioned by the SEC to police the American business industry for credit worthiness and financial soundness. Consequently, they have immense influence in America's markets.

Yet they also act as consultants to the very companies they rate, and they charge these companies for their ratings. Once again, I am not making a joke. We discover the fox is in the hen house. These organizations "did exactly the opposite of what they were meant to do: rather than expose financial risk they systematically disguised it."[16]

Here is one example of the creepy behavior of the rating agencies. In 1990, a financial firm named MBIA was rated AAA. Rightly so, as it insured municipal bonds, and had $931 million in equity and only $200 million in debt. By 2006 it had joined the bandwagon of insuring subprime-based securities and had $7.2 billion in equity and $26.2 billion in debt. The rating agencies made no move whatsoever to downgrade MBIA's rating. Yet other financial experts were publicly questioning MBIA's rating.

Again, why? Why has such a vital cog in America's financial wheel failed? Here's a clue:[17]

> ...a downgrade...was not in their short-term interest. A downgrade of MBIA would force the rating agencies to go through the costly and cumbersome process of re-rating tens of thousands of credits that bore triple-A ratings...It would stick a wrench in the machine that enriched them.

Measuring Credit Worthiness. Credit ratings—values assigned to borrowers—are called FICO scores (named after the Fair Issac Corporation, who invented it in the 1950s).[18] The highest possible score is 850; the lowest is 300. The average score around the time of the meltdown was 723.

The score is not accurate and can be manipulated. For example, by using a credit card and paying back the amount soon, a person can achieve a higher credit rating. In contrast, having no debt will not guarantee a high credit rating because a person has no credit history. Regardless of the validity of the FICO itself, let's take a look at how the rating agencies used it.

The rating agencies required the firms (that were packaging loans into securities) to furnish the *average* FICO score of *all* the mortgages in the pool. This approach meant there would likely be mortgages in the pool that were toxic; that were surely to default, but not so-identified. Yet if the average score for all borrowers in the pool was 615, it would be rated triple-A (again, the highest rating). It was later determined that a person with a score of below around 550 was almost certain to default on the loan, but if this loan were compensated by another loan of, say, 680 the security could be rated AAA.

What was the number of defaults that could wipe out this sort of financial instrument? Wall Street finally discovered—far too late in the game—*it was only 7 percent*. Many of these pieces of financial flotsam had far more than 7 percent of subprime loans packaged inside them.

What if these financial instruments were issued to the tune of billions of dollars? What if a lot of them went bad? What if billions of dollars of insurance (credit default swaps) had been issued on them? Answer: They would explode. As mentioned, the sage Warren Buffett called them financial weapons of mass destruction.

Beyond Saturday Night Live Parody. As the adjustable rate mortgages kicked in to produce higher interest rates and increased mortgage payments for home owners, the rating agencies did not change their assessments of these mortgages. They assumed the homeowner, who had little or no equity in the house, and maybe no income either, would continue to make payments on the loan! After all, the difference between 6 percent and 7.5 percent was "only" a few hundred dollars a month. These urban dwellers did not have such a cushion. They were cruising toward foreclosure city.

Equally bizarre, the mortgage backed securities paid more to the investors of these securities if the composite loans in the package had higher interest rates. Higher rates meant more money for the security owners. That makes sense, but the rating agencies gave higher ratings to securities that were backed by floating rate, subprime mortgages. They gave higher rating to these instruments than those containing fixed (lower) rate mortgages. In other words, they rated junk higher than they rated jewels.

Names to Mask Real Names. Critics of Wall Street firms claim these companies made up names to confuse regulators and investors; to divert attention to the contents and nature of complex, low-quality financial instruments; to have them appear as something different, when they were the same.

For example, a security was often repackaged pieces of other securities. So, it was nothing different, but by assigning a different name to it, it appeared to be different. To add to the complexity, and the resulting difficulty of assessing their values, loans often were packaged in a circuitous fashion.[19] Security A would have a part of security B in it. Security B would have a piece of security C in it. Security C would have a piece of security A in it.

Cutting the rating agencies some slack, given their limited resources and the complexity of the securities they were analyzing, it is not surprising they missed the boat. Well, that and the fact that banks paid the rating agencies large fees *if* they missed the boat.

The Deutsche Bank told an investigator/potential investor that it used the term Alt-A for "crappy mortgage loans for which they hadn't even bothered to acquire the proper documents—to verify the borrower's income, say." He also said, "The Wall Street firms just got the ratings agencies to accept different names for it so they could make it seem like a diversified pool of assets."[20]

Alan Greenspan had this to offer about the rating agencies, "What we have created in this world is an aura around the credit rating agencies about certification from them is the Good Housekeeping seal of approval. I will tell you the record of a lot of the forecasters of ratings have not been distinguished. They never were."[21]

We leave the rating agencies for now. But they are not off the hook. We'll return to them later.

Blame It on the Stones and the CRA

Some people in the industry have stated the financial institutions are not to be blamed for taking on so many toxic loans. They blame the federal government and the Community Reinvestment Act (CRA). This law, passed in 1977, is designed to discourage or eliminate redlining: the denial of loans in low-income neighborhoods.[22]

> The Act requires the appropriate federal financial supervisory agencies to encourage regulated financial institutions to meet the credit needs of the local communities in which they are chartered, consistent with safe and sound operation. To enforce the statute, federal regulatory agencies examine banking institutions for CRA compliance, and take this information into consideration when approving applications for new bank branches or for mergers or acquisitions.

The counter argument is that most subprime loans were made by banks and other institutions that were not subject to the CRA laws: "University of Michigan law professor Michael Barr testified ...before the House Committee on Financial Services that 50 percent of subprime loans were made by mortgage service companies not subject to comprehensive federal supervision and another 30 percent were made by affiliates of banks or thrifts which are not subject to routine supervision or examinations."[23]

I don't see how the CRA could not have had some influence and it was later amended with other legislation. Regardless of the CRA, in the first reports on this meltdown, I documented the causes of the financial crisis.

Alan Greenspan and the Federal Reserve

In earlier segments of these reports, I made the claim that two of the root causes of the financial meltdown were a long period of low interest rates and high liquidity. I briefly discussed the role of the Federal Reserve in keeping interest rates down; actions in which Alan Greenspan was instrumental.

I also made a passing reference to the Fed not fulfilling its oversight responsibilities. After posting this report, I read "The Financial Crisis Inquiry Report," published by the Financial Crisis Inquiry Commission. This body offered succinct words about the Fed:[24]

The prime example [of the financial crisis being avoidable] is the Federal Reserve's pivotal failure to stem the flow of toxic mortgages, which could have been done by setting prudent mortgage-lending standards. The Federal Reserve was the one entity empowered to do so and did not.

I have read Mr. Greenspan's *The Age of Turbulence*.[25] In this book, he makes the point many times that adhering to the rule of law is the only way a country can prosper. No one in the Western world would argue with this assertion. However, Greenspan has been heavily influenced by Ayn Rand and her philosophy of objectivism, which promotes a concept called *laissez-faire capitalism: Capitalism works best if private industry is not regulated.*[26]

I wish this assertion were true. In my heart, I am a quasi-libertarian, a laissez-faire proponent. I have reluctantly come to abandon this position. It comes not so much from any economic philosophy, but from the realization that we humans run amok if we do not place constraints on ourselves.

Unregulated capitalism is onerous and dangerous. We need rules by which to live. Markets need laws by which to function. An unregulated capitalist is little more than a fox in a hen house, or a Bernie Madoff in a Palm Beach country club.

Greenspan's job as chairman of the Federal Reserve Board was that of a regulator. But during the run-up to the meltdown, he was purposely asleep at the wheel. Those low interest rates in the early 2000s proved to be one of the matches that lit the meltdown's fire.

What is particularly disheartening about Greenspan's tenure is that he had the legal authority to prevent the subprime fiasco. In 1994 Congress passed the Home Ownership and Equity Protection Act.[27] It authorized the Federal Reserve to require all mortgage lenders to adhere to traditional banking standards: forbidding lending to people with poor credit or with no down payment. The law was passed because nonbank lenders were not subject to the stricter rules imposed on banks. Greenspan refused to use this law to regulate the emerging subprime market.

In addition, those financial weapons of mass destruction—namely, credit default swaps (see Report 8)—begged for oversight. In an astounding display of irresponsibility, Greenspan, working with Senator Phil Gramm (R-Tex.), helped guide the passage of a 2000 law named the Commodity Futures Modernization Acts. This act "virtually outlaw(s) the monitoring and regulation of many types of derivatives."[28]

Sidebar 7-1. Derivatives.

I have mentioned one derivative several times in previous reports: credit default swaps. But I have not defined the term. By using this quote, I am referring to my previous introductions to this specific derivative. But I am getting ahead of the game a bit by bringing up the general term of derivative. So, a brief diversion:

A derivative is a security. It is also a contract between two parties about their views on a financial instrument. For example it could be a bet, in the form of a credit default swap, for or against what will happen in the marketplace. It could be a security dealing with most any underling asset, such as a stock, a bond; even oil prices, or the price of rice.

The effect of this legislation was to allow the creation of unregulated, unmonitored credit default swaps. As of this writing, America's banks have increased their credit by 6 percent since September, 2008. But they are having problems "securitizing" the loans into mortgage backed securities because the financial industry is still in a state of shock and has no confidence in this unregulated market.

In addition, Greenspan's strong, influential support for the successful repeal of the Glass-Steagall Act and his loose approach to banks' increasing their risks resulted in banking houses taking on dangerous debt-to-capital leverages.

> **Sidebar 7-2. Leave the Punch Bowl on the Table**[29]
>
> After posting this report on the Net, a reader called my attention to an article with this information: The head of the Federal Deposit Insurance Corporation (FDIC), Sheila Bair, opposed Greenspan's approach, "The Federal Reserve Board was really the only authority that could set lending standards across the board—banks, non-bank lenders, any mortgagor...And it affirmatively did not do that."...She added, "The political pressure was to let it be."
>
> Bair did succeed in creating a set of "best practices" which the industry adopted, but they were largely ignored. Borrowers took out cash on the increasing values of their homes, which added more fuel to the consumption craze and the boom. She said, "It was hard to take the punch bowl away." But her blunt manner turned off other regulators, and until recently (covered in later reports), she was outside the circle of the "Big Three" (Fed chairman, Treasury secretary, president's advisors.)

Overseeing Banks' Leverage

The Fed and other government agencies are supposed to keep an eye on banks' balance sheets. While I was working at the Federal Reserve Board the most heavily used file was the Call Report. It contained data on commercial banks' assets, liabilities, and income. Its information helped regulators evaluate the soundness of a bank's financial position and was a vital oversight tool for assessing leverage. The Fed, as well as the FDIC and Treasury, kept a close eye on each bank's performance.

That was in the 1970s and early 1980s, during the tenures of Arthur Burns and Paul Volcker as chairmen of the Federal Reserve Board. What happened since those days? The oversight became more lax. As noted, Congress loosened or removed commercial and investment bank regulations. Alan Greenspan took over the regulatory helm and with his *laissez-faire* philosophy, piloted the banking industry into dangerous waters.

Now, the nation's big banks, after years of increasing their holdings of securities and loans, are so heavily leveraged they are in trouble. It is likely the FDIC will be handling more failures in the next few years than at any time since the S&L debacle in 1992.

Leverage and Margins

To see why, consider *the leverage ratio*, a topic discussed earlier, but used in a different context here. It is a measure of a firm's possible ability or inability to meet financial obligations. It is calculated in several ways, but in the main, it's the ratio of assets to liabilities.

Some ways to attain leverage are borrowing money, buying fixed assets, and using derivatives. For example, my company may borrow money and therefore, I will need less equity capital. Thus, any profits I make are shared among fewer people. As another example, Lehman Brothers used securities to leverage its assets. Its strategy was to make money, say, on $40 million of investments in securities by posting only $2 million as a *margin*. The margin procedure allows an investor to invest more than he has to take out of his wallet. It's really a loan.

A fine idea, so little invested with so much potential return. Yes, as long as the bubble kept expanding. Any glitch meant Lehman would have to come up with money to meet margin calls. (See Sidebar 7-3.) But it could not, as recounted in other reports.

> ### Sidebar 7-3. Margin Calls.[30]
>
> In volatile markets, prices can fall very quickly. If the equity (the value of securities minus what you owe the brokerage—on what is essentially a loan) in your account falls below the maintenance margin, the brokerage will issue a margin call. A margin call forces the investor to either liquidate his/her position in the stock or add more cash to the account.
>
> If for any reason you do not meet a margin call, the brokerage has the right to sell your securities to increase your account equity until you are above the maintenance

margin. Your broker may not be required to consult you before selling. Under most margin agreements, a firm can sell your securities without waiting for you to meet the margin call. You can't even control which stock is sold to cover the margin call.

Don't forget, with the repeal of Glass-Steagall, many financial institutions shifted their operations over to the investment side because of more lenient rules. Some lending firms had a 35 to 1 leverage ratio.

Our question to Mr. Greenspan is: What happened to your oversight? The leverage ratios you were reviewing in the Call Report could have come from a third world banking system. Granted, the Fed's reserve requirements pertain to checking deposits. But then, who—in the vast assemblage of government regulators and watchdogs—was looking at these trends, including the trends shown in figure 7-1? No one, because Congress had declared these financial instruments to be immune from oversight and parts of the ingredients to a bank's balance sheet were off the books, courtesy of Uncle Sam.

Mr. Greenspan's Invisible Regulatory Hand

Thanks to Greenspan's philosophy that banks can largely regulate themselves, figure 7-3 provides a survey of the current financial position of several big banks:[31]

Citigroup	**2009**	**2010**
Assets	$2 trillion	$1.9 trillion
Equity	$150 billion	$70.5 billion
Ratio	7.7%	3.8%

Conclusion? Citigroup will need $22 billion in additional capital.

JPMorgan Chase	**2009**	**2010**
Assets	$2.1 trillion	$2.0 trillion
Equity	$166 billion	$128 billion
Ratio	7.8%	6.4%

Conclusion? JPMorgan is fit, a point I made earlier… because of sound management.

BankofAmerica	2009	2010
Assets	$2 trillion	$1.8 trillion
Equity	$176 billion	$84.3 billion
Ratio	9.0%	4.6%

Conclusion? BofA will need $7 billion in additional capital.

Wells Fargo	2009	2010
Assets	$1.3 trillion	$1.2 trillion
Equity	$99 billion	$44.5 billion
Ratio	7.7%	3.8%

Conclusion? Wells Fargo will need $16 billion in additional capital.[32]

Figure 7-3. Condition of major U.S. banks.

Greenspan: The Regulator who Delegated His Job Away

Alan Greenspan accepted the job as chairman of the Federal Reserve Board to fulfill a position of a bank regulator. No one forced him to take the job, he came willingly. Repeating an analogy, but still apt: The fox got into the hen house and destroyed a lot of chickens and eggs.

During my stint at the Federal Reserve Board, Arthur Burns and Paul Volcker were its chairmen. They performed their jobs with distinction. There was also a Board employee who worked in the Division of Supervision and Regulation named Bill Taylor. He also performed his job well. I met Bill on occasion and during my two-year stint as the Board's ombudsman, I interacted with Bill regarding several employee issues in Bill's division. I found him to be quiet, composed, and fair.

Later, Bill became Greenspan's top advisor on bank regulation and, unlike Alan, did the job he was paid to do: regulating banks. Even before the 2008 banking crisis, he required Citibank to improve its capital position before issuing stock dividends. Imagine that! A regulator putting the brake on a bank's excess.

Bill later went on to become chairman of the FDIC (and died shortly thereafter). Greenspan never involved himself very much in bank regulation after the departure of Bill Taylor:[33]

In 1992 or '93, the Senate asked Greenspan, "With Taylor gone who is in charge of regulatory policy at the Board?" The answer surprised the Senate staff when it came back in writing because Chairman Greenspan said he had delegated the task to E. Gerald Corrigan, the president of the New York Fed.

For the first time, the Board was not managing its own supervisory policy...Instead it was delegating that important duty to the New York Fed, an organization that operated hand in glove with the banks it was supposed to regulate.

I wanted to insert another exclamation point to his testimony, but I will forego the temptation. I will vent my contempt and astonishment by saying that even after learning about Greenspan's gross and egregious incompetency, I am still dumbfounded by his admission. For now, we leave Alan to himself, but I'm not done with this man. He did too much damage to America's citizens to warrant only a couple pages in this book. We finish this report with another skewering.

SEC: Ineptitude and Shirking Responsibility

For this crisis, we need only look at the Securities and Exchange Commission (SEC) to witness another example of the failure of a governmental body to carry out its charter.

But before I perform the obligatory marring, a few words are warranted about the SEC manning levels. To be fair, the SEC has been underfunded and undermanned for years. It has not been given the tools to properly oversee and regulate the vast and complicated securities and financial world of America. Its technology to track possible fraud or even sudden crashes in the stock market are not up to the task.

The companies it regulates leave it lying in their dust in terms of market sophistication and manipulation. After filing this report, I read that its annual budget is less than the net worth of a man the

SEC has been investigating for insider trading. Nonetheless, it could have done much better with the resources it had.

The responsibility of the SEC is to protect "the public against malpractices in the securities and financial markets."[34] If the SEC is to meet this important responsibility, one would think this regulatory body would be quite concerned that the participants in these markets are solvent enough to operate—that they have sufficient capital; that this capital is of high quality (investment grade). To this end, the SEC decided in the 1970s to make certain that Wall Street firms and other dealers in bonds held investment grade instruments.

This worthy goal raised the question of who would certify the bonds as investment grade? The SEC selected the big three rating agencies to become the official sanctifiers of good and trusted bonds.[35] In effect, the SEC off-loaded one of its most important regulatory functions to someone else.

Because of the immense resources required to analyze and rate bonds and other forms of debt from America's thousands of companies, the argument can be made that Uncle Sam should not take on this task. Irrespective of one's opinion on this matter, the SEC's decision gave the rating agencies a monopoly on credit ratings. A corporation had no choice but to come to the rating agencies; otherwise, they could not market their bonds.

The Law of Unintended Consequences raised its head: The agencies—once paid by subscribers—began to charge the issuers of the bonds for rating those very bonds. It is difficult to understand the rationale behind this dangerous and absurd financial decision and why the SEC did not foresee its Kafkaesque outcome. The rating agencies were (are, but past tense is used here) profit driven and their profits depended on the number of bonds they rated. In effect, they were in competition with one another for snaring a company's bonds for their ratings analysis and grading. More ratings garnered more revenue. Furthermore, if a company did not like the rating of one agency, it could go to another.

This arrangement penalized a rating company for its strictness and objectivity. The more AAA ratings it gave the more business it took in. If the SEC believed it had to delegate this responsibility to another organization, it could have at least setup an arrangement that would not have led to a perversion of the rating system. Yet as described in the section about rating agencies provided earlier in this report, that is exactly what happened.

Asleep, but How? How could the SEC not have foreseen the emerging catastrophe associated with credit default swaps that insured mortgage backed securities containing toxic mortgages? How could it not have at least raised flags about the dangers of brokers dealing in billions of dollars of dangerous securities?

The commission was warned by noted experts such as Warren Buffett, yet it continued to let credit default swaps (and other financial instruments) go unregulated and unreported. I've read more than once that no one really knows how many credit default swaps are out there. *Wired* magazine claims, "At the end of 2001, there was $920 billion in credit default swaps outstanding. By the end of 2007, that number had skyrocketed to more than $62 trillion."[36]

From 2000 to 2008, an analyst/investor contacted the SEC five times about his findings that the Bernie Madoff's system was a Ponzi scheme. Each time, he upped the amount of money that was at risk. Each time, the SEC office in Washington, DC ignored him. Finally, in December, 2008, after a decade of warnings, the SEC took action. Madoff's story is told in other reports.

The SEC was Lehman Brother's main regulator. SEC reports indicate (on a monthly basis) that Lehman "had increased and exceeded risk limits."[37] What did the SEC do to corral Lehman's wild behavior? Nothing.

It's mindboggling. It would be the subject of slapstick jokes if the situation were not devastating to so many people. One of its former chairmen, Christopher Cox—like Greenspan—thought financial markets were largely self-regulating. The SEC chairman from 1993 to 2001 was Arthur Levitt. He has gone on to fortune, billing clients for his intellect at $900 per hour.[38] We can only hope his clients are getting more competent attention than he gave America's citizens during his stint as SEC chairman.

Beyond the Pale

The leverages in which banks placed themselves and their huge participation in the subprime/adjustable rate marketplace defy sound financial logic and common sense. We can excuse exuberance. We can appreciate how the mathematical models clouded judgment. We can understand why greed created a bandwagon/herd effect to make money while there was an opportunity. We can look to the Autocatalytic Process, the Threshold Lowering Syndrome, and the Law of the Instrument and say, "It was all part of human nature."

But how can we fathom that so many financial institutions accepted millions of subprime borrowers? How could the stellar companies not know that these poor, pathetic people, saddled with adjustable interest rates, would fail to make their future mortgage payments? How can we understand that our government was almost a ghost of a regulator? It does not compute.

Perhaps I have answered my own questions. Maybe it does compute. Maybe the Autocatalytic Process is also a cycle and a debilitating circle of three elements that have been discussed in these reports: risk, greed, and responsibility.

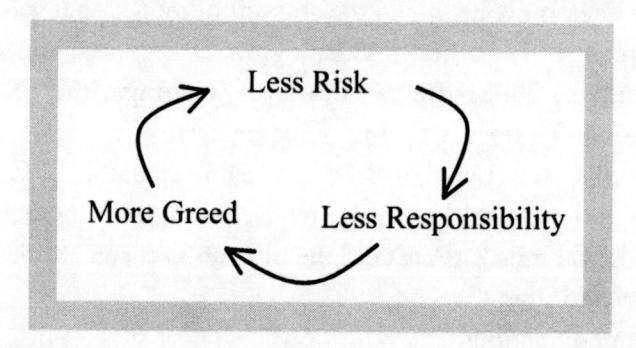

```
        Less Risk
      ↗         ↘
More Greed    Less Responsibility
      ↖         ↙
```

Perhaps so, but abetted first by Uncle Sam's support (liberals in power to open up the mortgage marketplace to most everyone), then later abetted by Uncle Sam as well (conservatives in power and ignoring the consequences of this resulting marketplace).

In the next report, I go into more detailed descriptions of the financial tools of the meltdown that have been introduced in earlier reports. I have attempted to keep the discussions as free of jargon as possible. And for this next report, if you are not interested in this detail, please read it anyway because it is important to understanding the financial weapons of mass destruction and America's nearly perfect financial storm.

---

[1] Wikipedia and http://www.opednews.com/articles/The-Real-Cause-of-the-Curr-by-Joe-Reeser-080926-83.html.

[2] Morgenson and Rosner, *Reckless Endangerment*, pp. 34-35.

[3] For the interested reader, the paper is titled, "Mortgage Lending in Boston: Interpreting HMDA Data," (HMDA: Home Mortgage Disclosure Act.)

[4] http://www.bos.frb.org/economic/wp/wp1992/wp92_7.htm.

[5] Morgenson and Rosner, *Reckless Endangerment*, pp. 37-39.

[6] Wikipedia. Key in "Fannie Mae."

[7] Charles Duhigg, "Pressured to Take More Risk, Fannie Reached the Tipping Point," *The New York Times*, October 5, 2008, p. 30.

[8] "How to Play Chicken and Lose: Finance Suffers from Reverse Natural Selection," *The Economist*, p. 14.

[9] Duhigg, "Pressured to Take More Risk, Fannie Reached the Tipping Point," p. 30.

[10] Ibid.

[11] Morgenson and Rosner, *Reckless Endangerment*, p. 5.

[12] Thanks to Morgenson and Rosner for their research on Fannie Mae's Partnership Offices. The statistics and findings in this section are sourced from pages 29, 61-68, 72-73, 76, 78, and 83 of their excellent book *Reckless Endangerment*.

[13] Duhigg, "Pressured to Take More Risk, Fannie Reached the Tipping Point," p. 30.

[14] Morgenson and Rosner, *Reckless Endangerment*, pp. 70-71.

[15] Amy Borrus, "The Credit-Raters: How They Work and How They Might Work Better," *Business Week*, April 8, 2002.

[16] Michael Lewis and David Einhorn, "The End of the Financial Word as We Know It," *The New York Times*, January 4, 2009, p. 9.

[17] Ibid.

[18] Lewis, *The Big Short*, pp. 99-101.

[19] Ibid., p. 131.

[20] Ibid., p.128.

[21] http://www.ritholtz.com/blog/2009/02/greenspan-blame-the-rating-agencies/.

[22] Wikipedia, key in "Community Reinvestment Act."

[23] Aaron Pressman http://www.businessweek.com/investing/insights/blog/archives/2008/09/community_reinv.html, September 29 2008.

[24] Financial Crisis Inquiry Report, p. *xvii*.

[25] Alan Greenspan, *The Age of Turbulence*, Penguin Press, New York, 2007.

[26] What happens to the rule of law? Is private industry exempt?

[27] Richard Katz, "The Japan Fallacy," *Foreign Affairs*, March/April, 2009, p. 10.

[28] Ibid., p. 12. Derivatives are so-named because they derive their value from something else, such as real estate. A derivative contract can be used to speculate about the value of its underlying asset, such as real estate and home mortgages. More about derivatives later.

[29] Ryan Lizza, "The Contrarian," *The New Yorker*, July 6 and 13, 2009, p. 32.

[30] Investopedia and Wikipedia.

[31] Stephen Gandel, "How Stressed Is Your Bank?" *Time*, March 2, 2009, p. 29. I am pleasantly surprised by this study. I thought the big banks were in worse trouble. If the projections are accurate, Uncle Sam *only* has to divvy up $45 billion more to Citigroup, BofA, and Wells Fargo. In addition, after I compiled this table, BoA's CEO Kenneth Lewis said his bank made a profit in January and February of 2009, and would not need any more government help. In addition, Citigroup and JPMorgan said they were in the black so far this year. Let's hope this is a trend. And for clarification, it is likely this money will be repaid...with interest. But this news does not expunge the fact that a supposedly capitalistic society is socializing risks and privatizing profits for major sectors of America, but only if they are too big to fail.

[32] In a speech to the San Francisco Chamber of Commerce last month, John Stumpf (CEO) said Wells Fargo would not require any more funds from the government. Let's hope so.

[33] Morgenson and Rosner, *Reckless Endangerment*, p. 44.

[34] Microsoft Encarta. All rights reserved.

[35] Lowenstein, *The End of Wall Street*, The Penguin Press, New York, 2010, pp. 39-40.

[36] http://www.wired.com/techbiz/it/magazine/17-03/wp_quant?currentPage=all.

[37] Financial Crisis Inquiry Report, p. 177.

[38] http://en.wikipedia.org/wiki/Brooksley_Born.

Report 8

Financial Weapons of Mass Destruction

Great deeds are usually wrought at great risks.
—Herodotus, Histories, VII, 50

So are great follies.

March 13, 2009

Hello, Your On the Street Reporter is here, still trying to sort out the mess of the 2008 financial meltdown. In this segment, we focus on the financial instruments that played a key role in the meltdown.

Earlier, we briefly examined mortgage backed securities (MBS) and touched on another instrument, credit default swaps (CDS). In this report, I expand on these introductions and introduce other condiments to the meltdown's stew.

Summary of Several Key Financial Instruments

After writing and posting this segment to my blog I added the illustration shown in figure 8-1. My readers were having difficulty comprehending the relationships of the major financial instruments involved in the meltdown. I hope the figure is helpful. Please keep in mind that it is a simple overview of a complex set of instruments, but it reflects their relationships. It acts as a frame of reference for the material in this report.

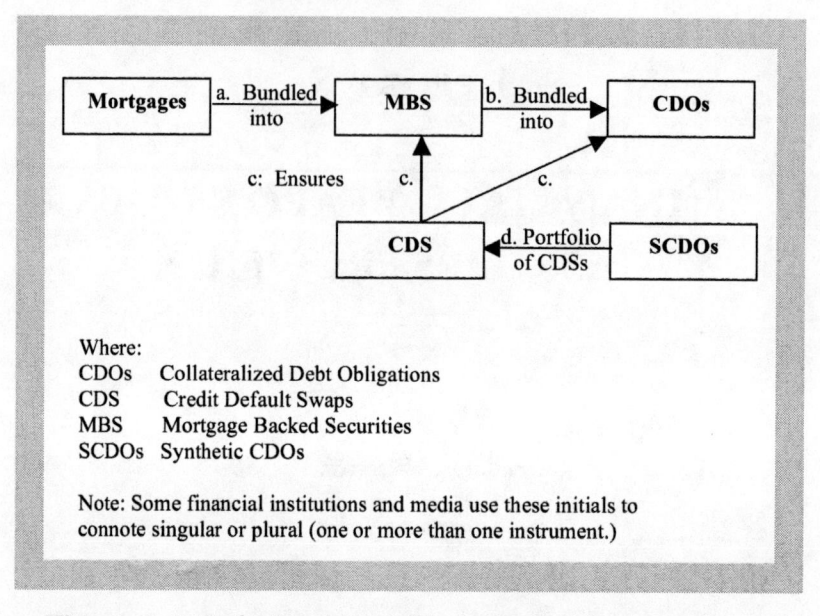

```
Mortgages --a. Bundled into--> MBS --b. Bundled into--> CDOs
                                 ^                         ^
                                 | c.                      | c.
                      c: Ensures |                         |
                                CDS <--d. Portfolio of CDSs-- SCDOs
```

Where:
CDOs   Collateralized Debt Obligations
CDS   Credit Default Swaps
MBS   Mortgage Backed Securities
SCDOs   Synthetic CDOs

Note: Some financial institutions and media use these initials to connote singular or plural (one or more than one instrument.)

Figure 8-1. Relationships of four financial instruments.

The next sections of this report review several terms and concepts covered earlier, but they are appended with more detailed explanations. Even if you are confident of your knowledge of the topics previously explained, I recommend you read this material. I have added additional information. I include some redundant material in this report, but I do so to lend continuity to the discussion.

Mortgage Backed Securities

For a brief review, recall that a mortgage backed security is backed by the principal and interest payments on a collection of mortgages. This pool of mortgages in the MBS is sold to investors. If the mortgages are solid, the investors make money.

In concept, mortgage backed securities are simple. But when thousands of mortgages are packaged into an MBS, the whole becomes more complicated than the parts that make up this whole. Each mortgage within the MBS has its own profile in relation to: (a) the amount of the loan, (b) the interest rate on the loan, (c) the equity invested in the loan, (d) the risk of the loan, and (e) its date to maturity. Plus, the MBS is affected when a loan is paid off because that part of the MBS is no longer making the MBS owner any money.

Consequently, the industry devised a variety of ways to evaluate and price an MBS, such as its weighted average coupon and its weighted average maturity. We need not go into these details to understand the MBS role in the meltdown.

Investors liked an MBS because its yield was usually higher than U.S. Treasury bonds, as it was based on the interest rates and equity of the packaged mortgages within the MBS. And the shakier the loan, the more interest it paid.

Mortgages are illiquid. A loan originator will not receive all the money on a loan until the loan is paid off. Whereas with an MBS, originators could sell the MBS to, say, Fannie Mae, and then have immediate funds available to make more loans and package-up more MBS.

In addition, by selling mortgages, a bank could remove assets from its balance sheet and reduce its risk. For the buyer, an MBS became another alternative for an investment beyond traditional debt and equity options.

Thus an MBS is in concept a great idea for the seller and the buyer. But after their creation in the mid-1990s, they began to be used for risky instruments and risky markets, such as Enron, WorldCom, and the more recent subprime home mortgage market.

How Wall Street Got into Mortgage Backed Securities. In the 1980s several Wall Street firms realized they could turn a handsome profit by dealing in mortgage backed securities. After all, mortgages were a huge business in America and mortgage bonds usually yielded more than corporate bonds. Thus companies such as Solomon Brothers began packaging, selling, and holding nongovernment mortgage backed securities. Because these instruments did not go through Fannie and Freddie, they were considered to be more risky than GSE-sponsored securities.

However, if the rating agencies came aboard and their evaluations became the authoritative stamp of approval for these private bonds, investors could invest and breathe easy. That is exactly what happened, especially because the SEC had long delegated its job of overseeing the security of financial instruments (to protect the security of America's citizenry) to the rating agencies.

Furthermore, because of the Savings and Loan debacle (courtesy of Uncle Sam and the Fed allowing interest rates to float), Uncle Sam came to the rescue of the very institutions it put into danger. After Volcker's speech (discussed earlier), interest rates skyrocketed and S&Ls immediately got into big trouble.[1] They were carrying thirty-year loans at, say, 8 percent but having to find money to support, say, a 12 percent (payout on customer deposits). After Volcker's declaration, the S&L industry nearly collapsed. The Law of Unintended Consequences raised its head again.

In 1981, to correct government's past mistakes, Congress passed a tax break allowing thrifts to sell their loans at a loss spread out over the *entire life* of the loans, which greatly inflated their actual worth. It was a dream come true deal for the S&Ls. In addition, the losses could be offset against any taxes the thrifts had paid for the last ten years. (I am continuously refraining from using exclamation points.) S&Ls went into a mortgage selling frenzy. Who was the purchaser? Wall Street.

Many of the S&Ls were staffed by inexperienced people who had spent their professional lives dealing with simple local home mortgages. They were babes-in-the-woods when it came to dealing with sophisticated financial instruments. They made poor deals with Wall Street firms, who ended-up making huge profits on these transactions. Nonetheless, these firms, in turn, were so enamored with this market that they bought a lot of poor-quality loans.

S&Ls and investment banks were (once again) aided by Uncle Sam and Uncle's Resolution Trust Corporation, (RTC). This organization relied on private industry (Wall Street) to package and securitize billions of dollars of residential mortgages. These mortgages were not up to the standards of Fannie and Ginnie (before Congress forced these GSEs to lower their standards). Today, they would be called subprime. Nonetheless, Wall Street took-on many of the assets of the S&Ls and made a bundle of money.

In a nutshell, Volcker's pronouncement led to the S&L crisis. Congress passed a tax break to save the nation's largest home mortgage lenders from collapse. This act led to the boot-strapping of the private mortgage backed securities industry (as well as subprime-based securities) and their presence on Wall Street.

Tranching. The private sector came up with the idea of using the rating agencies' contrived ratings to segment these mortgages into levels of quality, called "tranches," the French word for "slices".[2] Initially, there were two tranches in each package.[3] The highest quality tranche was the first to receive the principal and interest from the loans and was usually insured. The other tranche was not guaranteed.

Before long, mortgage backed securities contained many tranches containing groups of mortgages. They were ranked the highest (AAA) down to the lowest (BB). (Examples of S&P ratings: AAA, AA+, AA, AA-, A+, A, BBB+, BBB, BBB-, BB+, BB; with anything below BBB- considered as junk.) An MBS might contain thousands of mortgages, and as figure 8-2 shows, the income (the expected return) from the tranches depended on how risky they were. The riskier tranches yielded more income but in the event of problems, they were the first to go under.

The senior tranches were the highest rated. The mezzanine tranches were next. The so-called equity (or first-loss) tranches were the lowest rated and were the last in the queue to be paid if the MBS failed.

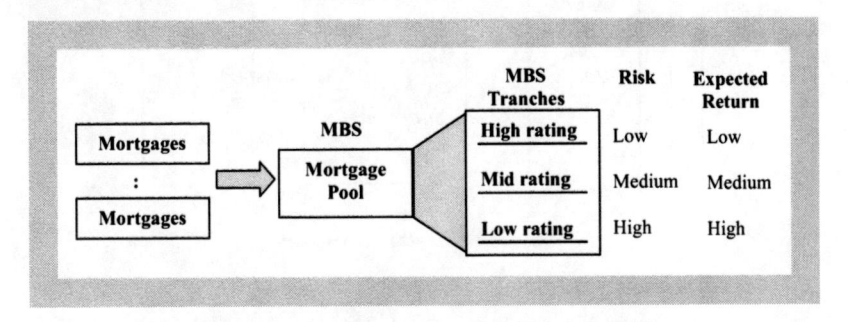

Mortgages → MBS Mortgage Pool	MBS Tranches	Risk	Expected Return
	High rating	Low	Low
	Mid rating	Medium	Medium
	Low rating	High	High

Figure 8-2. Mortgage backed securities.

Collateralized Debt Obligations (CDOs)

With the housing boom, millions of mortgages were pooled together in mortgage backed securities. Hundreds of these bonds were then placed into another instrument called the collateralized debt obligation (CDO).[4] Thus, millions of diverse loans were packaged into MBS and thousands of MBS were packaged into a CDO.

The reason for the creation of the CDO was to generate a new source of demand for the lower rated tranches contained in the MBS. These tranches provided a high return but because of their low ratings, they were difficult to sell. As well, some institutions were (are) not permitted to hold lower rated securities.

In the years from 2003 to 2006, BBB-rated securities became hot items as well as the CDOs in which they were packaged. By 2006, sales of mortgage-based CDOs had reached $225 billion.[5] Their popularity helped keep the mortgage industry and associated mortgage backed securities alive by injecting more cash into mortgage backed securities, which in turn provided the cash to originate mortgages.

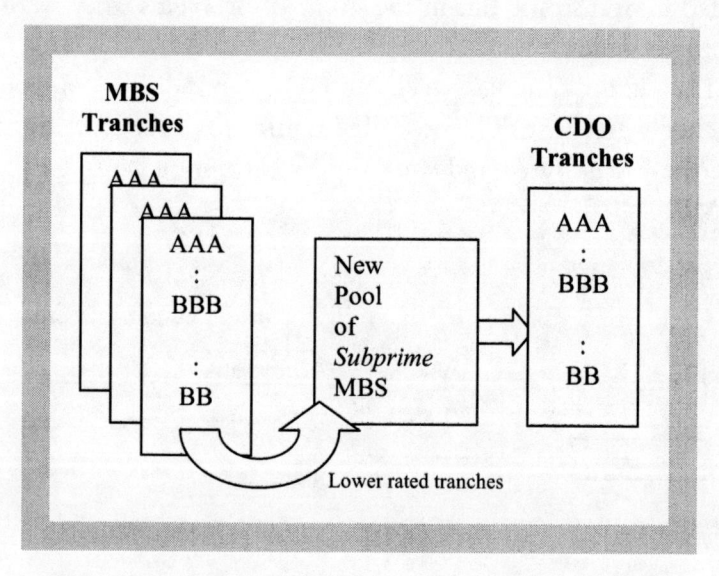

Figure 8-3. MBS tranches, packaged into CDOs.

As illustrated in figure 8-3 (and look again at figure 8-1), MBS were "sliced and diced" into CDOs.[6] These slices were also called tranches. With minor exceptions, BBB or A tranches were repackaged into the new CDO security with a higher rating. No, again I am not joking:[7]

> Approximately 80% of these CDO tranches would be rated triple-A despite the fact that they generally comprised the lower-rated tranches of the mortgage backed securities. CDO securities would be sold with their own waterfalls, with the risk-averse investors, again, paid first and the risk-seeking investors paid last. As they did in the case of mortgage backed securities, the rating agencies gave their highest, triple-A ratings to the securities at the top.

Once Again, Rating Junk as Jewels. These subprime mortgages were rated low; triple-B for example. But the CDO itself was rated AAA or AA. How could that be? Because the rating agencies were both shady and incompetent; because Wall Street created junk securities and gamed the rating agencies into mis-rating them.[8]

> Crappier pools of loans were cheaper to buy than less crappy loans…the Wall Street firm enjoyed a perverse monopoly. They'd phone up an originator and say, "Don't tell anybody, but if you bring me a pool of loans teeming with (low credit scores), I'll pay you more for it than anyone else." The more egregious the rating agencies' mistakes, the bigger the opportunity for the Wall Street trading desks.

> The market appeared to believe its own lie. It charged a lot less for insurance on a (supposedly) safe double-A-rated slice of a CDO than it did for insurance on the openly risky triple-B-rated bonds. Why pay 2 percent a year to bet directly against triple-B-rated bonds when they could pay 0.5 percent a year to make effectively the same bet against the double-A-slice of the CDO?

CDO Players. Figure 8-4 provides an illustration of the roles typically played by firms involved in bringing a CDO to the market.

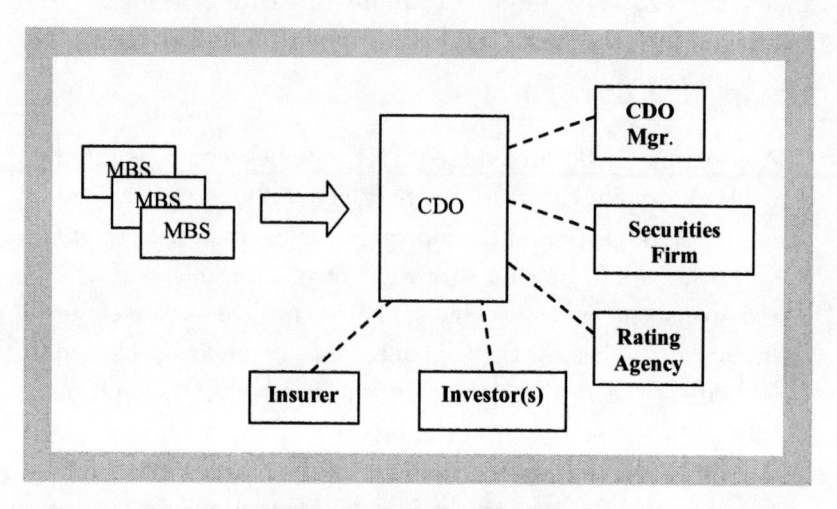

Figure 8-4. CDO process.

- The CDO manager studied the market and selected (or recommended) the mortgage backed securities that were to be a part of the CDO. The manager may also have managed the CDO on an ongoing basis.

- A securities firm, such as Goldman Sachs, Merrill Lynch, or Citigroup approved the selection and purchased the securities in the tranches (as mentioned, this procedure is called underwriting). I cite these three firms because from 2004 to2007, they handled roughly 30 percent of this market (along with two other major players, UBS and Deutsche Bank). The firm may have funded this purchase by taking on debt, such as issuing bonds. The securities firm also structured the various MBS into CDO tranches.

- A rating agency (maybe two) provided procedures for structuring the deal and performing the rating.

- The CDO's tranches were sold to investors.

- Investors hedged their risks by purchasing insurance on the CDO from an insurer, such as AIG. Many non-investors also shorted the CDO by taking insurance out on it.

Common Sense is Abandoned. While reading about CDOs, I was first puzzled about their use because I thought they were a simple repackaging of AAA securities into different bundles. I wondered why this repackaging was necessary. But upon further digging (and expressed by Mr. Lewis) it was evident the CDO was invented to find a way to pan off low-rated MBS tranches.

Nonetheless, Mr. Lewis' quotes above might lead one to believe the CDO creation was little more than a nefarious plot to dupe the unwary. Yes and no. Yes, it was a ploy to hoodwink uninitiated investors. No, in this sense: In an incredible breech of common sense, many smart people in both the securities firms (somewhat) and the ratings agencies (especially) believed that the pooling *together* of many lowly rated mortgage backed securities would somehow lead to less risk because the pool itself was diversified among different qualities of loans and kinds of people.[9] These ideas were based on faulty computer models and a lot of made-up assumptions.

In other words, because one security (say, MBS A) in a CDO might contain mortgages from one part of the country, its failure would not affect a security (say, MBS B) in the same CDO that contained mortgages originating from another part of the country.

Yet both MBS A and MBS B had nearly identical profiles. They (a) were constructed of poorly rated tranches, (b) containing subprime mortgages, (c) with adjustable rates ready to kick in and (d) render the mortgage underwater. These characteristics were found in both MBS A and B, regardless of where the mortgages originated. In what can only be described as self-delusion, the rating agencies did not think mortgage backed securities of nearly the same kind of content would exhibit similar behavior.

We can reasonably ask what happened to common sense? The rating agencies seemed to have little, while the securities firms had an abundance of it (as some of them, such as Goldman Sachs, bet against them). The rating agencies (and firms that issued insurance on this junk) were intellectually tarred and feathered by the smart bankers on Wall Street.

Don't Cry for Me. Moody's, S&P, and Fitch were not exactly on the bread line. The rating agencies welcomed the business of evaluating CDOs because they were more complex—thus, more lucrative—than simpler bonds. For example:[10]

> Moody's could earn as much as $250,000 to rate a mortgage pool with $350 million in assets, versus the $50,000 in fees generated when rating a municipal bond of a similar size.
>
> As CDO volumes soared, so did the ratings agencies' earnings. Moody's revenues from rating CDOs and other structured finance products totaled almost $900 million in 2006, up 63% from the $553 million generated two years earlier. In 2006, Moody's structured finance revenues accounted for fully 44% of its $2 billion in sales.

Fraud and Whoring by Any Other Names. One of the readers of this report (posted to me in 2009) wrote that no amount of rationalization could excuse the behavior of the investment banks and the rating agencies. She added, "This is a process classically called fraud." She also had this comment about the rating agencies, "How could they not know they were being bought?...Otherwise known as whoring."

Lots of Revenue, a Dearth of Resources. Part of the disorder with the CDO market stemmed from the rating agencies inability or refusal to staff sufficiently to support their increased business. For example, Moody's rated 220 CDOs in 2004, 363 in 2005, and 749 in 2006, but this revenue did not coincide with an increase in staffing levels.[11]

Because Wall Street's regulators and regulated are highly networked, it was not unusual for the lesser-paid rating agency employees to leave for a Wall Street firm, whose CDOs they may have once evaluated.[12] Moody's reported about 25 percent of its derivatives staff left the firm to work for commercial or investment banks.

For CDOs, Wall Street firms connived with the rating agencies to game poor stuff into highly rated stuff. They patted each other's back, sometimes inadvertently, but often intentionally. It is difficult to imagine a less healthy relationship in the business world. As one poet said, "And so we plow along, as the fly said to the ox."[13] The furrows they plowed created many furrows in the lives of millions of innocent bystanders.

But to Wall Street, as quoted in the Preface to this book, it was "a speed bump."

Credit Default Swaps (CDS)

Thus mortgage backed securities (MBS) and the associated collateralized debt obligations (CDOs) ended up carrying risk. As suggested at the beginning of this report, "Great follies are usually wrought at great risks." Consequently, yet another instrument, discussed generally several times earlier, was created to insure against the risk of investing in potentially chancy securities: credit default swaps (CDS). We've danced around CDS several times in this book. It's time to dance with them.

In 1994, JPMorgan was looking for a new way to mitigate risk on its loans and investments. In a meeting at the Boca Raton Resort & Club in Florida, JP's executives came up with the idea of an insurance policy in which a third party, say the insurance company AIG, would assume the risk of a loan going sour. (Or a package of loans in a mortgage backed security.) In turn, a bank, such as JPMorgan, would pay AIG premiums for this assurance, similar to an insurance policy.[14]

The idea is shown in figure 8-5. The CDS is a swap contract. The protection buyer of a CDS makes payments (premiums, like an insurance policy) to the seller. The payment is called a "spread" and represents the amount of money (monthly, quarterly, annually) the buyer of the CDS must pay the seller for the length of the contract.

If the instrument, such as an MBS, goes into default the buyer receives a payoff from the seller based on how much was insured to begin with.

If the protection seller's bet is correct that the MBS will remain solid until the expiration of the contract with the protection buyer, the seller has made a fine profit from the buyer's premiums without expending one red cent of upfront money. Of course, that is the very nature of insurance.

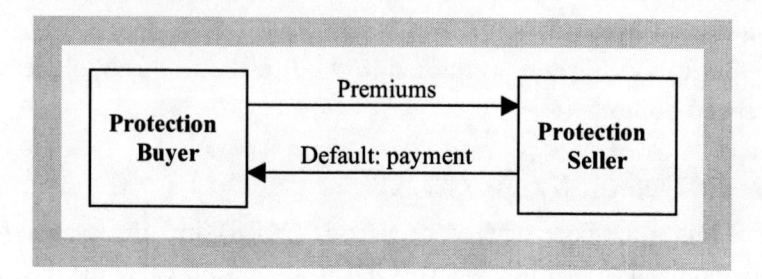

Figure 8-5. Credit default swaps.

Keep in mind that the CDS protection buyer (an investor) need not own the insured instrument itself. Thus, you might buy this "naked" CDS because you think someone else's mortgage backed securities or collateralized debt obligations are going to fail. You bet against those securities (you short them) and take money from the CDS seller if the securities tank.

Another Bet in Life. Reference was made earlier to the idea of betting that something we do not own, will fail. My friends who are experts in the fields of finance and banking tell me this practice is efficient because it keeps the market "lively and liquid." I am not one of these experts, so I bow to their views. But I remain leery of the idea of a person taking out insurance on something I own and he does not. In such a situation, he therefore hopes I will fail.

We humans are gambling creatures and the stock market is one of our many gambling venues. But the purchase of stock is of social value. While its purchase is a gamble, it also contributes to a socially enhancing infrastructure. And credit default swaps, taken out to protect one's own position in any type of risk, makes sense. But as discussed in this section of the report, a naked CDS, one in which a person can lawfully bet on a homeowner defaulting on a mortgage

REPORT 8: FINANCIAL WEAPONS OF MASS... 131

in which the person has no skin in the game is skating on thin ethical ice.

CDS Operations. Figure 8-6 illustrates the basic steps involved in executing a CDS transaction. I use ACME Inc. as the entity that is the object for the swap. Let's assume it's a delivery service such as UPS or FedEx. But the entity could also be a mortgage backed security, a major subject of these reports. I make this distinction to clarify that Wall Street can create instruments to wager on anything—even if the wagers are nothing more than bets on vacuous chattels.

Betting on thin air is all well and good, as long as Wall Street and Uncle Sam do not allow these bets to affect our pocketbooks, and as long as our tax dollars don't reward Wall Street's murky failures. But these two caveats are spitting in the wind. The truth is that Wall Street, an assemblage of financial whizzes, has no incentive to take care of us. Yet Uncle Sam, an assemblage of well-meaning, but often plodding bureaucrats—influenced by politicians who are subject to the largesse of Wall Street—has proven to be unwilling or incapable of overseeing this massive financial structure.

In figure 8-6, the credit-worthiness of ACME is analyzed by a rating agency, say Standard and Poor's. This agency disseminates its assessment to the public. An investor and a bank use the agency's appraisal in their transactions to possibly buy and sell a CDS on the reference entity.

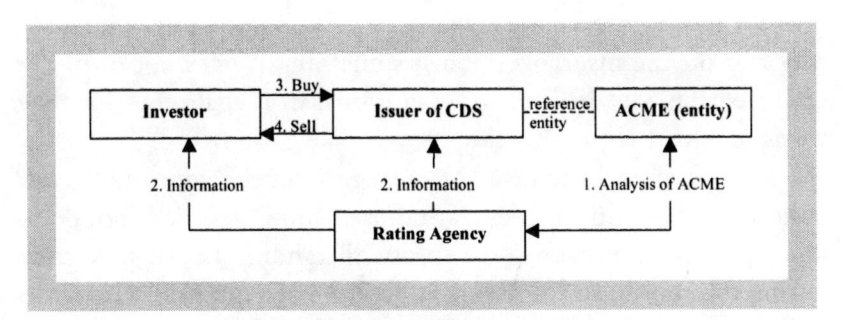

Figure 8-6. A CDS transaction.

The buyer of the CDS (the investor) hopes ACME will encounter troubles. If so, the buyer collects insurance from the CDS issuer.

The buyer also hopes (very much) that if ACME goes under, the issuer of the CDS does not. In a financial crisis it is possible that both the CDS issuer and ACME could default. If so, the investor loses its protection and the CDS is worthless. Its previously paid premiums on the CDS are gone.

In normal, non-crisis circumstances the investor of the CDS pays an amount to the issuer that is determined by the basis points of the spread (a basis point is = 0.01). If the spread increases, say, because ACME's delivery service is suffering from increased fuel costs for its delivery trucks, its credit worthiness might be down-graded by Standard and Poor's. If so, the amount paid for the insurance will increase. If ACME is having a good Christmas season, gas prices are low, and shoppers are shipping a lot of packages to their relatives, the spread will tighten (decrease) and the periodic payment for the CDS will be less.

For example, assume the investor buys $10 million for ACME protection from the CDS issuer. If the CDS is 40 basis points (a basis point is 100th of one percent), the investor pays the issuer $40,000 per period (say, a year). If ACME is evaluated by Standard and Poor's to be experiencing higher fuel costs because the Arabs and Canada have raised their oil barrel prices, the CDS spread might be set at 50 basis points, which would mean the investor would then have to pay the issuer $50,000.

Thus far, the situation is straight-forward and sensible. Sure, the investor has no ownership stake in ACME, so one might question why it is buying insurance against something it does not own. I've discussed this idea before, and will return to it again, but for now, we assume that is the situation.

The issuer and the investor must rely on the competence and honesty of the rating agency. If Standard and Poor's does not do its job, the process breaks down. Notwithstanding this dependency, during the run-up to this financial meltdown a (very) few investors did their own analysis by going into the innards of mortgage backed securities to discover how toxic many of the loans were. They bought as many credit default swaps as they could find. When the meltdown occurred, they became very rich.

Interlocking Gridlock. The situation described thus far is usually more complex, which leads to one of the major issues in the financial industry: the interlocking of financial instruments and institutions to one another, as well as to these institutions' customers.

A seller of this CDS (the issuer) usually buys insurance on it from another party (a different CDS). This is known as "hedging one's exposure." In addition, ACME might buy insurance on itself, and/or buy a derivative that will lock-in the price of gas for a given period. In turn, the sellers of these derivatives might hedge their exposure by also buying CDS derivates. In another turn, these sellers might do the same, and so on.

The situation can cascade into a byzantine set of interlocking, interdependent relationships. A CDS seller could be a CDS buyer from another CDS seller. This system is one of the main reasons the U.S. government has gone to such extensive measures to rescue AIG, car companies, and banks. Uncle Sam could not kick just one company out of bed because this company was actively engaged in mucking-with and mucking-over many bedmates' other bedmates ... and it was not about to get off the mattress.

Henry Paulson, former CEO of Goldman Sachs and the former Secretary of Treasury under Bush II, had this to say about the interlocking of big financial firms:[15]

> A (investment bank Bear Sterns) failure wouldn't just hurt the owners of its shares and bonds. Bear had hundreds, maybe thousands, of counter-parties—firms that it lent money or with which it traded stocks, bonds, mortgages, and other securities. These firms—other banks and brokerage houses, insurance companies, mutual funds, hedge funds, the pension funds of states, cities, and big companies—all in turn had myriad counterparties of their own. If Bear fell, all these counterparties would be scrambling to collect their loans and collateral. To meet demands for payment, first Bear and then other firms would be forced to sell whatever they could, in any market they could—driving prices down, causing more losses, and triggering more margin and collateral calls.

134 THE NEARLY PERFECT STORM

Prior to the meltdown, the naked CDS market—largely a casino bazaar—made up about 80 percent of the CDS market.[16] It was a speculator's fantasy: The sellers of the CDS could go long on a bond (bet for it) without buying the bond; just pay-out in the event of default. The buyers of the CDS could go short on a bond (as said, bet against it) without owning it either. Neither of the parties had a stake in the bond itself. The transaction did not raise any capital to build a factory. Again, speculation is fundamental to rational capitalism, and central to efficient human behavior. But in the meltdown, without the brakes of Uncle Sam, it was carried to absurd and tragic levels.

It was a fine idea from JP Morgan's brain trust for JP's benefit. Because the CDS was insurance—*but not called insurance*—it was not regulated by the Feds. In addition, because a swap was setup and negotiated between two private parties, no central records were kept to determine their value and quantity. This lack of information about the CDS market was a major problem, because it prevented investors from knowing what was going on; of making informed decisions.

Dark Matter. Some people call credit default swaps "dark matter" because it is not known where they may lie in hiding, waiting to blow up yet another balance sheet, or another company.

A telling example of CDS overuse is the company AIG. At the time it was bailed out, AIG held $440 billion of credit default swaps, more than twice the equity positions of any of America's largest banks.[17] Thus far, the government has ploughed in over $100 billion to keep AIG going.

Uncle Sam, prior to this charitable contribution to free markets, did not require AIG (or any other CDS issuers) to hold any reserve to pay off buyers of CDS. Thus, the AIGs of the world dealt in insurance-type products that were not regulated, or even tracked by the government, which of course, is exactly how the insurance companies wanted it. They were not required to hold reserves or post collateral against credit default swaps. Yet:[18]

> The reason that saving AIG was so costly was that the government decided to honor all of AIG's swap obligations,

lest defaulting on them plunge many of the company's counterparties (which included major banks such as Goldman Sachs) into insolvency.

Goldman got billions out of the arrangement, and shortly thereafter, was solvent enough to pay out millions to its employees as bonuses.

As mentioned, some CDS dealers took the path of managing their risk by acquiring offsetting CDS with other dealers; to hedge their exposure. All of it was off the record, with no regulation or accounting except between the consenting parties. Small wonder no one knows how deep the CDS iceberg is.

And it is not over. I have read that a quarter trillion dollars may have to be given to AIG, because it is too big to fail and its instruments are so closely linked (interlocked) to other financial firms.

Casino Bets with Your Money. Regarding the too big to fail issue: As you read about this subject, please keep in mind that the huge financial institutions today are not deemed too big to fail because of their social worth to society. They are too big to fail because of the casino bets they have placed with other big banks and the bets the other banks have placed with them. Except for their executives' bonuses and these *employees'* subsequent accrued wealth, their gigantic interlocking relationships have made them wards of Uncle Sam's bailouts.

But how could intelligent people display such arrogance and stupidity? (We keep asking this question.) Why would a company commit so much of its collateral and financial well-being to one instrument? Again, it appears the AIG savants never considered that an arrow pointing up was also capable of pointing down. The arrow pointing up was tracking the home mortgage market. As we know, the arrow began to turn downward around 2006. As more adjustable rate mortgages had their higher rates kick in (especially in 2007), the arrow began a deep downward turn.

Another of my blog readers wrote that these people may not have been stupid at all; that they knew the perilous path they and others were on. They were lining their pockets while riding the bubble.

This idea is substantiated in other parts of this book, with quotes furnished by Michael Lewis.

In addition, a substantial number of high-level people simply never factored such a possibility into their risk assessments. These officers were stupid and arrogant enough to think a bubble would never burst. Now we citizens are left to pick up the pieces.

I have taken an adversarial approach in this discussion of naked credit default swaps. To balance the discussion, I've also stated the supporters of naked CDS claim short selling in general has the beneficial effect of increasing liquidity in the marketplace:[19] "Without speculators buying and selling naked CDS, banks wanting to hedge might not find a ready seller of protection. Speculators also create a more competitive marketplace, keeping prices down for hedgers. A robust market in credit default swaps can also serve as a barometer to regulators and investors about the credit health of a company or country."

I agree about the bank's position. It might very well be prudent to take out a CDS on a loan it has made. But that is my point. The bank is protecting something it owns, not someone else's property. The idea seems to contain the notion that Wall Street cannot really function if it does not have pure speculators and hedgers. That's quite reasonable, as we all are gamblers when dealing with stocks, bonds, etc. Still, I close this part of the discussion harboring a distrust of credit default swaps. It comes from not how they were supposed to be used, but how they were misused.

Source of the term "Financial Weapons of Mass Destruction"

Appendix A of this report contains edited excerpts from the Berkshire Hathaway annual report for 2002 (edits were performed by Berkshire Hathaway.) It contains comments Warren Buffett made about derivatives and the CDS market. The material is more technical than the material in these reports and several terms about evaluating the worth of swaps are not discussed in this series. If you wish more details about this aspect of the nearly perfect financial storm, I recommend Mr. Buffett's explanation.

La La Loans for La La Land

I have discussed the variable rate mortgage (ARM) and how banks and mortgage brokers misrepresented it. This section introduces two more types of mortgage loans (a) interest-only loans and (b) negative amortization loans. As the Federal Reserve Board began to raise interest rates in 2004, the demand for heretofore cheap commercial and home loans declined. In addition, adjustable rate loans became less popular because their rates ratcheted up along with overall interest rates. The situation also led to a decline in the issuance of mortgage backed securities: For 2004, 40 percent fewer were sold than in 2003. If something were not done to revive this market, Wall Street saw trouble ahead. Million dollar bonuses might suffer.

To resuscitate the process, the system began hawking interest-only loans for home mortgages. This plan did not require the home buyer to pay *any* principal on the loan. In theory, the attractive aspect of this approach was to free money for the home owner to invest it in, say, high-yielding stocks. In reality, Joe and Josephine usually took this money to Best Buy to purchase another flat screen TV.

Meanwhile, there was zero equity being built into their home; the mortgage principal stayed the same. Meanwhile, adjustable rates on subprime loans were kicking in and defaults were occurring. Meanwhile, the values of homes began to decrease, leading to Joe and Josephine holding a mortgage whose outstanding balance was less than the value of the house.

To add to this toxic brew, the lenders and Wall Street came up with an idea to make more loans affordable: the negative amortization loan. The borrower could choose the amount he was to pay on the interest. The amount not paid was then added to the outstanding principal. Consequently, a loan that was likely going underwater had more weights attached to hasten its sinking.

The industry kept packaging these and other nearly worthless loans into securities and selling them to investors as AAA. Wall Street knew the nature of the underlying instruments; an investor did not.

I trust you now appreciate the subheading to this section: La La Loans for La La Land.

Structured Investment Vehicle (SIV)

Yet more fodder is added to banking's financial silage sleaze. It is called the structured investment vehicle (SIV).[20] Following Citigroup, many banks set up a SIV (a separate special purpose company). Next, the bank sold mortgage backed securities to the SIV. This action took the loans *off* the bank's balance sheets in order to assure regulators the bank was not taking on too much risk. It also isolated (in theory) the bank from any losses these securities might experience.

The regulators had trouble making any accurate assessment of this part of the mess because it was the intent of the banks to keep this practice as opaque as possible. For example, Citigroup named its satellite "Citi Alternative Investments" but changed the name to "Citi Capital Advisors" to make it sound more like a noble counselor and less like a cover-up.

Next, the SIV would issue bonds that were backed by the mortgage backed securities. When the subprime mortgage meltdown began, the SIV's income from the mortgage backed securities tanked. Once exposed, the banks were forced (avoiding a fantastic breach of faith) to place the securities back onto their balance sheets. Next, the banks' balance sheets tanked even more. Next, investors who had credit default swaps on the securities realized the issuer of the insurance on the securities might not be able to meet its obligation because so many defaults were occurring. Next, investors took any defensive actions they could, such as asking for more collateral from the insurer, or cutting off credit to the bank.

The Autocatalytic Process swung into action and Wall Street's financial boil, festering for many years, erupted and spilled its toxin onto America's Main Streets. Few escaped…except those on Wall Street who experienced a "speed bump."

Rerating Low Quality Mortgage Backed Securities

To compound the problems that were eventually (and inevitably) going to surface, Goldman Sachs went a step further.[21] As depicted in figure 8-3, within a CDO, the mortgage bonds (mortgage backed securities) were packaged based on risk and an associated expected return. The lower rated bonds (triple-B-rated) were harder to sell than the higher bonds (triple-A-rated) because they were the first to take losses. In Wall Street parlance, they were almost at the bottom—the ground floor—which was called the mezzanine or the mezz. (Others, limited in number, occupied a "basement.") As Lewis writes:

> But what if triple-B-rated mortgage backed securities—those containing subprime/ARM mortgages could somehow be rated as triple-A?
>
> ...there were huge sums of money to be made, if you could somehow get them re-rated as triple-A, thereby lowering their perceived risk, however dishonestly and artificially. That is what Goldman Sachs had cleverly done.
>
> ...they persuaded the rating agencies that these weren't as they might appear, all exactly the same things. They were another diversified portfolio of assets!
>
> The rating agencies, *who were paid fat fees by Goldman Sachs and other Wall Street firms for each deal they rated* [italics are mine], pronounced 80 percent of the new tower of debt triple-A.

In effect, subprime mortgages were now touted as prime mortgages. As the meltdown began in the summer of 2007, thousands of investors were surprised to learn "their stakes in triple-A-rated subprime-backed CDOs were worthless."

Synthetic CDOs

I wish the story about the folly of subprime CDOs and the venality of Wall Street's use of them could end here. But it does not.

We add another player introduced in Report 4: *synthetic CDOs*. They are called synthetic because they contain no hard assets. These instruments make reference to the assets that fueled the engines of the mortgage industry, but they did not finance the purchase of one single home. For the meltdown of 2008, a synthetic CDO represented an investment in credit default swaps, a shown in figure 8-1. A synthetic CDO used credit default swaps to generate income by betting if borrowers would or would not pay their mortgages.[22] The bottom line: They enabled casino betting on the value of mortgage backed securities. They were of no value to society, only to Wall Street gamblers.

Not everyone agrees with my claim about the vacuity of synthetic CDOs, and I admit that one of their characteristics had value: A conventional CDS usually referenced (insured) only one security, which meant an investor might be taking on a very large risk. In contrast, the synthetic CDO, by bundling multiple credit default swaps in its portfolio, diffused the risk by allowing an investor to pick and choose the specific component CDS and their associated MBS.

A synthetic CDO was (and is) a bundle (a portfolio) of credit default swaps. It was also securitized into various tranches, with progressively higher levels of risk. Thus, synthetic CDOs gave buyers the flexibility to take on only as much risk as they wished to assume. The investors could look at the referenced mortgages in the bonds and decide if they wanted to make a bet on their worth. The extent of the bet would determine the tranches they selected.

When I first came across the term synthetic CDOs I was confused because I assumed they contained something of value, such as mortgages or mortgage backed securities. As just mentioned, they only made reference to the mortgage securities through their component CDS, which *did cite* the specific mortgage backed securities.[23] Here is summary and comparison of CDOs and synthetic CDOs:[24]

> Party A wants to bet that at least some mortgage bonds and CDOs will default from among a specified population of such securities, taking the short position. Party B can bundle credit

default swaps related to these securities into a synthetic CDO contract. Party C agrees to take the long position, agreeing to pay Party A if certain defaults or other credit events occur within that population. Party A pays Party C premiums for this protection. Party B, typically an investment bank, would take a fee for arranging the deal.

In the event of default, those in the long position on either CDO or synthetic CDO suffer large losses. With the synthetic CDO, the long investor pays the short investor, versus the normal CDO in which the interest payments decline or stop flowing to the long investor.

The question is why would anyone create *mortgage-based* synthetic CDOs in the first place? To explain, we take another journey into Wall Street's La La Land. The increasingly frenzied pace of the mortgage bond market began to outpace the creation of the mortgages themselves—a danger to the continuity of the Autocatalytic Effect cycle and the accelerating income of Wall Street personnel.

Lenders were not able to find enough home buyers to whom they could grant subprime loans. There were only so many houses a migrant orange picker could afford on his orange picking income. Even if he made no down payment, there was the irritating aspect of the orchard worker not making his mortgage payments.

Granted, the tombstone names of deceased husbands, associated with the dead spouse's "current" income, provided a huge market for lenders to improve a widow's loan application. (This situation is explained in Report 10.) Nonetheless, the market for mortgage backed securities outpaced the availability of mortgages that were packaged inside these securities.

Wall Street's solution was to manufacture the synthetic CDO from thin air using another kind of financial instrument that was based on the cash CDO. It was constructed from artificial cloth so your writer likes to think it became known as a synthetic CDO (my own take on the name). Because there were no available mortgages or mortgage bonds to own, Wall Street's casino dealers created the synthetic CDO casino game: It bet on the performance of the credit default swaps...which bet on the performance of the CDOs.

The synthetic CDO, empty of anything productive, would "mirror the performance (through the CDS) of CDOs that did...An investor bought, instead of the actual bonds, a promise from some other investor to provide the same return; if the real-world bonds lost money, the buyer took a similar loss."[25]

Firms such as Goldman Sachs liked synthetic CDOs because they made money, and were cheap and easy to create, especially during the time when the supply of mortgages was drying up. Mortgage assets take time to assemble and finance into securities. As well, a lot of work goes into the packaging of mortgage backed securities and placing them into CDOs. With a synthetic CDO, a security firm could simply select a set of CDOs that already existed. The firm was no longer restricted by the supply of mortgages available.

Voila! Another casino game was created for the gamblers to bet for or against. Even better, synthetic CDOs produced income to those firms who did the underwriting, such as Goldman Sachs. An underwriting fee for a synthetic CDO ranged from 0.50 percent to 1.50 percent of the face value of the security. Between July 1, 2004 and May 31, 2007, Goldman sold 47 synthetic CDOs worth $66 billion.[26] A little bit here and a little bit there. Before long, synthetic CDOs were helping to finance those million dollar bonuses for Goldman's executives.

A couple years ago, I was playing Texas Hold'em at a Las Vegas casino. One of the players, after making a winning bet, offered this thought, "Damn! Every time I win a hand I lose money." I asked him why? He said, "Because I did not bet enough."

This mentality seemed to pervade firms such as Goldman Sachs. The firm's synthetic CDOs referenced 3,408 mortgage backed securities (and hundreds of thousands of mortgages). Not satisfied with this count and looking for yet bigger payouts, Goldman referenced 610 securities twice. One MBS was referenced in nine different synthetic CDOs![27]

Is it beneficial to our society for a firm to stake out nine bets on something that has already done its job of financing a home? It staggers my imagination, but then I do not possess the imagination of an investment banker.

How It Worked. As mentioned, anyone entering into a synthetic CDO transaction was betting for or against financial instruments owned by someone else (such as mortgage securities, existing CDOs, and commercial real estate loans). Thus, contending parties were involved (counterparties); one party thought the instrument would make money; the other party thought it would tank. It was really nothing more than a wager. Figure 8-7 shows this arrangement.

First, a broker, bundles up a group of CDS, which for this example, makes reference to CDO XYZ. The broker markets the instrument to both long and short parties. Party A shorts CDO XYZ (bets against it). Party C goes long (bets for it). Party A pays Party C premiums for the insurance, for the protection. Party C pays Party A if XYZ fails or is degraded. The transaction is more involved as amplified in this footnote, but my general description captures the important points.[28]

As stated, it was thin air in that the synthetic CDO did nothing to contribute to a nation's economic output. It contained no mortgages. It was a casino side bet, and a very big one. But then, it was after all a bubble: "...far more money was wagered on mortgage debt than the total of such debt in existence."[29]

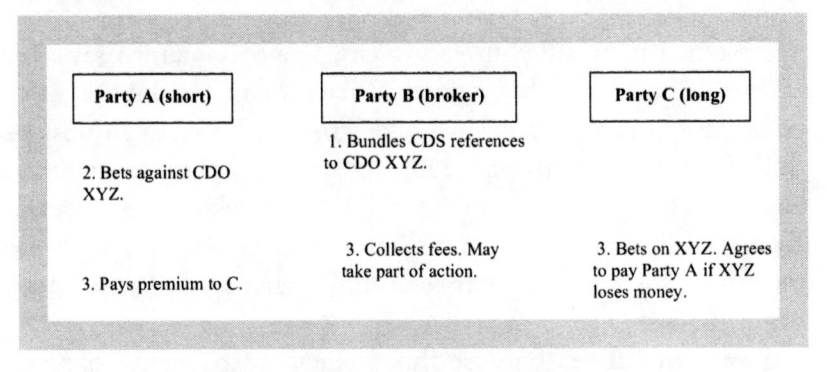

Party A (short)	Party B (broker)	Party C (long)
2. Bets against CDO XYZ.	1. Bundles CDS references to CDO XYZ.	
3. Pays premium to C.	3. Collects fees. May take part of action.	3. Bets on XYZ. Agrees to pay Party A if XYZ loses money.

Figure 8-7. Synthetic creations.

Packaging a Deal to Sell and Betting Against It. In 2004 Goldman created and sold a synthetic CDO called Abacus 2004-1. It was worth $2 billion, and referenced residential and commercial mortgage backed securities and well as existing CDOs. Goldman was the short investor.[30] You read correctly. Goldman created a package to sell to someone else and bet against the performance of this package. It purchased credit default swaps on the deal, mostly from AIG. The other side of the bet (some banks and security firms) forked out $195 million to purchase mezzanine tranches of the package. Goldman took on the good stuff. It kept $1.8 billion of the highest quality tranches, left the junk to others, and covered its exposure with insurance.

The FCIC hearings revealed the following facts:

- Goldman received about $930 million while the long investors lost "just about all their investments."
- An asset management firm paid Goldman $7.3 million as a result of CDS insurance Goldman purchased on the loss of Goldman's tranches.
- Goldman received $806 million from AIG as a result of the credit default swaps protection it had purchased on its high quality tranche.
- Goldman received $23 million, $30 million, and $40 million, and $24 million from various other companies with whom it purchased credit default swaps.

Goldman is staffed with very smart people. Goldman says, *Let the buyer beware*. Sure, that is good advice for anyone. But the buyer is often not as sophisticated as Goldman. The buyer might just be a hick-town retirement fund, looking for a safe place to invest its employees' 401(K) money. Goldman did not care about these nuances of ethical dignity. If you are skeptical of Goldman's pathetic arrogance, look at the congressional hearings and associated documentation.

Scope of Effect. Because this financial instrument's size and growth was not tied to anything that had inherent limits, such as the number of mortgages in America, its expansion was only limited by the number of gamblers who were willing to take it on. More gamblers in Las Vegas? Bring in more Texas Hold'em tables. More gamblers on Wall Street? Create more "synthetics." Make a million-dollar bet in Vegas? Find a caller to the other side of your bet. Make a million dollar bet on a Wall Street synthetic CDO? Find a caller to the other side of your bet.

Some institutions even bought their own mortgage companies to further relax loan standards in order to fuel the CDO and synthetic CDO fire.[31] Here are other thoughts about this subject:[32]

> To paraphrase the financial journalist, Michael Lewis, synthetic CDOs had as much to do with real estate as fantasy football had to do with the NFL…They built no houses and painted no walls; they simply multiplied the Street's gamble.
>
> In some cases, a single mortgage bond was referenced in dozens of synthetics. [As mentioned earlier] It was as if Wall Street, in all its mad Strangelovian genius, had found a way to clone armies of securities from a single strand of mortgage DNA.
>
> How many? By 2006, half of all CDOs were synthetic.

Shorting Ethics

Imagine, with forethought, effort, and expense, you assemble a synthetic CDO to sell to whomever wishes to take on this investment. However, in your assemblage of a $2 billion *nonasset reference* to tangible assets, you bet against the very objects of your invention. Yep. You are the short investor of a package you created to sell to a long investor. Do you think for one Wall Street second that your sales staff is going to peddle this stuff as low quality? If you do, I've a bridge near the Street that I'd like to sell you.

Anyway, you are both short and long because you have kept ownership of the high-quality tranches. You know the contents. So, go long on the good stuff and short the bad stuff.

Do your customers know what you know? You say they should know. After all, it's Darwin in Guccis. But many of your customers are not bedecked in Guccis. They toil away in penny loafers, reliant on your expertise and the integrity of your trading desk. They are retirement funds in Ohio; or groups of IRAs in New Mexico—ordinary people who have relied on your "hand-holding" of their financial future and security.

After all, is that not what you have told them? You will take care of them. No, that is not what happened.

Another Look at Interlocking Relationships

Before moving on, one more point should be made about CDOs and synthetic CDOs. They were not publicly traded, and therefore were not subject to examination by anyone other than the participating parties. If their effects were only between these parties, fine. But unlike most any other industry, the financial world is *very* tightly interlocked. As mentioned, competing institutions routinely borrow money from one another and engage in other cooperative activities that other industries would consider anticompetitive.

The experts tell me that tight interlocking is an important way for capital markets to operate efficiently; to allocate bank capital resourcefully. Banks routinely loan excess cash to each other. If bank A has excess cash and bank B needs cash for an upcoming loan, bank A loans cash to bank B. Later, the process might be reversed. Thus, credit is vital, not just for consumers, but for banks as well.

During 2008, banks became fearful about lending to one another because they were not certain about the soundness of other banks. By looking at the books of a bank, another bank could gain some sense of its position. But it could not really know all significant aspects of a balance sheet because the dark world of unregulated credit default swaps was hidden inside a black hole.

The House of Cards Comes Down

Billions of dollars were tied up in subprime loans, many tied to an adjustable interest rate. It was just a matter of time before millions of homeowners defaulted and were kicked out of their homes. As well, it was just a matter of time before the Law of Unexpected Consequences kicked in to put asunder a great part of America's economy and its infrastructure.

AIG and other credit default swaps insurers never saw the black swan until it was too late. The chain reaction began. For example, Lehman Brothers had made more than $700 billion in swaps, and many of them were backed up by AIG. But AIG could not cover its losses to Lehman and others. AIG was a big player, one of the numbers in the Dow Jones industrial average. AIG's "plunge" pulled down the Dow average and panic (with the loss of trust and confidence) rippled throughout the financial industry. Credit, the lifeblood of capitalism, froze up.

Keeping It Simple

We have only touched the surface of the arcane world of financial instruments. But we need not go into any more details. Keeping it simple works fine for these reports. I hope you were able to follow the discussions. It was somewhat technical, but I wrote it as a layman. I trust you did OK with the material. As mentioned earlier, Appendix A provides more details, courtesy of Warren Buffett. I also hope you read this appendix. It will provide a fitting summary to the topics of this report.

To conclude, the Law of the Instrument was a major factor in the meltdown. The instruments—modeling, mortgage securities, and swaps—came to be used without taking a more judgmental view of how they should indeed be used.

Risk was subordinated to greed; responsibility to stupidity. The child had the hammer in his hand and did the child ever pound it. This idea provides a convenient way to introduce the next report: "Greed, Stupidity, and the Herd Rule."

Appendix A: Warren Buffett on Derivatives[33]

I view derivatives as time bombs, both for the parties that deal in them and the economic system. Basically these instruments call for money to change hands at some future date, with the amount to be determined by one or more reference items, such as interest rates, stock prices, or currency values. For example, if you are either long or short on [an] S&P 500 futures contract, you are a party to a very simple derivatives transaction, with your gain or loss derived from movements in the index. Derivatives contracts are of varying duration, running sometimes to 20 or more years, and their value is often tied to several variables.

Unless derivatives contracts are collateralized or guaranteed, their ultimate value also depends on the creditworthiness of the counter-parties to them. But before a contract is settled, the counter-parties record profits and losses – often huge in amount – in their current earnings statements without so much as a penny changing hands. Reported earnings on derivatives are often wildly overstated. That's because today's earnings are in a significant way based on estimates whose inaccuracy may not be exposed for many years.

The errors usually reflect the human tendency to take an optimistic view of one's commitments. But the parties to derivatives also have enormous incentives to cheat in accounting for them. Those who trade derivatives are usually paid, in whole or part, on "earnings" calculated by mark-to-market accounting. But often there is no real market, and "mark-to-model" is utilized. This substitution can bring on large-scale mischief. As a general rule, contracts involving multiple reference items and distant settlement dates increase the opportunities for counter-parties to use fanciful assumptions. The two parties to the contract might well use differing models allowing both to show substantial profits for many years. In extreme cases, mark-to-model degenerates into what I would call mark-to-myth.

I can assure you that the marking errors in the derivatives business have not been symmetrical. Almost invariably, they have favored either the trader who was eyeing a multi-million dollar bonus or the CEO who wanted to report impressive "earnings" (or both).

The bonuses were paid, and the CEO profited from his options. Only much later did shareholders learn that the reported earnings were a sham.

Another problem about derivatives is that they can exacerbate trouble that a corporation has run into for completely unrelated reasons. This pile-on effect occurs because many derivatives contracts require that a company suffering a credit downgrade immediately supply collateral to counter-parties. Imagine then that a company is downgraded because of general adversity and that its derivatives instantly kick in with their requirement, imposing an unexpected and enormous demand for cash collateral on the company.

The need to meet this demand can then throw the company into a liquidity crisis that may, in some cases, trigger still more downgrades. It all becomes a spiral that can lead to a corporate meltdown.

Derivatives also create a daisy-chain risk that is akin to the risk run by insurers or reinsurers that lay off much of their business with others. In both cases, huge receivables from many counter-parties tend to build up over time. A participant may see himself as prudent, believing his large credit exposures to be diversified and therefore not dangerous. However under certain circumstances, an exogenous event that causes the receivable from Company A to go bad will also affect those from Companies B through Z.

In banking, the recognition of a "linkage" problem was one of the reasons for the formation of the Federal Reserve System. Before the Fed was established, the failure of weak banks would sometimes put sudden and unanticipated liquidity demands on previously-strong banks, causing them to fail in turn. The Fed now insulates the strong from the troubles of the weak. But there is no central bank assigned to the job of preventing the dominoes toppling in insurance or derivatives. In these industries, firms that are fundamentally solid can become troubled simply because of the travails of other firms further down the chain.

Many people argue that derivatives reduce systemic problems, in that participants who can't bear certain risks are able to transfer them to stronger hands. These people believe that derivatives act to stabilize the economy, facilitate trade, and eliminate bumps for individual participants. On a micro level, what they say is often true. I believe, however, that the macro picture is dangerous and getting more so. Large amounts of risk, particularly credit risk, have become concentrated in the hands of relatively few derivatives dealers, who in addition trade extensively with one other. The troubles of one could quickly infect the others.

On top of that, these dealers are owed huge amounts by non-dealer counter-parties. Some of these counter-parties are linked in ways that could cause them to run into a problem because of a single event, such as the implosion of the telecom industry. Linkage, when it suddenly surfaces, can trigger serious systemic problems.

Indeed, in 1998, the leveraged and derivatives-heavy activities of a single hedge fund, Long-Term Capital Management, caused the Federal Reserve anxieties so severe that it hastily orchestrated a rescue effort. In later congressional testimony, Fed officials acknowledged that, had they not intervened, the outstanding trades of LTCM – a firm unknown to the general public and employing only a few hundred people – could well have posed a serious threat to the stability of American markets. In other words, the Fed acted because its leaders were fearful of what might have happened to other financial institutions had the LTCM domino toppled.

And this affair, though it paralyzed many parts of the fixed-income market for weeks, was far from a worst-case scenario. One of the derivatives instruments that LTCM used was total-return swaps, contracts that facilitate 100 percent leverage in various markets, including stocks. For example, Party A to a contract, usually a bank, puts up all of the money for the purchase of a stock while Party B, without putting up any capital, agrees that at a future date it will receive any gain or pay any loss that the bank realizes.

Total-return swaps of this type make a joke of margin requirements. Beyond that, other types of derivatives severely curtail the ability of regulators to curb leverage and generally get their arms around the risk profiles of banks, insurers and other financial institutions.

Similarly, even experienced investors and analysts encounter major problems in analyzing the financial condition of firms that are heavily involved with derivatives contracts.

The derivatives genie is now well out of the bottle, and these instruments will almost certainly multiply in variety and number until some event makes their toxicity clear. Central banks and governments have so far found no effective way to control, or even monitor, the risks posed by these contracts.

In my view, derivatives are financial weapons of mass destruction, carrying dangers that, while now latent, are potentially lethal.

This writer thanks Warren Buffett for making his thoughts known to the public. For my readers, I hope you have discerned the Rules of Life in Mr. Buffet's piece. They were included in my reports before I read about Mr. Buffett's concerns and warnings. I offer this fact to (a) bolster my contentions in these reports, and (b) bolster my ego.

I regret Warren Buffett's thoughts were largely ignored by regulators and the finance industry. Let's hope the upcoming legislation will address this man's concerns and warnings.

---

[1] Lewis, *Liar's Poker*, pp. 125 and 130.

[2] Mathew Philips, "The Monster That Ate Wall Street," *Newsweek*, October, 2008, p. 46.

[3] Financial Crisis Inquiry Report, pp. 70-71.

[4] A more accurate term is collateralized mortgage obligation (CMO). A CDO may contain different debt obligations, which is a good idea, because it leads to diversification. In contrast, a CMO contains only mortgage debt obligations. CDO is used in this book because it is the prevalent term used in the finance industry.

[5] Financial Crisis Inquiry Report, p. 130.

[6] Wikipedia, key in "mortgage backed securities."

[7] Financial Crisis Inquiry Report, p. 127.

[8] Lewis, *The Big Short*, First quote p. 101, second quote p. 129.

[9] Financial Crisis Inquiry Report, p. 128.

[10] Morgenson and Rosner, *Reckless Endangerment*, p. 280.

[11] Financial Crisis Inquiry Report, pp. 149-150.

[12] In theory, an employee was not supposed to rate a security underwritten by a firm for which the employee was interviewing for a job.

[13] Henry Wadsworth Longfellow, *The Spanish Student*, 3.6, 1840. Secondary source: Frank, p. 387.

[14] Philips, "The Monster That Ate Wall Street," p. 46.

[15] Henry M. Paulson, Jr., *On the Brink*, Hachette Book Group, New York, 2010, p. 99.

[16] Dawn Kopecki, Shannon D. Harrington (July 24, 2009). Go to link: "Banning 'Naked' Default Swaps May Raise Corporate Funding Costs."

[17] Philips, ibid., p. 47.

[18] Posner, ibid., p. 57.

[19] Robert E. Litan, (April 7, 2010). "The Derivatives Dealers' Club and Derivatives Markets Reform: A Guide for Policy Makers, Citizens and Other Interested Parties", Brookings Institution, with this direct quote from Wikipedia.

[20] Posner, *The Crisis of Capitalistic Democracy*, pp. 54, 72; John Cassidy, *How Markets Fail*, Farrar, Straus and Giroux, New York, 2009, p. 214.

[21] Lewis, *The Big Short*, pp. 72-77, 175-177, 206, 210, 212. The quotes in this section are sourced from Lewis' book.

[22] Financial Crisis Inquiry Report, p. 142

[23] Lewis, *The Big Short*, p. 134.

[24] Wikipedia, key in "Synthetic CDO."

[25] Lowenstein, *The End of Wall Street*, pp. 55-56.

[26] Financial Crisis Inquiry Report, p. 145.

[27] Ibid, pp. 145-146.

[28] For the reader who wishes more details: The long side of the bet had two investors. The unfunded investor usually dealt with the highest quality tranches and received premiums on their investment. They did not put money up front but did swaps and made their profits if the referenced securities did not perform. The funded investors put in cash and did not participate in swaps, but were compensated with interest payments. If the referenced securities did not perform, they took loses before the unfunded investors. The Financial Crisis Inquiry Report, (pages 142-146) provides more details on synthetic CDOs, as well as more details on Goldman Sachs' machinations.

[29] Lowenstein, *The End of Wall Street*, p. 56.
[30] Financial Crisis Inquiry Report, p. 143.
[31] Nelson D. Schwartz and Eric Dash, blog entry, sent by a reader.
[32] Lowenstein, *The End of Wall Street*, p. 56.
[33] These are sourced at http://www.fintools.com/docs/Warren%20Bufett%20on%20Derivatives.pdf.

REPORT 9

GREED, STUPIDITY, AND THE HERD RULE

It is precisely the greed of the businessman, or more appropriately, his profit-seeking, which is the unexcelled protector of the consumer.[1]
— Alan Greenspan

The mortgage bankers said, "You know, it's kind of like the NRA— people kill people, not guns! It's not the mortgages, it's the borrowers!"[2]
— Sheila Bair

"Greed, leverage, and lax investor standards. We took conditions for granted, and we as an industry lost discipline."[3]
— Bank executive

March 14, 2009

Hello again from Your On the Street Reporter. The ninth report in this series about the financial meltdown begins by examining the quote above by Alan Greenspan, the former chairman of the Federal Reserve Board. Greenspan says that greed (clothed in profit seeking) is the unexcelled protector of the consumer.

His take on life reflects a flight from reality. Greed is the unexcelled *enemy* of the consumer. The very term greed conveys selfishness. It is not the so-called enlightened selfishness of *Atlas Shrugged*, but the destructive selfishness of Gordon Gekko.

What has made America a great economic power has been its ability to harness human greed and its associated practice of free enterprise with the reins of practical regulation. This approach has resulted in a rule of law encouraging competition, but one regulated by government. The system has led to a compromise, resulting in an effective and rewarding society; one based on *quasi*-capitalism with oversight and safety nets.

Nonetheless, Alan Greenspan thinks greed is good. Yet for eighteen years Greenspan played the role of regulator for many of the nations' largest banks. Implicit in this job—and delegated to the Federal Reserve Board by Congress—was supervising and regulating many major banking institutions.

The regulation of behavior, either that of a human or a human institution, necessitates placing a restraint on a human trait: greed.

After reading Greenspan's autobiography and reflecting on the research I did for these reports, it appears that Greenspan wrapped himself up in the fleece of a regulator but played his game as an unfettered, no-regulation capitalist.

Giving credit to the man's integrity, perhaps he was simply clueless to the attributes of human behavior; attributes that do not sway toward monetary altruism; attributes that assuredly do not lend themselves to self-policing and self-regulation.

I continue to write this phrase in these reports: "It's harder to imagine." Yet it still is. This ostentatiously inscrutable man declared that markets largely took care of themselves, as if the "invisible hand" of nonregulated commerce had no "visible mind" behind the hand's machinations.

In writing these thoughts I'm reminded of a movie I saw as a child, which scared the daylights out of me. It is called "The Beast with Five Fingers." In this movie, a solitary, severed hand stalks its prey, occasionally single-handedly playing the piano before leaping to its kill (it had a very powerful thumb). This hand had a mind of its own.

That idea seems to have been Greenspan's philosophy: Market forces (guided by the minds of humans) will magically lead to invisible hands taking care of the marketplace—of stabilizing it. It's an intriguing, almost metaphysical notion: Hands do it because they have a mind of their own. We will return to it this subject in the last parts of this book when we examine the philosophies of Adam Smith and John Maynard Keynes. For now:

Greenspan should never have taken the oath to carry out the duties of chairman of the Federal Reserve Board. Clearly, he was remiss in his duties of "supervision and regulation."

In hindsight, I wish Alan had heeded another sage's thoughts on greed. Aesop said that greed often overreaches itself. Greenspan failed to grasp that those bankers he was supervising might actually…gasp, be greedy for their *own* personal selves.

A part owner of a community bank near where I live in Idaho offered this thought to me: The idea cited in some media about harnessing "human greed and raw capitalism with the reins of practical regulation" might be amended to harnessing "human greed and raw capitalism with the reins of practical regulation and Christian/Judeo morality." He added, "Morality should play a huge role in business." I agree, and I think it usually does. But the ability of a few to do harm to many is evident with this meltdown.

How Much Is Enough?

Donald Trump, the producer of the TV show *The Apprentice* and a wizard of extravagance had this to say about greed, "The point is you can't be too greedy."[4] He backs up his philosophy with the opening theme music of this show. It is titled "For the Love of Money."

I am fond of money. I don't have a lot, but I have as much as I need. When I learned about the income of the CEOs of several commercial and investment banks, I said to myself, *What do those people do with all that money? Why aren't their stockholders coming after them and their boards of directors with a rope?*

REPORT 9: GREED, STUPIDITY, AND THE HERD RULE

Below is a survey of the compensation seven top executives received in relation to the performance of the firms they headed. CEO compensation is shown in millions (M); firm performance is shown in billions (B).[5]

Company	CEO	Compensation	Performance of Firm
AIG (1)	Martin Sullivan	1995-2007: $49.5M	2008: Lost $37.6B
Bear Sterns(2)	James Cayne	1998-2007: $290.4M	2007: Leveraged 35.5 to 1
Citigroup	4 previous CEOs	1998-2007: $483.1M	2007: Lost $18.7B
C'trywide (3)	Angelo Mozilo	1998-2007: $246.7M	2007/2008: Lost $3.9B
Lehman (4)	Richard Fuld	1998-2007: $255.9M	2008 (1st half): Lost $2.3B
Merrill Lynch	E. Stanley O'Neal	1999-2007: $157.7M	2007 (2nd half): Lost $35.8B
WaMu(5)	Kerry Killinger	1998-2007: $123.1M	2007 (4th qtr): Lost $8.0B

(1): Now a ward of Uncle Sam.
(2): Now a ward of JPMorgan.
(3): Now a ward of Bank of America.
(4): Now a ward of nobody.
(5): Seized by Uncle Sam; parceled out to JPMorgan and bankruptcy courts.

What happened to the idea of a company's return on investment being tied to the rewards (or no rewards) of a manager's performance? It would be reasonable to think these men would have some notion of meritocracy, perhaps some self-discipline, and place parts of their income into the hands of their stockholders. What did they do to earn these rewards? Some of them were fortunate enough to work for firms who were making fortunes engaging in Ponzi schemes in the real estate market.

They were not alone. In 2006 Goldman Sachs set aside $542,000 per employee in a bonus pool, over fifteen times the annual income of an average American.

The financial industry lobbyists, especially those for the investment bankers, are beginning to make comments (with subsequent pressure on Congress to follow) about the need to pay big in order to attract big brains. They are mounting an offensive to keep impending finance reform laws from establishing bounds on their bounty. K Street in Washington has never been busier.

I agree that government should not be in the business of overseeing payroll departments. But as discussed later, the present arrangement gives shareholders relatively little say in this matter. Whatever the final legislation may be, and it is being written as I write this report, it is in everyone's best interests (except these CEOs and their minions) for the stockholders to be able to at least have a say-so in employee compensation.

I recognize this suggestion might be opening a door for the "mob" to walk in and take over the castle. But I think the present system is skewed toward high-level employees, who—however talented—are just that: employees.

Stupidity Reigns Supreme

Suppose I were to tell you that with minor exceptions, the *only* people who had read the detailed prospectuses of the loans packaged in the mortgage backed securities were the lawyers who wrote them? That it was rare to find an analyst—even in the rating agencies—who had examined key aspects of the loans, such as proof of income of borrower, loan-to-value of the house, down payment, second lien, location of the house, etc.? That a study, even a general examination, was not performed on securities amounting to trillions of dollars?

What if I were to tell you that most people and companies never gave it a thought that insolvent homeowners would not repay their mortgages? That companies, such as AIG, issued billions of dollars of insurance on these mortgages, betting they would be repaid? That AIG mostly rubber-stamped these policies with the assumption it was business as usual? That AIG had not done due diligence by checking these worthless pieces of paper?

What if I were to tell you that a few very smart investors asked Standard and Poor's what was in the contents of a credit default swap and this rating agency responded, "Oh yeah, we're working on that." They were working on at least $400 billion of financial

REPORT 9: GREED, STUPIDITY, AND THE HERD RULE 159

instruments that were in the process of being bought and sold in Wall Street's secret netherworld.

What if I were to tell you that the CEO of one of the biggest banks in America did not understand the meaning of several line items on the balance sheet of his bank? That he had no idea what a subprime CDO was? That the top-notch bond traders at a now defunct investment bank did not know the difference between a corporate bond and a mortgage bond?

Okay, suppose I told you that Bear Sterns, a respected and sophisticated Wall Street firm, went into the overnight lending market (See Sidebar 9-1) for as much as $70 billion. That's a lot of money, even for a bank, especially because the bank's balance sheet showed $11.8 billion in equity versus $383.6 billion in liabilities. Incredible as it may appear, that was Bear's balance sheet and Bear had to renew the borrowing every day and pay interest on its borrowings.[6]

Here's one more: Let's say that by the end of 2007, Fannie and Freddie's combined leverage ratio "including loans they owned and guaranteed, stood at 75 to 1."[7] In layman's terms, this ratio equates to your writer having, say, $500,000 in assets with a leverage of loans and other liabilities of $37,500,000—on which I am paying interest.

> ### Sidebar 9-1. Overnight Lending.
> Banks commonly lend and borrow to and from one another on a daily basis to satisfy regulations regarding reserve requirements. On a given day, a bank may have too little liquidity or too much. This arrangement allows the banking system to adjust dynamically to a volatile world of deposits, withdrawals, and changing stock/bond prices. The interest rates banks charge one another for these short-term loans depend on prevailing rates, term length, and the overall liquidity of the market.

I suspect you might say "That couldn't be," or "How stupid!" But that's what happened.[8] A collective mentality took hold as the

Autocatalytic Cycle and the Threshold Lowering Syndrome took over peoples' judgment and restraint.

As I learn more about these strange flights from reality that led to the nearly perfect financial storm, I continue to recall an old saying that puts a brake on my otherwise positive countenance: "Against stupidity the gods themselves contend in vain."[9] With this thought in mind, we focus once again on AIG.

AIG: "Golden Goose for the Entire Street"[10]

I have spoken of the corporate giant AIG several times in these reports and cited instances in which it sold insurance in the form of credit default swaps to parties who wished protection or wanted to bet against mortgage backed securities. Before its demise, the company was the largest insurance company in the world, employing 116,000 people in 130 countries. It was rated Aaa and AAA by Moody's and S&P respectively. Only six private sector companies in the United States held these ratings.[11]

For conventional insurance procedures, government regulations required an insurance company to set aside reserves to cover possible losses. As we learned earlier, Wall Street firms devised credit default swaps so they were not subject to regulation. In addition, as told in more detail later, Congress passed legislation that kept these derivatives off the books. Consequently, AIG did not set aside sufficient reserves to handle potential losses.

And why should it have done so? After all, AIG's computer models proclaimed with 99.85 percent confidence that there would be no losses on the highest rated tranches of the CDOs the company insured.

But the black swan swam by and devastated the company. AIG could not cover its bets on defaulting subprime mortgages and their associated credit default swaps. Too many calls came from AIG's clients demanding the company pay off the other side of the bet. By 2005, AIG had written $107 billion in credit default swaps. By 2007, the figure stood at $379 billion.

In 2005, AIG lost its triple-A rating because auditors discovered the company had cooked some of its books on earnings. AIG might have gotten away with this major mishap if it had backed away from writing more credit default swaps. No, AIG's Financial Products department wrote another $36 billion of credit default swaps. Then, as Goldman and others looked at AIG's loss of AAA ratings, they demanded the organization post collateral on its swaps.

The Herd Rule

Another Rule of Life relevant to this report is the Herd Rule, briefly introduced in earlier reports. (It is also called the herding instinct or crowd psychology.) The rule states that if enough people do something, it must be okay for others to do it as well. "Okay" in that it is socially acceptable, even though the action may not be in our best interests. If we do something dim-witted but everyone else is doing it, too, it will not be harmful to our egos.

This idea seems absurdly stupid. Why would anyone do something that is self-damaging just because others are doing it? In relation to the nearly perfect financial storm, how could so many rational people behave irrationally in acquiring and granting subprime loans, in buying toxic mortgage based securities? Surely there must have been a large population of contrarians who went against this crowd mentality, who were able to mitigate the effect of the Herd Rule.

It is impossible to know how many people did not jump on the bandwagon, but very few individuals in the financial world saw the danger of massive subprime loans and associated problems. Lewis says fewer than twenty individuals made a direct bet against the subprime mortgage market.[12] Everyone else went along for the ride.

In the early 1950s, research conducted at Swarthmore College demonstrated how pervasive the Herd Rule can be. In June, 1990 a paper was published in *The American Economic Review* titled "Herd Behavior and Investment." The paper claimed, with supporting mathematical models, that investment managers often "mimicked the actions of others rather than trust their own judgments."[13] The paper was followed by several other studies that concluded:

Young fund managers who followed investment strategies that deviated significantly from their peers were more likely to lose their jobs, regardless of how their funds performed. The threat of being fired gave the fund managers a strong incentive to invest in popular sectors even if they believed they were overvalued.

I like most of what John Cassidy has to say in his book, but I read about these studies with skepticism. A fund manager is evaluated on one thing: Return. I cannot imagine a fund manager at Wells Fargo dismissing a person if the broker's portfolio is making money. I can understand the average guy on the street herding with the crowd and jumping on the investment bandwagon. But a maverick investment analyst getting fired for doing well seems too weird to be true. In fact, I would want a fund manager who does not follow the tape or do what the market is doing. I would want a manager who makes me money, bandwagon or not.

In any event, herd behavior has been shown to correlate to certain areas of the brain. Cassidy cites a study appearing in *The Journal of Biological Psychiatry* (2005). The conclusions of this study are not surprising because all humans' actions correlate to firings of synapses in various areas of the brain. What is fascinating about this study is the brain activity associated with the acquiescence of a person to a group's giving an obviously incorrect answer to a question. An MRI revealed this response created more activity in the visual cortex and the right intraparietal sulcus, areas associated with spatial awareness and perception respectively. When the test subject went against the crowd, there was more activity in the amygdala, which is associated with heightened emotions.

The researchers' conclusion was that peer pressure makes people perceive the world differently. That is an amazing inference, but clearly, something is going on in our gray matter that has to do with our herd behavior. It's really only common sense. Humans have survived for many years, partially because of our herd mentality.

John Maynard Keynes cited a beauty contest as an example of the Herd Rule. He stated a person will not choose the prettiest face

REPORT 9: GREED, STUPIDITY, AND THE HERD RULE   163

in a contest, but the face that others think is the prettiest. In relation to the financial market, most investors follow a herd mentality of doing what the majority of investors are doing. Even though the facts may reveal that the stock of company ABC is overvalued, an investor will buy the stock because others are buying it. The Herd Rule is one explanation of how bubbles form.

(A note made in this report after it was written. The Facebook IPO is another example of herd behavior. Did you participate? I was tempted to jump on the bandwagon. But I had earlier refrained from investing in dot.com IPOs in companies that had no coherent management structure or long range plan. I kept my distance from them and Facebook. For Facebook itself, I just can't see how it can sell advertising. People go to Google to look for products. They go to Facebook to look at one another.)

Skeptics of the influence of the Herd Rule on Wall Street need only look at the comments financial experts made about the debilitating effects negative comments, however untrue, can have on a company's stock. The company may be doing just fine, but even a rumor can create a run on the company's stock, leading to a deterioration of the company's credit position and a hindrance on its ability to raise money.

In late March, 2008 as events moved to a national crisis, Henry Paulson, then Secretary of the Treasury, remembers the events cited below. I paraphrase from his book because it reveals much about the Herd Rule and Wall Street, the interconnectedness of the financial industry, as well as the extent Uncle Sam was committed to bailout several key Wall Street firms (with the exception of Lehman Brothers). I also paraphrase this first paragraph because his direct quote uses terms not yet explained.[14]

> The bankers complained bitterly about speculators who were betting against their stocks (by taking out CDS insurance on them) and...in the CEOs' minds, all but trying to force some institutions under. [Writer's note: As well as spreading negative comments about the banks.] ...Dick Fuld (head of Lehman Brothers), whose face reddened with anger as he

asserted, "These guys are killing us." [Writer's note: Perhaps so Mr. Fuld, but your inordinate leverage and speculation furnished them with the weapons for Lehman's "assassination."]

As we left the dinner, Dave McCormick, who served as the main liaison to the G-7 and other countries' finance ministries, told me, "Dick Fuld is really worked up."

I told Dave I wasn't surprised. Lehman was in a precarious position. "If they fail, we are all in deep trouble," I said."Maybe we can figure out how to sell them."

Thus people learn that if other people are selling their stock in Lehman then, "Something must be amiss, I'd better sell also." In the example from Mr. Paulson's book, Fuld feared the feedback about Lehman's problems, fueled by short sellers, would result in a run on Lehman's stock. Which it did.

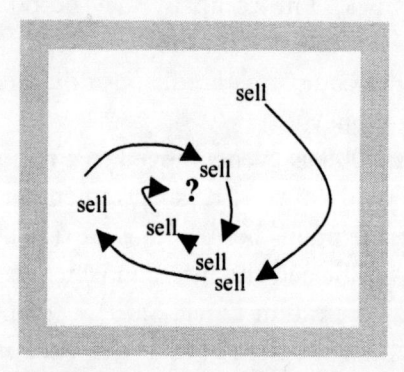

Figure 9-1. Keynes' feedback.

The Herd Rule and the Autocatalytic Process

During the nearly perfect financial storm, the Herd Rule worked in conjunction with the Autocatalytic Process, as illustrated in figure 9-1. Keynes made these observations but did not use the contemporary terms cited in this book. He said market economies were subject to feedback.[15] He said downturns had a tendency to spiral down as bad news and resultant loss of confidence, with (say) selling of stock, feed on each other: "Others are selling, so am I." As the process continued spiraling, the Autocatalytic Process amplified its effects, leading to decreased spending and the freezing of credit. The problem with a selling frenzy is that before long, there are no buyers. The system freezes. Lines of credit ice up. Merchants cannot pay their rent and we end up with the scenes shown in figure 1-1 in Report 1.

Accountability and Competency

During the time I was conducting research for these reports and receiving comments from my e-mail readers, I came across hundreds of sad, even tragic stories about the meltdown. They came from people who had nothing to do with creating the financial crisis. Like most citizens, they were small players—pawns if you will—in the big game of finance.

These people are angry. The more I delved into the meltdown, the more I understood and agreed with their anger. For this writer, it is not only the failure of government to oversee the financial markets in this specific instance, it is also the systemic incompetency of government to perform the very basic functions for which it is tasked: Bridge inspectors inspecting bridges after they collapse; flood disaster crews responding to floods days after a flood occurs; fighter aircraft—whose sole function is to respond to national emergencies—responding to 9/11 by flying off into the wrong direction, *without* armament.

Keep in mind that the bridge inspectors, flood relief crews, and National Guard pilots failed to perform the very job that was the sole reason for their having the job in the first place. Sure, we all make mistakes. But where do we citizens draw the line? And if we draw the line, what good will it do? Say what you will about the protests of the 1960s and 1970s, those people seemed to care. Nowadays, we roll with whatever punch is directed to our midsection with nary a howl.

Greed and stupidity played big roles in creating the nearly perfect financial storm. The Herd Rule blinded thousands of otherwise intelligent Wall Street analysts as well as the regulators.

Epicurus had this to say about greed, "Nothing is enough to the man for whom enough is too little."[16] Thomas Fuller had this to say about stupidity, "If you leap into a well, Providence is not bound to fetch you out."[17]

All true, except for many of the acts of stupidity associated with the 2008 meltdown, Uncle Sam was bound to do the fetching. Uncle Sam pulled much of Wall Street and others out of the well. As of this writing, it appears Uncle will continue his rescue operations for many years, trying to repair an Alice in Wonderland landscape from its own folly.

Speaking of Alice, we take a walk with her through this landscape, a subject for Report 10.

---

[1] Michael Lewis, "Beyond Economics, Beyond Politics, Beyond Accountability," *Worth*, May, 1995, Secondary source: Frank, p. 337.

[2] I came across this quote after writing this report. Sheila Bair is head of the FDIC and said this platitude was uttered to her by a group of mortgage bankers who met with her in 2007 to protest her pressure on them to modify their loans to prevent many homes from going into foreclosure. I hope Ms. Bair's response was, "Who did the credit checks on those borrowers? Who was responsible for the integrity of those mortgages?" The Bush administration said loan modifications would not achieve much. Its posture was, "Too many borrowers were in the wrong house, not the wrong mortgage." I hope Ms. Bair's response was, "Yes, and those who wrote the mortgages were instrumental in getting the borrowers in the house associated with those mortgages. You can't separate the two." Both quotes sourced from Ryan Lizza, "The Contrarian," *The New Yorker*, July 6 and 13, 2009, p. 34.

[3] Paulson, *On the Brink*, pp. 129-130.

[4] Frank, *Quotationary*, p. 338.

[5] Gretchen Morgenson, "Give Me Back My Paycheck," *The New York Times*, February 22, 2009, p. 7.

[6] Financial Crisis Inquiry Report, pp. xix and x.

[7] Ibid., p. x.

[8] With the exception of the Lehman and Fannie/Freddie examples, these stories are documented throughout Michael Lewis' *The Big Short*. This section is also sourced from several sections of his book, as well as Web blogs, and *The Wall Street Journal*.

[9] Friedrich von Schiller, *The Maid of Orleans*, 3.6, 1801. Secondary source: Frank, p. 831.

[10] Financial Crisis Inquiry Report, p. 139.

[11] Ibid., pp. 139-140.

[12] Lewis, *The Big Short*, p. 105.

[13] Cassidy, "How Markets Fail," p. 176, as well as the material up to the Paulson quote. After posting this report to my readers, I came across an article in *The New Yorker* (http://www.newyorker.com/reporting/2011/07/25/110725fa_fact_cassidy). The article is titled, "Mastering the Machine," and is about Ray Dalio, an immensely wealthy hedge fund founder (of Bridgewater Associates). I had read this article earlier in my subscription hard copy and was left with the impression that Mr. Dalio was smart but creepy. He was characterized in the article as running a cult. I watched Charlie Rose (PBS, October 21, 2011) and Dalio was the guest. He came across as a focused, intelligent man. He also came across as more than a bean counter of profits and losses, or as a predatory stalker of naïve IRA managers. He came across as a forthright inquiring person who, deeply knowledgeable in his craft, looks beyond it to a broader picture. I saw something in the man that Cassidy did not. Cassidy: "He is keen to be seen as something more than a billionaire trader. Indeed, like his sometime rival George Soros, he appears to aspire to the role of worldly philosopher." I disagree. Furthermore, I thought Cassidy's article hung disingenuously onto the vines of sour grapes.

[14] Paulson, *On the Brink*, p. 130.

[15] Lowenstein, p. 173.

[16] Frank, *Quotationary*, p. 337.

[17] Ibid., p. 831. Thomas Fuller, comp., *Gnomologia: Adages and Proverbs*, 2795, 1732.

REPORT 10

ALICE IN MORTGAGE LAND

A home without equity is just a rental unit with debt.[1]

March 15, 2009

Hello again. For this report, seven examples are used to focus again on the personal element of the meltdown. For a while, we are finished with technical topics, such as credit default swaps. We venture once more into the human behavior aspect of the Alice in Wonderland meltdown saga. Listed here are the case studies discussed in this report:

- Fixing Flats in a Flat Economy
- Flipping Houses in Florida
- Raising the Dead in California
- Closing Loans in Seattle
- "The Speculators Ran Me Out of Business."
- A Clip Joint Gets Clipped
- Making Hay in Palm Beach

Tinker Toys for Financial Tots

Before taking a journey into mortgage markets' stores, we take a side step into an equally bizarre bazaar. Previous reports described the separation (slicing and dicing) of whole mortgages into nearly

REPORT 10: ALICE IN MORTGAGE LAND

indecipherable pieces that were placed into mortgage backed securities. The rock stars of Wall Street went further. Looking for ways to create yet more financial snake oil from legitimate instruments—and thus earn more commissions on increasingly obfuscated junk—they separated a mortgage into separate interest only (IO) and principal only (PO) pools. Next, they pieced together various parts of unrelated IOs and POs to create bonds that had no connection to the real world. "Thus the 11 percent interest payment from condominium dwellers in California could be glued to the principal from homeowners in a Louisiana ghetto, and voila, a new kind of bond, a New Age Creole, was born."[2]

As expected, the mortgage bond salesmen sold the rights to the income from each pool. But unwary investors had no idea they were buying *pieces* of a mortgage. You may have owned the principal of my home loan; someone in China might have owned the interest. You and your silent Chinese partner were relying on stellar ratings from the rating agencies to insure the bonds containing my scattershot loan were rated AAA. Even better for Wall Street, this slicing and dicing made the securities even more difficult to understand—just what the Street wanted.

The Messiness of MERS

The booming home mortgage market led the country's large banks to set up (in 1997) an organization named the Mortgage Electronic Registration System (MERS). The idea was to eliminate the need to file assignments in the county land records and thus lower costs for lenders and consumers. MERS also provided (and still provides) a central database for tracking mortgage loans. It uses a mortgage ID and a service ID to uniquely identify the loans. Unfortunately, its database is not accurate or up to date. As mortgages were sliced and diced, it had become increasingly difficult to keep track of them. One set of IDs for interest only and another set for principal only? Repackaging them into other securities? It's a recipe for a messy meal.

Recently, MERS has been involved in foreclosing on mortgages, yet it owns no mortgages! It only holds mortgage liens for the actual owners. Consequently, a solid argument exists for MERS being charged with crimes. As of this writing, the MERS comedy is beginning to play-out, but I cannot imagine the ending will be a happy one for this organization.

Enough for now about Wall Street's Tinker Toys. Pour yourself a drink; you'll need it:

Fixing Flats in a Flat Economy

During a recent road trip to Glacier National Park in northwestern Montana, one of my tires picked up a nail. An AAA tow truck driver inflated the tire enough to follow me to a nearby repair shop. This business was a small setup, holding one car at a time in its garage. It was a two-person operation; one was the owner. I was behind a backlog, so the owner was kind enough to drive me to my hotel and pick me up later. During this time, we struck up a conversation about the economy in that part of the country.

I asked him how his business was faring during the downturn. His response spoke volumes about the effect America's financial meltdown has had on Americans (I use the present tense for the next part of the report):

His business is seasonal. Not much in the winter; most of it in the summer. His revenue has declined over the past two years. Fewer tourists are passing through and steady customers are driving longer on thinner tires. He's been dealing with the same local bank for over twenty years. He's never had a problem with his line of credit. He's now worried. His line of credit is almost exhausted and may be drying up altogether. He's scheduled for a meeting with a loan officer to discuss his situation. He says he can't operate without a line of credit.

This situation has been multiplied millions of times across America. It is steeped in irony: The man cannot get credit just when he needs it the most. The bank will not grant credit just when it should be granting it the most. Banks withdraw credit during lean times, which makes for even leaner times. It's a self-defeating spiral of the Autocatalytic Process.

As discussed in later reports, and contrary to the mistaken opinions of critics who oppose government intervention, the only entity with the motivation and leverage to break the downward spiral is the federal government.

Flipping Houses in Florida

In 2005 I spent a few days in Florida. Prior to leaving my profession of computer networking, I visited the state several times a year to explain the mysteries of the Internet to Gray Panthers. I had no time to learn about the state. Now that I am a Gray Panther myself, I take more time to check out where I am. Nonetheless, for my 2005 visit, I wrote these thoughts (in an essay, "Where Have All the People Gone?"):

> The state of Florida is in a sad state. Other than tourism, its only major industry is growth. The building industry (not factories, research labs, or dot com programmers) is the main industry. The economy depends on building more houses for more people to buy. Why are these folks coming to Florida? To build more houses for the people who have already come *because* of the building industry.
>
> It's a circuitous path to nowhere. The building of buildings should be undertaken because people are coming to town to work for a new automobile plant, or a new solar panel factory; not because people are coming to town to build houses for the people building houses. This surreal deck of cards is going to tumble down when the cycle can no longer feed on itself.
>
> If the building stops, a news commentator here said the Florida economy would stagnate. People might move out of the state to find jobs. Vacant houses would further collapse the building industry.

The building has stopped; the collapse has occurred. But not before thousands of (now vacant) residences were erected to decorate the landscape with empty pseudo-stucco Spanish-like casas. There's a friendly Spanish proverb that says, "Mi casa es su casa." (My house is your house.) After the meltdown, the "su" was not an invited guest. It was the local bank.

While under construction, these homes were sometimes bought and sold more than once. It's called "flipping houses." The market for residences was appreciating so rapidly a buyer could purchase a house, and sell it the next day for a huge profit. Here's a typical example:[3]

> On December 29, 2005, the house sold for $339,600. On December 30, 2005, it sold for $589,900. On June 30, 2008, it was foreclosed on. [A realtor] bought it for $325,000.

Hundreds of people in Florida (and elsewhere) got into the flipping houses business. Hundreds of people became mortgage lenders and/or brokers. Secretaries and yardmen had "five to ten investment homes—a thirty-five-thousand-dollar salary, and a million dollars in investments."[4]

I wish I were making up these stories. I wish they were part of a weird fictional novel. But no, the old saw that truth is stranger than fiction is applicable to Florida's real estate boom. Here's another:[5]

> ...more than ten thousand convicted criminals got jobs in the mortgage industry, including four thousand as licensed brokers...Felons lost the right to vote in Florida, but could still sell real estate.

Just Walk Away. Let me be clear about a matter touched on in an earlier report. The people buying these houses (even for keeps) were often not models of financial decorum. They overreached. Some had no savings, but "kept borrowing against the value of the house—with its apparently endless path upward."[6]

After the adjustable rate mortgage kicked in, the owners could not meet the monthly mortgage payment. They defaulted and/or abandoned the property, as did hundreds of thousands of others. The house went underwater: The value on the house went below the purchase price (or the loan price, which was often the same as the purchase price). The owners could no longer stay in the house but they had already made money on the venture with home equity loans. Many of them skipped town. Florida has a thriving bounty hunter industry.

Who was left with the responsibility for this loan? Whoever bought the mortgage backed security that contained it; say Citigroup. Or whoever insured the mortgage backed security with a credit default swap; say AIG. Or whoever placed guarantees on mortgages themselves; say Fannie and Freddie. Who is now bailing out AIG, Fannie, and Freddie with billions of dollars? That would be you and me.

Raising the Dead in California

A *60 Minutes* program was broadcast on CBS, February 15, 2009. It recounted how a bank in California named World Savings abandoned its once high standards for granting home loans to become a loan shark, an institution that engaged in predatory lending.

I know about these kinds of companies. Between my junior and senior years in college, I was a bill collector for one of these firms in the happy burg of Watts, California. (Another story for another time.) I learned how my employer, a finance company (AKA loan shark), took on the credit dregs that had been cast off by LA's commercial banks. The firm made every effort to approve a loan with huge interest rates. But even this company had minimum standards. It disapproved as many loan applications as it approved.

It is hard to believe, but World Savings lowered the loan approval bar of the loan sharks. It redefined subprime. And World Savings was not an exception, it was similar to other financial institutions in America. It granted home mortgage loans to people who had no chance whatsoever of ever paying back those loans.

Betty Towns was one of many who took out a loan from World Savings. She was sub-subprime and refinanced her home four times in four years. She was presented with several options for refinancing.

(It is called an option arm but World Savings called it "pick a loan.") She chose the smallest payment. She received $20,000 each time she refinanced.

The loans were back loaded with large deferred interest payments. Before long, the full payment was bigger than her total monthly income. World Savings told Mrs. Towns they would use her husband's income to help pad the new loan application (to pass the underwriters' review of her creditworthiness). The only problem with using her husband's income was that her husband had no income. Her husband was dead.

- Loan underwriter, "This loan application for Betty Towns looked pretty weak when I reviewed it last week. What's changed?"
- Loan broker, "Oh, we had forgotten to add Mr. Towns' income to Mrs. Towns' social security stipend."
- Underwriter, "OK. Eh, what does Mr. Towns do for a living?"
- Broker, "He works the graveyard shift at the local cemetery."
- Underwriter, "Great. Loan approved!"

One of the employees for World Savings (a Mr. Bishop) told CBS that things started to go wrong when World Savings "ran out of borrowers." He said that anyone who could fog a mirror was qualified for a loan. Not exactly Mr. Bishop. Betty Towns' husband could not fog a mirror. Betty got a loan anyway.

At the height of World Savings' Ponzi scheme, 60 percent of loans were being brought in by outside brokers, and 38 percent of the portfolio was in subprime loans. Standards continued to be lowered until the company exhausted its inventory of the local cemeteries' citizens. Once again, the Threshold Lowering Syndrome in action.

Closing Loans in Seattle

The people at Washington Mutual (WaMu)—a Seattle-based bank seized by the government last fall—set the standard for closing worthless loans. One of the bank's former underwriters, Keysha Cooper, had this to say, "At WaMu it wasn't about the quality of the loans, it was about the quantity. They [the bank officers and its CEO, Kerry K. Killinger] didn't care if they were giving loans to people that didn't qualify. Instead, it was how many loans did you guys close and fund?"[7]

Ms. Cooper said one of her subordinates was awarded a trip to Jamaica because he closed $3.5 million in loans in one month. WaMu was allowing brokers to take 6 to 8 percent of the loan. Hidden fees meant a broker could make between $20,000 and $40,000 on a $500,000 loan.

When Ms. Cooper complained to her bosses that she was being pressured to sign off on bad loans, she was "written up" and a formal letter was placed in her file. Later, she was placed on probation for refusing to approve a loan. Four months later, the loan was in default.

Let's pause for a moment and think about what Ms. Cooper has described. She was harassed for being honest. She was threatened for being ethical. Brokers even tried to bribe her. One man offered to give Ms. Cooper $900 to pay for her son's football camp if she would approve a loan that other banks had disapproved. She declined. Here's a topper:

One loan application showed a photo of a house that had a different street address number than the address in the loan. Ms. Cooper called the appraiser and asked him to investigate. He checked out the property, and said everything was in order. She disapproved the loan but was overruled by her superiors. Six months later, the $800,000 loan defaulted. When people went to the property to foreclose on the house, they found no house; just an empty lot.

We can only wonder where this loan ended up. The chances are it was packaged into a mortgage backed security and sold to an investor, say, Citigroup. The investor likely had it insured with a credit default swap by, say, AIG. Because AIG was leveraged well beyond what it should have been, AIG could not pay Citigroup the insurance on the defaulted loan. Because Citigroup would not recover the insurance from AIG, it could not recover the part of its mortgage backed security that contained this worthless paper. Citigroup had to write off this loan against its shareholder equity account because it had no other sources of funds...because it too, was overleveraged. The house of cards started falling down.

"The Speculators Ran Me Out of Business"

Recently I was in Las Vegas, conducting research on nightclub acts, hotels, and Texas Hold'em card games. On my way to the airport, I struck up a conversation with the taxi driver. He said he was from Minnesota. I asked him why he had moved to Las Vegas. He replied his business of raising and selling Holstein cattle failed and he had to do something else. I asked why his company failed. He said it was because of his inability to deal with the wildly fluctuating prices of corn. He then said, "The speculators ran me out of business." I turned on my recorder:

- Reporter, "Not sure I understand. What do you mean?"
- "Used to be that my father and later me could plan and budget for our feed. No longer. Nowadays, the speculators distort the market. I never knew what my feed bill was going to be. Couldn't plan; ended up over committing myself, 'cause I didn't know which end was up. Hell, it reached the point where I couldn't make payroll. I was playing poker but I wasn't in the game."
- "Funny in a way….but not funny."
- "Yeah. Anyway I got to playing online Texas Hold'em. Started making good money. My three hired hands joked when they saw me on line. One of them said, 'You playing today for my paycheck or for some corn for the cattle?'"
- "So that's why you came to Vegas? To play Texas Hold'em?"
- "Yep. Sold my farm. Been in the family since granddad. Came here to make a living."
- "So why are you not playing poker now?"
- "Still am. But I play in low stake games. Tourists watch TV and think they got it locked. I pull in a couple grand every two weeks. But my wife's got big bills from surgery; $30,000.

Need more money for the bills. Taxi driving is a good change of pace."
- "Yeah...Ever think of going back to farming?"
- "Yes I do. I miss it. My family misses Minnesota. Maybe someday....For now, nope. Frankly, I don't know how some of the small businesses handle the marketplace."

Was this man a victim of his own naiveté; his own ineptitude? In relation to futures on commodities, probably, but within his own world, he was neither. He was competent and knowledgeable. But he had become part of another world in which he was not an active participant. He never knew his predator until he was in deep trouble; by then it was too late. The short-time speculators were in the game: *Fuck the farmer. I'm cashing in on his cornpone reliance on corn. Why should corn prices be stable? Nothing else is.*

A Clip Joint Gets Clipped

My summer home is in North Idaho. I live in a relatively small urban area that includes the cities of Coeur d'Alene and Hayden. These cities convey some of the qualities of the small town where I grew up in New Mexico. For example, I'm a customer at a local barber shop in Hayden. The establishment is owned by a man who has plied his trade at a shop located on the main street of the town. He has been cutting hair for some 30 years. As an aside, this man actually *cuts* hair. There is a barber pole outside his shop.

His barber shop is frequented by many of the stalwarts of the community: mayors, some of my doctors, police chiefs, sheriffs, and so on. I usually come across some of them each time I have a haircut.

His business has decreased by 30 percent. Consider this statistic in relation to his comments: "Some of my customers are waiting longer to get a haircut. One told me he is budgeting for a sixteen dollar haircut."

He and his wife (*sans* children who are gone) spend about $1,000 a month on health care insurance. They have a $25,000 deductible and because of this high deductible, they have not capitalized on any of this service since 2006. I would say amazing but I know this profile well. Until I turned the magic 65 years of age, my family had a similar medical/financial profile. When I became eligible for Medicare, I entered medical welfare heaven.

With the meltdown, and the loss resultant loss of income, he is very close to deciding to cancel his health care insurance. He has six more years to go before he is eligible for Medicare, and as he said, as he was clipping my hair, "I've written this month's check, but I haven't sent it in. And I may not" He must decide on paying for health care or paying the rent and other bills. In the long run, he can't do both. He's running out of options.

The discussion and analysis of America's disgraceful health care system is beyond the scope of this book. The point is that the nearly perfect financial storm has made the system an even bigger sham and an American shame.

Making Hay in Palm Beach

I've saved the best for last. "Best" meaning the most egregious: Bernard Madoff, a man who is his own black swan. Not only did he defraud thousands of strangers, he also stuck it to his friends, and he seemed to do it with the aplomb of a guiltless person.

During my writing of *The Deadly Trinity*, I did research on the genetic and cerebral foundations of aggression. During this effort, I started to come around to the view that most of our behavior is determined by our DNA. I have had difficulty coming to grips with this idea because I like to think there is something ephemeral about who we are; about what makes us tick.

I recently read Malcolm Gladwell's, *Outliers*, and I've resisted his premise that all humans owe any success they may have to genetics and fortunate "social arrangements."(As well as hard work, with which I agree.) I want to think that greatness and creativity are dependent on more than the roll of the dice. I wish to believe the Einsteins and Shakespeares of the world are more than just a product of their genes and the company they keep.

But as DNA is deciphered, we learn that genetic and related cerebral underpinnings set the stage for who we are.

Trust and Mistrust. Many studies substantiate the commonsense notion that trust is one of the most important components of a healthy society. The most successful countries have trust built into their culture. I came upon research that shows an "ancient and simple molecule in the brain plays a major role" in trust.[8] The molecule is named oxytocin. Controlled studies have proved that higher levels of oxytocin produce more trust in people.

We can only sympathize with the many people who lost their nest eggs because of their trust in Bernard Madoff. Yes, you read correctly. Some of Madoff's investors had all of their savings in his hands. One wonders how much oxytocin these folks carry around in their bodies.

One individual who was not deceived by Madoff (and the hero in this report) is Harry Markopolos. From the beginning, he saw through Madoff's Ponzi scheme. If Mr. Markopolos is lacking a bit in the oxytocin department, we should all be thankful.

SEC: Trust? Mistrust? What me Worry? If oxytocin is part of an institution's make up, the SEC must be drowning in the stuff. Once again, the SEC failed to carry out its responsibilities. For lack of a better barb, it seems the SEC officials suffered from an overdose of ineptitude. The tale of Mr. Markopolos and his trying to alert the SEC to Madoff's scam reads like a John Grisham novel. But it is not fiction.

From 2000 to 2008, Markopolos contacted the SEC five times about his findings that the Madoff system was fake. Each time, he upped the amount of money that was at risk. Each time, the SEC office in Washington, DC ignored him. Finally, in December, 2008, after almost a decade of warnings, the SEC took action. Madoff is now under house arrest. (A later update from this dateline: He is now in prison.)

I have shied away in my writings from making innuendos about the "good old boy" network. In regard to the meltdown, its existence is obvious:[9]

Anything the SEC does to roil the markets, or reduce the share price of any given company, also roils the careers of the people who run the SEC. Thus, it seldom penalizes serious corporate and management malfeasance...Preserving confidence, even if that confidence is false, has been near the top of the SEC's agenda.

If you work for the enforcement division of the SEC, you probably know in the back of your mind, and in the front, too, that if you maintain good relations with Wall Street you might soon be paid huge sums of money to be employed by it.

Fees or Bribes?

If "network" sounds too conspiratorial, it is fair to say that America's financial industry operates with too many conflicts of interest. As one example cited earlier, the rating agencies are under the employment of the very companies they rate. They are paid to offer their supposedly independent assessment of a Goldman Sachs-sponsored security. Goldman pays for this service. If Goldman does not like the rating, it goes to another rating agency, adding a new meaning to "window shopping."

The practice of government and private enterprise commingling their efforts toward a common goal is often efficacious and laudable. The partnership of the Department of Defense and several universities spawned ARPAnet, which led to the Internet.

I'm not speaking of collaboration. I am speaking of collusion. It is impossible for a rating agency to work independently of an investment bank that writes a check to the agency for the rating.

In earlier times in America's financial industry, the same protocol was set up between the S&Ls, and Freddie Mac and Fannie Mae:[10]

> The thrifts paid a fee to have their mortgages guaranteed. The shakier the loans, the larger the fee a thrift had to pay to get its mortgages stamped by one of the agencies. Once they were stamped, however, nobody cared about the quality

of the loans. Defaulting homeowners became the government's problem.

American capitalism in action.

Sociopathy

I do not believe many of the people who helped create the financial crisis are sociopaths, but I have come to think a disproportionate ratio of them are unbalanced. But for now, we return to Madoff. The definition of a sociopath (or psychopath) is a person affected with a personality disorder, marked by antisocial thought and behavior, and a lack of remorse or empathy.

These people have been around since Cain. And sure enough, recent research and studies at the Western New Mexico Correctional Facility (Grants, New Mexico) on known sociopaths have established they have a deficit in the paralimbic region of their brains (more specifically, a dysfunction of the amygdala).[11]

Hundreds of people have taken tests, including brain scans, at this facility. And the researchers now have a rating system to tabulate just how sick these people are. (In case you are interested, the chances are quite good that you have come across a psychopath on more than one occasion. They are not uncommon. I think I've encountered some of them in the local grocery store checkout line.)

I would like to see Mr. Madoff take a brain scan on the equipment at that New Mexico facility. On second thought, maybe not. If the tests were to show him as a sociopath, his attorneys might get him off the hook because he had no control over his behavior.

Anyway, the subject is Madoff and the SEC. Do we need more regulation? Do we need more laws? With some exceptions, we do not. No question, mortgage backed securities and associated bonds must have oversight, and banks must be made to (once again) behave like banks. And the issues of interconnectedness and bigness must be addressed. Notwithstanding these facts, what we also need is for the people we pay to rein in the Wall Street misfits to simply do their jobs.

About those jobs. While Madoff was making off with billions of dollars, the SEC's head office of risk assessment had been vacant for more than a year. The former official had left for another job, a higher paying position on Wall Street.

I hope you enjoyed your drink.

---

[1] Lewis, *The Big Short*, p. 22.

[2] Lewis, *Liar's Poker*, p. 172.

[3] George Packer, "The Ponzi State," *The New Yorker*, February 9 & 16, p. 84.

[4] Ibid.

[5] Ibid.

[6] Ibid., p. 88.

[7] Gretchen Morgenson, "Was There a Loan It Didn't Like?" *The New York Times* business section, November 2, 2008, p. 1.

[8] Paul J. Zak, "The Neurobiology of Trust," *Scientific American*, June, 2008, p. 88.

[9] Lewis and Einhorn, "The End of the Financial World as We Know It," p. 9.

[10] Lewis, *Liar's Poker*, p. 135.

[11] John Seabrook, "Suffering Souls," *The New Yorker*, November 10, 2008, pp. 64-73.

REPORT 11

MEDIA DISTORTIONS

*I've heard a wise man learns from his mistakes.
True, and a wiser man learns from the mistakes of others.*
—anon

March 20, 2009

This is Your On the Street Reporter—pounding Wall Street in more ways than one. In this report, I address the comments from a number of media programs and articles about the meltdown and the bailout, and the bailout's consequences for our institutions. I also highlight Rush Limbaugh's ludicrous assessment of the recession. To begin, here are two definitions that will be helpful during this discussion:[1]

- Socialism: A political theory or system in which the means of production and distribution are controlled by the people (the state) and operated according to equity and fairness rather than market principles. (As an old saying goes, socialism is: "Cake for none until all have bread.")
- Capitalism: An economic system based on the private ownership of the means of production and distribution of goods,

characterized by a free competitive market and motivation by profit. (Stated another way: "Cake for me, bread for you.")

To prepare myself for writing these reports, I read many books and articles about this "great recession," a name given to the nearly perfect financial storm. I spoke with several financial experts. They have helped me with many technical aspects of the subject and offered suggestions for these reports. I spoke with many citizens and watched them grapple with the meltdown.

Starting as a curious reader with no axe to grind, I came to the conclusion that most of the prominent news media were presenting their views about the near disaster in an evenhanded fashion. As expected, *The Wall Street Journal* and *The Economist* editorials differed from those of *The New York Times* and *The New Yorker*. But these media giants offered sound ideas to backup their politically based opinions.

Right or Left, with No In-Between

Why do many left wing and right wing pundits start with sensible ideas and then alter them beyond any semblance of reality? I suspect it is because these thoughts are too closely aligned toward the middle, and therefore do not make for interesting, inflammatory diatribes that sell copies or bring in TV viewers. This report will focus on one example of this dangerous and pathetic extremism. Many others can be cited, but one is enough, as we have other matters to attend to. I just could not let this one go unchallenged.

Rush Limbaugh gave a speech last month to the Conservative Political Action Conference (CPAC). I read it and thought he had several fine ideas but he chose to lace them with misstatements. (The same holds true for the far left; they often overreach as well.)

Stimulus or Handouts?

From what I can gather from his speech, Limbaugh is against the bailout package because (a) it is fiscally irresponsible; (b) its contents will lead to America adapting European socialism; and (c) it has provisions that amount to handouts. I address the handout issue first.

I agree with Limbaugh about components of the bailout package. For example, the county in Idaho where I live (Kootenai) has received some of the federal stimulus largesse. It was allocated $1.2 million in transit funds. The money will be used to replace public transportation buses, put in wheelchair access in some of them, and buy a maintenance vehicle. A huge chunk will be for an environmental site study for a future transit center.

I would prefer the money be used to reduce our national debt. But the financial experts on Wall Street and Pennsylvania Avenue tell us we are in a fiscal and economic cycle that requires our going deeper into the money hole in order to get ourselves out of the money hole. Keep digging. At the end of the tunnel is China, salivating its chops to eventually eat our lunch, while relishing our irresponsibility.

I would also prefer the bailout money be used to repair America's infrastructure, such as bridges and roads; projects yielding tangible results. As opposed to environmental studies that might yield nothing.

One of my tennis friends told me it does not matter what the bailout project is, as long as it pumps money into the economy. He said the purpose of the bailout is to get money moving again in order to feed dollars to citizens and subsequent tax revenue to Uncle Sam. He said it is irrelevant where the money goes, just so it is spent and not hoarded. He went into a monologue about the recurring cycle of money and tax revenues; that each turnover of this $700,000 generated another round of tax dollars; that eventually, the $700,000 generated almost $700,000 in tax revenues. Afraid he was warming up for a lecture on the theory of the velocity of money and the Keynes multiplier effect, I suggested, "Serve 'um up!"

The point of this part of the report is the concern all of us should have about the long-term consequences of borrowing yet more billions of dollars. For the short run we are told we have no choice. In the long run, we cannot keep this up, a topic to which I return shortly.

Anyway, aside from my tennis buddy's theory on the subject, I have no argument with Rush's concern about continuing to spend money we do not have. On this issue, Rush and I have common ground. But we part ways, as discussed next.

Which Came First? Republican Socialism or Democratic Socialism?

The parts of Limbaugh's speech with which I take issue pertain to his attacking the present administration for the sins of past administrations. Here are five direct quotes from his speech, with my thoughts following the quotes.

Issue: Obama is fomenting anger and class envy

Limbaugh: "President Obama is so busy trying to foment and create anger in a created atmosphere of crisis, he is so busy fueling the emotions of class envy that he's forgotten it's not his money that he's spending."

Reporter: I have watched Obama's speeches and read his press releases. I detected nothing suggesting he wants to foment anger and class envy. Just the opposite; he goes out of his way to talk about the strength of America and its citizens; about pulling together as a team. My take on Obama is that he is excessively accommodating. Conservative ideas can stand on their own merits. Why engage in distortions?

Issue: Obama is spending wealth that does not exist

Limbaugh: "He's spending wealth that has yet to be created. And that is not sustainable. It will not work. This has been tried around the world. And every time it's been tried, it's a failed disaster."

Reporter: Mr. Limbaugh is correct in that (large) budget deficits cannot be sustained over a long haul. However, Rush acts as if America and Obama have recently decided to spend wealth that has yet to be created. Reagan did it. So did both Bushes. Ironically, the only recent president that did not was a free-spending Democrat named Bill Clinton—the antithesis of Rush.

A fact that Mr. Limbaugh should consider about spending wealth that does not exist: "Percentage of this year's (2010) federal budget deficit attributable to Bush-era tax cuts and the wars in Iraq and Afghanistan: 38."[2] One's support or nonsupport of the bailout and the two wars are irrelevant to the fact that Obama inherited the statistic of 38 percent. As the economy turns around, most of this money will be given back to Uncle Sam.

This deep recession will become a deep depression if money is not pumped into the economy. It is bitter pill for us to swallow, but swallow we must. In the meantime, let's remember that *both* Democrats and Republicans are at fault for letting this crisis occur. Furthermore, even arch-conservative economists acknowledge the bailout had to be done.

One of my advisors for these reports is a talented financial man, who is to the right of Attila the Financial Hun. He has said to me on numerous occasions that without the bailout (formally known as TARP, for Troubled Asset Relief Program) from Uncle Sam, America would have courted financial disaster.

Issue: People have a sense of entitlement

Limbaugh: "We can't have a great country and a growing economy with more and more people being told they have a right, because of some injustice that's been done to them or some discrimination, that they have a right to the earnings of others."

Reporter: I agree. But Mr. Limbaugh is referring to America's underclass and middleclass. He did not talk about America's upperclass. Specifically, the officials who walked away from the meltdown disaster with millions of dollars; or the incompetent CEOs of *public* companies who make over four hundred times the money America's average citizens take home, or the "lowly" employees of investment banks who are routinely granted year-end bonuses of over $200,000.

For the CEOs, it would be one thing if this compensation was based on merit, but it is not. In other reports, examples are cited about the ignorance of many executives about the very financial instruments their companies were buying and selling. The white collar executives at the banks have a sense of entitlement, no better and no worse than the GM blue collar employees. However, the execs' entitlements are considerably more lucrative and I've cited statistics on this excess in earlier parts of this book.

Rush also says, "They (think they) have a right to the earnings of others." I ask Rush, "Who is 'they'?" Is "they" Joe the unemployed plumber, who is living on his $255 unemployment checks; or Richard, the unemployed CEO, who is living on his $255,000,000 "performance" checks? (Notice the trailing zeroes.) Who was more competent in his job? Did Joe bring down his plumbing company? Did Richard bring down Lehman Brothers? I can only surmise that Mr. Limbaugh has not bothered to study America's tradition of meritocracy.

As for entitlement, many rich people pay less to the IRS than their maids, secretaries, and chauffeurs.[3]

Much of the income of the high rollers on Wall Street (for example, commissions and fees given to hedge fund managers[4]) is taxed as capital gains, which is 20 percent less than ordinary income.[5] This money is not capital gains. These people do not own the stocks; they've never held them; they only manage them. They are so-called rugged, freewheeling capitalists who do not even own the capital for which they say they deserve capital gains tax breaks. They are not capitalists. They're welfare wonks dressed in pinstripe suits.

Ordinary citizens pay 35 percent on taxable income above $379,150.[6] Limbaugh is correct in that "they" do not have the right to the earnings of others. But how about the hedge fund managers who pay 15 percent on their annual income of $5,000,000? Obama is proposing to raise this category, which brought forth this rebuke from a Wall Street patron, "It's like Hitler invaded Poland in 1939."[7]

Rush did not utter this inanity. A cofounder of a hedge fund company spoke it. But it's another example of how inflammatory comments agitate, but do not address the issue.

Issue: Socialism and Stalinism vs. Capitalism:

Limbaugh: "So here we have two systems. We have socialism, collectivism, Stalin, whatever you want to call it, versus capitalism."

Reporter: "...whatever you want to call it." If I were Rush, I would call for a new speech writer. But then, I don't think Rush prepares for his remarks; it might require thought. Off-the-cuff remarks are fine and reveal much about the person who makes them, but to ad-lib this sort of mistake is pathetic.

Mr. Limbaugh groups Socialism and Stalinism together. Coming from one of the most influential media stars in America, his statement represents ignorance and gross irresponsibility. Socialism permits dissent and allows freedom of expression. Stalinism repressed dissent and killed or tortured dissenters. It is probably useless to nitpick the comments of such a woefully uninformed man. If his drivel were not so influential, he could be ignored. But because of the inaccuracy of his propaganda and the size of his audience, his stupidity is frightening. I've heard that Rush Limbaugh is an intelligent man. Could be; he is certainly articulate. His rants remind me of the old saying, "The problem with being intelligent is thinking you are smart."

Issue: Debt

Limbaugh then offers, "They don't care about paying for it. All that's just words. All that's just rhetoric paying for it because (Obama) knows you have to worry about paying for it."

Reporter: Mr. Limbaugh, to fill you in, here are the facts: Figure 11-1[8] extrapolates a graph of the U.S. total federal public debt as percentage of GDP from 1900 to 2006—then to 2030. Does Mr. Limbaugh understand the significance of the line's sudden upward thrust, and that Obama did not draw it? This projection was made during the Bush II administration.

Does Rush possess the intellectual honesty to tell his listeners the truth that both Republicans and Democrats are the villains in this plot? Can he acknowledge that Obama is trying to fix a situation that has America in dire straits?

The meltdown and the fiscal crisis shown in figure 11-1 are not right wing or left wing problems. Nor are these problems the fault of a Bush or an Obama. They are the problems for all of us. And they are the fault of many of us. For decades, we've let our politicians run away with irresponsible budgets.

U.S. total federal public debt as percentage of GDP from 1900 - 2030.

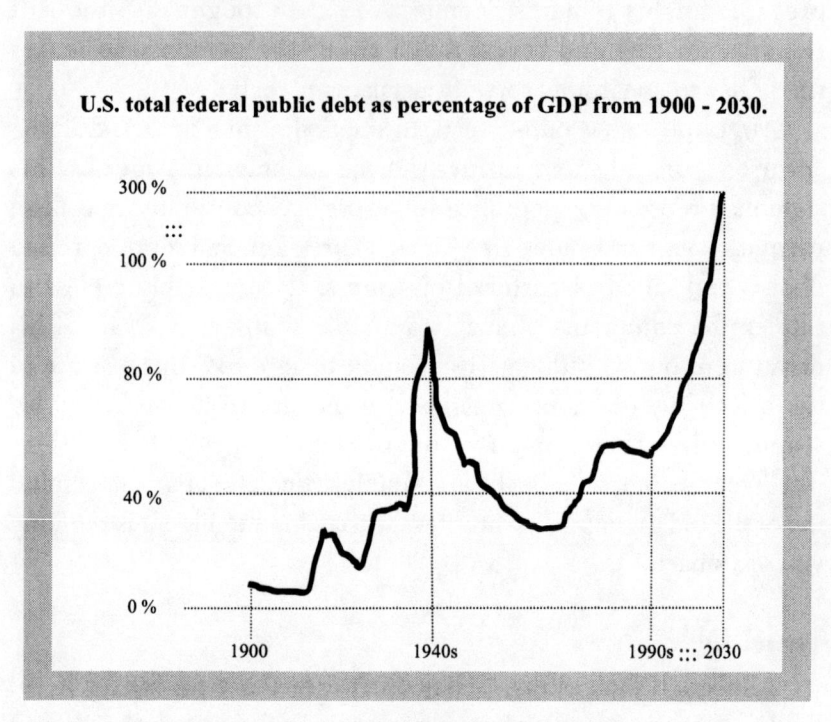

[Chart showing debt rising from near 0% in 1900, peaking around 80%+ in the 1940s, declining through mid-century, then rising sharply to 300% by 2030. Y-axis: 0%, 40%, 80%, 100%, 300%. X-axis: 1900, 1940s, 1990s, 2030]

Figure 11-1. Troubled waters ahead.

Speed Is of the Utmost Importance

Like Mr. Limbaugh, I think the bailout package contains items that are, at best, indirectly related to stimulus. That stated, I am not sure Rush and Uyless are qualified to know what will stimulate our economy and what will not, so I'm inclined to say, "We must get credit flowing again, and as soon as possible. If the package does it, and at the same time, builds an occasional bridge to nowhere, it's worth some inefficiency."

I read today that about 1 percent of the bailout money is for earmarks. That's a lot of money, but knowing the venality of Congress, I am not sure we could have expected a clean package. So, we citizens once again roll with the punches to our midsection.

America is embarking on the correct action by addressing the meltdown quickly. We learned from the mistakes that Japan made in the early 1990s with its slow reaction to its recession. Europe is dragging its heels; it had better initiate more stimulus packages very soon. I also read today that the nation's economists are giving Obama mostly Cs on the bailout. They think he is not giving enough money fast enough to the distressed banks.

Time will tell. Let's revisit this issue one year from now.

Cutting Some Slack

Again, I agree with Mr. Limbaugh that the present situation and the trends shown in figure 11-1 are not sustainable. My problem with the Rush Limbaughs of this country is that they choose to bury critical issues underneath an ideological agenda that has little to do with solving practical problems. In the final analysis, citizens of most nations are less concerned about the political mantras of politicians and pundits than they are about their physical safety, health, and security. If a government can provide its citizens these cocoons, the issue of a bank being nationalized is not on peoples' lists of concerns. Nor are many of the soft issues that keep the radical right and radical left employed.

The meltdown was not a failure of capitalism. It was the failure of those who were supposed to practice capitalism with at least a scintilla of ethics, intelligence, and restraint. The meltdown was also the failure of our regulators, such as the SEC and the Federal Reserve, to do their job; to rein in corrupt and destructive behavior. It was the failure of Congress to pass laws to protect the public from clearly dangerous financial instruments.

I'm rushing away from Rush. He's done America a great disservice with his distortions about this crisis.

Other Facts

Americans should be growing weary of the falsehoods of the media ideologues who routinely dish out inaccuracies about our current financial crisis. Deceptive pundits claim the present administration is leading America down the path to financial ruin, and they cite the current bailout as the culprit. More facts:[9]

- The bailout plan (TARP) and its money were initiated before Obama came to office.
- 85 percent of the projected deficit is attributed to pre-Obama administrations, principally that of Bush Jr.
- The period between Clinton and Bush leaving office (Bush's two terms) represents the biggest fiscal swing (to the negative) in the history of the United States.

I have had Rush Limbaugh in the crosshairs for this report. Charles Krauthammer is another example of the excess of the media. Both men have made statements about the bailout and resulting deficit that link the problem to the goings-on in the Obama administration. As if six months in office can create a national problem of this magnitude.

It is tempting to just laugh these men off because of their succumbing to the Ignorant Therefore Doctrinaire Syndrome. (They are smart yet ignorant about this subject.) Their problem is that they do not go through fact checking procedures to back their predisposed assertions.[10] They need to learn a rule of responsible journalism: They are entitled to their own set of opinions but they are not entitled to their own set of facts. Rush and Charles should keep this in mind: We find ourselves in the paradoxical situation of having to spend more now because we spent too much in the past. That past was during their leaders' residencies on Pennsylvania Avenue.

---

[1] Definitions are from Microsoft Encarta (with exception of the text in parenthesis). All rights reserved.

[2] Harper's Index, *Harper's Magazine*, October, 2010.

[3] Warren Bufett, the icon of capitalism, has so-proclaimed.

[4] This is the second time the term hedge fund has been used in the book; the first time was in a quote. For this introduction, these companies invest in various financial instruments, just like other companies. Their name comes from their frequent practice of hedging their risks by taking out insurance (such credit default swaps) on securities.

[5] One of my readers deals with hedge fund managers. He informs me these people routinely get a "carried interest" as part of their compensation package. This detail is not vital but you may be curious: The interest pays off when the fund increases and usually runs for a period of at least two years. Some of the people collect as much as $1 – 2 billion. Thus, allowing them long-term capital gains deprives the Treasury of more than $200-$400 million per person. My reader adds, "Of course, no payroll taxes are placed on this money either."

[6] Thanks to one of my reviewers (and a fine accountant) for correcting this figure in the report that was first sent to my readers.

[7] *Newsweek*, August 23 and 30, 2010, p. N10.

[8] http://en.wikipedia.org/wiki/United_States_pubic_debt. The 2030 information is sourced from Peter G. Peterson, *Running on Empty*, Picador Press, New York, 2004.

[9] From a Charlie Rose interview with Roger Altman on PBS, July 9, 2009.

[10] Sarah Palin is another example of this practice. During the health care debate, she claimed President Barack Obama was "making light of concerns over what she has called 'death panels' determining or denying care in the Democratic health care proposal." (Quote is from an AP dispatch, dated August 13, 2009). I read pages 424-430 of the bill that dealt with "pulling the plug on Grandma." Palin was completely incorrect. Not partially; completely. The passages in the bill gives grandma, and grandma alone, the right to pull the plug as well as consult with a doctor about death. It is sobering and even scary. Because of people like Palin, the majority of America's citizens think the bill did have death panel provisions. They are not going to take the time to read the bill. Nor, apparently, did Palin, yet she issued an outright falsehood. Who knows why? Ignorance? Malevolence? Whatever, she and her ilk are doing a great disservice to America with their incorrect bombasts.

REPORT 12

SURVEYING THE LANDSCAPE: WHAT'S NEXT?

*The richness of nations can be measured
by the violence of the crises
which they experience.*
—Clement Juglar, a 19th century Frenchman[1]

*The richness of nations can be measured
by mitigating the crises
which they experience.*
—anon

April 10, 2009

This is Your On the Street Reporter. I have not filed a report about the financial meltdown for a while. Things have somewhat stabilized over the past few months. I say stabilized in that not much of consequence has happened:

- Many Americans who seek employment are still out of work. Some have been seeking employment for well over a year.
- Homes continue to be foreclosed with the owners kicked out. Many people have abandoned their houses because the residences are (financially) underwater.

REPORT 12: SURVEYING THE LANDSCAPE:... 195

- America's debt continues to accelerate upward as Uncle Sam prints more bailout money.
- Wall Street employees continue to receive huge compensation packages—thanks partially to the tax payers' bailout.
- Tea parties are gaining traction. There are talks about mounting protests against Wall Street. Perhaps citizens are becoming weary of rolling with the punches that have been inflicted, first by John Maynard Keynes' governmental visible hand and later, by Adam Smith's private enterprise invisible hand.

Many shopping malls remain mostly empty, as seen in figure 12-1. This mall is located in Coeur d' Alene. It is a short distance from my home in Idaho. The small center has space for ten stores. Four are occupied. The signs in front of the other six shops speak to a better time.

Figure 12-1. Business as usual: empty lots, empty stores.

What's Next? Regarding the quote at the beginning of this report by C. Juglar, a 19th century Frenchman, one should not be surprised by his assertion of how violent crises define a nation's richness. Just before and during his time on earth, Juglar's country had a rich history of violent crises, often made more violent by the Frenchmen's zeal for showing excessive violence toward one another. Anon has the correct take on how a "rich" nation handles a crisis: doing its best to mitigate the effects of the crisis on its citizens.

I have reservations about aspects of the bailout package and as I've stated, I have reservations about the whole philosophy of bailouts. But as a whole, I think the bailout has been constructed in an attempt to meet the ideas behind anon's quote.

A Bleak Landscape

Since filing the first report on the meltdown last year, America's finances are not looking any better. As we come to grips with deteriorating conditions, we are beginning to understand the severity and depth of the crisis. It is starting to sink in that a recovery is going to take a long time.

I am beginning to believe that this meltdown, unto itself severe, has also exposed other dangerous vulnerabilities of America's infrastructure. As time permits, I'd like to reflect on this nascent thought, and perhaps file a separate report. For now:

Recently, I read an article that made predictions on how long it will take investors (those who held on to their stocks) to regain their losses:[2]

- Assuming annual returns of 10 percent, it will take eight years for the S&P 500 to climb back to its October 2007 peak of 15650.

- If investors were to sell their stocks now, and move their money to long-term Treasury notes, it would take 28 years to break even (assuming a current yield of 2.88 percent).

I consider the first forecast unrealistic. I think the stock market will make a faster recovery. For the second forecast, we can only hope to find short-term yields at 3 percent. Now, the yields are much lower, considerably less than 1 percent.

On another matter, from the perspective of an individual citizen, and not financial institutions, how can Uncle Sam preach the goodness and patriotism of savings when the Federal Reserve Board keeps interest rates so low? At a level that a bank depositor's return on a savings account does not even compensate for the rise in gas prices? Low interest rates help borrowers but penalize savers.

We are told by the Fed governors that low interest rates—for many years—will be required to aid in the nation's recovery. Meanwhile, Joe the Plumber pays 5 percent interest on a mortgage to a bank and the bank goes to the Fed's discount window for a loan at less than 1 percent. The Disproportionate Ratio in action.

Some people are moving their investments into real estate where there are many opportunities for bottom feeding. On the other hand, I saw a TV program last night in which a man and wife joked they were putting what's left of their IRA money under their mattress.

Who knows? Probably the tried-and-true idea of staying diversified makes the most sense. (If you have stakes in REITs, keep track of their purchasing depressed properties. In the long run, the strategy will translate into high dividends.) For all of us, I suspect it is a good idea to remember the Scottish proverb, "Better long little than soon nothing."[3] A reader suggested I add this old German saw, "Patience is a bitter plant that bears sweet fruit."

A Model across the Pond?

Earlier, the issues of migrating to Socialism were introduced (and more details follow in later reports). Every red-bloodied American is against this evil and Tea Party members are busting their tea bags at the thought. But from the correspondence I've received about previous reports, and from the views expressed by experts and laypeople on TV and in newspapers, I know of no one who thinks America's present setup is working.

Fixes

What to do? As touched-on in earlier reports: (a) Our regulatory agencies will have to perform their duties much better. (b) Congress needs to pass legislation that ensures effective oversight *and transparency* of the new financial instruments (such as credit default swaps), as well as the mortgage market. (c) A good dose of common sense is needed. If an institution looks like a bank, it should be regulated as a bank. (d) If a new financial instrument, whatever it may be, becomes large enough to affect the economy, it should be subject to oversight to prevent it from threatening the country.[4] (e) As discussed several times, the "too big to fail" idea must be examined. If a company is too big to fail, it should not be allowed to become big in the first place or its bigness must first of all: *Do no harm.* (f) The rating agencies need an overhaul. (g) Fannie and Freddie should be disemboweled. (h) The government should be empowered to close down any failed financial institution, not just commercial banks, but investment banks as well.

A Model Across the Border

Here's what our neighbor Canada is up to:[5]

- Canada is the only country in the industrialized world that has not had a bank failure during this crisis.
- It has not funded a massive government bailout for its financial firms.
- In 2008, the World Economic Forum ranked Canada's banking systems as the healthiest in the world. The United States came in fortieth.

Why? Because Canada's banks are well capitalized. They are leveraged at about 18 to 1; U.S. banks are leveraged at least at 26 to 1. Also:

- During the past year, the Toronto-Dominion Bank grew from the 15th to the fifth largest bank in North America.
- Over the last fifteen years, in contrast to the United States and Europe, Canada has kept tight rules (old banking practices) in place.
- House prices are down, but only one-half of what they are in the United States.

Why? Because mortgage interest is not tax deductible, yet 68.4 percent of Canadians own their own homes. In America, it's 68 percent (before the meltdown). Also:

- If you default on a home mortgage in Canada, it is not the bank that is responsible. It's you.
- Canada has had twelve years of budget surpluses.
- Canada's health care system accounts for 9.7 percent of its GDP. In the United States, it's 15.2 percent and climbing rapidly.
- Life expectancy in Canada is eighty-one years. Here, it's seventy-eight years.
- Car companies have been moving jobs to Canada because of lower health care costs.
- Canada has no limit on the number of skilled immigrants to whom it grants green cards. Thus, high-tech companies, such as Microsoft, have announced plans to open research centers in Canada so they can hire talented people to do work in their labs…and make Canada a lot of money.

Canada's "coddling" of its citizens would put Rush Limbaugh into an ideological frenzy. Meanwhile, America's clock on economic self-sufficiency is ticking away.

The Nearly Perfect Storm or the Perfect Storm?

We Americans have long prided ourselves in our self reliance, on making our own way. After all, ruggedness, tenacity, and independence have had a great deal to do with making this country the great nation that it is. I have an emotional tie to these ideas, as my family and I come from what is known as the cowboy culture; one of self-reliance and independence. Perhaps this streak shows in some of my writings. (Canada has also harbored these traits but with less bravado.)

On several occasions in these reports, I have expressed mixed sentiments about the consequences of this bailout. From a pragmatic viewpoint, I don't know how America's moribund economy can jump-start itself without the further (huge) loss of individual wealth and security. I am aware that history instructs us bailouts from a government have proven to keep a nation from going under.

But I find myself put off by the idea that my country is now in a situation where America is... let's admit it...rewarding malfeasance and incompetence; from the corporate side, as well as from the citizen side. That goes against the nature of our nation; certainly, my notion of what our nation should be.

Some of the responses to these reports have been adamant that the bailout is as repugnant as the actions that led to the bailout in the first place. One of my fine friends, and a first-rate financial intellectual, tells me the government made a mistake in doing any rescue. I try to absorb his idea. I think about his notion of a complete meltdown, of not a nearly perfect storm, but a perfect storm. I ask myself, could the system self-recover?

We will never know the answer to this question and my friend's assertion. I suspect it would not. We would suffer another great depression. Whatever the truth might be about this matter, America's welfare capitalism train has left the station, and it started its departure with the New Deal.

I've also given thought to the possibility that the bailout, which was orchestrated by people who pass through the revolving doors of government and Wall Street, was done on behalf of the financial industry. By and large, Wall Street was saved, as was big business. Main Street and small business were the bodies that really suffered. The thought continues to bother me and we will never know the answer.

I've taken the talk show ideologues to task in the last report, but not because they have strong ideals and ideologies. My concern is their debasing America's debates with bombastic near truths or outright falsehoods. It is important that we have honest, open debates on how to move forward, about how much legislation is passed, and to make certain the proper legislation is indeed passed.

We need to scrutinize our current laws and determine if they are (or are not) sufficient. We need to find a way to ensure current and future laws are enforced. This chore is largely a matter of competency, which cannot be legislated.

The danger we face these next few months is to have a knee-jerk reaction to the meltdown and go for legislative overkill. As one who thinks a free market is vital to a society but also as an opponent of *laissez-faire* capitalism, I think the saying, "A government that governs best governs least," is catchy but incorrect. Somewhere in our past, in a moment of rare clarity, we humans created government to protect us from ourselves (and the Bernard Madoffs who will always stalk us).

The rule of law is fundamental to a civil, wealthy society. Creativity and innovation—abetted by the rule of law—are a vital source of that wealth. Financial creativity and economic innovation are part of this equation. Thus, in attempting to repair the damage from the meltdown, and to make laws to prevent another one, let's make certain we allow Wall Street to continue creating and innovating.

During the last year or so, I have watched the meltdown saga unfold with both regretful and amused eyes. I am regretful because it has been devastating to millions of innocent people. I am also regretful because many unethical people became rich at the expense of millions of ordinary citizens who put their trust in a system that did not live up to that trust.

I am amused because the meltdown saga reflects many aspects of human nature, as reflected in the Rules of Life. Thus, no matter how many laws we may pass, no matter how well they may be enforced, we will never be able to prevent ourselves from creating hammers and lowering the thresholds for what we pound.

---

[1] "Fixing Finance," *The Economist*, January 27, 2009, p. 22.

[2] Adam Shell, "Stock Recovery Will Be a Long Haul," *USA Today*, March 9, 2009, p. B1.

[3] James Kelly, *A Complete Collection of Scottish Proverbs*. Secondary source: Frank, p. 866.

[4] "Fixing Finance," *The Economist*, January 27, 2009, p. 23.

[5] Fareed Zakaria, "Worthwhile Canadian Initiative," *Newsweek*, February 16, 2009, p. 31.

REPORT 13

SOBERING STATISTICS FOR FINANCIAL ROCK STARS[1]

*If you wanna be a rock star,
you gotta make it past your one hit single.*

May 10, 2009

Hello from Your On the Street Reporter. I had intended that the previous reports would constitute what I had to say about the current financial crisis. However, several readers have asked if I would continue writing about the financial meltdown. Thanks for the request and yes, the story is not yet finished. So here is an update.

This report's focus is on several subjects: (1) Statistics about Wall Street's well-being in relation to Main Street. (2) The requests to Uncle Sam from several financial institutions to pay back their bailout money early. (3) The tests administered to the nineteen largest U.S. banks to evaluate their loan portfolios. (4) The role of financial institution board members. (5) The rock star mentality of Wall Street's actors.

Bailing Out of the Bailout

One reason the financial institutions offer for paying back their bailout debt is because the loan carries with it restrictions on compensation to their employees. The banks and investment firms claim it is hurting their efforts to attract and hire talented people. It is yet to be seen, but I'm betting these organizations' officials will make this issue one of their most intense lobbying efforts during the debates on crafting legislation to rein in Wall Street.

Better reasons can be advanced for not having debt. Employee compensation is a poor tool to bolster their argument. First, its validity is open to question. Second, it is a public relations mistake. The main reason for paying back debt is to improve a shaky capital position, not to pay employees more in wages and bonuses.

I also grant that the mechanics of Wall Street are not for the intellectually faint. Gifted minds are needed to create and then grease the wheels of financial mechanizations. But for this story, capitalizing on the innovations of these minds involved hiring the very minds who created debilitating financial schemes.

To expand on this idea, we examine some recent events, followed by more details on the requests from the financial sector. To begin, it was noted in earlier reports that the share of profits from the financial industry as a share of overall U.S. business profits has been increasing since such records were kept. Figure 13-1 shows a snapshot of this trend.[2]

Financial Industry Profits (%) of Overall Business Profits

Year	Financial Sector Share
1948	8%
1958	14%
1968	18%
1978	16%
1988	17%
1998	23%
2006	42%
2007	28% (reflecting the meltdown)

Figure 13-1. Sharing the profits.

Keep in mind that much of this revenue was derived from engaging in activities having nothing to do with anything but gambling on and hoping for the misfortune of someone else.

Forty-two percent of America's business profits in 2006 came from the financial industry. Almost half of the revenue of the United States' powerhouse economic engine came from smoke and mirrors. Granted, I'm overstating as parts of the 42 percent came from productive infrastructure-enhancing activities. But much of it was not. To view the problem another way, look at the growth of the financial derivatives market.

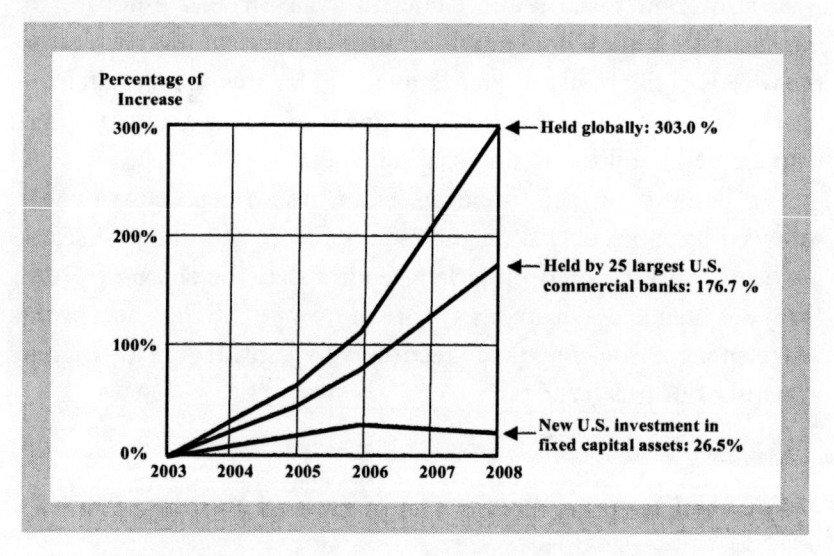

Figure 13-2. Growth of financial derivatives.

Figure 13-2 shows the relationship of the value of certain financial instruments (derivatives, such as mortgage backed securities) to the value of capital assets (nonderivatives, such as factories, equipment, bridges, buildings, and highways.)[3] Using 2003 as a beginning benchmark, these soft financial instruments have dwarfed the investments in hard projects and labors that are critical to a nation's well-being. Alarmingly, the investments in capital assets are decreasing. In the near future, as Congress begins the process of trying to fix this disproportionate ratio the bank executives are going to dig in to protect their lucrative turf.

Figure 13-2 is another example of the Disproportionate Ratio Effect. To review, it is the ratio n:m, where the value of n is small and the value of m is large. For this illustration, n represents capital investments in America and m represents investments in toxic based mortgages in America.

This view is a relative one. Wall Street would not consider this ratio disproportionate; its streets are pristine, suffering no neglect. But Main Street sees the truth of this ratio. Its streets are (increasingly) lined with a lot of potholes.

Disproportionate Compensation

Some of the financial derivatives made many people rich, but they did nothing to improve the physical infrastructure of America. So why do the titans of finance think they deserve more money? In light of their *relatively* meager contributions to society, do they deserve to make millions of dollars a year when some of this money could be distributed to the actual owners of the firms: the stockholders?

The people in the financial sector are well compensated. A sizeable portion of the profits of their companies docs not go to the stockholders of their company. These profits go to the people at the loan and investment desks. This money also goes to their bosses—the people who helped light the meltdown fire.

Figure 13-3 shows the pay per financial sector worker as a percentage of the average for all private industry: "From 1948 to 1982, average compensation in the financial sector ranged between 99 percent and 108 percent of the average for all domestic private industries. From 1983, it shot upward, reaching 181 percent in 2007."[4]

Pay Per Financial Sector Worker as a Percentage of Average U.S. Compensation

Year	Financial Sector Share
1948	103%
1958	100%
1968	101%
1978	100%

1988	123%
1998	143%
2006	178%
2007	181%

Figure 13-3. Dividing the wealth.

Stress Tests

Figure 13-4 shows the top ten stressed-out banks of the largest nineteen banks that were examined as part of the federal government rescue project. This week, the public learned three of the largest banks (Bank of America, Wells Fargo, and Citigroup) did not pass the government-mandated stress test for financial soundness. They are likely to be given tens of billions more dollars in order for them to perpetuate their current practices. Morgan Stanley, one of the banks wanting to pay their officers more money, is in the top ten list of the distressed banks.

The Top Ten Stressed-Out Banks

Bank	Additional Needed "Cushion"
1. Bank of America	$33.9 billion
2. Wells Fargo	$13.7 billion
3. GMAC	$11.5 billion
4. Citigroup	$5.5 billion
5. Regions	$2.5 billion
6. SunTrust	$2.2 billion
7. KeyCorp	$1.8 billion
8. Morgan Stanley	$1.8 billion
9. Bancorp	$1.1 billion
10. PNC	$0.6 billion

Figure 13-4. The top ten.

Who are the people at Morgan Stanley prodding Uncle Sam to allow the bank to give more money to officers? It's not the bank tellers.

The stress tests inform the banks and the public how much capital these firms need to raise to achieve a reasonable level of security if loans continue to go sour. The disturbing news is the banks themselves did not initiate their own tests, an indication of their head-in-the-sand mentality. The good news is that Uncle Sam's loans will likely be paid back in full, with interest.

What Should a Board Member Do?

Since I've taken up the pen and computer to write social commentary, I have shied away from writing about the so-called "good old boy" network (in any system). So-called because I've held the view that humans are too stupid to conjure up and maintain such networks. But I have come to believe these networks exist—usually not through conspiratorial design, but through evolutionary default. (I saw them in operation when I held the position of ombudsman for the Federal Reserve Board.)

I served on several boards of companies when I was an active participant in the computer networking industry. I was chosen for my technical skills as well as my knowledge of the industry, to act as an overseer of start-up companies, to offer suggestions to the design teams, and to suggest ideas in relation to my views about computer networks.

One such enterprise was created to build a machine that would compete with Cisco routers. It was highly risky (and succumbed to Cisco's deserved dominance). But it was worth a go. In relation to the capital investment, the potential rewards were enormous. The firm attracted a lot of venture capital around the San Jose area.

I was vetted. I was asked about my ties to other companies and memberships on other boards. I was told of the reason for my being on the board: to protect the venture capitalists' interests.

I dug in. Unlike crony board members of many companies, I sat with the design teams. I even looked at code. Granted, board members do not ordinarily go to this level, nor should they. But they should do more homework. Board members should be chosen, not because of their fame in their profession, but for their specific knowledge of the products produced by the company they are obligated to serve and for their insights into that marketplace.

Concentration of Mutual Compensation: Board Memberships

As it is often constructed today, the board room is the opposite of the situation just described. An aspect of the problem is encapsulated by one of my friends, and a reviewer of these reports. He is an accountant for large firms, and an expert on the subject.[5]

> The problems in the board room come about as a result of several factors. Shareholder apathy (pay my dividends, run up the value of my shares, and I'll remain in my stupor) is a key.
>
> Another key is the interconnected (crony) directorships and executive positions. At the top of the corporate ladder there is an "elite" group of people, mostly men, who have a history together. Ben is the CEO of X; Jerry is a director of X. Coincidently, Jerry is the CEO of Y and Ben is a director of Z, the parent of Y. And so it goes. When Ben's compensation package comes up before the board Jerry considers the rippling impact this might have on his own package when Ben is in the director's chair.
>
> Companies often choose a famous person (the rock star metaphor) to sit on their board of directors. The star is often a gem of talent in his field of excellence, but he does not know a hill of beans about the products of the company for which he is a board member. Granted, the star should not be looking at a coding sheet, as I did in one company. But he should have sufficient savvy to be able to get his hands dirty enough to understand and guide the company.

Many Wall Street managers, traders, and salesmen pride themselves as belonging to an in-crowd—a network—as well as coming across as white collar mavericks, of having a derring-do attitude toward life. As mentioned earlier, during times when critical decisions are being made about "betting the ranch" on a deal, the attitude of one of the founders of the mortgage bond market—sitting in a meeting with his good old boy network—replied, "Sure what the fuck, it's only a ranch."[6]

As regards the meltdown, here is one take on the "good old boy" network that I cited in an earlier report:[7]

> Anything the SEC does to roil the markets, or reduce the share price of any given company, also roils the careers of the people who run the SEC. Thus, it seldom penalizes serious corporate and management malfeasance... Preserving confidence, even if that confidence is false, has been near the top of the SEC's agenda.
>
> If you work for the enforcement division of the SEC, you probably know in the back of your mind, and in the front, too, that if you maintain good relations with Wall Street you might soon be paid huge sums of money to be employed by it.

Take a look at the career paths of SEC and Wall Street people. The path is a two-way conduit through revolving doors into and out of the regulator's offices and the offices of those who are regulated. Robert Rubin was once cochairman of Goldman Sachs and was also the Treasury Secretary. Later, he was named chairman of Citicorp's executive committee. Henry Paulson was CEO of Goldman Sachs and was also the Treasury Secretary. Alan Greenspan is now a consultant to Pimco, a huge player in the international bond markets.

Regardless of the reputations of these men, I can't see how they can avoid conflicts of interest. I can't see how their insider information will not be used when they enter (or reenter) private enterprise. How can these people remain above the capitalistic fray between the regulator and the regulated when they alternately play both roles?

The potential problem for conflict of interest can be mitigated when a person leaves private industry and goes into government by this person divesting his/her holdings. Henry Paulson sold all his Goldman stock before coming to the Treasury. He kept only an insignificant retirement fund.[8]

While I question the transparency of the revolving door scheme, I do not question the honesty and integrity of Henry Paulson. Since writing this report, I have learned more about this man and of his actions during this crisis. He is brilliant, slightly eccentric, and a straight-shooter. Andrew Ross Sorkin makes this point in his *Too Big to Fail*. Mr. Paulson's book, *On the Brink* shows him to be a dedicated, conscientious man. (References are available in the Bibliography.)

We ordinary citizens must rely on the character of these people in the finance industry. Like it or not, we are dependent on them for our well-being. Still, I do not back off from the themes of these reports: Greed, ignorance, and government incompetence ran amok to create this nearly perfect storm. On page fifty-seven of his book Mr. Paulson says, "In short, Fannie and Freddie were disasters waiting to happen. They were extreme examples of a broader problem that was soon to become all too evident—very big financial institutions with too much leverage and lax regulation."

Here's an example of the problems faced on Wall Street with potential and actual conflicts of interest. The chairman of the board of Federal Reserve of New York (Stephen Friedman) resigned this week over questions of his ties to Goldman Sachs.[9] Goldman Sachs received permission from the New York Fed to become a bank holding company in September, 2008 and received a $10 billion capital injection shortly thereafter. Freidman is also on Goldman's board. Mr. Friedman may be as pure as the driven snow and as clean as the Ivory Snow girl, but it is inconceivable that he would even think of sitting on both boards when decisions are being made at the Fed about the fate of his employer!

On the other hand, how can, say, the Secretary of the Treasury hope to manage the Treasury Department if he or she has had no experience working in commercial and investment banks—and being successful in them? It can be done, but it is unusual. One example is the current Treasury Secretary, Timothy Geithner. It is my understanding he has never been in private industry but he is as knowledgeable and capable as any Wall Street executive.

One-Hit Wonders

I have watched the TV pundits offer answers to America's Wall Street woes. I have read *The Wall Street Journal*'s solutions and those of *The Economist*, as well as others. I posed some ideas on this subject of compensation to these stars in earlier reports. Another approach was suggested to me by one of my brokers, who is now called a "wealth manager" (and who has the wrong client): Tie compensation to long-term performance, not an immediate sell.

I like the idea. Let's say my wealth manager calls to tell me I should get into werewolf stocks and bonds because lycanthropy is making a comeback. I toss in some money and my broker gets his commission. Later, it turns out I did not dodge the (silver) bullet. Lycanthropy Inc.'s stock hits the skids. What happens? My broker must return some or all of his commission.

Not realistic? I don't think so. It's like many jobs today. We get paid for long-term performance. It's similar to a rock star. A one-hit wonder brings in some big time cash, but unless he sires a Hannah Montana, his meager creativity and output will not continue to be rewarded.

I've no idea how the logistics of all this would work, or if the concept is even feasible. It's just that, an idea. But I am certain we cannot continue to operate in a world in which failure goes unpunished.

Some of my readers, especially stockbrokers, have told me my ideas about brokers/wealth managers not being tied to long-term performance is not accurate in today's world. They say (quoting one of them who is also my friend): "Most advanced and conscientious wealth managers today don't work on commission, but rather on a percentage fee based on the investor's assets. Then, when an investor loses money, the advisor loses income. They are sitting on the same side of the table. And if the investor loses a lot of money, he moves his account elsewhere, and the advisor loses a lot of income!"

That makes sense. But I'm not speaking of day-to-day stock market trades. I'm speaking of selling toxic securities containing subprime junk that bring millions of dollars in near-immediate commissions to the salesman. Later, when the securities go belly-up, the salesman has safely ensconced his money inside an untouchable larder.

Recent Events

Last week, CNN aired a segment on a plan in the bailout package to give several thousand dollars to any citizen who would trade in their old car for a new one. Why? To jump start the moribund American automobile industry, one that has continuously shot itself in the foot.

This past week, Charlie Rose (one of the best programs to be found on television) hosted some of the big players in the financial crisis. I tuned-in to one of the programs featuring a Bush administration Treasury Department official. He had done a splendid job in helping to contain the floodwaters of the meltdown. Because he was leaving his government job, Mr. Rose asked him what he was going to do. Charlie smiled and then predicted the official would go into the private financial sector, where he would make "tons of money."

The man responded that he was taking some time off, and yes, he would probably go into the financial sector. He did not second Charlie's prediction, but he knows he will indeed make tons of money.

Does it matter? I hope I have convinced you that it does. It isn't his compensation that is the issue. It is the accepted idea (from Charlie Rose and our society) that Wall Street is our friend, that we can plug-and-play the players into and out of banks and the agencies that are chartered to regulate banks. After my research on this subject, I am having reservations about the merits of this idea.

But the truth is, I don't know of an alternative. We can only hope the noble intentions of these folks will somehow keep them immune from capitalizing on their inside knowledge of how to "game" the system. I'm not optimistic. Gaming can be done in so many subtle ways. Even in ways that appear ethical, but are nothing more than taking advantage of the good old boy network. Here's the underlying meaning of this part of that interview (the quotes are mine):

- Charlie Rose, "OK. You've done your job as America's public servant. Now—using your inside knowledge obtained at taxpayer expense—go out and make some real money!" (Writer: You've labored in the chorus long enough. It's time for you to be a rock star!)

- Former public servant, "Thanks Charlie. That is exactly what I intend to do."

Idealism aside, unless you work on Wall Street, let me assure you that Wall Street is not your friend. If you are an investor, the *only* job of Wall Street is to sell you its products. It is not there to offer friendly "financial advisor" advice. It is there to sell you something. Wall Street wealth managers are no different from used car salesmen. They both work on volume. They both work on return.[10]

Summary Thoughts

America is not being held hostage to the financial sector. I hope this report has not been that apocalyptic. But we have let banks and other investment companies gain too much leverage about passing or not passing laws to oversee their operations. As well, the wealth passed to the financial sector—even by my entrepreneurial standards—is ridiculous. If I still have doubts, I ask you to review the figures cited earlier in this report and consider this recent editorial:[11]

> While the [stress test] results have focused mainly on the 10 banks that need to raise capital, some of the banks deemed well capitalized have seized on the results to suggest that they should be freed from the extra government control that came with the bailouts. They seem to believe that if they repay the original bailout money from last year, they should be allowed to resume business as usual.

The editorial continues with these thoughts: How about the government guaranteeing billions of dollars of the banks' debt? How about the billions of dollars indirectly funneled to them by bailing out AIG? What about the backing from the FDIC? What about the fact that the Treasury is going to provide about $1 billion to help investors buy banks' toxic loans?

The banking industry continues to leverage the regulators. As another example, they recently succeeded in defeating an attempt to let homeowners have their mortgages decreased in bankruptcy court.[12]

America's mistake was letting the financial sector become so powerful in the first place. We put financial institutions into a position where they are now too big for our own good. Can any of us fathom the implications of this idea being part of America's principles: You cannot be allowed to fail. Yet we not only see this trend in the business world, our educational system and many schools are reluctant to issue "Fs" to our children: Can't have them fail, it might hurt their feelings.

Our founding fathers are turning over in their collective graves. Collective as in "applying to many" and not as in "under state supervision."

What do we do now? We can ignore the problem. We can keep our TV primed with "American Idol" singers and "Dancing with the Stars" dancers. We can ignore Charlie Rose's attempts to confront our problems. We can continue to permit the Wall Street egoistic geeks to behave as if they were intellectual heroes and financial rock stars—while they go about their venal creations of synthetic capitalism.

Or we might consider getting rid of the oligarchs and restructuring the banking system. We might think about eliminating the perverse welfare capitalism networks the oligarchs created for their own benefit. Now *that* would be cause for some serious singing and dancing.

---

[1] Thanks to Greg Venit for this title and idea.

[2] Simon Johnson, "The Quiet Coup," *The Atlantic*, May, 2009, p. 49.

[3] David J. Lynch, "U.S. May Face Years of Sluggish Growth," *USA Today*, May 8, 2009, p. 1B.

[4] Johnson, "The Quiet Coup," p. 49.

[5] E-mail from an accountant and expert in the field of corporate finance. Name withheld for privacy considerations. Name will be furnished on request and subject to permission from source.

[6] "How to Play Chicken and Lose: Finance Suffers from Reverse Natural Selection," *The Economist*, p. 16.

[7] Lewis and Einhorn, "The End of the Financial World as We Know It," p. 9.

[8] Mr. Paulson had to sign a waiver that he would not be in contact with Goldman for a year. When the financial meltdown reached the crisis point, he needed (almost desperately) to be in frequent contact with the major players, including Goldman. He had to get (a very fast) waiver in order to be able to talk on the telephone with Goldman. Had he not had this waiver, he could not have done his job. The waiver was timely and appropriate.

[9] Ray Goldbacher, "N.Y. Fed Chair Resigns Abruptly," *USA Today*, May 8, 2009, p. 4B.

[10] Some of us have the good fortune to have brokers who break this stereotype. I've gone through a number of these folks. My current "financial advisors" are top rate. No pressure. No phone calls at the end of the month to meet quotas. They occasionally offer advice, but pretty much leave me alone. They break their own stereotype and I am glad they are not only my advisors but my friends as well.

[11] "After the Stress Tests," *The New York Times*, May 10, 2009, p. 7.

[12] Ibid.

Report 14

The Mortgage Market and Regulation

*The banker will always be one step ahead of the regulator.
The banker invents circumvention to a regulation;
only then can the regulator regulate it.*

*We find ourselves in the paradoxical situation of having to spend
more now because we spent too much in the past.*

July 8, 2009

Hello again. This segment of the nearly perfect financial storm reports on the issue of financial institution regulation in relation to the current financial meltdown.

Even Bigger

I'll not rehash the issue of bigness in detail, as it was covered earlier, but a general review is pertinent to this discussion. It is now obvious this meltdown has resulted in creating even bigger banks. The folding banks have been folded into other (and now larger) banks. Jurist Louis Brandeis was on the mark in 1914 in a book titled, *Other People's Money—How the Banks Use It:*[1]

Size, we are told, is not a crime. But size may, at least, become noxious by reason of the means through which it is attained or the uses to which it is put.

The Regulation Puzzle

I've dwelled on the problem of the bigness and interconnectedness syndromes several times in these reports. Forgive this repetition, but it should be kept in mind during the next few months as the financial system tries to repair itself. There will be efforts to keep the financial industry unregulated, free to do what it wishes. The reasoning is: "Regulators make things worse."

The other side of the debate says, "You had your chance. You blew it. We're taking over."

The truth is both sides blew it. The regulators had the means to regulate, to prevent the meltdown, and they failed. The current Secretary of the Treasury (Timothy Geithner) says:[2]

> These companies were large, highly leveraged, and had significant financial connections to the other major players in our financial system, yet they were ineffectively supervised and regulated.

This comes from a former president of the New York Fed! Some of the companies he describes in his statement were under his supervision.

As of this writing, it appears the Obama Administration is leaning toward repairing the system with "enhanced regulatory oversight" but not downsizing, or restricting the size of financial institutions, or limiting their interdependencies.[3] The experts tell us it is too late to put the genie back in the bottle. So, we will witness the system getting repaired. A few years from now, another debacle will occur.

The Regulators Continue to Tussle with Each Other

More laws? Better regulation of existing laws? Competency in regulation? How much is enough? How much is too much? As I write this report, the decision makers and their lobbyists are debating these issues. The sides are roughly aligned as follows:

> Fine-tune the system: Leave the system mainly intact and let banks continue with business as usual, accompanied with new laws about how they must behave.

> Tank the system: Restructure the system, accompanied with new laws about how banks must behave.

The fine-tuners represent the mainstays in the Obama administration. They think the system can operate effectively if its ailing institutions are bailed out and a lot of laws are written. Their rationale is that the problem is one of liquidity.[4]

They also state the government has no authority to take over a bank holding company. (Which includes the large banks, which own other non-bank companies.) Plus, the arduous process would have a "disruptive effect on market confidence."[5]

In other words: Americans can't have the Dow Jones go down, even if it means correcting a systemic flaw in America's financial infrastructure.

The fine tuners also say their approach is vindicated by the fact that JP Morgan Chase and Goldman Sachs have paid back their bailout money, they're doing just fine, and they're now doing business as usual. Sure, but these two banks are not in the top ten list of stressed-out banks, as described earlier.

Business as usual? That's disconcerting. The "businesses as usual" are keeping America's financial engine temporarily stoked, while truly productive efforts to invest in our infrastructure go unattended.

The tankers include Paul Volcker, Sheila Bair, and Joseph Stiglitz. They think the current bailout approach is little more than putting bandaids on a gaping wound. They say the insolvent companies should be nationalized, have their bad assets sold off, and then re-privatized. They believe any company that is too big to fail will always be guaranteed a government bailout at the expense of America's citizens and to the detriment of America's position in the world market. This writer agrees.

Stupidity, Ideology, and Vested Interests

Laws will not protect citizens if the people who enforce the laws are stupid or slothful. Laws will not help if regulators are ideologically opposed to regulation, or excessively networked to the industry that is supposed to be regulated.

It is a somber scenario. If laws are not in place, the unregulated institutions will find a way to game the system. That's the nature of human behavior and the profit motive. But the laws are only as effective as those who enforce them. The SEC could have stepped in on numerous occasions to dilute the effects of the nearly perfect financial storm. The same goes for the Federal Reserve and the Treasury Department.

With the exceptions of some diehards in the financial community, misguided Greenspan ideologues, and ill-informed Limbaugh groupies, most knowledgeable people accept that more regulation is needed in the financial market.

I believe some additional legislation is needed but I also believe a fundamental restructuring of America's financial system is at the heart of the solution; not the patchwork "increased regulations" philosophy that is emerging from Obama and Congress. I am not in favor of another regulatory body. The ones we have today have proven they are not up to their tasks. Why should we think another agency will solve the problem?

Banks must be reorganized. The effects of their failures must be contained. The effects of their actions must be localized, which is anathema to modern business philosophy.[6] If they remain as they are, they will continue doing what they have been conditioned to do since America lost the anchor of the local bank. What this might do to the globalization nirvana needs to be examined as well. So should globalization.

When the failure of a single investment bank (Lehman Brothers) can rock the foundations of the world's financial system, something is drastically wrong and needs to be changed.

As stated at the beginning of this report: The banker will always be one step ahead of the regulator. The banker invents circumvention to a regulation; only then can the regulator regulate it.

Maybe we are tilting at windmills. Perhaps the nature of financial institution regulation is to always be behind the creative inventions of the financial institution. If so, the institution should not be allowed to bring down anything but itself. That philosophy should be the guide post for the current debates about regulation.

---

[1] Eric Dash, "If it's too big to fail, is it too big to exist?" *The New York Times*, June 21, 2009, p. 3.

[2] Gretchen Morgenson, "Too big to fail, or too big to handle?" *The New York Times*, June 21, 2009, p. BU 1.

[3] Ibid., BU 3.

[4] Lizza, p. 34.

[5] Ibid.

[6] Last night on television, a CEO of one of the big banks said growth and associated expansion were essential to his bank's survival. He meant buying other banks, which he did. Where does this path lead? Is there a point in the capitalistic cycle where it can be said, "Enough is enough?" If not, the end result is one Goldman Sachs for all, one Walmart for all, one Taco Bell for all…and zero competition.

Report 15

Give Me Liberty and Give Me Bailouts: No Creative Destruction Please!

Bulls and bears make money; but pigs get slaughtered.[1]
—Edwin Lefevre

Not quite correct. The pigs have golden parachutes.
—Your writer

The mistake I made with my failed company was not growing large enough to become a ward of Uncle Sam.
—Your (less than wealthy) writer

August 26, 2009

Since the last report, several leaders in the financial industry have gone public with their views on the financial meltdown and the subsequent government bailout. At the heart of the matter is the issue of the role of government in the markets of capitalism: banks, Wall Street, credit cards, the airlines, Detroit, and so on. The (extreme) positions of both sides of the issue can be summarized as follows:

- Proponents of no government involvement: Government participation in the marketplace is unnatural. It curtails innovation and competition. It leads to inefficiency. Humans regulate themselves because their self-interests lead to socially acceptable behavior.

- Proponents of government involvement: Left alone, the marketplace will behave the same way humans behave. After all, they're running the markets. Humans will take whatever actions are needed to protect their own interests, often to the detriment of other humans, which is socially unacceptable.

Some readers of these reports know me personally and are aware of my professional background. Others do not. I'm inserting a brief resume into this report in hopes it will help explain how and why I have come to my views on the issue and also to provide a backdrop for some comparisons.

A Brief Aside.

I spent three decades of my life as a self employed businessman. I created three companies (the first was in concert with four other men). I came to appreciate that the creation of a commercial enterprise, small or large, is a difficult and risky proposition. For all three of these startups, they could have easily gone broke and taken away much of my savings and security. But if they succeeded, I was convinced (as are all entrepreneurs) they would make me rich. (They did not, but they gave me the cushion to be writing this report without worrying about selling it.) Such are the dreams of entrepreneurs. However unrealistic they may be, they stoke the fires of capitalism. I'll add some thoughts to this introduction shortly.

"Give Him Liberty, but not a Bailout"

The heading in the line above was taken from the title of an article appearing in *The New York Times*.[2] The "him" is John A. Allison IV, Chairman and former CEO of the BB&T bank. The article centers on his allegiance to the philosophy of Ayn Rand. In short, her philosophy of "objectivism" promotes *laissez-faire* capitalism: Capitalism works best if private industry is not regulated.

Mr. Allison is a supporter of this approach. He is a popular speaker. He travels widely to express his views and explain how BB&T has prospered because he fostered Randian operations at the bank while he was in charge.

Success and Bigness in Today's World

During the past few decades, we have been told by company executives that their companies cannot succeed in the world economy if they are not big. Time and again, a corporation acquires another enterprise for the sake of supposedly increasing efficiency, reducing overhead, and reaching other markets—achieving economies of scale.

Mr. Allison became CEO of BB&T in 1989. At that time the bank had $4.7 billion in assets. He retired in 2008. During this tenure, his bank made 60 bank and S&L acquisitions and now has $152 billion in assets. BB&T is the 11th largest bank in the nation.

Mr. Allison is not in favor of government intrusion. He and the Rand objectivists believe the scenario in her book *Atlas Shrugged* is unfolding now as the government takes over a collapsing economy.

BB&T was one of the banks that did not need TARP. But it was forced to take the money, which is irksome to Mr. Allison. I cannot understand why the government forced some banks into TARP that did not need any money. It's distasteful. Mr. Allison said the interest on the "loan" will cost BB&T about $250 million.

But that is what is happening in America. BB&T aside, which is obviously well-run, we are increasingly protecting people and institutions from their own ineptitude. We can't let capitalism take its natural course to what Joseph Schumpeter calls "creative destruction."

Creative Destruction

In his book *Capitalism, Socialism and Democracy* Joseph Schumpeter uses the term creative destruction to describe the process of radical change that accompanies competition and innovation. In Schumpeter's vision, entrepreneurs—if given free reins—are the driving force behind economic growth. This dynamic may destroy established companies, along with their employees and stockholders. But in the long run, it contributes to a better and more affluent society.

I agree. Even in my small commercial enterprises, my innovations forced my competitors to improve their products. And before they did, before they reached my level of service to customers, I made more money than they did. But one company got ahead of me on the competitive treadmill, eventually forcing me to close one of my businesses. The closure rebounded into: fewer contactors that I had hired to peddle my products; the contractors' lessening of their purchases at various stores because they were no longer receiving a check from me; the stores cutting their inventories, and so on. But because I was small, this ripple effect did not create much of a stir. I was small enough to fail. In that enterprise, I did fail.

My company and its ultimate fate is a good example of creative destruction. I "out-created" for awhile and bested my competition. I "under-created" for a while and paid the price. Someone came along with a better competitive strategy and my company was out of business before I could counter their new approach. I was creatively destroyed.[3]

Where's the Destruction?

Proponents of Ayn Rand sometimes go off course in their defense of her credos. But in fairness to Ms. Rand, she was forming her philosophy (1950s-1970s) before the massive mergers of companies took place; before globalization took hold; before the interlocking of companies created a devastating economic domino effect if they failed.

Let's assume the validity of the present canon that our large institutions cannot be allowed to fail and that they cannot be allowed to be destroyed. Where do we draw the line? Who is allowed to fail and who isn't? How much creative destruction can we handle?

We don't know. Because the experts tell us we don't want to know. They tell us the bailing out of failed companies must be done to prevent the economy from...well, failing.

I wish I were an economist or some other financial whiz. The logic above makes no sense: *Companies must be allowed to become big in order to survive. But once they're big, they can't be allowed to fail. Because? They're too big.*

Say what you will about Ayn Rand and her views, she was an original thinker. I'm taken with many of her ideas. They do not play well into today's gargantuan, networked world. At least with the current mantra, as we're told we can't allow destruction because it would actually destroy. Let's take another view of the issue.

Interconnectedness Destroys Creative Destruction

I am impressed with Mr. Allison and how he directed the operations of BB&T. He's a competent manager. He was conservative enough to avoid the toxics. If all bank managers were as prudent and competent as he, we would not be in as big a mess as we are.

He understands the wisdom of restraint. His bank supports the teachings and research on "the moral foundations of capitalism." He quotes Rand's concepts of the "trader principal" where life is about trading value for value. Of course it is. That's the foundation of any successful business transaction. What else could one teach? How long will a business relationship exist if one party is being taken to the cleaners? Not long.

But here's the catch, what if it is long enough for the other party to make a lot of money and the pilloried party to be left in ruin? The losing person is left with underwater home mortgages, depleted IRAs, no jobs, and no life lines. With so many citizens barely meeting their monthly bills, a deep recession to wring-out or destroy that which should be wrung-out or destroyed is not allowed.

As for the second part of the "catch," we've come again to your writer's dilemma: *Too small to survive; too big to fail—if the failing firm is highly interconnected to like firms.* The mistake I made with my failed company was not growing large enough to become a ward of Uncle Sam or interconnecting myself to big banks.

Do you think for one North Carolina minute that BB&T would have been allowed to fail twenty years ago with only $4.7 billion in assets? How about now, as the nation's 11th largest bank with thousands of interlocking relationships with other financial institutions? It would be interesting to see what Mr. Allison would have done if his bank had been in deep trouble. If he is what he claims to be, he would have let his bank be creatively destroyed.

The thoughts of Ayn Rand and the performance of John A. Allison IV are worthy. But they (and we) cannot have it both ways. We can't let the AIGs of the world become so big and interconnected that we must protect them from their own foibles. We should, but I'm told we can't. So, how do we contain the rare bad apples that game the system; that look to distort the wise "value for value" premise?

In times past, their excessive behavior would do them under—and them alone. They might take down some unfortunate bystanders, but the effects of their destruction—like my company—would have been contained. The repercussions into other systems would not have been of much consequence.

In today's world, the interlocking of financial relationships—the networking of fiscal cabals—the idea of creative destruction appears to have been rendered obsolete. But we don't know because our government does not allow the theory to be tested.

The current administration is not addressing the fundamental problem of bigness or that of interlocking relationships. By allowing big banks to absorb other big banks, it is compounding the problem. Unless financial institutions are required to hold much more capital and deal transparently so they can be monitored, Bailout 101 will eventually become Bailout 102.

How can such a system be managed? Do we force companies to divest, to become smaller? That's yet more government intrusion. Do we restructure the banking and financial industry to make institutions less interlocking? Do we adapt a Rand philosophy and have no oversight of the capital markets? I have made the case in previous reports that non-regulation of over-the-counter derivatives market led to disastrous results.

As discussed in later reports and Part II of this book, there are solutions to these problems. But based on recent history of the national political process, it is likely Congress will kick the can down the road. It is likely our children and grandchildren will be faced with the same set of problems; if not the same set, then the same kind. If Congress and the White House do come up with laws that address the situation described in this report, past history also tells us the legislation will be complex, verbose, and require the creation of yet more government oversight agencies. These agencies will likely overlap current agencies' charters, resulting in another layer of bureaucracy that does not perform its job properly.

---

[1] Alan Greenspan, *The Age of Turbulence*, The Penguin Group, New York, 2007, p. 28.

[2] Andrew Martin, "Give Him Liberty, but Not a Bailout," *The New York Times*, August 2, 2009, pp. BU Y 1 & 6.

[3] Truth in disclosure: The competitor that put me under did not have better products. They succeeded in signing a contract with two trade magazines whose mailing lists I purchased to mass mail advertisings about my products. The two mailing lists (with tens of thousands of addresses) were the life blood of my company. The contract had my competitor purchase advertising space in these magazines with the agreement that the magazines would not allow me to purchase their mailing lists. These lists resulted in 50 percent of my business. Within two months, I closed this firm. My products were better, but I was still "creatively destroyed." Very creatively!

Report 16

Other Pieces to the Meltdown Puzzle

May 12, 2010

Hello from Your On the Street Reporter. It has been a while since my last report on the 2008 financial meltdown. Like many citizens, I have sat back and watched Wall Street and Uncle Sam jostle with each other. In so doing, I decided it might be helpful to introduce other embers that helped enflame the financial meltdown.

For this report, I will usually resort to the past tense, because I am writing about events that took place prior to 2010. However, present tense is used on occasion, because some of the past events and related situations are still extant.

Clearinghouses

A clearinghouse provides clearing and settlement services to financial institutions (the parties) for financial transactions, such as bond trades and various derivatives. The term clearing describes the activities beginning with a formal commitment for a trade until the trade is settled. The term settlement describes the delivery of the securities from one party to another.

A clearinghouse stands between the two parties, called clearing firms. Its job is to reduce the risk of a firm not honoring its obligations. Using a variety of methods, the clearinghouse acts as a go-between to insure all goes well with the trade and the proper transfer of titles and funds for it. It also provides transparency to the trade.

Because the clearinghouse takes on the risk of settlement failures, it must be well capitalized to prevent the possibility of a defaulting clearing firm or a market crash bringing down the clearinghouse. Another advantage of using clearinghouses is that they are usually funded by the parties using them, who must be mindful of their risks.

Hedge Funds

To help in understanding the current financial situation on Wall Street, and therefore America's finances, hedge funds and hedging (discussed generally thus far) are now examined in more detail. Hedge funds are similar to other funds in that their strategy is based on investing in certain financial instruments. The name comes from some of their activities which seek to hedge their risks by taking on derivatives such as credit default swaps.

Hedge funds are significant players in the financial world. In Report 9, I described how Richard Fuld, chief of Lehman Brothers, accused hedge funds of doing Lehman in. As he said, "These guys are killing us." ...by shorting Lehman Brothers. He was saying the negative evaluation of Lehman by the hedge funds was doing Lehman great damage. True, but Fuld and Lehman themselves are to blame for their demise. The hedge funds merely sped up the process.

A hedge fund typically borrows money for its operations on margin. Some companies borrow very heavily. Thus, the fund can be heavily leveraged. If a hedge fund has borrowed $9 for every $1 received from investors, a loss of only 10 percent of the value of the investments of the hedge fund will wipe out 100 percent of the value of the investor's stake in the fund, once the creditors have called in their loans.[1]

They also engage in short selling, which we learned is a bet that, say, a stock price will go down. If it does, they make money. Again, win or lose; a zero sum game (the bold text in this quote is added by this writer):[2]

In most jurisdictions hedge funds are open only to a limited range of professional or wealthy investors who meet certain criteria set by regulators but, in exchange, **hedge funds are exempt from many regulations that govern ordinary investment funds**. The regulations thus **exempted** typically include restrictions on short selling, the use of derivatives and leverage, fee structures, and on the liquidity of interests in the fund. **Light regulation and performance fees are the distinguishing characteristics of hedge funds**.

Please read again the paragraph above. For hedge funds, the gloves are off. Darwin meets Guccis. *That is, until these companies (if they are large) get into trouble. Then, the U.S. government picks up the pieces with our tax dollars.*

Risking excessive metaphor (admittedly again, but the subject begs for it): Wall Street's Gucci-toed citizens stay well-heeled by Uncle Sam's Dickens-like laws which give them fantastic unregulated latitude to game the system to their benefit.

Let's say the stock in Uyless Black Lectures Inc. is going down (I've gone public with a stock offering). I had a couple cities in which my mailings did not pan out. I'm still the same company and subsequent cities will prove profitable. Nonetheless, a hedge fund groupie sees the sparse attendance at New York and bets against my future (and me) in the form of swaps.

These sorts of activities can create a rundown on a company's stock price, because it breeds skepticism. It can create severe stress on a company or even an economy, as evidenced in 2008. I still have a very fine company, but it does not matter. My fate is dictated by press releases and associated herd stampedes.

These activities may be secret. Certain derivatives are off the books.

Market Trends and Trading

If you think derivatives are not beneficial to your life (and your depleted IRA), the trend in the market for derivatives does not paint a pretty picture. Returning to the *The Wall Street Journal* report, here are some statistics on derivatives, as seen in figure 16-2.

Gross Market Value of Derivatives Contracts Outstanding

(Trillions of Dollars)

1999	3
2001	4
2003	8
2007	11
2009	20
2010	25

Figure 16-2. Gross.

You might say, why not? The more the better, and the more they are traded, the more flexibility an investor has to enter and leave the market. Nowadays, the investment banks do more trading than investment banking. After all, with all this trading, the investment banks are helping to provide liquidity to the marketplace. In-and-out, almost at will. Buy-and-sell, almost at will.

Maybe, but maybe not. There is a school of thought that markets suffer from too much trading because it leads to short-term speculators—who do not care about the underlying merits of a stock—overwhelming long term investors. Short-term speculation creates gyrations in stock prices that do not reflect the "fundamental value" of the instruments.[3] A friend and an expert in the stock market told me, "Volatility scares long-term investors."

As an unseasoned Wall Street participant, I cannot see the value of short-term speculation. It remains my impression that the function of stocks and bonds is to provide a means to raise money for ventures that might enhance the building of an industrial and economic national infrastructure; not to pad the bank accounts of gamblers. I have the same opinion about high frequency trading.

High-Frequency Trading[4]

High-frequency trading creates volatility in the marketplace. It gives the term "short" in short-term speculation a meaning beyond what many people can comprehend. It uses powerful computers to engage in millions of trades during a very short time, in mere seconds; more often, in fractions of seconds.

Short term? Millions of dollars can be made by making trades and flipping stocks within a millisecond window. Sometimes, it is even less. Nanosecond windows are not that big a deal when dealing with the speed of computers. Paraphrasing from Duhigg:

> For most of Wall Street's history, stock trading was fairly straightforward: buyers and sellers gathered on exchange floors and dickered until they struck a deal. In 1998, the SEC authorized electronic exchanges to compete with marketplaces like the New York Stock Exchange. The intent was to open markets to anyone with a desktop computer and a fresh idea.
>
> But as new marketplaces have emerged, PCs have been unable to compete with Wall Street's computers. Powerful algorithms execute millions of orders a second and scan dozens of marketplaces simultaneously. They can spot trends before other investors, changing orders and strategies within milliseconds.
>
> Loopholes in market rules give high speed investors an early glance at how others are trading. And their computers can essentially bully slower investors into giving up profits—and then disappear before anyone even knows they were there.

In addition, these traders can make a boatload of money just by trading, regardless if they lose or gain on the transaction. Stock exchanges pay a small fee to big volume traders. Spread over millions of shares, the income can be millions of dollars. Thus, the game is gamed to encourage even more frequent trades. Nice work if you can get it. In 2008, high-frequency traders turned a profit of about $21 billion.

Some advice, if you are surfing the Net to check out prices of stocks, bonds, etc. on your home computer and you are relying on your Intel processor and Microsoft Excel to assist you in excelling in your Wall Street speculations: find another profession. You are on the second tier of a two-tier hierarchy. By the time you make your buy or sell, the high-frequency traders have already eaten your profit margins.

Short-Term, High-Frequency Speculation: How it Distorts the Market

Two business executives testified before Congress recently about short-term speculative trading in energy stocks and bonds, and how this practice has raised their costs of doing business. Their thoughts also pertain to high-frequency trading. They have taken out insurance to protect against the huge swings in energy prices and passed the overhead to their customers.[5] These men describe the situation (the following material is paraphrased from the cited article):

- Robert Fornaro: "Rampant and unregulated speculation in commodities" has created a "casino like atmosphere for the end user."
- Sean Cota: Shortly after the derivatives market was deregulated (2003) his company was paying 3 to 6 cents a gallon to buy a derivative as a hedge against extreme and rapid swings in the price of heating oil. Today, the same security costs 50 to 75 cents per gallon.
- Cota says the increase is because of speculation in the marketplace, where hedge funds, traders, and Wall Street firms account for the buying and selling of derivatives contracts.
- He further states that 2,000 to 3,000 energy derivative contracts are bought and sold to produce one tank of gasoline.

Whether we accept (which I do) or reject this premise is irrelevant to the fact that investment banks have moved away from their time-honored job of helping firms find money to build things. They still perform these services, but not as much as in the past.

Discount Window

Banking institutions who are members of the Federal Reserve System are allowed to use the Fed's discount window, which is a lending facility. It gives a bank quick access to credit and liquidity.

During the 2008 crisis, several investment banks were allowed by the Federal Reserve to convert to bank holding companies, thus giving them access to cheap credit at the discount window. This strategy was part of the bailout to help investment banks that were having liquidity problems.

How cheap is a discount window loan? Much less than a loan you and I will get from our bank. It varies, but as of this writing, it is less than 1 percent.

Uyless Black Lectures, Inc. would like to convert to a bank holding company; so would everyone else. We could gain access to dirt-cheap money and use this money to invest in stocks, our businesses, etc. Let's assume the spread between the discount window and this investment is one percentage point. If a bank borrows millions of dollars from the Fed and invests it in most anything, the profit runs into hundreds of thousands of dollars. Where does this money go? It goes to Goldman Sachs, which recently became a bank holding company, and to other organizations that have placed Uncle Sam's protective umbrella.

Loan Shark Windows

In the meantime, the prolonged low interest rates you and I are getting on our checking and money market accounts—money we make available to the banks—are several percentage points below what our banks charge us for taking out a loan—money that they make available to us. With discount window rates, banks have almost free capital to lend back to customers at much higher rates.

The situation just described is even more ridiculous. Banks charge us a fee for holding our money. They use this money to make loans, on which they charge interest. Got it? The banks charge you for holding your money, then use that very money to charge you for borrowing it.

But not if you are liquid! By holding a minimum amount in the bank ($25,000 is the minimum at my bank), you will not be charged a fee. You will be paid interest on this money. I obviously do not know the liquidity position of your account, but statistically, few folks in America have the means to keep $25,000 laying around in an account that draws less interest than America's inflation rate.

But of course, we are not bankers. We are depositors and maybe borrowers. Banks are also borrowers, but banks borrow from Uncle Sam. We borrow from the banks. Cited below are more examples of the Disproportionate Ratio in action:

Recently, I purchased a CD from a local bank. Its interest yield is less than one percent. This earning does not even beat America's current inflation rate. I'm doing my duty to save, a patriotic gesture. Yet my loyalty to the cause is rewarded by my deposits declining in value.

This same bank will lend me money on my home at 0.045 percent. As of this writing, this bank can go to the discount window to obtain a loan at 0.0075 percent. That represents a spread of 0.0375 percent, a gift from Uncle Sam to the banking system. "Capitalism" in action, courtesy of the U.S. government. That is to say, the American taxpayer.

The situation is similar in Europe. As an update to this report, I came across this article in *Newsweek*:[6]

> Now, near-zero interest rates are drawing hundreds of billions from the pockets of savers and depositing them in the coffers of banks and their investors.
>
> ...near-record profits are being channeled into dividends, bond redemptions, bonuses, and the continued propping up of zombie banks [note: failed banks]. Case in point: one of the world's biggest gamblers on toxic assets, Germany's WestLB, is engineering a profit this year by spinning off a $106 billion "bad bank" to taxpayers. That profit, however, will go to bondholders (i.e., insurance companies and other banks) who have only taken losses on the investments. Cheap

money is supposed to be a stimulus, but it's looking a lot more like a sickly financial addiction.

There is no fairness in these scenarios. Granted, they are biased toward macroeconomics—the big picture of rescuing the banks overall—and policy makers must look at the big picture. But Joe the Plumber cares less about the big picture. He only knows the current mantra of saving being a long-term solution to America's woes is doing nothing more than depleting Joe's already meager assets. Small wonder Joe and others are perplexed and angry.

What's Next?

For a few days, we will wait it out. The next reports will discuss investment banks in more detail and the ongoing debates about legislation on financial reform.

---

[1] "Lessons from the Collapse of Hedge Fund, Long-Term Capital Management." Riskinstitute.ch. http://riskinstitute.ch/146490.htm.

[2] Wikipedia, key in "hedge funds."

[3] Roger Lowenstein, "Who Needs Wall Street?" *The New York Times Magazine*, April 21, 2010, p. 16.

[4] This general discussion is sourced from an article by *The New York Times* correspondent, Charles Duhigg, "Stock Traders Find Speed Pays, in Milliseconds", July 23, 2009; from Time's website.

[5] David M. Herzenhorn and Edward Wyatt, "Banking Bill Negotiations Begin Again," *The New York Times*, April 21, 2010, p. B1. The executives are Robert Fornaro, CEO of AirTran Airways and Sean Cota, CEO of Cota and Cota (a heating oil company).

[6] *Newsweek*, October 11, 2010, p. N.

Report 17

Investment Banks, Underwriting, and Goldman Sachs

Where there is too much, something is missing.
—A Jewish proverb

Investment banking:
The process by which banks redistribute the national income, among themselves.
—Paraphrase of a quote by Leo Rosen[1]

July 16-18, 2010

Hello from Your On the Street Reporter. The votes are in: the Senate passed a financial reform bill. The fix is in: The SEC struck a deal with Goldman Sachs to resolve a fraud complaint against the investment bank. This report provides more information on investment banks, followed by a discussion about SEC and its case against Goldman Sachs. In Report 18, also dated July 16-18, 2010, we examine the legislation coming out of Congress.

Investment Banks, Then and Now

In the past, investment banks, such as Goldman Sachs, helped companies raise capital to build factories, shopping centers, computers, etc. They advised these organizations on how to issue securities (for example, corporate bonds) to obtain money from investors. They participated in the issuance of these securities. Much of their income came from consulting as well as their conduits to the securities marketplace, which they made available to their customers.

These Wall Street firms performed a valuable service for executing complex financial arrangements. They acted as middlemen between those who needed money and those who were looking to invest money. The arrangement (likely) helped Apple find funds to market the Macintosh computer, Intel to build the Intel chip, and Google to fund the development of its search engine. The investment banks' role was to help companies find capital for productive enterprises. They were integral players in fostering the Internet revolution of the 1990s.

Investment banks still perform this vital service, but they do not do as much of it as they did in the past. They do not deal in bonds so much as they deal in the creation and trading of financial instruments. In fairness, many of their financial products are quite useful to society, so I am in no way suggesting investment banks are of no value.[2] Indeed, since the days of Babylon, no progressive society has been able to function without banks.

Nonetheless, as discussed in earlier reports, some of these instruments are of no value to society. For example, they do not contribute to the building of a factory. But they have proven to be fantastically profitable to the investment banks and the banks' investors. They are of huge commercial value (billions of dollars).

The financial transactions with these instruments are a zero sum game. Someone wins; someone loses. That's fine, except for one point. The manner in which these securities have been set up has translated into loses not just at the casino table where the parties are placing their bets. It has cascaded into the lives of nonparticipants: you and me.

It's akin to the two of us sitting at a poker table betting against each other. At another table across the room, someone makes a bet that is completely unrelated to our game and wins. The house comes over to our table and takes away our chips and transports them to the other table.

Win-lose on Wall Street is not a big deal if it is restricted to the contending parties. Otherwise, it is a shell game affecting unwary innocent bystanders. That is the crux of the matter, and that is the reason the average citizen in America has such a deep distrust of Wall Street.

Goldman Sachs and the SEC

The recent SEC accusation against Goldman Sachs has drawn a lot of attention. The SEC states Goldman created a security and traded it as if it were AAA when Goldman knew it was not AAA. On the other side, it hedged against it because Goldman knew the security was trash. The SEC claims these actions constitute fraud because Goldman was misleading clients. It was going short with securities it marketed and sold to customers. Some of Goldman's customers lost millions of dollars.

Goldman's response is threefold: First, the investors were sophisticated and knew what they were getting into. Second, trading at both ends of the win-lose contest is part of the game. (In so many words, let the buyer beware.) Third, Goldman did not realize the market was basically ill-founded, but when it became aware, it took action. This excerpt is taken from Report 5 of this series.[3]

> In December 2006, (computer) models were producing output indicating that something was amiss in the housing market. Nothing of major consequence, but the company had lost money ten days in a row on mortgage business. The officers concluded the situation was worthy of more analysis. The risk managers at Goldman Sachs spent the better part of an afternoon going over the firm's trading positions. They concluded the mortgage backed securities market did not "feel" right. So, they took actions to rein in their risk.

Prior to the SEC ruling, most experts said the case was weak and Goldman would either prevail in court or opt for a settlement. Still, I'm troubled by Goldman's actions. If I were one of Goldman's clients, I would be incensed. If I were Lea County's comptroller who bought these phony AAA products, I would believe I had been deceived.

Goldman is dead wrong. Not all purchasers of their "products" are experts. Some rely on the integrity of Goldman and must trust this firm's judgment. For example, the Lea County School District.

But cutting some slack to Goldman and other investment bankers, we can admire Goldman for being one of a very few companies who had the foresight to see where the mortgage market was heading and to (a) get out of the market and (b) bet against it. And it is not at all unreasonable for a firm to hedge against exposures. During the Senate hearings, a Goldman spokesman said it was Goldman's standard, prudent practice to hedge.

For the sake of argument, let's assume Goldman did not see the subprime meltdown coming before its customers bought lousy securities that were underwritten by Goldman. Let's assume that going long and going short at the same time is ethically acceptable. As claimed, I think it is not only acceptable, but wise, However, I do not think it is ethical to knowingly peddle a low quality security to customers as being AAA, then bet against it. But I'm not an investment banker.

If I were on the panel of the current congressional hearings, I would pose this scenario to Goldman, "If your interpretation of these events is correct—that you did not know the market would tank. But when you did, you got out of it and also bet against it. Did you then go back to your customers who had bought these securities, and advise them to do the same? That is, did you take actions to also rein in the risks of those customers who were trading with you—those who trusted your sales pitch? If not, why not?"

The answer to these questions would have a lot to say about investment bankers' ethics and honesty. But it will not happen. What trader is going to go back to customer and say, "I was wrong. Get

REPORT 17: INVESTMENT BANKS, UNDERWRITING... 241

out of the deal."? Hmm, maybe the trader will. It might lead to another commission.

Besides, my hypothetical situation did not happen. Goldman knew all along that it was hawking securities as prime that were subprime.

It is revealing that trading and investing produced 76 percent of Goldman's income in 2009. Investment banking, "which raises capital for productive enterprise, accounted for a mere 11 percent. Other than that, it could have been a hedge fund."[4]

Underwriting

An investment bank going both short and long on the securities it *underwrites* is skating on thin ethical ice. To see why, consider that the underwriting of financial securities is a means for investment banks to raise capital for their customers (corporations, governments):

- An investment bank's customer issues a security to obtain money.
- The investment bank underwrites the security. That is, it takes on the risk of holding it. But it hopes to sell the security to an investor, which is another customer.
- The underwriter takes a piece on the difference it pays the issuer (customer A) and what it sells to the investor (customer B). Or it takes a commission. Either way, it makes money on the trade.
- In order to sell customer A's security to customer B, the investment bank must convince customer B the security is of high quality. So the investment bank goes long on the security. It often takes to the road to market the offering.
- But to hedge its position on the security, the investment bank takes out insurance on it. A prudent and wise strategy.
- This action is not really going short in the sense of betting against it, as the investment bank has no reason to think the security is of poor quality.

Nonetheless, regardless of a person's wisdom and prudence in going short on something a speculator went long on, the situation can be morally hazardous. As one example (paraphrased from the Senate hearings:[5]

> In May 2007, Goldman executives were discussing problems facing the debt deal it had helped underwrite called Long Beach Mortgage Loan Trust 2006-A, according to e-mails the Senate panel released.
>
> Among the Senate documents is an e-mail from a Goldman executive to Michael Swenson, then a Goldman managing director in the firm's mortgage group, about the 2006-A bond deal. In an 8 a.m. e-mail, Goldman executives circulated a securities report that showed loans inside the pool had soured.
>
> Six minutes later, a Goldman executive wrote, "bad news...(the price decline in the bonds) costs us about $2.5 mm," adding, "good news...we make $5mm" on a derivatives bet against the bonds.
>
> The Senate panel, in a statement over the weekend, said the e-mail showed how the soured Long Beach bonds "would bring [Goldman] $5 million from a bet it had placed against the very securities it had assembled and sold."

Something is wrong here. Recovering from a loss with an insurance policy is one thing. Making a profit from a loss with an insurance policy is another. It's akin to my home insurance company paying me two dollars for every one dollar of loss I experience on my home. I can hardly wait for my house to burn down.

For Goldman Sachs, more than enough was not enough. We can only wonder what the Goldman executive was thinking. I can only conclude that this kind of culture leads to even well-intentioned people not really caring about some of their actions. Either way, they are going to make money. But giving them the benefit of the doubt on these specific practices, there is another variation on going long and short that is not very pretty:

Underhanded Underwriting

Here's another scenario (which actually happened):

- An investment bank's business associate (a hedge fund manager) informs the bank he wants go short and bet against a security containing subprime mortgages (the mortgages have a low quality rating of BBB).
- The investment bank knows of some potential customers who would go long on the security (buy them).
- The hedge fund manager puts together the security and the investment bank markets and sells the security to investors. The investment bank receives huge fees by acting as middleman for the trades.
- The investment bank does not inform its customers the party who put together the security is (a) a hedge fund manager, (b) who knowingly packaged the security with junk, and (c) and has shorted the security by taking out credit default swaps on it.
- When the meltdown comes, the investors lose their investments on the security. The investment bank keeps its fees. The hedge fund manager makes millions of dollars on his shorts.

The marketplace is not for the fainthearted. Some financial experts, described shortly, state that it is not for Wall Street to govern itself, but to make money and help grow the economy. They say it is the job of Uncle Sam to govern Wall Street.

But where is the line drawn to separate risk taking and innovative speculation from downright dishonesty? Going short with credit default swaps to protect one's long position is sound. Going short with credit default swaps to bet against something one peddled to a customer as being long is not just shady, it's fraudulent.

Your Stockbroker Is Shorting the Stock He Is Longing to Peddle

You get a call from your stockbroker (eh, wealth manager). He tells you he has a recommendation on a financial instrument. It looks good; it looks solid. He convinces you to buy. So you do. By the way, this instrument has been created and packaged by your stockbroker's company.

On the other side of your stockbroker's office is another department. As mentioned, these folks are using the very offering you just bought. That's fine, except for one small point. They think the package will tank. So, they hedge against it.

You are supposed to trust your wealth manager. After all, he is managing your wealth. But you are also supposed to know better. You are supposed to know more about the market than your wealth manager. Does this situation make you feel uneasy? It does for me. It makes me think of salesmen peddling snake oil and touting it as an elixir.

Wall Street Shoves It to Main Street

I started research on these reports two years ago with a neutral view of the subject. I was a financial *tabula rasa*. I had no opinion about so-called Wall Street, exemplified by the investment banks. I did not come to my conclusions and opinions lightly. But I have now come to them firmly.

Earlier, I outlined a theoretical scenario of how my childhood home place in Lea County could easily be duped into investing into worthless financial instruments. I made the point that investment banks were basically at moral and ethical odds with themselves in how they went about dealing with Lea County. The July 5, 2010 issue of *Time* magazine provides a nontheoretical example.[6] The article is titled, "How Goldman Trashed a Town."

The article states how Goldman Sachs created a bond (to go long) that the company (initially allegedly, now admittedly) rigged to fail (to go short). The bond (called Abacus) was constructed with the help of a hedge fund manager named John Paulson. (For the now sophisticated reader, it was a synthetic CDO.) What vexed the SEC, not to mention the buyers of the stuff, was that Goldman did not inform investors that Paulson played a role in its creation or that Goldman knew it was faulty.

Goldman initially defended its actions by claiming buyers had "sufficient skill to evaluate its risks." Eventually, the instrument found its way into another instrument and was sold to unwary investors, such as the city of Cedar Rapids. This city saw an AAA rating from the rating agencies and bought $2.6 million of the bonds.

According to this *Time* article, Goldman was aware the bond was suspect, yet its trading desk traded it. And Goldman tells the public it did nothing wrong. *To hell with the customer to whom it sold the junk. He should know better.* In this situation, the investment tanked, Cedar Rapids had to raise its fees for trash removal to get rid of the debt on trash, and Paulson banked $1,000,000,000 (as in $1 billion) for his sterling work.

Goldman claimed no wrong. *Let the buyer beware.* Yet Goldman was instrumental in creating synthetic financial instruments referencing CDS insurance on subprimes and then gamed rating agencies into rating them highly:[7]

> And so, to generate triple-B-rated subprime mortgage bonds, Goldman Sachs did not have to originate $50 billion in home loans. They needed simply to entice (market pessimists and other speculators) to pick 100 different triple-B-bonds and buy $10 million in credit default swaps on them. Once they had this package (a "synthetic CDO," it is called), which was the term of art for a CDO composed of nothing but credit default swaps, they'd take it over to Moody's and Standard & Poor's. "The rating agencies didn't really have their own CDO model," says one former Goldman CDO trader. The banks would send their own model to Moody's and say, "How does this look?" Somehow, roughly 80 percent of what had been risky triple-B-rated bonds now looked like triple-A-rated bonds. The other 20 percent, bearing lower credit ratings, generally were more difficult to sell, but they could, incredibly, simply be piled up into yet another heap and reprocessed yet again into more triple-A—rated bonds. The machine that turned 100 percent lead into an ore that was 80 percent gold and 20 percent lead would accept the residual lead and turn that into gold, too.

Is there anything wrong with this scenario? According to the experts in this field, it is legal. And after all, Goldman was merely being a facilitator between a short party and a long party, merely dealing the hand. But the deck was stacked against the long party.

Should the long party have done its own due diligence? That's the position of Goldman Sachs. Everyone is a big boy and responsible for his actions. But most people and institutions assumed the rating agencies were the guys doing due diligence. They made trustful assumptions. But smart people such as Goldman Sachs (and around twenty brilliant individuals) made millions of dollars by buying CDS on these crappy securities by shorting them.

How about the thousands of pension funds that have relied on the rating agencies and Goldman for their honesty? How about cities, such as Grand Rapids, Iowa, which lost millions of dollars because it bought only AAA securities that were rated AAA by the rating agencies?

On Wall Street, it's Darwin in Guccis. Tough grits for the penny loafer, cornpone folks in Grand Rapids. Besides, Wall Street informs us these events are only speed bumps.

For its efforts Goldman took about 2 percent of the transaction for playing its society-enhancing role as a financial facilitator. As a result, Goldman made millions of dollars for its contribution to America's financial infrastructure.

Underhanded Underwriting II

Risking overexposing you to this fiasco, let's use the scenario cited above and substitute the Goldman gnomes for the imaginary personnel:[8]

- John Paulson (the hedge fund manager and also a player in the Cedar Rapids story, cited earlier) informs Goldman he wants go short and bet against securities (Abacus again) containing subprime mortgages.
- Goldman knows that German Bank IKB would likely go long on the security.

- Paulson—working with and behind a cover organization (ACA Management LLC), which was selected by Goldman to hide Paulson's identity—puts together the securities. Goldman trades them to IKB and others.
- Goldman does not inform IKB (or even ACA) the security is (a) junk, and (b) that Paulson has shorted it.
- When the meltdown came, IKB lost almost all of its $150 million investment. Goldman pocketed about $15 million in fees. Paulson took away about $1 billion.

Goldman Games a Gamer

One final point about this specific subject. I spoke earlier of AIG and its key role in the nearly perfect financial storm. AIG, the big insurance kid on the worldwide block, was "nearly the only buyer"[9] of subprime lead that Goldman gamed into prime-time gold. AIG was the long side of the short CDS buyer. Yet, because of its size and influence in the market, if it failed it would have repercussions of great consequence.

America, the land of rugged capitalism pretty much owns AIG. Let's hope we citizens get paid the bonuses the AIG executives paid themselves. By the way, billions of dollars of our bailout money that went first to AIG went second to Goldman Sachs so that AIG could pay off Goldman's credit default swaps.

Mea Culpa...Now Leave Me to My Sordid Details

Today (July 16, 2010), the news media announced the SEC and Goldman Sachs settled the suit.[10] The company agreed to pay a $550 million fine and admit it did not provide vital information to investors about Abacus.

One moment. The Abacus investors lost about $1 billion. Goldman was penalized just over half of that amount. And the SEC gets $300 million of that figure. Goldman's fine is less than 5 percent of its net income, and less than 2 percent of its net cash balance. Fantastic.

Did the city of Cedar Rapids get any of the money? Not one red cent. The bribe was paid to sophisticated investors: The Royal Bank of Scotland and IKB Deutsch Industriebank. It's amazing. The organizations "who should have known better" are compensated. Organizations who could not possibly have known better get nothing.

Goldman's chairman Lloyd Blankfein, not a proponent of the buck stops here, keeps his job. Instead, a lowly Goldman VP has been named in a separate fraud complaint. Goldman has agreed to help the government in its suit against this man. Whatever happened to accountability? This episode is offensive to an outside observer.

Charlie Rose and Rose-Colored Glasses

This evening, (July 16, 2010) Charlie Rose had three financial experts on his program. He asked them about this settlement. Their answers grouped around these observations:

- Goldman did nothing illegal.
- The SEC had little or no case.
- Corporate America saluted Goldman and was moving business their way.
- Main Street America (the Cedar Rapids of this world) was taking its business elsewhere.
- These experts seemed a bit perplexed. As they adjusted their rose-colored glasses they said they were puzzled about the bad press that had come to Goldman Sachs; about why Main Street was in an uproar.
- Goldman would easily weather the storm, and before long, it would be business as usual.

What was not mentioned:

- Goldman deceived its customers and one of its business associates.
- It operated with conflicts of interest.
- Although within the bounds of legality, any thought of a Christian/Judeo morality and associated responsibility to the

marketplace were absent. (The documentation about Goldman from the hearings does not make for pretty reading.)
- The incompetent and dishonest performance of the rating agencies further deceived potential buyers of the bond.
- While Joe the Plumber is collecting unemployment, Joe at AIG (responsible for billions of dollars of losses to taxpayers' money because of his keen sense of never-ending bubbles) has retired with millions of dollars in his bank account.
- The Goldman executives are once again bringing home millions of dollars of bonus money.
- While they are cashing their checks, hundreds of thousands of individuals do not have a check to cash.
- Yet, these men are perplexed about it all.

In Report 16, I made the point that much of this hedging is taking out a policy on a neighbor's house and betting on a fire—or setting the fire. It seems to me that Goldman essentially set up an incendiary situation, bet on a fire, and waited for the flames. I am still wrestling with why it is considered a sound idea for people to be able to take out insurance on something they *do not own*. (I hope my more erudite readers will educate me about this matter.)

Worse still, this modest slap on the wrist will only encourage more reckless and unethical behavior. Other Wall Street firms must be breathing a deep sigh of relief. Yet it appears so many people don't know what happened with this settlement. Maybe they don't care.

Warren Buffett and Charlie Munger

I have mentioned Warren Buffett several times in these reports. I have great respect for the man, especially because of his warning of the dangers of unregulated derivatives (See Appendix A, in Report 8). He is an icon in the financial industry and one of the richest people on this planet. I've not read or heard one single word about him that was negative. An all-American guy, he plays ping pong, strums guitars, and cheers for the University of Nebraska football team.

I admire Mr. Buffett but I am puzzled by some of his statements and actions. During a meeting with his company, when asked to comment of the financial problems and the role of Goldman Sachs, he responded, "I haven't seen anything in Goldman's behavior that makes it any more subject to criticism than Wall Street generally."[11] Faint praise, as he then went on to say that Wall Street is a "very defective system."

He defends Moody's, and says the organization has "incredibly wonderful businesses." Yes, Moody's, a firm that through both greed and incompetence, allowed billions of dollars of worthless securities to be fostered-off onto unwary investors who actually believed AAA meant AAA...when it really meant junk.

His partner Charlie Munger admits Wall Street (the tiger) is defective, but blames a dysfunctional government (the tiger keeper) on the problems, "When the tiger gets out and starts creating damage, it's insane to blame the tiger, it's the idiot tiger keeper" that deserves the blame.

Does Mr. Munger mean a firm can do anything it can get away with? It has no ethical obligation to anyone but itself and its stockholders? Any sense of imposing a scintilla of morality into its practices is the responsibility of the government?[12] I hope not and so should you. We are pawns on the chessboards of the Buffetts and Mungers of the world. Much of our welfare is interconnected with and dependent upon their behavior.

By the way, Buffett's company owns twenty percent of Moody's and has invested in Goldman as well. Another by the way: For the tea party folks, I would be careful about wishing for the dismantlement of the government. You may get what you wish for.

If I were not such a proponent of free enterprise, the Goldman Sachs story recounted in this report would lead me to check out the book *Das Kapital* from the library.

A Pragmatic Broker's Perspective

After filing Report 17 in this series, one of my friends, who is in the "wealth management" business, sent me these thoughts.

The way I see it, there are many roles in the "Wall Street industry":
1. Investment Banker
2. Broker-Dealer
3. Trader
4. Sell-side Researcher (i.e. rating stocks for potential buyers)
5. Investment Advisor (Fiduciary)
6. Bond Credit Rater
7. Asset Manager (mutual funds, hedge funds, etc)
8. Commercial Banker

Currently, Goldman Sachs and Morgan Stanley play all roles except #6. BofA, Citigroup, UBS, and JP Morgan, all play in five or more roles. Most of these roles bear inherent conflicts of interest, because there is so much "customer overlap." Much of the overlap is at the institutional level, and doesn't directly impact the individual investor. [My note, Yes, but the so-called institutional investor often sells his wares to the Lea Counties and Cedar Rapids of this world.]

But, imagine playing at a full poker table and discovering that all the other players at the table were a team!!

I am truly a conservative free market advocate, but my sense of unfairness is piqued. If earlier conservative U.S. governments can force Standard Oil and AT&T to breakup, what is our current liberal government doing? The ineptitude under Obama and the current Congress leadership is mind-boggling! These people are merely a bunch of poll-watching populists with no direction or values other than their own self-promotion. An aside ... read "Game Change" to get a feel of what our politicians stand for.

Now, what does all this mean for the retail investor (you) and the retail advisor (me)?

I play only one role, the Fiduciary, i.e. one who puts his client's interest first. I haven't and won't promote products developed by my own employer, whether they believe in them or not.

I do not allow my clients to engage in a "principal trade", i.e. where the counter-party is my employer. Any of my client trades are "agency", i.e. where my employer acts as a middleman dealing with some external party.

I use only research from third-party providers, and I recommend only mutual funds that are managed by a third-party. The vast majority of my clients pay a fee based on the value of their assets with me, and do not pay any transactional charges.

My only motivation is to see my clients' assets grow in a risk-controlled manner ... and, consequently, my compensation.

You, as a retail investor, can rest assured that your interests are well served if your investments advisor subscribes to most or all of these principles. Then, all you need to worry about are ... the markets!!

If only all wealth managers and investment bankers operated this way. In subsequent reports, I change the pace to examine on a more general level what is happening to America and its foundations of republican, democratic capitalism. For now, let's look at recent Capitol Hill financial reform activities.

---

[1] Whose original quote was "private banking" and not "investment banking." See "Political Lexicon," *New Republic*, July 3, 1945.

[2] Electric cars, fuel-cell technology, wind farms, to name only three.

[3] And sourced from: Joe Nocera, "Risk Mismanagement," *The New York Times Magazine*, January 4, 2009, p. 27.

[4] Lowenstein, "Who Needs Wall Street?" p. 16.

[5] Compiled from congressional e-mails by Mark Gongloff and Serena Ng of *The Wall Street Journal*.

[6] Stephen Gandel, "How Goldman Trashed a Town," *Time*, July 5, 2010, pp. 32-33.

[7] Lewis, *The Big Short*, p. 76.

[8] Reuters, "Factbox: How Goldman's ABACU.S. Deal Worked," April 18, 2010.

[9] Lewis, *The Big Short*, p. 83.

[10] David Lieberman and Matt Krantz, "Goldman Sachs Concedes Mistake, Settles SEC Suit," *USA TODAY*, July 16, 2010, pp. B1-B2.

[11] Scott Peterson, "Mr. Bufettt Goes to Bat for Goldman, Moody's," *The New York Times*, May 3, 2010, p. C1. Quotes in next two paragraphs are also from this source.

[12] One reader of this report took me to task with my opinion about Mr. Munger's opinion. He told me, "It is insane to blame a tiger for being a tiger when the keeper allows it to roam freely amongst the sheep....History is a hard task-master and it informs us that each and every time you loosen the leash on the tiger, you get bitten in the ass, at best." I agree with his second assertion. I have reservations about his first. If business has no ethics by which it operates, no number of leashes from Uncle Sam can control what will become social chaos.

Report 18

Financial Reform: Putting the Wrappings around Legislation

*We are told by Wall Street that greed is good.
We are told by Uncle Sam that greed must be regulated.
Who regulates Uncle Sam?*

July 16-18, 2010

Hello from Your On the Street Reporter. This report is devoted to the congressional bill dealing with financial reform. The bill comprises 848 pages. It is not yet a formal law. It will be expanded and the current text will likely be revised.

The legislation, known as the Dodd-Frank Wall Street Reform and Consumer Protection Act creates at least one new government agency and several committees and oversight groups to monitor the financial industry. At this time, no one knows how many additional Uncle Sam's minions will be recruited to build yet more Dickensian bureaucracies.

From my initial and general review, it is certain the legislation will result in more government overhead, more red tape, and additional expense for Americans to do business with banks and other financial institutions. Some of its provisions will prove to be burdensome to both banks and bank customers. Let's hope it will also at least curtail (if not eliminate) some of the Wall Street excesses described in previous reports.

Laissez-faire government-stay-away fans are upset. Keynesian government-intervention fans are ecstatic. Regardless of their views, one thing is clear. As always, if an industry does not regulate its excesses, the government will step in, usually accompanied with its own excesses. And that is what has happened in this instance. Wall Street fell on its own sword.

But how big is the sword? Will it cut into the huge profits being gained by the investment banking industry; profits that have abetted Wall Street's lobbying influence on Congress?[1] Will it guide the industry's actions back to its past practices of performing services useful to America's infrastructure? Will it mitigate Wall Street's surreal compensation to people whose services are irrelevant to America's GNP? Can it moderate Wall Street's condescending behavior toward common America? It is not just an issue about money or wealth. It is an issue about ethics and fair play.

My initial conclusion is maybe, if the final bill does the following:

- Forces Wall Street and its CEOs to fully fund its own failures.
- Forces the rating agencies to be honest (and at least reasonably competent) in their assessments.
- Allows a company's stockholders to determine the compensations of senior management—not just advise. Creates an ombudsman to represent the mom-and-pop stockholders' interests *vis-à-vis* the board of directors, the CEO, and organizations that have large blocks of shares (such as unions and retirement funds).
- Requires officer compensation to be tied to long-time performance of the company but does not stipulate the specifics of compensation. The officer in a publicly traded company must be held personally accountable for his actions, just as he or she is in a privately held enterprise.

- Insures a person does not sit on the boards of companies that have interconnections, such as is stipulated in the tax code's "related parties."
- Forces mortgage companies to actually look at the creditworthiness of a prospective home buyer instead of the fog-a-mirror check.
- Denies lenders getting into bed with mortgage brokers to encourage risky loans.
- Brings transparency to the trading of over-the-counter financial instruments and hedge funds.
- Requires banks to separate themselves from self-serving trading, to force them to be more like commercial banks: serving their *walk-in customers*. This includes restrictions on proprietary trading.
- Prevents banks from off-loading all their mortgage loans onto someone else.
- Increases the capital for banks to hold.
- Takes away the deceptive practice of off-the-books record keeping.
- Revamps Fannie Mae and Freddie Mac.
- Allows Uncle Sam to step in and break up a financial oligarchy with the associated costs apportioned to the stockholders and the consortium(s) (for example, a clearinghouse) to which the financial oligarchy belongs.
- Establishes rules on government employees revolving in and out of the doors of the buildings on K Street (lobbyist's doors).
- Addresses the issues of bigness and interconnectedness.

If existing agencies would do their job properly, the legislation could accomplish these goals by using the current governmental apparatus. However, the embryonic bill states that some new bureaucracies will be created. We can only hope the law does not create agencies to do what current agencies should have been doing in the first place. I have made the case that many of the problems pertaining to the role of government in this crisis stemmed from the fact that government did not perform the job it was mandated to do.

The enactments I have listed above will only be as effective as the competence by which they are administered. In the past, the regulators were in place with their rules but they did not perform their jobs properly.

Will they do it now? Probably for a while, and then bureaucratic languor will set in.[2] Rules will be ignored or circumvented. An Ayn Rand administration will ascend to the throne and another storm will ensue, with different financial instruments creating the mayhem. Then, an anti-Ayn Rand president will take over. The process will start again with more governmental filters set up, which will further dissipate the already vanishing flow of free markets in America.

The bill supposedly addresses the issue of too big to fail. I read where it will require $50 billion to be accumulated by a community of banks to address a failure. But the very size and interconnectedness of this industry makes this amount of money a drop in the bucket in what would be needed to do another bailout. For example TARP was $700 billion. I am not sure the bill addresses the fundamental issues of too big to fail and welfare capitalism.

Even if the final enactments on this legislation address the too big to fail issue, Congress is not known for its clairvoyance. Eventually, another meltdown will occur. It will likely not be of the sort we just experienced. Big business will figure out a way to game Pennsylvania Ave. and Capitol Hill. It always has. Just consider: Enron, Internet bubble, Teapot Dome, Hunt's silver market, on-and-on. And it always will.

That's it for now. We'll take a more detailed look at the legislation and keep track of how Congress and the regulatory bodies are putting the details into the law—as well as the reactions of Wall Street to these activities.

Report 18, Segment Two
October 16, 2010

Hello from Your On the Street Reporter. I've been in hibernation, ensconced in a self-made cocoon, trying to veer away from the tumults of the current financial depression that continues to knock on the door of my IRA.

Call it what you will, "recession", "great recession", "quite large, yet not quite as large as the really big one in 1929". Whatever its label, it's big. Just ask those citizens, almost 10 percent of the working-force population, who cannot find a job.

I have also spent a few hours looking over 848 pages of the Dodd-Frank Wall Street Reform and Consumer Protection Act. Thus, the lapse between this segment of the report and the first segment. I have also reviewed comments from industry experts and businesses about this legislation.

In this segment, I will attempt to write a nontechnical summary of the bill. For better or worse, the opinions are mine, and as the old saying goes, people often accumulate opinions about a subject when their understanding of the subject is at its weakest. At this stage of my research on the nearly perfect financial storm and my experiences in banking and business, I trust these opinions are well founded. So, here goes:

New Government Agencies, Committees, Bureaus, and Offices

The Dodd-Frank act calls for the creation of thirteen new forms of governmental bureaucracies! The act calls for the abolishment of *one entity*, the Office of Thrift Supervision. But its functions (at taxpayer expense) remain intact and its employees are being transferred to the comptroller with their jobs guaranteed. Congress regaled these people as being "dysfunctional." Therefore, to reward their dysfunctional performance, they stay on the taxpayer payroll. Preposterous. Another Charles Dickens farce.

Advanced Warning Council Dropped from the Act

The preliminary press releases from Congress about the act discuss the creation of a new entity named the Advanced Warning Council. It is not included in the final act. I suspect because it (notes in parentheses are mine) "creates a council to identify (does not say how) and address (does not say how) systemic risks posed by large, complex companies, products, and activities (does not explain anything about large or complex) before they threaten the stability of the economy."

Perhaps this part of the act was dropped because the legislators realized they might be creating an organization whose mission was impossible to define.

New Governmental Entities

Listed below are the thirteen additions to Uncle Sam's crown, followed with a brief summary of their responsibilities. A qualification to what follows: Many of these entities are taking on tasks that were supposed to have been performed by current government institutions. Some appear to be stepping on the turf of existing bureaucracies. Time will tell, but it appears there will be considerable confusion and overlap between the new and old organizations.

My descriptions use italics to highlight passages from the legislation. For ease of reading, some text has been edited and shortened.

1. Financial Stability Oversight Council
2. Office of Financial Research
3. Consumer Financial Protection Bureau
4. Office of Financial Literacy
5. National Consumer Complaint Hotline
6. Office of Vice Chairman for Supervision
7. Central Clearing and Exchange Trading
8. Office of Minority and Women Inclusion
9. Office of Housing Counseling
10. Office of Credit Ratings

11. Federal Insurance Office
12. Investment Advisory Committee
13. Congo Conflict Minerals

1: Financial Stability Oversight Council

This council will be composed of a body of regulators and advisors who are tasked with what current government agencies should have been doing all along: *(A) to identify risks to the financial stability of the United States that could arise from the material financial distress or failure, or ongoing activities, of large, interconnected bank holding companies or nonbank financial companies, or that could arise outside the financial services marketplace; (B) to promote market discipline, by eliminating expectations on the part of shareholders, creditors, and counterparties of such companies that the Government will shield them from losses in the event of failure; and (C) to respond to emerging threats to the stability of the United States financial system.*

Comments: This charter represents what the Federal Reserve Board, FDIC, SEC, and Treasury have been created to carry out. I grant that it brings together the heads of the major agencies but these people should have been working together anyway.

The body is allowed to regulate (and divest) any company in the United States if the company's holdings pose a financial threat to the stability of the United States. That's a very big stick.

Trust busting? I'm not convinced clauses (B) and (C) are compatible, because by the very nature of the financial system, it does not respond to bubble bursts and credit freezes. In order to achieve these goals, the system would have to be disemboweled.

2: Office of Financial Research

This office is to be created within Treasury and is to be staffed with, as stated in a press release: *a highly sophisticated staff of economists, accountants, lawyers, former supervisors, and other specialists to support the council's work by collecting financial data and conducting economic analysis. Through the Office of Financial Research and member agencies the council will collect and analyze data to identify and monitor emerging risks to the economy and make this information public in periodic reports and testimony to Congress every year.*

Comments: Again, these responsibilities are supposedly already in the hands of the financial regulatory agencies. The Federal Reserve alone has hundreds of economists who do nothing but financial research.

3: Consumer Financial Protection Bureau

This new bureau will be led by an independent director appointed by the president and confirmed by the Senate. It will be funded by the Fed. The bureau will be able to autonomously write rules for consumer protections governing all financial institutions—banks and nonbanks (with assets over $10 billion)—offering consumer financial services or products.

Comments: Currently, the following government bodies provide consumer protection: Office of the Comptroller of the Currency, Office of Thrift Supervision, Federal Deposit Insurance Corporation, Federal Reserve, National Credit Union Administration, the Department of Housing and Urban Development, and the Federal Trade Commission.

The act directs this new kid on the block to consolidate the responsibilities of seven separate consumer protection fiefdoms! Why not do it right, and dismantle these disparate turfs and start over? It's the only way to get a clean slate. As best I can tell, not very much is dissolved with this act. What is clear is that a lot of redundancy has been added to functions that were ill functioning to begin with.

4: Office of Financial Literacy

As part of the Consumer Financial Protection Bureau, the Office of Financial Literacy will: *In consultation with the Financial Literacy and Education Commission,* (develop) *a strategy (including, to the extent practicable, measurable goals and objectives) to increase the financial literacy of investors in order to bring about a positive change in investor behavior.*

Comments: What might this change entail? We can only hope America's citizens will be bombarded with enough financial literacy propaganda to become ashamed to hock themselves into near insolvency with huge credit card, mortgage, and Best Buy debts.

"Positive change in their behavior": I won't dwell in this report on how many parts of the act have Uncle Sam once again taking the reins of responsibility for what should be the responsibility of a private citizen.

5: National Consumer Complaint Hotline: State Appraiser Certifying and Licensing Agency, and Financial Institution Regulator

The act provides for the establishment of a toll-free hotline and an Internet address for consumers to send in complaints about financial institutions. Databases are to be created to store the complaints and all government financial agencies are to have access to the data. Complaints will be handled by a State Appraiser Certifying and Licensing agency, and a financial institution regulator.

Comments: What the final effect of the hotline with this agency and current institutions will be is anyone's guess. Clearly, America's consumer finance system is broken. Usurious credit card rates and obscene adjustable rate mortgages are two examples—not to mention the recent revelations of mortgage companies throwing away original mortgage papers and employing "robo-signers" to attest to the accuracy of the "papers."

Something needs to be done to protect the unsophisticated innocent from the sophisticated crook. But how many hotline operators in India will be required is a big question mark. What is not a question is, once again, the fact that more overhead is being added to doing business in America.

6: Office of Vice Chairman for Supervision

This person will be appointed by the president and will be a member of the Federal Reserve Board. The job will be to shadow the Fed's supervisory and regulatory operations and report to Congress and the president about them. This job is what the Fed Chairman, also appointed by the president, is tasked to perform.

Comments: I call this office "The Shadow Fed Chairman" because it does indeed shadow the FRB chairman. It was created because of Alan Greenspan, who proved to be a shadow of a regulator.

7: Central Clearing and Exchange Trading

This part of the act (from a congressional press release): *Requires central clearing and exchange trading for derivatives that can be cleared and provides a role for both regulators and clearinghouses to determine which contracts should be cleared.*

Requires data collection and publication through clearinghouses or swap repositories to improve market transparency and provide regulators important tools for monitoring and responding to risks.

Adds safeguards to system by ensuring dealers and major swap participants have adequate financial resources to meet responsibilities. Provides regulators the authority to impose capital and margin requirements on swap dealers and major swap participants, not end users.

Comments: This is one of the most important actions in the Dodd-Frank bill. The huge trades in financial securities[3] that were expressly exempted from oversight by Congress and examination by the public will be subject to review. However, it appears the clearinghouses that will be established from this act will have Uncle Sam's arm around their shoulders. Section 806 of the act establishes that the Federal Reserve will avail a clearing house (or any other financial institution) "discount and borrowing privileges" under "unusual or exigent circumstances."

Clearinghouses are not immune from collapsing. One almost did in 1987: the Chicago Mercantile Exchange. Financial clearinghouses are connected to the overall banking system, so I have trouble with this part of the act. I see why such a clause is in the act from a political standpoint, but I think putting this burden of bailout once again onto the taxpayer is wrong. It continues a precedent that in the long run will undermine citizens' support of a system that many already view as ethically bankrupt. Section 806 is a positive part of the act but it supports the notion of too big to fail.

8: Office of Minority and Women Inclusion

The act requires each government financial institution to create an Office of Minority and Women Inclusion, to provide: *(A) equal employment opportunity and the racial, ethnic, and gender diversity of the workforce and senior management of the agency; (B) increased participation of minority-owned and women-owned businesses in the programs and contracts of the agency, including standards for coordinating technical assistance to such businesses; and (C) assessing the diversity policies and practices of entities regulated by the agency.*

Comments: What these noble sentiments have to do with the financial meltdown and Wall Street failures is beyond me. It's another example of (likely) getting irrelevant legislation (irrelevant to the issue of the act) into the act in order to gain support for the act. It matters little that this part of the act has nothing to do with financial reform, or that it clearly impinges upon the charter of the ongoing Equal Employment Opportunities (EEO) Commission.

9: Office of Housing Counseling

This entity is also called "Expand and Preserve Home Ownership through Counseling Act." The head of this group has an Orwellian moniker: Director of Housing Counseling. This senior executive position will be placed in the Department of Housing and Urban Development (HUD) to provide the: *establishment, coordination, and administration of all regulations, requirements, standards, and performance measures under programs and laws administered by the Department that relate to housing counseling, homeownership counseling (including maintenance of homes), mortgage-related counseling (including home equity conversion mortgages and credit protection options to avoid foreclosure), and rental housing counseling, including the requirements, standards, and performance measures relating to housing counseling.*

Comments: First, HUD already performs many of these functions. Second, and again, why should taxpayers pay for such services? Third, I have come to the conclusion that government should not be in the business of promoting home ownership, nor should mortgage interest payments be tax deductible.

This financial crisis has highlighted one of the big problems associated with large home ownership populations: lack of mobility. If a homeowner cannot sell his home, he has trouble relocating to another job.

By the way, socialistic Canada and Europe do not allow interest to be deducted from taxes. Only in free market America is this practice part of the landscape.

10: Office of Credit Ratings

This office will operate under the SEC, which will be doing what the SEC should have been doing all along: *Promote accuracy in credit ratings issued by nationally recognized statistical rating organizations, and ensure that such ratings are not unduly influenced by conflicts of interest.*

Comments: These reports have made the point several times about the huge role the credit rating agencies played in the meltdown. As well, the incompetence of the SEC in its lax oversight of the agencies has been described. But giving some benefit of the doubt, I'm told the SEC is underfunded and understaffed. Also, its new management is a breath of fresh air and appears to be taking hold of its responsibilities.

11: Federal Insurance Office

One of the major reasons for the nearly perfect financial storm was the absence of regulation on insurance instruments called credit default swaps (CDS). These derivatives became one of the largest, if not the largest, financial instruments in the world. Because they were used to short (bet against) toxic mortgage backed securities, lack of oversight and regulation has spelled financial disaster for many businesses and people.

It appears the act addresses this gap: *Monitor all aspects of the insurance industry, including identifying issues or gaps in the regulation of insurers that could contribute to a systemic crisis in the insurance industry or the United States financial system;*

Comments: I cannot discern how this office will interact with the fifty state governments. It mentions "consultation," which will not be enough. Perhaps other additions will clarify this aspect of the act.

12: Investment Advisory Committee

The lobbyists prevail once more. This part of the act creates a committee composed of investors whose job is to advise the SEC on how to regulate and deal with investors. I'll wager my last mortgage backed security that the "investors" will not be mom and pop folks who trade with Chuck (Charles) Schwab. They will be high-end Wall Street movers, shakers, and traders.

13: Congo Conflict Minerals

In a final feat of irrelevance to this financial crisis, the act requires anyone doing minerals securities business with the Republic of Congo not to do it illegally. It requires the State Department to "address" the Congo illegal minerals trade. What about other countries with minerals? Why in this act? This clause will likely hinder this country's position with its competitors. The lobbyists on K Street being paid by Nigeria are licking their chops. So is Nigeria. It can only be concluded that the Nigerian lobbyists forked out more golf trips, NFL tickets, money to fund raisers, *ad nauseum* to Capitol Hill than did the Congo lobbyists.

Studies

In addition to the major actions cited above—in many cases, the associated creation of governmental bodies—the act stipulates conducting the following studies (I may have missed some):

- A study of the effects of size and complexity of financial institutions on capital market efficiency and economic growth.
- A study to evaluate the definition of core deposits for the purpose of calculating the insurance premiums of banks (This study includes four other "sub-studies.")
- A study of the effect of drywall (!) presence on foreclosures. Specifically, the impact that drywall imported from China from

2004 to 2007 had on a bank kicking a homeowner out of his house. We can only guess how such irrelevant topics find their way into pieces of legislation. Maybe the plaster wall lobby was involved.
- A study to evaluate how effective a currently existing interagency task force is combating foreclosure scams and loan modification fraud scams. It matters little that all states currently have their legal departments aggressively pursuing the very same subject.

How many studies have been conducted by the federal government resulting in no action? Thousands. How many labor hours and how much tax money had been wasted on these studies? Billions. For my readers who have never worked in the federal government, it might seem impossible that a study would result in *nothing happening*. After all, the purpose of the study is for something *to happen*. My readers who have worked in Washington, DC know what I am talking about.

Cutting Congress and Wall Street lobbyists some slack, the conclusion of this report takes on a more positive note.

Room for Hope

As mentioned, the act requires central clearing and exchange trading for derivatives. As stated in a congressional press release, *it provides a role for both regulators and clearlinghouses to determine which contracts should be cleared. It requires data collection and publication through clearlinghouses or swap repositories to improve market transparency and provide regulators important tools for monitoring and responding to risks. It adds safeguards to the system by ensuring dealers and major swap participants have adequate financial resources to meet responsibilities. It provides regulators the authority to impose capital and margin requirements on swap dealers and major swap participants, not end users.*

It does not cover all items I listed at the beginning of this report. It duplicates past incompetency on the part of Uncle Sam, but does rein in some of Wall Street's fickle underhandedness. Nonetheless,

I do not see how the bill will avoid creating yet more roadblocks to efficient commerce.

In addition to conventional banks and bank holding companies, the bill does contain clauses that allow regulators to tear-down other financial institutions. If done properly, this part of the act will allow Uncle Sam to place a failed company into bankruptcy. The stockholders should take the bath with such an action, as well as bond holders and holders of commercial paper, not the taxpayer. Let's see who wins on this part of the bill.

As we can see, the legislation is heavy-handed, but then, so is Wall Street. Tit-for-tat.

---

[1] And the ability for a corporation to exercise "free speech" with its massive campaign contributions.

[2] Some good news. As of this writing, the Federal Housing Finance Agency (overseer of Fannie Mae and Freddie Mac) has issued sixty-four subpoenas to various financial institutions, seeking documents about securities these organizations bought. The actions are intended to determine how mortgage securities were packaged, with or without fraud intent, and then to go after the fraudulent companies. Fannie and Freddie are following in this wake as well. See Gretchen Morgenson, "Holding Bankers' Feet to the Fire," *The New York Times*, July 18, 2010, p. BU-1.

[3] It is not known exactly how big the financial derivatives market is because it has not been subject to public disclosure. *The New York Times* states (from the Bank for International Settlements) that this market had a gross credit exposure of $3.5 trillion at the end of 2009. See Gretchen Morgenson, "Count of Sequels to TARP," *The New York Times*, October 3, 2010, p. BU 1.

Report 19

Synthetic Capitalism

In America, the only respectable socialism is socialism for the rich.
—John Kenneth Galbraith

December 5, 2010

Hello from Your On the Street Reporter. I return to a subject I have made passing references to in earlier reports: The myth that America—that is, big company America—operates on capitalistic, free market principles.

Low Interest Loans for (Big) Failures of (Big) Companies

I have made the point several times that during a financial bubble burst, banks will do just the opposite of what they are supposed to do. They will withdraw credit. Because the financial industry is so tightly interconnected, banks will also stop trading with each other as well. This situation makes it more difficult and sometimes impossible for small businesses and individual families to gain credit from them. Essentially, the market freezes.

It is left to the federal government to come to the rescue. But to whom: big business, small business, or families? To the sector that started the mess in the first place, but that can't be allowed to fail? That would be big business.

Recently, the Dodd-Frank law forced the Fed to make public the firms that received emergency lending during the 2008 crisis. No surprises, as the biggest recipients were the large commercial and investment banks, courtesy of the Primary Dealer Credit Facility, those firms too big to fail; thus "primary dealers."[1]

These firms had to post collateral for the loans, some of which were of dubious quality. Of course, the firms had become credit risks in the first place. Hmm. Sounds similar to the subprime mortgage market: lend money to unqualified parties, all the while knowing it would be risky. But the subprime lenders made sure they got a very high return for this risk. Not so for Uncle Sam. As one example, during the last two weeks of September, 2008 the Fed was loaning money to the tune of $100 billion a day at a 2.25 percent interest rate.

Any sensible lender would have charged at least 7 percent. But the system was in trouble and supposedly could not afford to pay a high interest rate, so the taxpayer lost about $325 billion during that one period alone.

Meanwhile, Joe the plumber cannot get a loan from his bank. Meanwhile, you and I are being paid less than one percent on our CDs and saving deposits at the local bank. It's little more than a mugging. The government and big business are the muggers. You and I are the mugged.

Fannie Mae and Freddie Mac: Socialistic "Fairness" in Action

I made reference at the beginning of the report to the common misunderstanding in America that this country operates on capitalistic principles, and that the rest of the world (especially, gasp, Europe!) is socialistic. Here are two definitions introduced in an earlier report that will be helpful during this discussion:[2]

- Capitalism: An economic system based on the private ownership of the means of production and distribution of goods, characterized by a free competitive market and motivation by profit.

- Socialism: A political theory or system in which the means of production and distribution are controlled by the people (state) and operated according to equity and fairness rather than market principles.

Given these definitions, several European countries do indeed practice socialism and considerably more than the United States. Nonetheless, market principles are integral to Europe's economies. But the control of the state over many institutions (utilities, health care, etc), with associated high taxes, has come to define the modern notion of socialism.

Sidebar 19-1: Balancing the Views.

I have been persistent in these reports regarding my criticism of America's financial infrastructure. I have done so with the hope of having repairs made to a historically vibrant system. In fairness, when our banking system and overall competitive culture is compared to countries such as Greece and Italy, we can be thankful we have a long way to go before reaching the point of government indolence and taxpayer torpor that exists in these nations and other places around the world.

The phrase in the definition of capitalism, "a free competitive market" has begun to ring hallow for America. Fannie and Freddie epitomize the situation: "9 out of every 10 new mortgages are sold to, or *guaranteed* by, arms of the U.S. Government; the majority of them to Fannie and Freddie."[3]

Even though these institutions were privatized during the Johnson administration, they have always been considered to have the backing of the U.S. government. Other countries consider them an extension of Uncle Sam.

I have made points in this regard in previous reports. For now, given Fannie's and Freddie's role in America's finances, our so-called free enterprise mortgage market is little more than a governmentally subsidized bazaar.

Here is an update to previous reports about Barney Franks' Favorite Follies:[4]

- Fannie Mae needs another $8.4 billion in federal money to cover continuing high rates of mortgage defaults

- The taxpayer costs of supporting Fannie and Freddie is now at $145 billion since Uncle Sam took them over in late 2008.

- Estimates are now at $154 billion to rescue the organizations.

- However, these figures do not include dividends that are to be paid to the U.S. Treasury based on its ownership of preferred shares in the companies. If these amounts are included, by 2013, Fannie and Freddy are expected to need $221 to $363 billion.

- The good news is that all parties belong to the U.S. government, so it's a "Rob Peter to pay Paul situation." But in this situation, "Peter" is you and me. "Paul" is Uncle Sam.

- More good news: Previous estimates had the tab at $400 billion.

The United States Government has taken an 80 percent ownership in each company and the Treasury Department now controls them. It's an example of nationalization. And here's more:

Updates

This section summarizes recent events that have taken place between Uncle Sam and several financial institutions. Once again, it deals with interconnectedness of large institutions.

AIG. Because of AIG's sensationally inept management, the Fed took over a 79.9 percent equity stake in the company. As mentioned earlier, Goldman Sachs received $13 billion of this money because it had shorted AIG's securities. A few months after this time, and after Goldman had recovered, it paid out eight-figure bonuses to its high-level executives.

Bear Sterns. During 2008, the Fed engineered JPMorgan Chase's takeover of Bear Sterns (Bear). Morgan did not want to take ownership of Bear's toxic mortgages. So, the Fed agreed to shoulder $29 billion of garbage that Morgan rejected.

Why not let Bear fail? The government almost did but after going over Bear's books, it was determined that the firm had about 150,000,000 trades on its book with more than 5,000 companies. If Bear went under, so might other firms.

This example is symptomatic of the nation's and the world's financial system. By its very nature the collapse of big banks will invariably spillover into the economy as a whole. As John Cassidy puts it, it was an acknowledgment that "some of the losses from the subprime debacle would have to be socialized."[5]

GM and Chrysler. Likewise, the U.S. government rescued GM and Chrysler. If it had not, several hundred thousand workers would have been out of work and eligible for Uncle Sam's unemployment doles.

Citigroup, Bank of America. I could continue this farce but it is too depressing. Okay, two more: the federal government has shouldered further losses on $306 billion of toxic assets owned by Citigroup and $118 billion owned by the Bank of America.

Robosigners. AKA Forgers. Many lending institutions purposely lowered the standards for lending. They forged documents, discarded originals, and hired gnomes to "robosign" papers the gnomes did not understand (nor likely read). I cannot interpret these actions as honest mistakes. I interpret them as fraud. Will the guilty go punished? If so, only the corporate side will suffer. Fines will be taken from the shareholders' premiums. Most of the individuals behind this sleaze will go scot-free.

Even worse, Robert L. Christensen, an expert on finance says, "There may be reluctance to challenge the banks because of the overall fragility of the financial system."[6] Joseph Schumpeter, the author of "creative destruction" is turning-over in his grave.

Bailing out Whom?

Given the monolithic system the United States has created and fostered over the past few decades—passing laws allowing increasingly huge concentrations of near monopolies on the Street—the bailout was needed. America hoisted itself onto its own petard. Its laws to protect the taxpayer did not keep pace with its passing laws to curtail the Street's excesses. There was no set of laws or set of procedures in place to "wind down the systemically important bank-holding companies that were at risk of failing."[7]

Part of this process came down to the screwing that Uncle Sam administered to you and me. Our government ended up protecting the debt holders of Wall Street institutions above that of the taxpayer.

Sheila Bair, the former head of FDIC,[8] had this to say about bailouts:

> "Why do we do the bailouts," she went on. "It was all about the bond holders," she said. "They did not want to impose losses on bondholders, and we did. We kept saying, 'There is no insurance premium on bondholders,' you know? For the little guy on Main Street who has bank deposits, we charge the banks a premium for that, and it gets passed on to the customer. We don't have the same thing for bondholders. They're supposed to take losses."

Bair continued:

> She had a second problem with the way the government went about saving the system. It acted as if no one were at fault—that was all just an unfortunate matter of "a system come undone," as she put it.

> "I hate that," she said. "Because it doesn't impose accountability where it should be. AIG was badly managed. Lehman Brothers and Bear Stearns were badly managed. And not everyone was as badly managed as they were."

Pass the Capitalistic Contribution Plate Down the Aisle

Bond holders, the owners of securities, are in the game because they know the risks associated with their investments. If they are naive investors, such as a local teachers' union retirement fund, they should be able to rely on the accuracy of a rating by the rating agencies. For this discussion, irrespective of the sophistication of an investor, Wall Street was protected because the Fed and Treasury did not want to destabilize the stock market.

During the Bear Sterns rundown (which was precipitated by Bear's huge illiquid holdings of mortgage assets based on subprime ARM mortgages), the New York Fed and Treasury worked with JPMorgan for JP to take over Bear. Why? Because Bear was sufficiently large and excessively interlocked to other banks and security firms on the Street to *not* allow it to fail.

Do we see any concerted, planned partnerships of the Fed and the Treasury with JPMorgan to keep a local business on Main Street in operation? To keep in operation what many experts consider the real engines of capitalism? Not that I've come across. The state of America's financial chains to Wall Street defies the imagination:[9]

- On March 16, 2008, JPMorgan informed the Fed and Treasury that it was interested in helping Bear. But only if this helping hand included a handout from the government.

- Therefore, the Fed *purchased* $29.97 billion of Bear's (mostly) mortgage related securities to get them off Bear's books. They became part of the New York Fed's books.

- For this amount, JP Morgan took on risk of the first $1.15 billion of loses. Any further losses of up to $28.82 billion would be taken in by the New York Fed.

- With these financial arrangements in place, JPMorgan announced it would buy Bear Sterns for $2 a share. The low price was reportedly made because Uncle Sam would not support a higher buyout in which Bear's equity holders received any taxpayer money to bailout stockholders. After all, buying stock is speculation. Let the buyer beware.

- A few days later, all parties agreed to a price of $10 share. So much for the issue of "moral hazard" of the federal government padding capitalism.

When has it become the responsibility of our government to insure the stability of the stock market? The practice is a contradiction of free market participles.

Big Business and Big Government

I wish I could close this report on a positive note. Wall Street and other financial institutions have failed, big time, which will lead to more government intervention into the marketplace. Yet, existing government institutions also failed: The Federal Reserve's obsession with prolonged low interest rates; its loose regulation; the SEC's stupendous incompetence; the venal behavior of the rating agencies; Barney Frank's pressure on Fannie and Freddy to give away a home to every semi-living body in America.[10] On and on, I've recounted these woes in earlier essays.[11]

The institutions of Freddie and Fanny are perversions of capitalism. They make so-called socialistic Europeans look like predatory capitalists. They should be disbanded, with their functions taken over by regulated (but not protected) private enterprises. There is no question that government should take measures to abet commerce and business, but the creation of crossbred organizations that have been hybridized into closely interlinked government/private entities is little more than, shudder, European socialism at its worst. In reality, it's akin to "the crony capitalism that one finds in countries like Russia and China."[12]

In the meantime, it's business as usual. In the future, if measures are not taken to fix Wall Street, the 2008 meltdown will be a pansy when compared to the next financial storm.

We find ourselves outraged by what has happened. And what we find equally ridiculous is the illusion that America is a bastion of free market capitalism. We continue to live a lie about the pervasive role Uncle Sam plays in most aspects of our lives. In order not to have another deep recession (when the market is allowed to run its course), we must continue to rely on the federal government to keep credit and liquidity going—especially during the "fragile" times.

For certain, the banks won't do it, yet that is their very job. When America most needs credit, the banks are most reluctant to furnish it. It's irony in action, or inaction.

---

[1] Gretchen Morgenson, "So That's Where the Money Went," *The New York Times*, December 5, 2010, p. BU 1, 5.

[2] All definitions are from Microsoft Encarta. All rights reserved.

[3] Roger Lowenstein, "Cracked Foundation," *The New York Times Magazine*, April 25, 2010, p. 12.

[4] *USA Today*, May 11, 2010, p. B1; with updates: October 22, 2010, p. B1.

[5] Cassidy, *How Markets Fail*, p. 320.

[6] Ibid.

[7] Joe Nocera, "Sheila Bair's Bank Shot," *The New York Times Magazine*, date not cited in article, circa July, 2011, p. 29.

[8] When this report was first written, Bair was the chairwoman of FDIC. She has since retired. This quote is from Joe Nocera, "Sheila Bair's Bank Shot," *The New York Times Magazine*, as noted above, date not cited in article, circa July, 2011, p. 29.

[9] Financial Crisis Inquiry Report, p. 290.

[10] Even dead people, as mentioned earlier.

[11] And not mentioned in this report is the underlying problem of America's debt to China and India.

[12] Posner, *The Crisis of Capitalistic America*, p. 255.

Report 20

Financial Cabals

Monks do not dissolve monasteries.
Bureaucrats do not dissolve bureaucracies.
Bankers do not dissolve banks.
They enlarge their monasteries, bureaucracies, and banks.

Perhaps no business is as profitable today as derivatives.
Not making loans.
Not offering credit cards.
Not advising on mergers and acquisitions.
Not managing money for the wealthy.[1]

December 25, 2010

Hello from Your On the Street Reporter. Merry Christmas! Sorry, Happy Holidays! Anyway, I had intended for these reports to branch out from the specifics of the meltdown, but recent events persuaded me to stick with the details of the nearly perfect financial storm. This segment is devoted to the issue of establishing openness and competition in one of the most lucrative and influential instruments in the world's financial system.

This part of the economic engine is a derivative that was explained earlier. Specifically, it is the credit default swap. These financial instruments were also explained earlier and I'll review them briefly in this report. But we need not dwell on their details again. The main thrust of this report is to once again expose the shady mentality of Wall Street.[2]

To set the stage for what I hope is a topic that will encourage even my non-writing readers to write Congress, here's an example familiar to most citizens. It deals with the healthy openness of selling and buying a home. However, this *altered* scenario mirrors the derivatives marketplace.

Hiding the Price of a Home

Let's say you want to sell your home for $300,000. You contact a broker who finds a buyer. However, the broker does not list your home publicly. Through a closed network of other brokers, he finds someone who might like to buy a home in your neighborhood. The potential buyer does not know your selling price of $300,000. The buyer only knows the price the broker quoted. Let's assume it is $350,000.

You read correctly. The seller and buyer are not aware of each others' thoughts about the potential financial transaction, one that is between the seller and the buyer. Nor do the buyer and you know about the prices of other homes in the neighborhood. Nor will the two of you ever learn what the final sell/buy price is. Nor will you ever know the other prices of homes; not just in your neighborhood but anywhere. The seller and buyer of this residence only know what the broker tells them.

For this scenario, the broker tells the potential buyer the price is $350,000. The buyer counter offers with $325,000. The broker tells you he found a buyer for $300,000 and pockets the $25,000 difference.

The broker's fees are secret. You and the buyer have no idea about this marketplace. Both of you are at the mercy of a closed system. It's a distortion of the free market concept where dealings are transparent (known to the public).

This scenario is unheard of in the mortgage industry. Yet this scenario is how some of Wall Street's mortgage-based derivative markets work. Even worse, nine large Wall Street firms, anticipating the Dodd-Frank Wall Street Reform and Consumer Protection Act passed a few weeks ago, have set up what can only be characterized as monopolies in one of the most lucrative financial operations in the world.

Brief Review of Derivatives

Derivatives are so named because they derive their value from something else, such as the prices of real estate, corn, heating oil, etc. The derivatives emphasized in these reports have been credit default swaps and they are the main subject in this report. They are used to hedge against the value of an underlying asset (such as mortgage backed securities). They act as insurance on these assets.

Derivatives are also valuable in allowing a company to lock in prices for a given period; say on heating oil that a heating oil company uses and sells during its winter months of operation. They are vital to commerce.

They are immensely profitable to brokers who buy and sell them. And they are a huge factor in America's economy. In an earlier report, I quoted one estimate from the Bank for International Settlements of their notional value at $680 trillion. This organization states this value *is more than ten times the GNP of all the countries in the world.*[3]

Publicly traded derivatives are many, including stock options, commodity futures, and stock index options.[4] These instruments serve an important economic function and are highly regulated. Many derivatives, such as stock option/purchase plans, are established privately between employers and employees. They serve an important albeit closed market function.

But many derivatives are not publicly traded. We have dealt extensively with credit default swaps in these reports. They are largely privately traded and Wall Street is making every effort to make sure they stay this way.

Hiding the Price of a Derivative: No Transparency

Here's a summary of the problems with hidden derivatives taken from Louise Story's article:[5]

Banks' influence over this market, and over clearinghouses like the one this select group advises, has costly implications for businesses large and small, like Dan Singer's home heating-oil company in Westchester County, north of New York City.

This fall, many of Mr. Singer's customers purchased fixed-rate plans to lock in winter heating oil at around $3 a gallon. While that price was above the prevailing $2.80 a gallon then, the contracts will protect homeowners if bitterly cold weather pushes the price higher.

But Mr. Singer wonders if his company, Robison Oil, should be getting a better deal. He uses derivatives like swaps and options to create his fixed plans. But he has no idea how much lower his prices—and his customers' prices—could be, he says, because banks don't disclose fees associated with the derivatives.

"At the end of the day, I don't know if I got a fair price, or what they're charging me," Mr. Singer said.

Too bad. If Mr. Singer does not like this closed arrangement, he can go to another broker and find out about the overall market. But it is not that easy because nine big banks control major parts of the system. They have created the rules for how derivatives are created and managed, as well as which banks can participate in these activities. Their clearinghouses to handle this business clear transactions only within their closed system and their customers. Other investment banks are excluded. The government wants to change this situation but lawmakers who receive largesse from Wall Street are against this sort of reform. (A key subject in Part II of this book.)

Yet this closed system, one in which the public and Uncle Sam have been locked out, created the huge dark-matter cloud of unregulated, secret derivatives; especially credit default swaps. The dark matter was and continues to be anti-free market and monopolistic.

The banks that participate in these clearinghouses have blocked the efforts of other organizations (mostly hedge funds) from publicly pricing the trading of derivatives and from joining the closed cabals.

Consider the New York Stock Exchange and NASDAQ. If someone wants to purchase a specific derivative contract, the prices of the derivatives are listed. But many derivatives are not listed on public exchanges, and the Cabal of Nine want to keep it this way. Openness could lead to cutting out the banks as middlemen.

So what? It's none of my business to know the markup and profit on a private business product, say, a Costco lawn mower. And if Wall Street sets up cabals, that's part of capitalism.

Wall Street cannot have it both ways. If it wants independence from Uncle Sam, it should not come back to Uncle's welfare swill in bad times. It should not be allowed to become a bank holding company and take out loans at the Fed's discount window for less than 1 percent while it charges us three to five times as much for our loans.

I know nothing about Costco's lawn mower pricing practices. But then, if Costco goes broke, I do not have to bailout Costco. Nor does Uncle Sam (using our money). Any company that takes our money should not be allowed to secretly line its pockets with our loot.

Since I began these reports, the big banks have maneuvered themselves into a position in which they dominate "not one, but two of the most prominent new clearinghouses in the United States":[6]

> That puts them in a pivotal position to determine how derivatives are traded. Under the Dodd-Frank bill, the clearinghouses were given broad authority.

> The risk committees there will help decide what prices will be charged for clearing trades, on top of fees banks collect for matching buyers and sellers, and how much money customers must put up as collateral to cover potential losses. [Writer: The fox is in the hen house again.]

Perhaps more important, the risk committees will recommend which derivatives should be handled through clearinghouses, and which should be exempt.

If you or I buy or sell shares on a stock exchange, the price and fee are known. It's called electronic trading. Such openness leads to more competition and lowers the cost of doing business. After NASDAQ was forced to go public with its prices, fees on NASDAQ trades dropped from about 1.15 percent to 0.15 percent.

If I were a member of JPMorgan Chase & Company, Morgan Stanley, Deutsche Bank, UBS, Barclays, Credit Suisse, Goldman Sachs, Bank of America, and Citigroup, I would be protecting my prosperous turf with as much opaqueness and closeness as possible.

But I'm not so employed. Nor likely are you. If you and I are profit oriented, we put our businesses up in the wrong location. We opted for Main Street to build something of social value. But Wall Street is where the money is, often building nothing at all.

It is not too late for Congress and the regulatory bodies to take measures to bring more competition and transparency to the credit default swaps derivatives industry. If Uncle Sam cannot release itself from Wall Street lobbyists' bribes and foster competition for these new clearinghouses, at least it can require their murky transactions to be known to the public. Thus far, it appears it will be business as usual as Wall Street will continue to control the United States Congress.

---

[1] Louise Story, "A Secretive Banking Elite Rules Trading in Derivatives," *The New York Times* Web site, December 11, 2010, p. 1. Statistics and direct quotes for Report 20 are sourced from this article.

[2] As stated earlier, not all of Wall Street, but many of the large investment banks.

[3] Notional means what the derivative has been pegged at. For example, if I use a derivative to lock in a price for 50 gallons of heating oil at $100, the notational value of this instrument is $5000. This value is also used to determine, say, what the cost will be of insurance I might purchase on the

derivative. In the financial world, *notional* value is used to calculate the payment on the instrument, such as premiums. For insurance, a credit default swap. The term notional is used because money on the instrument itself does not change hands; only money regarding its notional value. (That is, unless a default occurs, then it's no longer "notional"!) Some readers have taken me to task about using the term worth. Good point, but it's not my quote, and perhaps the term price might be more fitting. But keep in mind the definition of notional, just cited. Also, the estimates about outstanding derivatives vary. I came across a *Slate Magazine* article that quoted a figure of $596 trillion (see http://www.slate.com/id/2202263/).

[4] Comments in this paragraph came from a blog reader who works with derivatives.

[5] Story, "A Secretive Banking Elite Rules Trading in Derivatives," p. 1.

[6] Ibid., p. 11.

REPORT 21

WRAPPING UP THE REPORTS

*John Maynard Keynes started the meltdown
and Adam Smith finished it.*

November 12, 2011

Hello from Your On the Street Reporter. I took another (long) break from reporting on the nearly perfect financial storm to wait and see how America might recover from the 2008 financial meltdown.

Thus far there is not much good news to report. High unemployment remains a major problem. America's shopping malls are still populated with many empty stores. I took the photos in figure 21-1 in an area near my home in Hayden, Idaho. Business as usual, translated to no business. It's amazing. I am writing this report five years after the 2008 meltdown began and signs of recovery are faint.

From talks with citizens and from my personal observations, it appears saloons and churches are still doing a thriving business. While touring the malls, I paid a call on a sex apparatus store, seen in the right photo of figure 21-1. I asked how business was going. The owner informed me:

- "Business has been steady."
- "No slack in trade?"

- "Nope. I had to close another store down the street. It was a dress shop. But I'm doing just fine with this store."
- "Hmm. So sex is immune to business downturns?"
- "Business keeps on humming!"

At last, some good news to a small segment on Main Street. The nearly perfect financial storm was a mere speed bump to the Adam and Eve sex shop. You've survived. Congratulations on choosing a recession-free product line.

Figure 21-1. Empty stores, continued from figures 1-1 and 12-1.

The only new stores up here are two tattoo parlors and a Walmart outlet. Walmart bashers cannot claim the opening of this facility led to the closure of the shops shown in figures 1-1, 12-1, and 21-1. These businesses closed before Walmart came along.

The big news these past few weeks has been the deadlock between liberals and conservatives about raising the debt limit. As of this writing, no resolution is in sight. In the long run, we can only hope this elevated debate will at long last wake up our citizenry. But I am not optimistic as most of the polls indicate Americans are for decreased taxes with no cuts in social services. Even an Archie Bunker can see the illogic to this supposition.

Watching the spectacle of debates between red and blue ideologues is not much different from watching a vending machine in operation. Put in a blue coin, out comes liberal platitudes. Put in a red coin, out comes conservative platitudes.

But this report is not about the topic of America's debt, whose unfunded obligations is now $534,000 per household.[1] Let's return to the happier subject of the financial meltdown.

Was It Worth It? (The Law of Unintended Consequences)

I have made the case that the foundation for the 2008 financial meltdown in America stemmed from concerted White House efforts and congressional laws to encourage and sometimes force mortgage originators and Fannie Mae to enter into the residential mortgage market for marginally qualified or unqualified mortgage applicants. Almost all parties were willing participants in the feast. The banks came willingly. So did Fannie Mae and home buyers.

Was it worth it? In the end, did formerly low-income renters and squatters who moved into their homes come out ahead?[2]

> A study issued last week on the widening wealth gap between minorities and white Americans points to the costs of predatory lending [writer: and clueless home buyers]. Conducted by the Pew Research Center, a nonpartisan organization, the study noted that housing woes were the principal cause of precipitous declines in household net worth among both Hispanics and blacks from 2005 through 2009. The organization found that, adjusted for inflation, the median wealth of Hispanic households fell by two-thirds during that period The wealth of black households declined 53 percent. The net worth of white households fell only 16 percent.

All that work and so little gained. Four million home mortgage foreclosures. An additional four million home mortgages remain in precarious straits, subject to foreclosures.

Adam Smith's invisible hand? John Maynard Keynes' visible mind? Both: Keynesian regulated public governments started the process and Smith's unregulated private sector finished it.

Status of Legislation and Wall Street Doesn't Get It

At this writing, Congress is working to place the details into the Dodd-Frank Act, which I summarized in Report 18 (its early form). One only can guess how many pages it will eventually contain. Even in its initial form, it appears to be the introduction of yet more inefficient bureaucratic processes: Overlaying more laws onto existing laws that were not followed in the first place; adding more bureaucracies to existing bureaucracies that did not do their jobs.

Banks are resisting parts of the legislation. Financial institutions are lobbying to have the law diluted. One major effort on the banks' part is to prevent regulators from opening up the derivatives marketplace, to keep this marketplace opaque to the public. As discussed in these reports, it was this market—and its secrecy—that created many problems. As the crisis loomed, the financial industry, as well as the regulators, had no idea of the magnitude and impact of these instruments, because Congress had previously made them immune to all but Wall Street's eyes.

I hope this part of the bill will not be compromised. If it is, much of Wall Street will go about business as usual. Also, there must be more control of the assumption of risk in proprietary trading (where a bank trades on its own behalf and not a customer). During the meltdown, some traders did not even know from one day to the next how much they were in the hole.[3]

I hope I have convinced you in these reports that the financial industry in general, and investment banks specifically, have long since gone off the rails of behavior that is financially sound for our society. If not, here is one more attempt:

Thus far, the emerging act establishes that loan originators must—get this—actually grant loans to people who might make their monthly payments! The debates revolve around this idea: If a mortgage backed security contains high quality loans, the bank can off-load all loans in a security. What would be considered high quality loans? The same loans that were granted before mortgage securitization came along: (a) 20 percent down payment; (b) the mortgage does not exceed 28 percent of household's monthly income, and (c) total debt does not exceed 36 percent of household's total income.

The change would be like the old days when banks were respectable lending institutions and not originate-and-sell loan sharks. But we must wait it out and see what happens. As a skeptic of huge bills in general, I expect the ability to get a loan will swing to the other extreme. Even qualified buyers will be swamped with unnecessary paperwork and requirements.

The good news: If some of the loans are not of high quality, the bank (the underwriter) will be required to keep five percent of the issue on its books. This idea is just common sense. One of the big problems surrounding the meltdown was the fact that mortgage originators became careless because they could off-load trash, and thus had no skin in the game.

One would think that a bank would want to improve its reputation; to make up for past travesties; that it would be in the bank's best interest to make high quality loans. But the American Bankers Association (ABA) is resisting this part of the act.[4]

The ABA and its banks cry foul. Such restrictions would "undermine the goal of expanding homeownership."[5] How noble, and full of absurd nonsense. Do not for one Wall Street minute think these people give a hoot about home owners. In the meantime, you and I are still picking up the tabs of billions of bailout dollars to make up for the rapacious greed of the subprime, interest-only, adjustable mortgage rate loan predators.

And further: The current president of the Mortgage Bankers Association (David Stevens) states the proposed requirements (including other restrictions) are unnecessary and not worth the social costs to America's citizens. Which citizens is Stevens talking about? Not me. I'll bet not you either. Our "social" costs are still being tabulated in amounts of, say, over $150 billion being paid out to Fannie and Freddie.

By the way, Mr.Stevens was a former high-level official at HUD. During his time there, he had polar opposite views, which leads to the last Rule of Life for these reports: *Where one stands, depends on where one sits.* And that tidbit is also the last example of the revolving-door networking between government and Wall Street.

Status of Bigness

No changes here. Banks continue to get bigger. The bailout even encouraged more bigness. The bright spot (which admittedly will be passed to the consumer) is the likelihood of increased reserve requirements, especially for large banks.

I am reaching the conclusion that my heavy emphasis in these reports on "too big to fail" has been sparring with windmills. While correct in its contradiction to capitalism's creative destruction and fair play to small companies, too big to fail reflects the reality of (a) allowing bigness to come about in the first place, and (b) the inability to reverse course. Big banks operate at an advantage to small banks (unfair), yet small banks are not large enough to do big deals across international boundaries (reality).

I also wish I knew the answer to the question of the often unhealthy relationship between the commercial and investments sides of a bank. Breaking them apart might do nothing more than create two separate institutions that are too big to fail. Nonetheless, during the next months, governments around the world are addressing this problem and looking for ways to protect their citizens from another nearly perfect financial storm.

Status of Paychecks[6]

No changes here. Executive pay continues to increase, while Joe the Plumber remains on Uncle's dole. I've discussed this topic in these reports because of its debilitating effects on the morale and moral fiber of this country.

In 2010, executive compensation increased by 13.9 percent. Of this survey ("S&P 500 Executive Pay: Bigger than ...Whatever You Think It Is") 2,591 executives were identified as having received $14.3 billion. A figure that is larger than the GNP of many countries.

The claim that compensation is commensurate with performance is not correct. Studies show that executives continue to receive raises even when the stock values of their companies go down.

And for our story, when the stock values tank, the executives have already taken their millions of dollars by the time you, Uncle Sam, and I pull out our wallets for a bailout.

But I am beating a dead horse here. By now, I trust I have enlisted you to my cause of your insisting you have more say in the compensation packages of the executives operating companies in which you have stock.

Chained but Untamed[7]

Regardless of what the regulators do, they can only tame banks temporarily. Before long, the bankers will make an end run around their barriers and devise yet more schemes to circumvent laws. Perhaps this is the natural order of our modern society. I have stated that government and private enterprise are natural enemies. My hesitancy in accepting this sort of dominance game is my belief that both parties should act in concert to be wards to—not just citizens and stockholders, but to ethical free market capitalism. In this regard, I think I can justly claim that many examples in this book showed the bad side of both parties.

As mentioned, I delved into the project of writing these reports with some background in banking but I did not know a lot about the subject. Most of my experience was with my small mortgage brokerage company and with my stint at the Federal Reserve Board. All in all, I had respect for the banking industry.

My respect has diminished, especially after immersing myself in the details of the 2008 financial meltdown. Still, as I declared earlier, the banking industry is not the lone fox in the hen house. These reports have chronicled a pack of foxes that did the raiding. We humans are the self-defeating predators in this story.

Here is another quote to finish this take on banks: "Bankers are like suicide bombers, who must be appeased because they are threatening to blow everyone else up."[8]

Yes, and if they are not appeased, they will.

Unchained and Untamed

If the banks can be characterized as chained but untamed, Uncle Sam can be characterized as unchained and untamed. Government can put the bridles on business. Who can put the bridles on government? In theory, that is the job of citizens.

How extensively have the citizens' views been taken into account during the recent debate in Congress about raising the debt ceiling? Very little. The politicians, ideologically bedridden by gerrymandering and zealotry, will not compromise. And compromise with regard to America's debt is what the vast majority of America's citizens wish. Compromise moves us forward toward solving what is in reality a simple problem. Gridlock does not.

In the meantime, government creates laws that are (a) not enforced by the government, (b) not even tracked by the government for adherence, (c) ignored by business, and (d) gamed by business. Here is a classic example of all four of these events occurring based on one single law. It is a 2004 tax break to encourage U.S. corporations to (1) bring foreign profits back home and (2) create more jobs.[9] The law required this money to be used only to stimulate job growth and other investments, but not for the multinational company to use it to reward employees or stockholders.

The law was supported by many businesses and Republicans who claimed the legislation would create several million jobs and add as much as $1 trillion to the economy.

A recent Senate panel study concluded this break did nothing to create jobs or increase investment. Instead, from 2004 to 2006 (even *before* the meltdown):

- Firms cut jobs.
- Firms cut research spending.
- Firms raised stock buy-back prices for their stockholders.
- Firms raised executive pay.
- Some firms moved operations overseas to take advantage of the tax break (by sending their profits back home). Very smart of them. The companies reduced their tax liabilities without

changing much of anything. This switch of venue also led to the loss of jobs in the United States.
- The government required *no* documentation from a firm to prove the company was adhering to the law.

The U.S. Chamber of Commerce takes issue with the Senate study, stating stock repurchases and dividend payouts indirectly boost consumer spending, which helps strengthen the economy and bolster employment.

But that is not what the law stipulated! These multinational companies, who are very large businesses, broke the law or at least (unethically) circumvented it. It appears to this writer that laws were broken and those executives should be hauled into court.

These large businesses were taxed 5.25 percent on this income, instead of the customary 35 percent. I have an idea: Uncle Sam gives a tax break to any small business that hires new employees. Better yet: give my small company and yours green dollars for each and every new job we create. That way, you and I will not have to pay one red cent for these workers. We, not big business, would keep the bribe.

What is the significance of this type of situation? Big business can't be trusted to manage itself to conform to the spirit of a law. Government can't be trusted to manage big business for adherence to that law. Meanwhile, Main Street remains the last-man-out, often ignored when the dole is passed around.

One Last Anecdote

My next door neighbor up here in Idaho worked for a mortgage title firm. I've known him long enough to attest to his intelligence, social skills, and graces. He has read most of these reports and has offered helpful thoughts and insights.

Early in 2011, he was "let go" by this firm because of the financial meltdown. After over seven years of loyal and fruitful service, he was given two weeks of severance pay and compensation for accrued vacation days. He lost sixty days of accrued sick leave, which might have made him a bit ill.

No gold watch. No party. But as Wall Street tells us, his trip to the unemployment line is just a "speed bump."

It's a Wrap

It is time to wrap up these reports and find other ways to burn my calories. I hope the Rules of Life were helpful to you during these reports. They took us beyond a specific industry and into humans' behavior within the institutions that were players in the nearly perfect financial storm.

I had been putting off the completion of this project by terminating these reports. But new issues came up so I kept adding more essays. The subject, suffused with so many elements of human foibles, is almost intoxicating in the context of its moral tales about human behavior.

While it is time to put these reports to bed, I suspect I will be writing more from a layman's view of Wall Street and this financial debacle.

Thank you for taking this journey with me. We began March 1, 2009 with the first essay. The process was almost three years in the making. I hope my learning experience was one for you as well. I hope the incremental approach helped you understand this great and tragic event in our lives. It worked for me. I trust it did for you.

One last quote, taken from an on the street comment from a Wall Streeter to a Main Streeter: "What is greed to you is ambition to me."

---

[1] *USA Today*, June 7, 2011, p. A1.

[2] Gretchen Morgenson, "Some Bankers Never Learn," *The New York Times*, July 31, 2011, p. BU 6.

[3] "Where Angels Fear to Trade," *The Economist*, May 14th, 2011, p. 13.

[4] Morgenson, "Some Bankers Never Learn," p. BU 6.

[5] Ibid.

[6] Gretchen Morgenson, "Paychecks as Big as Tajikistan," *The New York Times*, June 18, 2011, pp. BU 1 and 3.

[7] Heading taken from *The Economist*, May 14, 2011, p. 3 of "Special Report: International Banking."

[8] John Cassidy, "Paging J.P. Morgan: Who Should Pay Korea's Bills?" *The New Yorker*, January 19, 1988.

[9] Paul Davidson, "Study: Tax Break Didn't Create Jobs," *USA TODAY*, October 12, 2011, p. B1.

Part II

Reflections

Chapter 22

The Storm's Aftermath

Wife to husband, "Honey, we now own a 401(k)!"
Husband to wife, "Great! How many pistons does it have?"

I am writing Part II during the mid months of 2012. I decided to continue my work on what some people call the Great Recession. Some of my readers and friends suggested I continue doing research and make my findings and opinions known. I was encouraged by their support and decided to stay with the project for a while.

For most of Part II, we leave the invisible hands of Adam Smith, the visible hands of John Keynes, and broaden our investigation into more pragmatic subjects: America's politics and social fabric, problems associated with the Union, and America's will to solve these problems.

Part II contains eight chapters. I have named them "chapters" instead of "reports" because they are less about reporting facts than they are about subjective essays.

Persistent Squalls

Squalls of the nearly perfect financial storm persist. The storm's aftermath continues to be felt. Long unemployment lines at welfare offices have become routine events. Some five million people have been seeking employment for over two years.[1] The news media publishes daily stories about hapless citizens who have lost most of their material possessions and a great deal of their self-worth.

In Europe, a gallows humor joke recounts documented instances of "suicide by economic crisis." The suicide rate in Greece has increased by 27 percent since 2007. In Ireland, it's a 16 percent increase; in Italy, 52%. In America, statistics are unavailable on suicides caused by the economic crises, but little has changed in the political system to alleviate or eliminate the problems discussed in Part I.

Given these conditions, I thought of postponing Part II until I could write about a growing U.S. economy and a less corrupt—or at least repaired—financial/political system. I hoped to finish this project on a positive note.

However, that is not to be, so I have decided to forge ahead and complete this undertaking. I do not want to spend these later years of my life on one subject. The effects of this nearly perfect storm will be around for a long time. As just mentioned, little has changed to prevent a future financial storm or for that matter, to mend the political ills that contributed to this meltdown.

To begin the second part of this book, we briefly revisit the subject of interconnectedness.

Interconnectedness: Fact or Falsehood?

Some financial experts have stated the rationale for the bailout was based on the erroneous premise that the interconnectedness of financial institutions necessitated a rescue. They claim the fear of a toppled domino toppling other dominos was incorrect. To cite one example, in *The Wall Street Journal*, Peter J. Wallison, states, "There's no evidence that any of the financial institutions that were rescued...were weakened by their exposure to Lehman."[2]

I wish this claim were true but it is not. I cited many examples in Part I that refute this contention, such as statements by Henry Paulson (in Report 15).[3]

The article by Mr. Wallison also claims that because interconnectedness is a myth, the government does not "need or should have the powers that Dodd-Frank (the financial reform act) conferred on it."

He and I are in alliance about Dodd-Frank. As you know, I am skeptical the act will do much in the way of righting America's financial ship. It creates a huge set of bureaucracies and as of this writing, it does not address several of the major problems that contributed to the storm.

The Wallison article is published in a newspaper (*The Wall Street Journal*) noted for its bias toward business and skepticism of Uncle Sam's visible hand. I have the same leanings but Wallison's suppositions are incorrect.

Let's grant Mr. Wallison his illusion. If financial interconnectedness is a myth, what is to be made of the thousands of unemployed citizens emerging suddenly in 2008/09? Did they spring from nowhere, a spontaneous generation in a vacuum? No. They sprang from a source over which they had no control, one to which they were interconnected without their say, nay or yea.

I resurface the subject of interconnectedness in order to share with you a survey I conducted pertaining to the nearly perfect financial storm. It is summarized in the following section.

Main Street and Destructive Interconnectedness

One emphasis in this book has been the welfare Uncle Sam provides for big business, especially in relation to small companies. One of my blog readers, who knows me well, made a comment about how liberal these reports have come across (because of my comments on big business). He said it seemed at odds with what he knows about my political leanings. I pointed out that I skewered Uncle Sam as well. I also placed small business in a favorable light (my own bias as a small business owner). He has yet to reply, so I'll assume he agrees.

There is better reason to favor small business. Small companies (with fewer than five hundred employees) create more jobs than larger companies. From 1992 through 2010 small business employed 55 percent of the American private-sector workforce yet created 64 percent of new jobs.[4]

I have mentioned that I play tennis. Single tennis, played with an adroit opponent, is as fine a game as any I have come across.

With its large court area, it requires speed, acceleration, strength, keen hand-to-eye skill, as well as stealth to keep the opponent at bay. But I usually play doubles now as my body is more frequently doubling over from the rigors of playing singles. Still, on occasion, I have flashes of mediocrity.

I bring up tennis because many of my doubles partners are small business owners. A few weeks ago, I asked these men to answer a short questionnaire. They did. In my travels to gather information for this book, I have asked other small business owners the same questions. I bring these facts to your attention to note that this survey is anecdotal, but it rings true to my observation of the meltdown. I asked the small business owners five questions, with the answers shown in Table 22-1.

Table 22-1. Survey of Meltdown's Effects on Small Business

1. Has the financial meltdown affected your volume of business?

    Yes: 100%   No: 0%

2. If yes, has your business volume increased or decreased?

    Increased: 20% Decreased: 80%

3. To your knowledge, have any of your competitors gone out of business?

    Yes: 80/%   No: 20%   Don't know: 0%

4. If yes, do you know if you took over some of their business?

    Yes: 40%   No: 20%   Don't know: 40%

5. Has the increase or decrease of your business volume affected the purchases you make from your suppliers? (That is, if you buy from suppliers.)

    Yes: 85%   No: 10%   Not Applicable: 5%

There is more to glean from this set of questions than the straight-forward answers. The men and women I surveyed deal with products that contribute to America's economic engine. Their output is not synthetic. Their products drive the micro pistons of America's macro engine.

These businesses are plying their trades, selling their wares, and contributing to America's infrastructure. All the while, they find their livelihood is dictated by strangers. As I have said in the reports in this book, the bulk of America's businesses and many citizens have been blindsided by forces beyond their control. Irrespective of the article in *The Wall Street Journal*, interconnectedness of large institutions and the effect of their behavior on small business is a serious problem.

Globalization

Shortly, we examine proposals that address the problem of interconnectedness. But it is important to understand and acknowledge that attempting to eliminate inter-institutional dependence is akin to putting toothpaste back in the tube. It cannot be done. For several decades the world's financial systems have been evolving toward closer ties and mutual dependence. Globalization has led to the extensive integration of international economic organizations.

Nonetheless, measures can be put in place to avoid the contagion that came about (partially) because of the interdependence of financial institutions. I'll have more to say on this subject in later chapters.

Should the Bailouts Have Been Done?

One of the issues covered in Part I of this book was my support of the rescues of investment and commercial banks, as well as GM, Chrysler, Fannie Mae, and AIG. I am no longer certain government's intervention to *preserve* an existing financial system will result in a healthier society. We are told a financial disaster has been diverted. As a layman, I suppose I must accept this notion. Perhaps you do, too. We will never know what might have happened if creative destruction had been allowed to take its course. The experts state that the absence of Uncle Sam's bailout would have resulted in a financial tragedy akin to the Great Depression.

With the hindsight of over three years of studying this recession, I am not so sure about the long-term effectiveness of the financial system bailout. First, runs on banks' deposits by the general populace in America would not have occurred because of FDIC insurance on the deposits themselves. The run on banks was one of the straws that broke the back of America's financial camel in 1929-30.

Second, if inept institutions are rescued, they become "zombie banks." The U.S. government (with tax money from you and me) keeps them on life support while they continue to haunt and drain our (money) crypts.

Third, almost five years after the meltdown *and bailout*, shopping malls remain populated with abandoned stores. The unemployment rate has not gone down. Many businesses are still in trouble.

Millions of people have been unemployed for over two years. Some have given up trying to find employment. The financial and psychological damage inflicted upon these citizens cannot be calculated. This writer cannot fathom what the effects would be for having no income or job for years. I cannot help but think this chronic unemployment would damage both my pocketbook and ego. Self-sufficiency is an important factor in having self-worth.

Once a proponent of bailouts, I have doubts about their long-term effectiveness. I say long-term, in the sense of decades. Bailouts solve immediate problems and temporarily stabilize the financial world. By their nature, they are short-term efforts. But this short view is akin to putting bandaids on a gaping wound.

This immediate aid may calm the populace for now. But most citizens sink into TV indolence. Their leaders in Washington continue to be unable or unwilling to take on the more difficult long-term effort of cleansing the wound and starting over. That task is left to the next generation.

The Chickens Are Coming Home to Roost, But the Moral Hazard Still Looms

Finally, here is some good news. Lawsuits are coming forth. The list below represents a snapshot of the situation.[5]

- The Federal Housing Finance Agency (FHFA) has named seventeen banks that this agency claims sold around $200 billion in fraudulent mortgage backed securities to Fannie Mae and Freddie Mac. Among those seventeen revered institutions, responsible for greasing the cogs of America's financial wheels, are Goldman Sachs, JPMorgan Chase, Bank of America, Citigroup, and Morgan Stanley.

- Bank of America has agreed to pay $8.5 billion to settle claims by investors who lost money on mortgage backed securities purchased before the U.S. housing collapse. The payment will be the largest such settlement by a financial services company to date.

- Parts of the litigation against many of the banks and mortgage companies deal with mortgages granted that fell outside underwriting guidelines. Estimates vary but it is thought that about 25 percent of home loan mortgage documentation was incorrect.

- UBS Americas Inc. is being hauled to court for allegedly misleading investors about the worth of mortgage backed securities.

- The SEC has begun to live up to its charter and is pursuing lawsuits against several firms.

Yet the moral hazard issue has not been resolved. With the exception of a few insider trading arrests, only in rare occurrences are individuals being held accountable for their behavior. They are shielded by their corporations, which are now granted the right of free speech.

America's Realities

Let's review the bets that have taken place around the financial storm's gambling table. Here is what the American citizen faces today, even though he or she is not sitting at this casino table:

We live in a society in which large institutions that are tightly interconnected and dependent on one another will be given resuscitation by the federal government if they get into trouble. Small institutions will not be offered this life-line.

Our nation and its lawmakers have created (and continue to do so) a legal system that is so complex to follow it is leading to scenes reminiscent of a Charles Dickens novel. And like the Dickens' characters, the rules are circumvented or ignored with yet more legalistic machinations.

We live under the illusion that our country is a capitalistic society. We are so blinded by media falsehoods and our post Cold War mental superiority that we are intellectually incapable of seeing some of the attractive aspects of other countries. Why? Because they practice socialism.

We refuse to learn from others or use their models, such as Finland, which has the best educational system in the world. Or Canada, which practices capitalism as much as America does, but with less fanfare.

All the while, capitalism's "creative destruction" in America is selectively applied to specific institutions and particular classes of people.

We continue to wave our hubristic, anti-socialism flags. Ensconced in a self-hoax cocoon, we wave these flags *while often practicing outright welfare*. Not only welfare for the single mom tied to six kids, but welfare for large companies tied to each other. This mentality has led to:

A Dysfunctional Combination

The United States government owns a significant segment of America's supposedly free enterprise companies and the huge quasi-government agency Fannie Mae. Uncle Sam's support of these bastions of capitalism is *similar* to socialism. After all, in socialistic countries the government controls the nation's production and distribution systems.

The word *similar* is important. America's practice of rescuing and sometimes out-right buying banks, car manufacturers, and insurance companies smacks of socialism. But it is not socialism. If truth be told and if America's citizens were aware of this truth, they would come to understand that the U.S. government's ongoing operations are an affront to both socialism and capitalism.

If the actions cited above are not acts of socialism (or capitalism) what are they? They are acts of misguided charity. Uncle Sam gives hand-outs to failed enterprises, shakes his finger at them: *Do not do that again!* Sam walks through their doors to stay a few months to put a bandaid on the place. Sam then walks out, leaving the organizations intact, mostly whole, and positioned to repeat their performances.

America's actions during the nearly perfect financial storm—as well as other past financial storms—have led to a dysfunctional environment. To illustrate further, let's assume Uncle Sam informs a failed free enterprise company:

- You have been operating on capitalistic principles. They have led to a precarious position on your part. You may be creatively destroyed. (capitalism)
- But I will rescue you. (welfare)
- The hand-out money I will give you must be repaid…if you are able. (welfare)
- I will take over your company to keep you functioning. I will take control of the executives who make decisions about your production and distribution. (socialism)
- To prevent America's unemployed proletariat from coming after your officers with a rope, I will require your executives to take pay cuts.[6] (socialism)
- But I will not do much in the way of changing your structure or the ways in which your company interconnects with other institutions. (capitalism)

- Nor will I stay inside your doors indefinitely. After the storm has passed, I will exit. You will continue to exist but I will not be overseeing your operations. Your executives can even recoup their pay cuts. You can remove the bandaid I put on. By and large it will be business as usual for you. I will not alter your business model that led to my hand-out in the first place. (dysfunctionalism)[7]

America is not practicing capitalism. It is not practicing socialism. It is operating in a dysfunctional netherworld. One of taking-on the patina of both philosophies, but one instilled with a hands-off welfare mentality that distorts the integrity of each.

If this approach to governance is going to be a permanent way for America's economic wheels to grind, let us at least be honest with ourselves and admit it.

To be discussed in Part II:

With Part I of this book in mind, Part II is devoted to the following contentions:

- America's magnificent rule of law concept has been greatly compromised by the actions of the very people who make and enforce these rules: the United States Congress and the Supreme Court.

- Increased income inequity, coupled with citizens' sensing America's rule of law is increasingly favoring specific classes and institutions, are creating disrespect and resentment among the citizenry.

- Tax cuts of the past two decades have not led to increased revenue for the masses, but to increased revenue to those who already have a lot of revenue to begin with.

- Because of its debt to itself and other countries, America increasingly finds itself in danger of not being able to sustain its place in the world, or even being capable of sustaining its citizens' standard of living.

- The right to free speech, now granted to non-persons (corporations, unions, and such), is eroding the nation's republican foundations. It is eroding the power—and associated integrity—of the individual voter.

- The continued use of gerrymandering is leading to the re-drawing of voting districts based on political/religious/cultural ideologies. This practice is leading to ideologically based campaigns in which many issues have nothing to do with America's security and well being.

- America's citizenry has identified the issues it asks our government to address. But because of the influence of lobbyists and massive amounts of money given to politicians by special interest groups supporting different issues, the citizen's concerns are taking a back seat to the lobbyists and their supporters' agendas.

- America's citizens are unable to understand and accept this somber truism: For this country to get back on the right track, sacrifices must be made; both in the reduction of services and an increase in revenues.

- Meanwhile, because of the events cited above, the issues facing the United States are not being addressed in any meaningful way because the political process is in a state of ideological dead-lock.

- As a result, America is sinking more deeply into debt and its once-vaunted political process continues to unravel.

My Bailout Plan

I close the first chapter to Part II on a more positive and lighter note. I offer my own financial bailout plan. My idea deals with fair play by taking turns being morally hazardous.

Some experts state a sizable amount of the bailout money should have been directed—not to the banks, but to home buyers. It is a provocative argument with the proponents of rugged capitalism claiming any leniency shown to a home buyer will raise the scepter of a moral hazard. This opinion may be true, but it does seem appropriate to help the people who were deceived with false claims about their mortgages.

America is known for its fairness. So we should pass the moral hazard baton around to someone else. Wall Street and other big businesses have had the baton long enough, accompanied by $1.2 trillion of moral hazard bribes and dirt-cheap borrowing from the Fed to these institutions.

Here is my bailout suggestion: With the unemployment benefit vaults of Uncle running out of inventory, let's give moral hazard money to you and me. Oh. Already spent? That is of no concern. Sam can print more money and go deeper into debt.

With this money, divided up among our citizenry, each man, woman, and child in America will receive over $300,000 to bail out the economy.

This capital will be the gas needed to jump-start America's engine. Just think of the boom that will occur when we citizens queue up at Best Buy to purchase a yet larger flat screen TV, or at a sports shop to buy our fourth dirt bike. On and on, tax revenues will explode.

Should we save some of the 300 grand? Start a 401(k)? Put some of this money in a savings account? Invest in America's rotting infrastructure? Go to school to learn a new skill? No way. After all, our leaders are telling us to spend, spend, and spend! Keep that money going around, especially in consumer goods. Every go-around gets taxed. Besides, interest rates are so low what's the point of being thrifty?

Absurd? No more absurd than the subject matter of this book: How the nearly perfect financial storm came about from ignorant or self-indulgent consumers, from a debased and corrupt political system, and how many of the storm's perpetrators not only stayed out of prison, but also became rich because of their greed, unethical behavior, or moral vacuity. Take your pick.

The following quote by the British philosopher Herbert Spencer sums up many of the themes of this book: "The ultimate result of shielding men from the effects of [their] folly is to fill the world with fools."[8]

For the nearly perfect financial storm, many people were shielded from the effects of their folly, and while they might be called fools, they ended up rich fools.

For this story, perhaps Mr. Spencer would not have tagged as fools those who were rescued and shielded from their folly. Perhaps he would have tagged as fools those who did not act foolishly, but also did not shield themselves from the folly of others.

---

[1] CNN TV news item, June 9, 2012.

[2] Peter J. Wallison, "Dodd-Frank and the Myth of 'Interconnectedness,'" *The Wall Street Journal*, February 30, 2012, p. A15.

[3] Paulson, *On the Brink*, p. 99.

[4] Carl Bialk, "Sizing Up the Small-Business Jobs Machine," *The Wall Street Journal*, October 15-16, 2011, p. A2. These figures include the loss of jobs as well.

[5] Taken from several newscasts, within the AOL home page citations; as are the other direct quotes in this chapter, unless otherwise cited.

[6] The federal government ordered AIG, Ally Financial Inc. and General Motors to reduce the compensation of their high level officers by 10 percent. This penalty came about because these companies had not paid back all the bailout money. The sacrifice for these officers is heart rending. The General Motors CEO earns about $9 million annually. Ally Financial's CEO earns about $9.5 million. Source: *The CDA Press*, April 7, 2012, p. B5.

[7] I will rescind this harsh indictment if Dodd-Frank's final rules result in containing the scope of effect of bigness, interconnectedness, and secret dealings in derivatives.

[8] Excerpted from *The Economist*, October 15, 2011, p. 98.

CHAPTER 23

INCOME DISPARITY AND FREEDOM OF SPEECH

The eagle suffers little birds to sing.[1]
—Shakespeare

Micro Consequences of Income Disparity

Report 9 in Part I of this book documents the huge compensations paid to CEOs of failed companies, some that were bailed out by taxpayer money. We also posed the hypothetical question, of "So what?" If Joe the Plumber does not like his paltry salary for fixing toilets, he can become Joe the banker. After all, making a choice about an occupation is part of life. We make the decisions and we live with the consequences.

But as America is now constructed, we do not have free market capitalism, a point I have made clear in the reports in Part I. We also have a system that is increasingly migrating toward deep financial inequality within our citizenry; one that gives even more leverage to those who already have leverage. Let's update the data in Report 9:[2]

- 1980: The wealthiest one percent of Americans took ten percent of national income.
- 2007: The wealthiest ten percent of Americans took fifty percent of national income.

A relatively few people are making a lot of money and a lot of people are making little. But that's capitalism. The "capitalists" on Wall Street inform us: "Those who can do the job get the prime rib. Those who can't do the job get the bone." In concept, I agree, but the situation is not that simple:[3] The average increase in real income for the bottom 99 percent of American families between 1973 and 2006 was 8.5 percent. The richest one percent saw a 190 percent increase in income.

From 2000 to 2010, the median income in the United States, after adjusting for inflation, decreased by seven percent, the worst ten-year performance since records were kept (back to 1967).[4]

These facts are disturbing. First, they reflect a great disparity in how our society rewards its citizens in the context of their contributions to society. A mortgage broker makes hundreds of thousands of dollars a year gaming the subprime market with false mortgage applications. A bond salesman makes several million dollars a year hawking toxic mortgage backed securities. A plumber, an electrician, or a carpenter find themselves unemployed partially because of the greed and poor judgment of the mortgage broker and bond salesman.

Macro Consequences of Income Disparity

Again, that's life. Nothing is fair. Take care of yourself. The micro management of your own welfare is fundamental to your survival and security. Nonetheless, many years ago in a moment of practical wisdom, we humans created halters to place around the mouths of our hungry, self-interest appetites. For a society to be able to thrive—and abet an individual's chances of survival—some form of income (re)distribution would have to be made. For two reasons:

First, if for nothing else, to keep the starving peasants from rioting and killing the landed gentry (which has been known to happen on occasion): "If they don't have cake, we had better *at least* give them bread. Otherwise, they'll come after our cake." Second, we humans have slowly evolved into a more benevolent species.[5]

We've come to accept the idea of the distribution of wealth to the less fortunate members of our species.[6]

I make these observations to focus on two aspects regarding modern-day America: (a) Unequal income distribution without associated risk taking is creating disrespect, even animosity among America's citizens. This contempt is being directed toward big business for doing it, and government for fostering it. (b) Unequal income distribution—leading to disparate political payoffs—is leading to an erosion of America's republican foundations.

And of major import: By propping up unsuccessful enterprises, other companies are denied opportunities to foster their ideas and sell their products. They are placed at a further disadvantage by Uncle Sam's actions.

The sense of fair play for Americans—hackneyed as it may be—is taking a big hit by the nearly perfect financial storm and its aftermath. It is creating resentments that will not be easily healed. It is fostering movements such as the street occupiers and tea party associations.

Unequal Campaign Contributions

Until recently, I had given no thought to the notion of a company having the right of free speech in the context of the First Amendment. It hit home after reading about the United States Supreme Court ruling (January 21, 2010) that corporate funding of independent political broadcasts in candidate elections cannot be limited under the First Amendment right of free speech. In Part I, I wrote a couple paragraphs about this ruling. Let's examine it in more detail.

Justice Kennedy wrote the majority opinion by stating, "If the First Amendment has any force, it prohibits Congress from fining or jailing citizens, or associations of citizens, for simply engaging in political speech." He also said it was not possible to distinguish between media and other corporations and a restriction would allow government to suppress political speech in newspapers, books, television, and blogs.

I agree with these general sentiments. After all, where is the line drawn? My problem with this ruling is the fact that a corporation is not a citizen with inherent constitutional rights. Even more, the Court took on a narrow issue and *purposely* broadened it to overturn decades of rulings and practice.

Furthermore, the majority opinion gives corporations an additional lever against the individual citizen, which is a repudiation of the one person, one vote legacy.[7] A private citizen can make campaign contributions and go to the voting booth to cast one vote. A corporate citizen can exercise this same right and then go to his office to make additional campaign contributions from business coffers. For certain, the private citizen can also contribute to campaigns but he cannot come close to matching the deep pockets of large companies.

The heart of this issue comes down to this fact: The amount of money given to a campaign is a significant factor in determining the outcome of an election. (Supporting statistics are cited later in this chapter.)

The Supreme Court opinion states that spending is a form of free speech. Thus, a heretofore fictional being of commerce (the corporation) is given the patina of a private citizen. Corporations are speakers who have the same constitutional rights as you and me.

Part of the minority opinion rang true with what is eroding in America: common sense:

> At bottom, the Court's opinion is thus a rejection of the common sense of the American people, who have recognized a need to prevent corporations from undermining self government since the founding, and who have fought against the distinctive corrupting potential of corporate electioneering since the days of Theodore Roosevelt. It is a strange time to repudiate that common sense. While American democracy is imperfect, few outside the majority of this Court would have thought its flaws included a dearth of corporate money in politics.

What does this issue have to do with Wall Street and the financial industry? It gives large organizations, such as banks, much greater power in America's politics. Equally serious, it further distances the individual citizen from the classical concept of a republic:[8] "A state in which supreme power is held by the people and their elected representatives."

Corporations should not be vested with the same constitutional rights of individuals. We will witness backlash in the future, because the ruling means the definition of a republic is now, "A state in which supreme power is held by those who have the deepest pockets."

The Court could have issued a narrower ruling. (As it was asked to do by the lead attorney for United!) But it did not. The majority also said, "The appearance of influence of access, furthermore, will not cause the electorate to lose faith in our democracy."

This claim is a fantastic assumption. The ruling will lead to large companies, especially those held privately by political zealots, buying elections without regard to anything other than ideological, single-issue topics.

The ruling will become a major factor in America's politics. Pro-business Republicans, along with antigovernment right wingers will initially gain more control of the political process in America, and further extend their reach into the ever-increasing gerrymandered wards and districts of this country.

Not to be denied of their now constitutionally guaranteed soapbox, the radical left will lick its wounds, form Super PACs, and mount their own freedom of speech campaigns. You and I will have the pleasure of watching increasingly scurrilous ads on TV, interspersed with the TV commentators lamenting the ads that will be funding their lamentations.

Do these scenarios trouble you? I suppose it depends on your political leanings. It should trouble all of us because it further removes individual citizens from the political process.

Perhaps my prediction for this future is not so far-fetched. With the dependency of political success increasingly based on massive advertising, the electorate has already been detached from exercising "supreme power" as the deciding political agency. The deciding political agencies are now corporations, PACs, unions, and social networks funded by large campaign contributors.

The personal door-to-door "Howdy, I'm running for Congress!" glad-handing protocol is being rendered irrelevant. It is only effective if it is played back on TV ads; ads funded by PACs.

Meet Mr. and Ms. Inc.

If corporations are granted citizen rights, they should also be granted citizen responsibilities. But how do you put a corporation in jail? With rare exceptions, the malfeasance of corporations results only in puny fines (relative to their net worth), with none of the guilty people spending any time behind bars. Quite the opposite occurs. The money for the fines is taken from the coffers of the stockholders. The guilty parties' incomes stay intact, often even increasing as bonuses continue to accrue. As described in later chapters, these legal fees may even be taken on by taxpayers.

I have made the claim several times in this book that the power of K Street's lobbyists is undermining the integrity of our governmental institutions. This ruling will greatly abet this dangerous trend.

In view of America's present corrupt congressional/lobbyist cabal, the Supreme Court's decision will prove to be a dangerous extension to the notion of free speech. Insult is added to injury when corporate crooks are insulated from incarceration by sitting behind their corporate shields.

Voters: Not What They Used to Be

Meanwhile, the Supreme Court decision is beginning to show its head. Recall from the last section that the Supreme Court has ruled that corporations and other nonpersons have the same right as persons to make independent campaign contributions. However, unlike persons who are allowed to spend up to $2,500 on a candidate, nonpersons can spend an unlimited amount of money for or against a candidate.

The supposed counter to this decision is that these contributions must be made independently. That is, they cannot be coordinated with the candidate. The individual candidate must remain aloof from these contributions. According to the law, a candidate must have nothing to do with these fund-raising organizations.

How can this facade possibly hold up? The candidate need only proclaim he is "For Issue X" and a "For Issue X" political action committee (PAC) will spring up, with a network that is able to bring in millions of dollars.

One of the leaders of this pack of attack dogs is Larry McCarthy, creator of the Willie Horton ad, a slam that helped wreak havoc on the 1988 presidential campaign of Michael Dukakis. (Granted, Michael's pose wearing a helmet while sitting in a combat tank did not help his cause).

McCarthy is good at this job: skewering the opposition with innuendoes, allegations, and outright purposeful distortions. Yet he proclaims, "I'm not allowed to communicate with Super PACs (explained shortly) in any way, shape, or form. If we coordinate in any way whatsoever, we go to the big house."[9]

We can only express amazed contempt for the blatant disregard for civility displayed by the Larry McCarthys of this world. Anything these people can get away with, they will do. They have no respect for the simple notion that a candidate's philosophies can be addressed by speaking about those very philosophies, that their ideas stand or do not stand on their own merit.

More Fodder for the Fire

Here are two examples of the effect of the Citizens United ruling from the Supreme Court. In North Carolina, Art Pope and his family's privately held company (Variety Wholesalers) are becoming an even larger force in state politics. Republican Pope, his family, and their organizations targeted twenty-two legislative 2010 races in North Carolina. The Republicans won "eighteen, placing both chambers under Republican majorities for the first time since 1870."[10]

Pope discounts the idea that money determines the outcomes of elections. Really? In the 2008 races, 93 percent of the House races and 94 percent of the Senate races were won by the candidate who spent the most money.[11]

In the 2006 election cycle, independent expenditures totaled $37,394,589. In the 2010 election cycle, they totaled $210,912,167.[12] That gain is more than a fivefold increase, resulting in yet more negative ads on television and more citizens voting for dancers than for politicians.

The Supreme Court did not make its decision based on corporations being persons, about which I regaled earlier. The Court stated that Congress did not have the right to limit this kind of political "speech"; that is, speaking with money.

Under America's present political campaign system, the ruling is leading to further erosion of the republican concept of one person, one vote. Justice Kennedy, who we learned wrote the majority opinion, used an earlier thought for this ruling: "Favoritism and influence are not...avoidable in representative politics. It is the nature of an elected representative to favor certain policies, and by necessary corollary, to favor the voters and contributors who support those policies."[13]

Contributors? Is that what James Madison and his colleagues had in mind? Consider the absurdity of this idea. Goldman Sachs is not a voter but a contributor. Goldman cannot cast a vote in the voting booth. But through its campaign contributions, it has extraordinary influence on whose names are on the ballot sheet that Joe Citizen supposedly chooses, as well as on the candidates themselves. This winnowing process is not determined by voters. It is determined by large campaign contributors, such as Goldman.

Okay, but what if the interests of Goldman and Joe Citizen overlap? It makes no difference as the practice is still a distortion of the Constitution. Besides, they do not overlap (unless Joe owns stock in Goldman...which he cannot afford to buy).

To illustrate the huge gap between the public's view of America's problems and the views of K Street lobbyists—who reflect special interests and have tremendous influence on Congress—see Table 23-1.[14]

This study compares the percent of K Street's lobbying efforts to the average responses to a Gallup poll question, "What is the most important problem facing the country today?" (The percentages do not add to 100 percent. These issues were the most frequently cited.)

Table 23-1. Responses to Gallup Poll question: "What is the most important problem facing the country today?"

Issues	Lobbyists' Focus	Public Response
Law, Crime, and Family Policy	5%	25%
Macroeconomics and Taxation	3%	20%
Health	20%	8%
Environment	17%	2%
International Affairs and Foreign Aid	2%	10%
Transportation	8%	0%
Banking, Finance, and Commerce	8%	0%
Science, Technology, and Communication	7%	1%
Foreign Trade	6%	0%
Education	5%	10%
Social Welfare	2%	7%

Why are the lobbying efforts on Congress so different from the issues that concern voters? The authors of this study do not answer this question directly. To this writer, the study shows a detachment between what shallow-pocket voters want and what deep-pocket special interest groups want. Who gets the attention of a congressperson, a $10 donor or a $10,000 donor?

The issues important to voters are not the issues bringing in lobbying money. I cite two of the big differences. Banking: big dollars to Wall Street and largely off the scope of Joe Citizen. Health: big dollars to insurance companies and not in Joe's vision as long as he has this company's Blue Cross or Uncle Sam's Medicare.

Joe remains unconcerned. On the surface, he is being taken care of. Below the surface, his taxes and health care premiums are funding an enormous contest for billions of dollars of revenues to Wall Street and health insurance companies.

The average voter does not realize he/she is being taken to the cleaners by the banking and health care industries. How can the voter know the arcane details of thousands of pages of almost unreadable lawyerese? I read many of these pages, and I often come away baffled. Yet the wording in these documents affects the well-being of each voter.

Does this voter get a shot at writing the passages in the laws? No. After all that is the job of elected lawmakers. But the lobbyist has a hand it them. He often helps craft the text. If not the lobbyist, then congressional assistants who will shortly be employed on K Street. All participants' ultimate livelihood—lawmakers, lobbyists, and assistants—are funded by huge donations from special interest groups.

Which brings us back to the Supreme Court decision. It is obvious there is little overlap between, using Justice Kennedy's words—the "voter" and the "contributor." They are often at odds with each other. As I will amplify later, campaign contributions have corrupted Congress, which has grown dependent on them. In addition, they have contributed to the public's distrust of our government. The process, which is reinforced by the Supreme Court's ruling, is symptomatic of an anti-republican state:

- The campaign funds of huge contributors determine the candidates for Congress.
- The voters vote on the candidates who were selected by the contributors.
- The contributors' K Street lobbyists help Capitol Hill fashion legislation, usually for the benefit of the contributors.
- Eventually (and frequently) Congress members and their aides transfer jobs, going from Capitol Hill to K Street. At K Street, they take up where they left off at Capitol Hill.

This scenario is not what constitutes a democracy, much less a republic. A voter should not only get an equal vote for a political candidate, the voter should have an equal say in who gets on the ballot in the first place. But it is the big money that determines who the ultimate candidates are.

Of course, the suppositions based on the list above are anecdotal. I have no hard data to back up these claims. But I am writing this book, not as a political scientist, but an average person who knows, "If it walks like a duck and quacks like a duck, it is not a chicken." The connections and resulting distortion of America's vaunted republican ways are too obvious not to be known.

We voters are not so stupid to have learned that it is Justice Kennedy's "contributors" who call the shots. In disgust, because we think we have no real say in the process, we vote less and less and watch "Dancing with the Stars" more and more; a formula for further erosion of America's political process.

As cited earlier, in Justice Kennedy's statements in Citizens United, he tells us, "The appearance of influence or access...will not cause the electorate to lose faith in our democracy." The justice is behind the times. The electorate has already lost faith in our democracy. Through what process can he make such a subjective and preposterous claim? We can only ask, what world does he inhabit?

Goldman Sachs is (once again) licking its chops. Goldman, and others of its ilk, have left the politicians to do their own *geographical gerrymandering*. With their access to huge quantities of funds, the large banks will reshape (even more) the *financial gerrymandering* landscape, aided and abetted by the increasing influence of wealthy contributors. As Bob Dole said, "Poor people don't make campaign contributions."[15]

Super PACs

Largely because of the Supreme Court decision, the way has been opened up for virtually unlimited spending by anyone. Thus, the name of Super PACs has come into being. Here are some examples of this spending:[16]

> Edward Conard, a former colleague of Mitt Romney's at Bain Capital, gave the Republican front runner a $1 million

contribution. Jeffrey Katzenberg, CEO of Dreamworks Animation, gave President Obama $2 million. And Las Vegas casino magnate Sheldon Adelson gave Newt Gingrich $5 million.

Technically, these contributions did not go to these men. The money was given to a Super PAC, which can accept unlimited donations to spend "as much as it likes to support a particular candidate (or tear down his or her opponent.)"[17]

As mentioned, this money must go to an "independent" organization, with no formal link to a candidate. Nonsense, this idea is a complete illusion. Even if Mr. Conard never talks with Mr. Romney, his $1 million will not find its way into Newt's coffers. Where will it go? To Mitt.

To throw salt on the wound opened up by the Supremes, the Super PACs are now routinely engaged in creating hardball ads about an opponent. But these ads are not associated with a political candidate. The candidate remains a noble politician, above the fracas of personality assassination. The candidate no longer must say, "I approved this message." The setup is little more than political pornography.

Obama is joining the fray:[18]

> The president's advisers have signaled to donors that he will soften, for the time being, his long-standing opposition to the outside groups, in hopes of assisting their fundraising efforts and leveling the campaign finance field heading into the general election. Obama's campaign staff will go so far as to appear at super PAC events—though they will not be explicitly raising money. The president will not attend those events, a source confirmed.

Obama is no different from any other big-time politician. He must raise a lot of money if he is to remain in office. He has declared he does not accept contributions from registered lobbyists but those very lobbyists have immense influence on the White House.[19] While donors fete on $17,900 dishes at a patron's home, Barak explains to the diners that the nation's capital should be "more responsive to the needs of the people, not the need of special interests."

Meanwhile, Barak's White House hospitality suite harbors other "people." A study shows that "those who donated the most to Mr. Obama and the Democratic Party since he started running for president were far more likely to visit the White House than others."

Among donors who gave $30,000 or less, about 20 percent visited the White House. Those donors who gave $100,000 or more, the pay-a-call-on-Obama figure rises to about 75 percent. However, these statistics do not include the donors who pay a call on the White House by standing in the mass-attendance visitation line. This assemblage is what Barak gratuitously refers to as the "people."

I digress to offer that a politician, even clothed as a people-oriented Democrat, is still a politician. Returning to Super PACs: A Democrat political pollster described the impact of these organizations:[20]

> It's become a situation where the contest is how much you can destroy the system, rather than how much you can make it work. It makes no difference if you had a "D" or and "R" after your name. There's no sense that this is about democracy, and after the election, you have to work together, and knit the country together. The people in the game now just think to the first Tuesday in November, and not a day beyond it. ...Now you can hide behind super pacs [sic] that have no future responsibility to govern.

Unequal Representation

Before closing this topic, here are a few more examples of the effect of the Supreme Court decision:[21] Nevada ranks 25th in the nation in its residents' donations to presidential candidates. It is second in the nation in donations to Super PACs. One person, Sheldon Adelson, has donated $25 million to Super PACs. Adelson's spokesman informs us, "[Adelson] is not looking to have a role in the public debate." How can anyone utter such a falsehood? By his massive contributions, Adelson has greatly influenced the tone of the public debate pertaining to the Super PACs to which he has contributed.

The securities and investment industry has donated $31 million to Super PACs, the most of any sector. $31 million? Just a tad more than Joe the Plumber contributes. Whose issues get the grease, Joe or K Street? I have documented these facts. See Table 23-1.

The Super PACs are going after politicians who do not fit their political color. In electoral races, they are outspending, and therefore usually defeating their lesser-funded opponents. (As Robert Dole told us earlier, poor people don't make campaign contributions.)

I've documented specific outcomes of the Supremes' decision in the main body of this book. I bring it up again to ask you to take note of this travesty: A republic cannot remain a republic if its dictates are controlled by those who have the most money. In this regard—after much self-imposed resistance—I stand in the camp of finding a way to publically fund campaign contributions.

Income, Education and Training Disparity

Income. While doing research for this book, it became obvious that America's present financial and social setup is leading to a fading middle class and a growing upper class. Middle class Americans are hunkering down, while the more affluent citizens are hunkering up. In addition to the information cited in the reports in Part I, here are some more statistics:[22]

- Fortune 500 directors (on the board of directors) will receive a median pay of $234,000 in 2011,
- for putting in about 4.3 hours per week of work,
- on subjects about which the directors are often clueless.

On the other side of the street, citizens are moving out of their former homes, downgrading their dens, and selling off their dirt bikes. Here are some updates to the reports in Part I: [23]

- From 2006 to 2010 census, data reveals the number of middle-income families in America shrank. In metro areas, the middle-class share of income dropped by more than 2 to 1 to those families who had an increase of income.
- In the 1970s, 53 percent of the nation's income went to the middle class. In 2010, the figure was 46.3 percent.
- Three decades ago, the difference between the starting salaries of teachers and lawyers was $2,000. Today the difference is $125,000.[24] Guess which profession is on top?

Earlier, I made a joke about the staying power of churches, saloons, and sex shops. I recently passed by a local watering hole in Hayden, Idaho named The Beer Hunter. It was a popular hangout. I use the word was, as it is now boarded up. What's the next door to be closed? Maybe it will be a door to a church, or the door to the Adam and Eve sex apparatus store. (At this late stage of my life, it's a coin toss about which building I am rooting for.)

I have had several conversations with those who tell me I am wrong about my criticism of rewarding high level executives with large payouts. They say (a) these people work a lot, (b) make decisions that gain their shareholders more income, and (c) are skewered in bad times, but ignored in good times. They tell me shareholders cannot have it both ways; that highly paid people need to be highly paid all the time in order to keep them around.

One of my friends framed his argument with Steve Jobs. He asked me, "How many shareholders care if Jobs rakes in millions?" My answer, "No one cares, because Jobs created Apple and personally drove the company to its present vaunted status."

Education. Slacking off from my skewering of high level executives in general, the people on most boards make their way into the broad rooms because they are talented. Most of them are well educated. I am not suggesting America's income disparity is because of the wealth of Wall Street. The problem is partially due to the deterioration of the nation's educational system. Consider these facts:[25]

- 35 percent of people between 25 to 54 years of age with no high school diploma have no job.
- High school dropouts are three times more likely to be unemployed than college graduates.
- Americans between 25 to 34 years of age are less likely to have a degree than Americans between the ages of 45 to 54.
- Children from upper class families are far more likely to get high level educational degrees than children from lower class families; that is, in comparison to what happened in the past.

The education divide in America is becoming more pronounced. To a large degree, this divide has fueled the income divide.

The Fact Remains

Nonetheless, the discrepancy of compensation to a person in relation to this person's worth to society's financial wheels is what is seeding much of the outrage expressed by the members of Occupy Wall Street. These people cannot connect the dots behind the rationale of a synthetic financial instrument—devoid of societal value—yielding over *one billion dollars* to the person who sells it under shady pretenses.[26]

These people are rightly confused. Before I delved into this book writing project, so was I. Yet many of America's citizens believe these protesters, while meaning well, are ill-informed malcontents. I agree with the idea that some of these people make misinformed claims. But their basic concerns in regard to the themes of this book are on target.

---

[1] Shakespeare, *Titus Andronicus*, 4.4.83, 1593. Secondary source: Frank, p. 295.

[2] Roger D. Hodge, "Readings," *Harper's Magazine*, October, 2010, p. 14.

[3] Ibid., and *Time*, using IRS data for adjusted gross income, October 3, 2011.

[4] Phil Izzo, "Bleak News for Americans' Income," *The Wall Street Journal*, October 14, 2011, p. A6.

[5] Or is it a matter of our having more than ten future meals stored on our shelves?

[6] Studies show that charitable activities activate feel-good feelings, which are associated with neural activities in the brain.

[7] It is beyond this book to delve into detail about the illusion that America practices the one person, one vote concept. The Electoral College guarantees disproportionality. Nonetheless, for this discussion this admirable idea is further debased.

[8] From Google Dictionary.

[9] Jane Mayer, "Attack Dog," *The New Yorker*, February 13 and 20, 2012, pp. 42-43.

[10] Jane Mayer, "State for Sale," *The New Yorker*, October 10, 2011, p. 93. It is immaterial to this writer if the winner is Republican or Democrat.

[11] OpenSecrets.org: http://www.opensecrets.org/news/2008/11/money-wins-white-house-and.html.

[12] Lawrence Lessig, *Republic, Lost*, Hachette Book Group, Inc., New York, 2011, p. 361, footnote 42.

[13] *Citizens United vs. Fed. Election Commission*, 130 S. Ct. 676, 910. Secondary source, Lessig, p. 363, footnote 51.

[14] Frank Baumgartner, Jeffery Berry, Marie Hojnacki, David Kimball, and Beth Leech, *Lobbying and Policy Change*, pp. 257-258. Secondary source: Lessig, ibid., p. 349, footnote 60.

[15] George Packer, "The Broken Contract," *Foreign Affairs*, November/December, 2011, p. 29.

[16] *USA TODAY*, January 12, 2012, p. 6A.

[17] Ibid.

[18] http://www.huffingtonpost.com/2012/02/06/president-obama-super-pacs_n_1258925.html.

[19] Mike McIntire and Michael Luo, "White House Opens Door to Big Donors, and Lobbyists Slip In," *The New York Times*, April 15, 2012, p. 1.

[20] Mayer, "Attack Dog," p. 49.

[21] Fredreka Schouten and Gregory Korte, "A Few Rich Donors Fuel Super PACs," *USA TODAY*, May 3, 2012, p. 5A.

[22] Marisol Bello and Paul Overberg, "The Fading Middle Class," *USA TODAY*, October 26, 2011, p. A1.

[23] Ibid., p. A6.

[24] CNN program on education in America, November 13, 2004. Commentary by Fareed Zakaria.

[25] Ragburam Rajan, "The True Lessons of the Recession," *Foreign Affairs*, May/June, 2012, pp. 74-75.

[26] I once again emphasize: The individual who takes the risks himself deserves any amount of money his risks engender. The individual who takes the risks with the money of stockholders does not.

Chapter 24

Corrupting Influences

"A jackass can kick a barn down, but it takes a carpenter to build one."
—attributed to Sam Rayburn

A ship that cannot be steered is a ship that will sink.
—Lawrence Lessig[1]

Public service. A noble thought. The phrase is a mantra for almost every politician. In one form or another, it is invoked during their campaigns for election and during ribbon-cutting ceremonies for earmarked projects in their districts.

The two words are used along with another phrase: self-sacrifice. This term conveys the idea of taking a financial loss to serve the public and foregoing time at the family hearth while toiling away at the remote capitol.

It is not my intent to stereotype the entire political profession, but it must be said that significant aspects of America's state and national political/financial systems are dysfunctional. I have provided examples in Part I and will provide others in this chapter. These examples, some so egregious they seem imaginary, reveal that "public service and self-sacrifice" are often masquerades for unashamed, corrupt lifestyles—at the expense of society.

To balance the scales, it should also be emphasized that America is one of the least corrupt nations on earth. But it is not blameless.

According to Transparency International, the United States ranks nineteenth in the world in a "corruption perception index."[2] Not even in the top ten.

This chapter and the next point out weaknesses in the U.S. political/financial system. I am not unearthing new revelations but framing them in the context of the subject matter of this book. Anticipating that so-called patriots will assail these thoughts because they are un-American, I again state that I write them because I am a partisan of America.

Bribes by Any Other Name

On *60 Minutes* (November 6, 2011) Leslie Stahl interviewed the former lobbyist, Jack Abramoff who spent time in prison for some of his dealings.[3] He said his K Street lobbying firm had an influence on one hundred congressional offices. Although Mr. Abramoff did not say so, it was obvious the interview revealed "influence" meant bribing congresspeople or senior members of their staffs.[4] Abramoff said he thought a lobbyist considered this number a failure because he had less or no influence in 325 other offices. Here is an excerpt from this interview:

> Stahl: "But the "best way" to get a congressional office to do his bidding - he says - was to offer a staffer a job that could triple his salary."

> Abramoff: "When we would become friendly with an office and they were important to us, and the chief of staff was a competent person, I would say or my staff would say to him or her at some point, 'You know, when you're done working on the Hill, we'd very much like you to consider coming to work for us.' Now the moment I said that to them or any of our staff said that to 'em, that was it. We owned them. And what does that mean? Every request from our office, every request of our clients, everything that we want, they're gonna do. And not only that, they're gonna think of things we can't think of to do."

Abramoff spoke of his success in altering a very small part of a bill that gave "a backdoor license to an Indian casino owned by one of Abramoff's clients." Here is the exact wording in the bill that made this happen: "Public law 100-89 is amended by striking section 207 (101 stat. 668, 672)."

That's it, and someone got a casino license! Abramoff said no one really paid much attention to such details. Except those who were bribed.

Do we think the national lawmakers actually know about the thousands of details in a law, such as the financial reform bill covered in Report 18? Hardly, and that is where the corruption of congressional senior aides comes into play. We saw a likely example of this practice with the Congo Conflict Minerals clause in the Dodd-Frank bill. In this instance, I would wager it was someone other than a staff person who had this clause placed into this legislation.

Here are a few more Abramoff quotes:

You can't take a congressman to lunch for $25 and buy him a hamburger or a steak of something like that. But you can take him to a fund raising lunch and not only buy him that steak but give him $25,000 extra and call it a fundraiser. And have all the same access and all the same interaction with that congressman. So the people who make the reforms are the people in the system.

...the system hasn't been cleaned up at all.

Stahl: "He says the most important thing that needs to be done is to prohibit members of Congress and their staff from ever becoming lobbyists in Washington."

Will this idea clean up the mess? Somewhat. Consider that since 1998, 43 percent of people who left Congress ended up on K Street.[5] That figure is an amazing statistic that says a great deal about our politicians and our political system.

But this action unto itself will not solve the corrupting influence that lobbyists have on sitting congresspeople. It will not diminish significantly the significance the Supreme Court decision will have on the rich buying elections.

Insider Trading

A model. To introduce the subject of congressional insider trading, we look to the past, to the behavior of a legislator, Sam Rayburn. Next, we compare his ethics with those of current members of Congress.

At the onset of this discussion, I emphasize that in Rayburn's times, his ethics were not of the norm. Graft and greed were as endemic to Congress then as they are now. I am not suggesting that things have changed all that much. I am proposing that Rayburn's approach to conflicts of interest should be a model for all members of Congress to follow.

Rayburn refused to accept money from companies for which legislation was pending. He was a partner in a law firm during his time as a Texas legislator. If he were given a check made out to his law firm from a company that was involved in legislation of which he was aware, he refused to accept the proportion of the check that reflected his partnership.

Here we go. Hold your nose.

Another Model. In addition to the lobbying extremes discussed in the previous section of this chapter, some members of Congress are outright political pickpockets. *60 Minutes* aired a program on November 13, 2011 about the access that many congresspeople have on inside information that affects stock market prices and many other financial aspects of America. The program provided several examples that I extracted directly from the associated Web page (I have made small changes to improve readability):

> Former House Speaker Nancy Pelosi and her husband have participated in at least eight IPOs. One of those came in 2008, from Visa, just as a troublesome piece of legislation that would have hurt credit card companies, began making its way through the House. Undisturbed by a potential conflict of interest the

Pelosis purchased 5,000 shares of Visa at the initial price of $44 dollars. Two days later it was trading at $64. The credit card legislation never made it to the floor of the House.

If you are a member of Congress and you sit on the defense committee, you are free to trade defense stock as much as you want. If you're on the Senate banking committee you can trade bank stock as much as you want. This practice is prevalent in all committees; no restraints whatsoever.

During the health care debate of 2009, members of Congress were trading health care stocks, including then House Minority Leader John Boehner. (Writer: Boehner bought tens of thousands of dollars of health care stocks, including stocks in heath care insurance companies.[6] Need we infer? The public option for health care insurance never made it.)

Former New Hampshire Senator Judd Gregg, helped steer nearly $70 million dollars in government funds toward redeveloping a defunct Air Force base, in which he and his brother both had a commercial interest.

In the past few years a new and unregulated $100 million industry has grown up in Washington called political intelligence. It employs former congressmen and former staffers to scour the halls of the Capitol gathering valuable nonpublic information then selling it to hedge funds traders on Wall Street who "refine" their investment portfolios accordingly.

Illinois Congressman Dennis Hastert became speaker of the House in 1999. He was worth a few hundred thousand dollars. He left the job eight years later a multimillionaire; worth close to $11 million. (Writer: On the salary of a public servant? Perhaps it was due to a $207 million earmark he had inserted into a federal highway bill for a road near land he owned.)[7]

CHAPTER 24: CORRUPTING INFLUENCES 335

I trust most readers are now aware of the misleading machinations of America's political leaders in Congress. If not, here is more information for further persuasion:[8]

> Senator Max Baucus played a central role in forging the health care reform bill. As he was negotiating with the pharmaceutical companies and putting his imprint on legislation, Baucus was also buying and selling health care stocks.
>
> John Kerry and his wife Teresa Heinz Kerry made numerous trades in health care stocks, buying almost $750,000 in Teva Pharmaceuticals in November 2009 alone, while Kerry pushed Obama-care as a member of the health care committee.
>
> Representative Jared Polis sat on two committees central to the crafting and language of Obama's health care bill. At the same time, he invested millions of dollars in stocks and related funds to health care and pharmaceuticals.
>
> After a briefing with Henry Paulson and Ben Bernanke, Representative Shelley Capito sold between $100,000 and $250,000 shares of Citigroup. She and her husband accrued as much as $50,000 in capital gains from Citigroup transactions made throughout the crisis.

Are you surprised? I was astounded. I naively assumed there were rules prohibiting members of Congress from insider trading. Some of these people should be in jail. Absence of rules, it is important that a legislator remove himself from any legislation that affects the lawmaker's wallet. Either have the person remove himself or make sure the person is distanced from and cannot participate in blind trust.[9]

Other Facts. The CBS News website (http://www.cbsnews.com.) lists two studies about this issue. One study "shows that Senators' stock sales and purchases combined outperform the market by 97 basis points per month, or 12.3 percent per year."[10] The other study "shows that members of the U.S. House of Representatives' stock sales and purchases combined outperform the market by 55 basis points per month, or about 6 percent per year."[11]

Even if we discount these facts, which I do not, the very idea that these lawmakers would continue to participate in pending legislation that affects their investment portfolios says a lot about their lack of sense of fair play and their contempt for insider trading laws. Irony in action once again: Laws that these politicians sponsor have lead to non-politicians being sent to prison for insider trading.[12]

Only Upon Experiencing Public Disgust

I begin this section with a quote from *The New York Times*:[13]

> In an effort to regain public trust, the Senate voted Monday to take up a bill that would prohibit members of Congress from trading stocks and other securities on the basis of confidential information they receive as lawmakers.
>
> Senators of both parties said the bill was desperately needed at a time when the public approval rating of Congress had sunk below 15 percent.

It was not conscience that led the Senate to vote on an issue that represents a lynchpin of the stock market. It was political expediency. These lawmakers finally (after decades of self-serving plundering) succumbed, not to their shame, but to the publicity about their duplicity.

Even with their admission of the contempt held for them by America's citizens, they had the gall to maintain their interests in making laws pertaining to what they have in their investment portfolios:

> However, the bill does not subject lawmakers to a second type of restriction suggested by Mr. Obama, who said Congress should "limit any elected official from owning stocks in industries they impact."

So much for the integrity of blind trusts. A lawmaker knows which stocks and bonds are in his investment portfolio upon it being placed in a blind trust. Unless he is Jesus in a suit, the lawmaker cannot possibly remain unbiased about pending legislation that will affect his financial security. He will eventually leave office, at which time he will once again take over his former blind trust. Surprise! His health care stock gained over 100 percent during his tenure on health care lawmaking committees.

For government to function properly, its elected representatives must act as trustees of that government on behalf of the public. These representatives must place the public benefit before that of their own.

In a fine example of the Law of the Graveyard Shift, Congress is finally passing laws that forbid them from doing what they should never have been doing in the first place. All the while, their asymmetrical approach to ethics and fair play has put insider trading lawbreakers behind bars. The lawmakers—being the makers of these laws—remain on the other side of the bars.

State Legislatures' Self Generosity

USA TODAY conducted an investigation of the pensions provided to state legislators.[14] While some states are circumspect about this matter and have reasonable control over this pension money, many states do not. According to this study:

> More than 4,100 legislators in 33 states are positioned to benefit from special retirement laws that they and their predecessors have enacted to boost their pensions by up to $100,000 a year...Even as (they) cut basic state services and slash benefits for police, teachers, and other workers, they have preserved pension laws that grant themselves perks unavailable to voters they serve or workers they direct.
>
> Lawmakers in several states start collecting their retirement benefits while still in office... while also collecting legislative paychecks.

Several states' lawmaker pensions allow lawmakers to base their pensions on expenses, per-diem allowances, and stipends to their base salaries.

Many states' pensions for legislators are higher than other state workers. These lawmakers—*who wrote and enacted the very laws supporting their legal corruption*—can retire earlier than their civil service counterparts. In addition, many states pay extra to a lawmaker if he/she assumes a position beyond being just a legislative drone. For example, the New York legislature rewarded James Tedisco in this way: "(He) improved his $79,500 legislative pay by taking on the minority leader with its $114,000 salary."

Try to imagine this wacky concept: Minority or majority leaderships in a legislative body are positions bestowing esteem and power on the leader. Such positions provide the holder with fantastic accesses to influence and sources of largesse from K Street and other "freedom of speech" supporters. I'm using Tedisco as an example. He may be as pure as New York City snow. Yet taxpayers are bilked for funding a position that is coveted for what it brings the position holder.

Defenders of generous pensions for "retired" lawmakers say these lawmakers must be sufficiently compensated in order to discourage them from engaging in graft. "One has to eat, even if one is a public servant."

I am amazed by this view of what can only be characterized as lawful bribery. But I also understand if we citizens want lawmakers who live among the mainstream of America's salaried masses, we must pay the rank-and-file legislators for time spent in their capitols.

About that time spent. Most state legislatures are in session three to five months during a year. Again, defenders of the system state the legislative process is a full-time job. Most state lawmakers have income from other professions and they spend time on those professions while at home...and while making laws in their capitols. Nice part-time work.

I close this part of my criticism with one more finding from the fine reporting done by Thomas Frank.

CHAPTER 24: CORRUPTING INFLUENCES 339

Connecticut legislators can add mileage reimbursements to their salary for the calculations of their pensions. All told, the Connecticut lawmakers use this gimmick to boost their salaries about $1.6 million a year. And the next year; and the next...

Can you imagine the amount of corporate muck that would hit the fan if we proposed to our company that our retirement plans factor in the gas we purchased for a corporate business trip? Gas that the corporation paid for in our last payroll check? I hope it astounds and repulses you. It does me.

Trust in government, one in which politicians—even local state legislators—routinely exploit their constituents? The tea parties continue to assemble.

Gerrymandering

For sake of illustration, let's suppose you and I live in the 17th congressional district of northern Illinois. Some of America's political wards are as irregularly shaped as a Rorschach ink plot, with the 17th district shown in figure 24-1.[15] The dark-colored part of the figure represents this district.

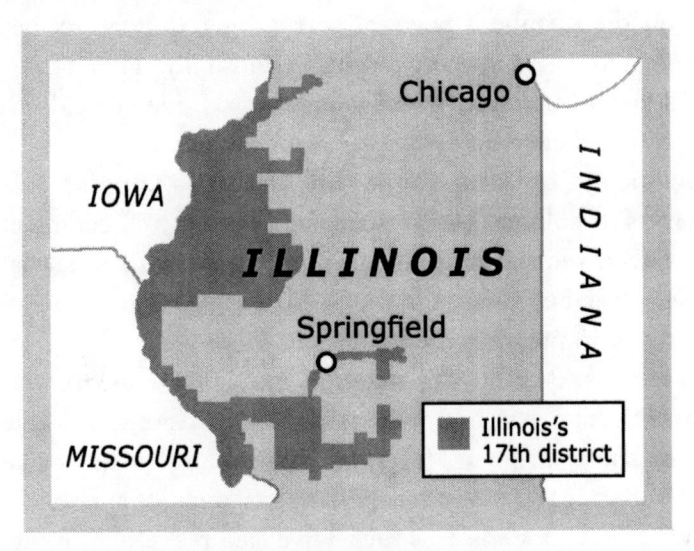

Figure 24-1. A Gerrymandered ward.

One alderman appoints the ward superintendent who directs the trucks and obliges many special pickup requests that meander through byzantine routes:[16]

> Revamping the city's collection system...would strip officials...of key powers...[Yet] garbage trucks often travel down alleys that switch from one ward to the next and back, each with different trash schedules.

I am an opponent of the practice of many states (forty-four of fifty) allowing party politicians to determine the boundaries of electoral districts. Some people disagree with my stand, and studies are available that state politically based gerrymandering has no effect on "electoral competition."[17] I disagree. It allows what should be demographically based decisions to be subjugated to political preferences. Because redrawing electoral boundaries is based on the ten-year census results, the practice gives a party in power a ten-year-long advantage.

Politically based gerrymandering has led to the current situation of radial, ideologically based politics. After all, if a district is redrawn based on the member's political persuasions, the district becomes more aligned with a specific political philosophy. This leads to safe districts for a candidate, which reinforces the ideological biases of both voter and candidate. One feeds on the other.

Again, my opinion about this matter is contested by the supporters of political gerrymandering. They say, "Leading experts have proven redistricting has nothing to do with polarization." Furthermore, they claim it is impossible to divorce politics from the process, not to mention the expense to do so.[18]

In the past decade, 96 percent of House incumbents who have sought reelection have been successful. Why? Answers: (a) big money, (b) pork barrel projects, (c) good performance of lawmaker, (d) gerrymandering, (e) name recognition/personal interaction.[19]

What are your choices? I say all five factors are significant. I will also take a guess you and I are in agreement that (c) and (e) are practices and attributes that need fostering and (a), (b), and (d) represent major obstructions to America's republican foundations.

Time Sharing: Campaigning and Occasionally Governing

Scholars such as Lawrence Lessig claim the corrupted system described thus far is not as it is because the participants are necessarily evil. He says an institution can be corrupted when its members become "dependent upon an influence that distracts them from the intended purpose of the institution. The distracting dependency corrupts the institution."[20] He calls it dependence corruption.

The idea has merit but I am uneasy with the notion that members of Congress, who benefit from this corruption, were the very people who put it in place and continue to keep it in place. After all, the basic function of a congressperson is to govern, not to get reelected.

The time spent by a legislator in legislating pales to his/her time in looking for money to stay in office. Even if all of our state and national congressional members are politically pristine, the fact is they do not spend much time doing the jobs for which they were elected. That alone should convince even the most doubtful that substantial reform is needed.

Campaign Contributions and Legislation

There is a direct, positive correlation of campaign contributions to that of laws passed on behalf of the contributors. Here are three examples, among many:

High fructose corn syrup, a sugar substitute, was never tasted by a consumer in 1980. In 2006, it accounted for 35 percent of sugar consumption. Forty percent of the products we buy in the supermarket have high fructose in them. Why? America makes the cost of corn cheap because its production is subsidized. "In the fifteen years between 1995 and 2009, the government spent $73.8 billion to ensure that famers produced more corn than the market would otherwise bear. That corn then got used to produce lots of high-fructose corn syrup, at an increasingly low price."[21] The campaign spending from the corn industry during this time went from $9 million to $19 million.

As another example, America's public school system is a disgrace. The major reasons are the inability to fire incompetent teachers and the low pay for competent teachers. It is not rocket science. Finland has one of the best teaching systems in the world. The country pays its teachers well and makes sure they are competent. Why can't we solve this relatively simple problem? Unions. By the way, teachers' union contributions to political campaigns went from about $5 million in 1994 to about $12 million in 2010.[22]

In Part I of this book, I wrote several pages about the demise of the Glass-Steagall Act. For this discussion, we turn to another politically motivated financial fiasco, touched on in Part I: the exemption of most over-the-counter derivatives from federal regulation—a lapse that was one of the key ingredients of the nearly perfect financial storm.

Wendy Gramm, upon departing as chair of the Commodity Futures Trading Commission, signed an order for this exemption. A few months later, she was "named a director of Enron, an active trader of natural gas and electrical derivatives."[23] During this time, K Street lobbyists using their financial leverages succeeded in killing four anti-derivatives bills in Congress. "From 1998 to 2008, the financial sector spent $1.7 billion on campaign contributions and $3.4 billion on lobbying expenses; the securities industry alone spent $500 million on campaign contributions and $600 million on lobbying."[24] The financial sector's contributions dwarf the combined contributions of the health care and defense industries.

I could go on with many more examples. I trust my point is made. To conclude this chapter, let's return to Sam Rayburn. I cite three paragraphs from Wikipedia, with minor edits for clarification (except the direct quote from Rayburn).[25]

Legislator, Heal Thyself by the Role Model of Sam Rayburn

Although many Texas legislators were on the payroll of public service companies, Rayburn refused to take part in this arrangement. He recounted his ideas on this matter in a speech during his congressional campaign.

"When I became a member of the law firm of Steger, Thurmond and Rayburn, Messrs. Thurmond and Steger were representing the Santa Fe Railroad Company, receiving pay monthly. When the first check came after I entered the firm, Mr. Thurmond brought to my desk one-third of the amount of the check, explaining what it was for. I said to him that I was a member of the Legislature, representing the people of Fannin County, and that my experience had taught me that men who represent the people should be as far removed as possible from concerns whose interests he was liable to be called on to legislate concerning, and that on that ground I would not accept a dollar of the railroad's money, though I was legally entitled to it. I never did take a dollar of it. I have been guided by the principle in all my dealings."

This practice of refusing to accept fees from clients who had interests before the legislature was "virtually unheard-of" at the time. Later, while serving in Congress, a wealthy oilman had a very expensive horse delivered to Rayburn's farm in Bonham. No one apparently knew the oilman delivered the horse except him, Rayburn, and a Rayburn staffer. Rayburn returned the horse.

Compare the actions of Sam Rayburn in this section of the chapter to the actions of other lawmakers cited in previous discussions. The brazenness and unabashed shamelessness of the current members of Congress in fleecing the very people who elected them is astounding. They were elected to protect the interests of their voters. Their misuse of their offices goes beyond uncaring. It borders on callousness.

Yet well meaning and smart scholars, such as Lawrence Lessig, tell us these people are victims of dependence corruption. Yes. Dependence on a system they themselves have created, one they continue to perpetuate, and one that is mostly immune to the wishes of the voter.

In the meantime, Wall Street has built a $300 million eight-hundred-mile optic fiber system that links the Chicago Mercantile Exchange with the New York Stock Exchange. The path "shaves three milliseconds off high-speed, high-volume trades—a big competitive advantage. But passenger trains between Chicago and

New York run barely faster than they did in 1950...We can upgrade our iPhones, but we can't fix our roads and bridges."[26]

Pennsylvania Avenue and K Street are well paved. No potholes whatsoever.

---

[1] Lessig, *Republic Lost*, p. 1.

[2] "Another Great Leap Forward?" *The Economist*, March 13, 2010, p. 28.

[3] http://www.cbsnews.com.

[4] I am not taking liberties here. He did not explicitly say so. But watch the interview. His gestures and intonations say much more than the words I put on paper.

[5] Wikipedia, key in "Lobbyists."

[6] *Newsweek*, November 21, 2011, p. 35.

[7] Ibid.

[8] Ibid.

[9] Before inserting this idea, I spoke with a blind trust expert. He explained the various ways this system prevents, say, a lawmaker from exploiting his blind trust portfolio by his/her legislative actions. I disagree, and will explain why later in this chapter.

[10] Alan J. Ziobrowski, PhD, Ping Cheng, PhD, James W. Boyd, PhD, and Briggitte J. Ziobrowski, PhD, "Abnormal Returns from the Common Stock Investments of the U.S. Senate," *Journal of Financial and Quantitative Analysis*, December. 2004.

[11] Alan J. Ziobrowski, PhD, James W. Boyd, PhD, Ping Cheng, PhD, and Briggitte J. Ziobrowski, PhD, "Abnormal Returns from the Common Stock Investments of Members of the U.S. House of Representatives", *Business and Politics*, May 2011.

[12] Three examples: Danielle Chiesi (thirty months); James Fleishman (thirty months); Raj Rajaratnam (eleven years).

[13] Robert Pear and Jonathan Weisman, "Bill to Prohibit Insider Trading by Members of Congress Advances in Senate," *The New York Times*, January 31, 2012, p. A15. Other quotes in this section are sourced from this article.

[14] Thomas Frank, "How State Lawmakers Pump Up Pensions in Ways You Can't," *USA TODAY*, September. 23, 2011, pp. 1A, 8A – 10A. Statistics and quotes in this section are sourced from Frank's article. Thank you Mr.

Frank. Your superior "legwork" and "brainwork" should be a model to "reporters" who pirate your findings and make money on your labors.

[15] "Time to Bury Governor Gerry," *The Economist*, October 9, 1010, p. 20.

[16] Douglas Belkin, "Chicago Mayor Trashes Politics of Waste Removal," *The Wall Street Journal*, October 12, 2011, p. A1

[17] Wikipedia, key in "gerrymandering".

[18] *USA TODAY*, editorial published October 22, 2011, p. 8A.

[19] Most likely 50 percent of the 4 percent who did not win reelection found employment on K Street.

[20] Lessig, *Republic Lost*, p. 15.

[21] Ibid., p. 49.

[22] Ibid., p. 65.

[23] Ibid., p. 72.

[24] Ibid., p. 83.

[25] From Wikipedia, key in "Sam Rayburn." Primary sources for these excerpts are: The direct quote of Rayburn is form H.G. Dulaney and Edward Hake Phillips, *Speak, Mr. Speaker* (1978). Other material in this section is from: Anthony Champagne, *Congressman Sam Rayburn* (1984), and Anthony Champagne, *Congressman Sam Rayburn* (1984).

[26] Packer, "The Broken Contract," p. 22.

Chapter 25

The Rule of Law, Its Misrule, and Resultant Loss of Faith

You can do very little with faith, but you can do nothing without it.
—Samuel Butler

Trust in God, but tie your camel.
—An old saying

I have mentioned that litigation is forthcoming against banks and mortgage companies. The lawsuits pertain to falsifying legal contracts. This writer, an admitted naive legal waif, is astounded by the very idea that an institution—not just one person—would even consider engaging in on-going fraud.

These companies approved mortgages that fell outside underwriting rules. Estimates vary, but studies claim that about 25 percent of home loan mortgage documentation written in the early 2000s was incorrect. Not just technically incorrect, lawfully incorrect. This statistic is a thought-provoking number, remindful of a third-world country: *One-quarter* of all home mortgages were written unlawfully.

The success of a community—for this discussion, a nation—depends on many factors. Benevolent geography and ample natural resources are two of these factors. They are usually contributors to a vibrant society. But some countries have benign climate and ample minerals, yet are mired in social chaos and poverty.

A successful nation, perhaps bestowed with gifts from Mother Nature, exhibits three traits in its everyday dealing with its citizens. These traits pertain to a concept called the rule of law: First, the society has a well known set of rules (formal decrees or other accepted codes of behavior) by which the citizens are expected to conduct their lives. Second, the citizens trust those rules to the extent they adhere to them and live their lives accordingly. Third, the institutions of this community also adhere to these rules and administer them fairly to the citizens.

Of course, if a community (again, for this discussion, a nation) has no rules to begin with, it cannot hope to function. Likewise, if a country's citizens have no regard for the rules that are meant to structure their communal behavior, the people are not much better off than having no rules at all.

For a nation to flourish, it must provide security and peace of mind for its citizens. It must have rules that are fair to all. It must codify and practice a set of laws that protect the citizen. The laws' enforcement must also be efficient and implemented in such a way that moves the society forward in a competitive world. And regardless of the extent and clarity of these laws, if their implementations are tainted with corruption, they will do as much harm as they do good.

Trust

The bedrock of a successful society is also trust. Trust means a citizen has faith in the rule of law of his/her country and a trust in the leaders who *create* the rules. It also means trusting the people who *enforce* these rules.

As well, trust means that in knowing these rules, however distasteful to an individual's whims and aspirations, the citizen believes they are dispensed without prejudice toward an individual or a group of individuals. And if prejudicial laws do come about, if they are unfair and detrimental to a citizen, the rule of law provides a means by which they will be rescinded or corrected.

Trust in the rule of law has its ups and downs. Sometimes you win, sometimes you lose. But in the end, you know the cards that have been dealt to you were cut before they were dealt.

Exclusivity

A key to the success of a lawful society—perhaps the most important key—is non-exclusivity of a nation's laws. They apply equally to all. No exceptions. It is a culture in which all the cards are dealt-out equally.

A clean deck of cards is a fitting analogy to that of a just set of rules. If certain card players at a poker table are discovered to having been dealt favored cards, the other players will take measures to even the odds. They may resort to cheating. They may leave the game. They may kill or maim the crooks. Whatever their actions may be, they lead to a dysfunctional card game.

The same holds true for a society. Applying laws in an exclusive way leads to a dysfunctional culture. However complex; however arcane; however unintelligible, if a nation's laws do not rule fairly, the citizenry will come to know of this unfairness and rebel against them. Maybe the populace will not kill-off the lawmakers (as they did in the Russian and French revolutions), but they will surely undermine the formal governmental structure (as in modern-day Russia, India, and many other extralegal societies.)

On a less onerous note—I do not foresee citizens storming Capitol Hill and lynching legislators—but pertinent to my points: many laws of our land grant exclusivity to selected groups of citizens.

What is new? Exclusivity is part-and-parcel of legislation. But it can be taken to the extreme, leading to tea party and occupy street movements. I will amplify this assertion in the remainder of this chapter.

The Mystery of Capital and the Rule of Law

Hernando De Soto has written a book titled *The Mystery of Capital*. He explains why capitalism succeeds in some countries and fails in others. In his opinion, the most important factor in this success is property rights laws:[1]

Every parcel of land, every building, every piece of equipment, or store of inventories is represented in a property document that is the visible sign of a vast hidden process that connects all these assets to the rest of the economy. Thanks to this representational process, assets can lead an invisible, parallel life alongside their material existence. They can be used as collateral for credit.

Americans take property rights laws for granted. Yet De Soto states the vast majority of people in the world reside in countries that have weak, corrupted, or no property rights. Consequently, citizens often create their own extralegal society because they have been shut out of opportunities to own a business or buy a house.

The result can be seen all around the globe: huge cities of slums operating "illegally" next to the landed gentry's plush downtowns and suburbs. Consider India, one of the fastest-growing countries in the world:[2]

One massive problem in India is that few people can prove who they are. They have no passport, no driving license, no proof of address. They live in villages where multitudes share the same name. Their lack of identity excludes them from the modern economy. They cannot open bank accounts, and no one would be so foolish to lend them money.

Sharing the Wealth through Transparent Processes

In De Soto's studies, another fact stands out. Prosperous countries have found a way for the majority of its citizens to share in the wealth of the nation, as well as for the citizens to understand the source and nature of the distribution of the wealth. That is, the process, through the rule of law, is transparent (not secret) to its citizens.

These countries have their super rich, but the number of poor people is relatively few. America is such an example. India is the opposite. China sits in the middle. While China has a huge population of impoverished citizens, in the past thirty years, it has moved forward with land reform and has also improved its property rights laws.

In addition, adherence to the rule of law has been found to lead to a more prosperous nation. "A country's income per head rises roughly 100 percent if it improves its governance by one standard deviation."[3]

Several countries, including the United States, are models for how the rule of law is practiced. I make this statement because I wish to emphasize this point in relation to some unsettling trends, discussed in the remainder of this chapter.

Disturbing Tale

In other parts of this book the subject of Goldman Sachs' problems with Congress and the SEC were highlighted. This section provides more details on this subject. To briefly review, the company was accused of misleading investors by hiding information about its going both short and long on several financial instruments.

During the congressional hearings, the following conversation took place between Senator Carl Levin (D-Michigan, chairman of the Permanent Subcommittee on Investigation) and Lloyd Blankfein (CEO of Goldman Sachs):[4]

- Levin: The question is did you bet big time in 2007 against the housing mortgage business? And you did not.
- Blankfein: No, we did not.
- Levin: OK. You win big in shorts.
- Blankfein: No, we did not.

As discussed earlier, e-mails in Goldman's files are unambiguous in refuting Blankfein's statements. Even more disturbing is this part of Blankfein's opening statement for this hearing, "Much has been said about the supposedly massive short Goldman Sachs had on the U.S. housing market. The fact is, we were not consistently or significantly net-short the market in residential mortgage-related products in 2007 and 2008."

CHAPTER 25: THE RULE OF LAW, ITS MISRULE... 351

Senator Levin offered these thoughts about Goldman, "They don't give a damn about appearances...The bottom line: They have lied."

I have substantiated the claim that Goldman's analysts were very smart in persuading the company to lessen its exposure to the toxic mortgage backed securities. To be fair, Goldman did down-mark its securities. It claims it is quite precise about this matter. However, it was also betting against them at the same time (making about $4 billion on the short bets).

Most of the other investment banks did not have sufficient profits during this time to offset the ripple effect of Goldman's actions. By the necessity to take Goldman's new marks into account, Wall Street had major problems coming up with the money to meet margin calls on financial instruments:

> The shock waves of Goldman's lower marks quickly began to be felt in the market. The first victims—of their own investment strategy, as well as Goldman's marks—were to Bear Stearns hedge funds that had invested heavily in squirrelly mortgage-related securities, *including many packaged and sold by Goldman Sachs* [emphasis is mine]...The Bear Stearns hedge funds were required to average Goldman's marks with those provided by traders of other firms.

William Cohan (quoted and footnoted earlier) goes on to say, "Understandably, Goldman does not like to talk about the role it had in pushing other firms off the edge of the cliff." True. But that's too bad for those less-intelligent, even clueless bankers, who mostly fell on a sword they themselves held. Goldman covered its bets. It was not the job of Goldman to cover the bets of anyone else.

However, for Goldman, the "anyone else" included not only its competitors but some of its customers as well. Therein lies the shame of this sorry episode and the mockery of the culture in which Goldman is allowed to exist: the flaunting of the rule of law.

Don't forget, Goldman became a bank holding company during the crisis and was given access to the Federal Reserve's low interest rate short-term loans. A few days after becoming a bank holding company "Goldman raised $5 billion from Warren Buffett....and another $5.75 billion from the public."

Did Goldman make any effort to ward off the desolation that its securities' marking created? No, that is not the way the system works. The bleeding was not stopped by the industry that largely created the wound. It was stopped by the United States government, courtesy of United States citizens.

Double Standards and the Exclusivity of the Rule of Law

I have resurfaced the Goldman situation to relate it to the rule of law. The SEC case against Goldman was settled without any of the company executives serving jail time or paying fines from their own pockets. The quotes above of the exchanges between Levin and Blankfein can only be interpreted as Blankfein lying to a congressional committee.

Blankfein is still walking the streets and working Wall Street's naive customers. Martha Stewart lied to federal authorities and she was sent to prison. Perhaps Blankfein was not under oath when he testified to Levin and the other lawmakers. So he could lie with impunity?

In addition to the Goldman situation, I have made the case that congressional representatives have engaged in insider trading. Even if they have not, many continue to sit on committees and vote on issues in which they have financial stakes. While these people remain immune to the laws forbidding insider trading, less fortunate souls are sitting in jails. It's another example of the misuse of the rule of law.

The disturbing aspect of these stories is the imbalance of how America's laws are often applied. "The law says one thing but actually means different things for different people."[5] What is the message these interpretations of the law convey to the American citizen? *It is the perversion of the rule of law by the practice of a double standard*

The imbalance can also be illustrated with the initial public offering (IPO).

The IPO: Nice Work if You Can Get It

IPOs usually take place through one or more investment banks, called underwriters. A company, such as BlacksStreets.com, wants to raise money by selling shares in the company. It signs a contract with an investment bank to sell these shares to the public. The initial offerings are often made to the banks' preferred customers. The underwriter (or underwriters) charges a commission for these efforts, usually 7 or 8 percent.

I have not been approached to be one of those insiders to buy Facebook IPO shares. I have not because I am not a big time customer of Wall Street's IPOs. I am not an institutional investor. I am not an insider.

The founder of Boston Beer Company, Jim Koch, learned that an IPO is typically controlled by investment banks and is set up "to reward the banks and the favored institutional investors."[6] He was concerned that these banks set the price for the offering and "allocated the shares to their favored clients at a favorable price." Consequently, he circumvented the banks to offer his tailored IPO. He set up an IPO auction in which more people would have fairer access to buying shares in his company.

He says, "The laws and regulations were set up to make this kind of thing very difficult." But why? Koch had decided to give his customers an inside track instead of investment bank customers (institutional investors). He had the audacity to sell shares at two prices: $15 per share to his beer drinking customers and $20 per share for those who bought at the opening price at the IPO—maybe wine drinkers.

Investment banks do not like this practice. As one fund manager said, "So I'm going to buy shares for $20 while you're selling them to these cat-and-dog investors for $15? I always get the lower price. You've turned things upside down."

This arrogant and pouting statement could well have come from the same Wall Street mental midget who claims the 2008 meltdown, which ruined thousands of families, was a "speed bump".

One more quote from Jeff Sommer's article: "Wall Street will always hate [Jim Koch approaches], because Wall Street is all about insider access, and these auctions take it away."

And I add: A further distillation of the Rule of Law. If not the rule itself then certainly its intent.

The investment banks have succeeded in forming their own private financial world, where they make their own rules. If you have forgotten, the huge market of many derivatives operate in a closed world, governed by a handful of investment banks.

Misuse of Rule of Law:
Illegal bank Activity and Regulator Collusion[7]

To establish the groundwork for this discussion, let's once again pose a few hypothetical questions. Suppose I were to tell you that several of the largest banks in the world have been engaged in the illegal manipulation of an index that is used to control the interest rates of at least $800 trillion-worth of financial instruments? That this activity has been going on for several years? That the banking traders involved in this activity were so blatant, they went about it almost openly? That the Federal Reserve of New York warned the overseers of the index that something was amiss, but the overseers took no action. Suppose I were to tell you that this illegal activity likely affects the interest you pay on your home mortgage, car loan, and credit card debt. That it affects your yields on Wall Street investments? Suppose I were to tell you that the regulators who are supposed to prevent this sort of illegal activity knew about it and cast a blind eye; even tacitly supported it?

Your response (and mine) would be one of astonishment. But the hypothetical events cited above took place. As this book went to hard copy and e-tablets, here is the latest on what happened with this massive deception (the final outcome will play out over many years):

The (interest) index under discussion is LIBOR (the London inter-bank offered rate). It is used by financial institutions as guidance for setting interest rates as well as a benchmark for banks to negotiate

CHAPTER 25: THE RULE OF LAW, ITS MISRULE... 355

fees and rates among themselves and their customers. It is set by banks submitting to authorities an estimate of the costs of their borrowing money (from other banks). The word "estimate" is emphasized because the figure is not based on actual borrowings. Thus, it is subjective. Here is a summary of the situation:

> ...damning evidence has emerged...that employees [of several banks]...tried to rig the [LIBOR] number time and again.
>
> As many as 20 big banks have been named in various investigations or lawsuits alleging that LIBOR was rigged. [JP Morgan and Citigroup have been named. Barclay's has been fined $450m by American and British regulators. The Swiss bank UBS has reached an immunity deal with the U.S. Justice Department.[8]]
>
> ...those involved in setting the rates have often had every incentive to lie, because their banks stood to profit or lose money depending on the level at which LIBOR was set each day. [Not to mention the banks' traders.]
>
> The suspicion is that at least some banks were submitting low LIBOR estimates with tacit permission from their regulators. [In order to calm the markets.]

The potential effect of this scandal has been characterized as global finance's "tobacco moment," referring to the lawsuits against the tobacco industry in 1998.

For decades, the LIBOR index has been a vital benchmark; one that we think has been honestly and earnestly computed. While an ordinary citizen has not known about this financial yardstick, its value has affected his everyday life.

What are commonplace citizens to make of such a massive fraud, one that took place among some of our most trusted institutions? One in which the vaunted values of self-responsibility and self-policing are cast aside, often to the citizens' detriment?

It is another example of the misuse of the rule of law, which can only lead to the further misuse of the rule of law by citizens who begin to realize the game is rigged against them. The danger of letting lawbreakers break the law with impunity is that it leads to more lawbreaking by them and others.

In both parts of this book I have cited several examples of lawbreakers being shielded by their corporations from paying fines or going to jail. I have made the case that the Supreme Court's decision about the corporate right of free speech—in light of these corporate shields—makes a mockery of accountability and due process.

The U.S. Justice Department has begun the process of building criminal cases against the offending institutions and their employees who may be responsible for these acts. These cases will likely provide an impetus for the banks to reach a settlement with the regulators. The settlement will cost the banking industry an immense amount of money, but this money will most likely be extracted from the corporation, not the individuals. The offending corporation will not go to jail. The corporation will still retain the right of free speech and continue to shield its members from the responsibility of their actions.

A democracy cannot survive if its people do not own-up to personal responsibility. An infinite number of laws can never successfully govern a nation. That must come from the behavior of its citizens. We are told, "The price of democracy is self-responsibility." Yet:[9]

> The prospect of criminal cases is expected to rattle the banking world and provide a new impetus for financial institutions to settle with the authorities.

Note the phrase "financial institutions" and not "employees of financial institutions."

As stated earlier in Part I, many banks (especially their traders) have come to consider themselves operating in their own private financial world. One in which they can ignore tried-and-true ethics and make their own rules. The LIBOR fraud is another example.

And as a short preview of the last chapter in this book: The banks that used LIBOR were trusted to do their own bidding honestly—to *discipline themselves* to adhere to the rule of law (Adam Smith raises his right hand). But many of them did not. Consequently, they will be subjected to more rules of law, which *will attempt to contain* their avaricious behavior (John Maynard Keynes raises his left hand). The consequence of the latter act will be more laws such as those described in the next section:

Examples of too many Laws

The rule of law can be distorted by having too few rules. It can be compromised with too many. The remainder of most of this chapter provides examples of the latter.

A report filed by Jesse Eisinger states the proposed legislation (the Volcker Rule) against financial firms trading on their own behalf with others' money is hopelessly bloated and open to loopholes:[10] This important concept, one that would "curb risky proprietary trading by banks includes 383 questions that break down into 1,420 subquestions."[11] While America's firms are busy filling in these forms, foreign competitors are busy grabbing these firms' business.

Nonetheless, Volcker type rules are appearing: "The proposal specifically prohibits a bank or institution that owns a bank from engaging in proprietary trading that is not at the behest of its clients, and from owning or investing in a hedge fund or private equity fund, as well as limiting the liabilities that the largest banks could hold."[12]

Crushing Regulations Are Crushing Productivity

De Soto and his team of researchers spent considerable time analyzing the laws and associated bureaucracies of several countries. His findings should be heeded by America's regulators: Congress has become so fixated on specific details of a law that the lawmakers are creating impediments to the efficient practice of the intent of a law.

The legislation I studied for this book (Frank-Dodd financial reform and the health care legislation) will result in a bewildering set of new legal rules, as well as untold bureaucrats to enforce them. I use the word untold because both pieces of legislation are now being filled-in with specific, concise regulations. No one knows how many civil servants will be hired to monitor adherence to them.

Let's return to De Soto. He and his team opened a small garment workshop on the outskirts of Lima, Peru. In order to establish the business in accordance with local laws, they spent six hours a day at the effort. The business was registered and allowed to operate legally 289 days later. Here is De Soto's description of the ordeal:[13]

> Although the garment workshop was geared to operating with only one worker, the cost of legal registration was $1,231—thirty-one times the monthly minimum wage. To obtain legal authorization to build a house on state-owned land took six years and eleven months, requiring 207 administrative steps in fifty-two government offices. To obtain title for that piece of land took 728 steps. We also found that a private bus, jitney, or taxi driver who wanted to obtain official recognition of his route faced twenty-six months of red tape.

De Soto had similar experiences in other countries. He learned that underground economies and extralegal societies spring up—not because the citizens are willing lawbreakers, but because they *can't* survive if they *don't* break the law.

In Report 18, I wrote about my impressions of the 848 pages of the Dodd-Frank law, which is twenty-three times longer than the Glass-Steagall act passed after the Wall Street crash in 1929. I claimed that Dodd-Frank would lead to yet more bloated and inefficient government. It mandates four hundred new rules for doing business in the financial world.[14]

Four hundred new rules. Legislation such as this is akin to a third world country described by De Soto.

CHAPTER 25: THE RULE OF LAW, ITS MISRULE... 359

Sections 404 and 406 of the original legislation (dealing with financial firms filling out forms) run to about three pages of text. (I copied and pasted these PDF-formatted sections into WORD, eliminated some formatting notations, and expanded the congressional law format across the page to obtain the count of three pages.)

Two years after it was approved, sections 404 and 406 of the legislation have been expanded to 192 pages![15]

The Economist states hedge fund firms will spend $100,000 - $150,000 for the first effort to comply with sections 404 and 406, and $40,000 annually thereafter.[16] How many sections does Dodd-Frank contain? I did a quick count: about 350. Granted, not all the sections will be expanded several-hundred-fold. Nonetheless, the expansion of sections 404 and 406 are instructive as to the effect government's increasingly detailed laws is having on eroding the rule of law. Jonathan Macey of Yale Law School puts it well:[17]

> Laws classically provide people with rules. Dodd-Frank is not directed at people. It is...directed at bureaucrats and it instructs them to make still more regulations to create more bureaucracies.

At the risk of offering a self-serving compliment, my observations and predictions about Dodd-Frank are coming true. The patently partisan, earmarked section dealing with Congo mining will affect 1,000 to 1,500 companies' operations at an estimated cost of $71 million.[18] Granted, Congo mining operations are controversial but why is the issue contained in a financial reform bill?

Estimates from the banking industry put the cost of adhering to Dodd-Frank at over $500 billion annually. And this figure cannot take into account that many sections of the law have yet to be completed

On the back row of the chessboard of the Rules of Life the players are vying for control and power. Dodd-Frank details are forthcoming, loopholes are forming, lawyers are salivating. Meantime, Joe and Josephine citizen sit as pawns on the front row, trying to come to grips with America's decline into a self-defeating triad of capitalizing gains, socializing risks, and shirking self-responsibility.

America's rank and file citizens are increasingly befuddled and angry. These manifestations of crony free market capitalism are leading more people to question the rule of law as it is practiced in this country.

Sidebar 25-1. Examples of Absurd Laws.

I've a friend whose company builds boat docks. He tells me he can only place piles into water at certain locations during certain times because the government has placed time limits on this construction in order not to bother fish. His docks must now have decks that are corrugated to permit light to shine below because fish do not like to swim in shadowed waters! He is restricted in the noise he makes in his constructions, so as not to bother several eagle nests posted high above his operations. Too noisy the government says; too disruptive to the eagles. These birds sit in their nests, watching from afar, going about their ways undisturbed.

In the meantime, government creates yet more rules to protect fish...who *seek* shadowed waters and eagles that are far removed from the trivial goings-on below their nests.

Business Pushes Back...Sam Pushes Back the Push

As expected, the emerging new rules being placed around legislation are being contested by the big banks. As one example, a fed rule to limit credit exposures between banks is cited by the banks as an unnecessary rule that would limit their activity. This kind of law is essential if the dangerous interconnectivity of large financial institutions is to be addressed. Specifcally, the rule, "would limit net credit exposure between any two of the largest financial firms to 10%

CHAPTER 25: THE RULE OF LAW, ITS MISRULE... 361

of a company's regulatory capital. The banks contend that rule would harm the financial system."[19]

Perhaps it would be harmful to the financial system, but it is certainly open to debate if it would be harmful to America.

The banks' statements also indicate that they continue to lobby for their shadow banking world. While beyond the general treatise of this book, the unregulated world of short-term lending pertaining to money market funds came close to unraveling the bailout effort.[20] This inter-bank credit granting averages about 1.4 trillion a day.[21] As the 2008 meltdown evolved, Uncle Sam came to understand this part of Wall Street—and its associated freezing of short-term funding—had become a huge and dangerous part of the overall problem. Because of the tight interconnections of the banks, they lost the ability and nerve to grant credit to each other.

The banking industry had the option of coming up with their own solution to a major interconnectedness problem. The government said the banks' proposal was not acceptable. Thus, the regulators step in and state, "It now falls to the regulatory agencies to take appropriate regulatory and supervisory measures to mitigate these and other risks."[22]

Other risks? A blanket statement unto itself. Likely resulting in more laws pouring out of the chambers of Capitol Hill.

Intrusive Government + Abusive Big Business = Business as Usual

The financial reform legislation continues to expand, resulting in more overhead to be added to American commerce. With a few exceptions, the financial reform law does little more than add regulations to similar laws. It creates new bureaucracies to perform the functions current bureaucracies should be performing.

The lawmakers claim more laws are needed to control the financial industry and improve citizens' lives. Yes, legislation is needed to (for example) make the trading of financial instruments more transparent. Nonetheless, if the regulators had performed the jobs they were being paid to perform, little additional legislation would have been needed. The situation is not one that engenders optimism about the future of government and business interactions and the effects they will have on the citizenry.

Business circumvents laws. Government creates more laws to prevent business from circumventing these laws. Business finds ways to circumvent the new laws. Government creates more laws to prevent business from circumventing its new laws, a never-ending cycle:

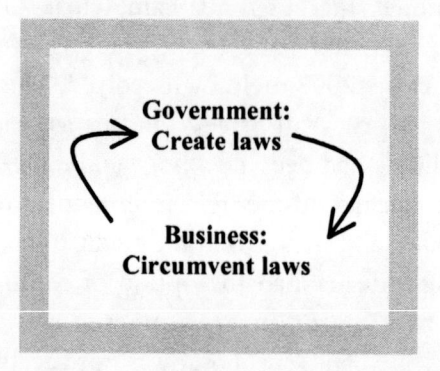

```
        Government:
        Create laws

        Business:
        Circumvent laws
```

During 2010 alone, the government added 81,405 pages to the Federal Register. This addition to an almost incomprehensible library of rules and regulations costs the U.S. economy $1.7 trillion a year in tying to comply with these laws.[23] Not to mention the overhead of devising ways to circumvent them and in many instances, outright flaunt them.

Who pays for this overhead? America's citizens. Who becomes disenchanted with America's once-vaunted rule of law? America's citizens.

Warning Shots Across the Bow

The occupy Wall Street movements owe their existence to their members sensing the rule of law is being applied inequitably. They have come together because they understand they are being denied a part of America's political process that affects their security and well being. They sense the rule of law, as it is being practiced today, is inequitable. As discussed in this book:

- For the political system: K Street influence, Super PACs determining campaign outcomes, congressional insider trading, gerrymandered lifetime jobs for lawmakers, exclusionary pension and medical plans for Congress.

- For the financial system: Too big to fail banks, closed IPOs, secret trading in derivatives, banks trading on their own behalf, deceitful mortgage contracts, illegal collusion among banks' employees.

America's citizens may not understand the many arcane details of these distortions of the rule of law. But they understand enough to know that their country's increasing exclusivity and its partitioning of favors to selected segments of the citizenry is leading to their disenfranchisement.

Less obvious to the citizens, but also burdensome, is a larger and more restrictive yoke being placed on private enterprise by lawmakers passing complex and convoluted laws.

---

[1] Hernando De Soto, *The Mystery of Capital*, Basic Books, New York, 2000, p. 6.

[2] Ibid.

[3] "Order in the Jungle," *The Economist*, March 15, 2008, p. 83.

[4] William D. Cohan, *Money and Power: How Goldman Sachs Came to Rule the World*, Anchor, Books, New York, 2012, pp. 6-8. Direct quotes in this section pertaining to Goldman Sachs are sourced from this book.

[5] Jonathan Turley, "Do Laws Even Matter Today?," *USA TODAY*, June 15, 2010, p. 9A.

[6] Jeff Sommer, "No Bitter Aftertaste from This Stock Offering," *The New York Times*, February 19, 2012, p. BU-3. The other quotes in this section are also sourced from this article.

[7] Unless otherwise cited, the source for this section is: *The Economist*, July 7, 2012, pp. 14, 25-27 and Damian Paletta at damian.paletta@wsj.com.

[8] Ben Protess and Mark Scott, "U.S. is Building Criminal Cases Over Rate-Fixing," *The New York Times*, July 15, 2012, pp. 1 and 4.

[9] Ibid, p. 1.

[10] Jesse Eisinger, "The Volcker Rule, Made Bloated and Weak," *The New York Times*, February 23, 2012, p. B4.

[11] "Over-Regulated America," *The Economist*, February 18, 2012, p. 9.

[12] *President Obama Calls for New Restrictions on Size and Scope of Financial Institutions to Rein in Excesses and Protect Taxpayers*, http://www.whitehouse.gov/the-press-office/president-obama-calls-new-restrictions-size-and-scope-financial-institutions-rein-e, retrieved from Widipedia. Go to http://en.wikipedia.org/wiki/Volcker_Rule.

[13] De Soto, *The Mystery of Capital*, pp. 18-20.

[14] "Over-Regulated America," p. 9.

[15] I did not copy and paste this amount of nearly unfathomable legal cipher into WORD. The 192-pages report comes from the source footnoted below. I suspect this page count reflects the congressional format. Nonetheless, from my admittedly detailed attention to this matter, the expansion represents sections 404 and 406 containing at least eighty pages.

[16] "Over-Regulated America," p. 22.

[17] Ibid.

[18] Ibid., p. 24.

[19] Dan Fitzpatrick, Liz Rappaport, and Victoria McGane, "Well, That was Awkward," *The Wall Street Journal*, May 3, 2012, pp. C1 & C3.

[20] For the reader who wishes to delve into more details, the operation is known as the tri-party repro.

[21] David Reilly, "Getting Fed Up with the Repro Man's Loans," *The Wall Street Journal*," May 3, 2012, p. C12.

[22] Ibid.

[23] *The Wall Street Journal*, October 14, 2011, p. A4.

CHAPTER 26

DEBT AND RESPONSIBILITY

Debt: Who owes how much to whom? The headlines in newspapers, blogs, Twitters, Faces, Tubes, Huffington's virtual investigations, and other media report how much money America owes to other countries and individuals.

The news also states how this debt is leading the United States down the road to insolvency. Associated with these forecasts are statistics that lead the reader to one conclusion: America is in trouble.

I agree. If we do not curtail our borrowings and reduce our federal debt, we U.S. citizens will in the not too distant future find ourselves in a situation in which we must reduce our standard of living. Our national debt, as a percentage of gross domestic product (GDP), is one of the largest of first world countries. Only Ireland, Iceland, Greece, Portugal, and Italy exceed the debt-to-GDP ratio of the United States.[1] These countries are considered fiscally inept. Increasingly, so are we.

Responsibility: Who pays how much to whom? For that matter, who is responsible to whom and under what conditions? Responsibility is a cornerstone of a democracy. Its importance is described well by Elbert Hubbard with his simple statement, "Responsibility is the price of freedom."[2]

As recounted in Part I, some people make the claim that it is the responsibility of government to make sure private business is responsible for its practices. I disagree. As stated in Chapter 25, self-responsibility on the part of business people (and private citizens) is vital for a democracy to succeed. If our society must rely on government to police every business deal to gauge the ethical worth of the transaction, we will drown in laws, rules, and associated paperwork. From reading the previous chapter, it is obvious we are headed down that very road.

None other than Jesus—no slouch in the responsibility department—said in Luke 12:48, "For everyone to whom much is given, from him much will be required."

Nonetheless, in this nearly perfect storm it is evident that individuals and institutions were given much and looked for ways to be given more. By seeking more, they often abandoned any pretext of self-responsibility. In many instances, these actions manifested themselves with the parties incurring debt beyond their means to pay or finding ways to pass the debt onto others. I provided several examples in Part I. In both parts of this book, I have provided examples of institutions and individuals shirking-off other aspects of self-responsibility; many having a huge negative impact on America and its citizens. Thousands of these acts went unpunished. In this chapter, I expand the discussion.

Bank Responsibility

If a company, say, Smith Brother's Plumbing Supply on Main Street goes broke, this single failure does not put the economy of the entire country into a tailspin. Contrast that with the failure of the Lehman Brothers' investment bank on Wall Street.

As said several times thus far: Too big to fail, too interconnected to fail. The large banks are aware of this truth. This quote, which was used in an earlier report, sums it up well: "Bankers are like suicide bombers, who must be appeased because they are threatening to blow everyone else up."[3] Appeasement often leads to irresponsibility.

If not for the bailout, the failure of one investment bank (exhibiting outrageous irresponsibility with its huge debt) might have taken down the banking industry and many other enterprises. This codependency of so-called competitors would be akin to Smith Brother's failure also taking down its plumbing supply opponent

CHAPTER 26: DEBT AND RESPONSIBILITY

down the street, other plumbing supply stores, as well as other businesses. Taken in this context, an industry built on competitor interdependency—to the point of depending on one another for their very existence—could be one devised by someone with a mad-hatter mentality; certainly not by a rational mind.

An e-mail reader wrote that my comparing the finance industry to the plumbing supply industry was like comparing apples to oranges. Banks are designed and legislated to be interdependent. Companies in other industries are not. My friend spoke about interbank lending to maintain liquidity and the flow of money, as well as the interdependency financial institutions have among themselves in buying and selling securities.

We are told by other experts that interconnectedness is the way the banking industry must operate and the only way it can exist. Because most of us are bank depositors, not bank stockholders or fiscal wizards, I suppose we must bow to their expertise,

Nonetheless, one more attempt. Let's substitute small stores for large stores. The situation in the banking industry, if extrapolated to Costco and Walmart, would mean the failure of Costco would drive Walmart to bankruptcy. But not just Walmart, the nation's entire economy! How bizarre is that?

For an actual example: Borders Books recently closed. Barnes & Noble is rejoicing.

But the idea is more widely applicable. Let's take one example: the airline manufacturing industry. As disruptive as it might be to many people, the failure of Boeing aircraft would not take down Airbus. Granted, it would bring financial ruin or near ruin to thousands of people and "4,500 factories in 40 countries" that are contracted to Boeing.[4]

But planes are being built because airlines need them. I venture a guess that many of these 4,500 factories could retool their factories to build to the Airbus specifications. The companies could creatively resurrect themselves, based on creative destruction.

The system is a mess. The Occupy Wall Street protesters are onto it. They may not know the details of the mess, so I hope they read this book.

Whatever becomes of the financial reform bill, until the two problems of bank size and interdependency are addressed, America will continue to be tracked down by financial storms. Its actors, not shouldered with responsibility, cannot be expected to act responsibly. It goes against human nature.

Investment Bank Responsibility

The previous section deals with banks' responsibility in general. Much of this book's focus is on investment banks. Accordingly, in this section we examine the issue of investment banks' responsibility to their customers and the public.

Two years ago, my wife and I took a rafting trip on the Flathead River in the Glacier Park area. We camped next to the river, where we shared food and talk with several other rafters. During a campfire dinner, I struck up a conversation with a man who had recently left employment at a large Wall Street investment bank. I told him about the research I was doing on the meltdown and asked his opinion about the subject. As a former high level officer at the bank, he was privy to the firm's management culture.

I quote verbatim the first statement of his response, "I left the bank in disgust." During dessert and coffee, he explained how he witnessed the firm's culture change. It evolved from a customer-oriented focus—with concern for revenue secondary to concern for the customer—to a single-minded focus on revenue. He said the bank paid attention to customers, but it came to placing the customer second to profits.

I countered, "All companies look for revenue first. That is the reason they exist." His answer was an expected truism, "If you don't take care of your customers, you will not have revenue."

As he polished off his coffee, he polished off this company, "I couldn't work there anymore. They lost their bearings." His simple confession reflected an ethical declaration. It came from a person who could have stayed in the company to become wealthy. (Perhaps he was already wealthy. I did not pursue this aspect of his ethics.)

The next day, as we were preparing to take on the Flathead River again, I had a chance to talk with his wife. I paraphrase her comments as my recorder was in my backpack, *Bonuses were what mattered. Everything was for the bonus.*

Case Study. My rafting companion's story reflected that of another former Wall Street executive. I learned about this person while reading a newspaper article.[5] The man featured in this op-ed column (Greg Smith) left a golden handcuffs job at the Goldman Sachs investment bank. He departed for the same reason my rafting companion did. He was disgusted by the company's culture of gaining revenue for itself at the expense of its customers' revenue. He spoke of ways to become a leader:

> Execute on the firm's "axes," which is Goldman-speak for persuading your clients to invest in the stocks or other products that we were trying to get rid of because they were not seen as having a lot of potential profit.
>
> "Hunt elephants." In English: get your clients—some of whom are sophisticated, and some of whom aren't—to trade whatever will bring the biggest profit to Goldman.

Case Study Refuted. As expected, Greg Smith's yin was assailed by a yang. An article in *The Wall Street Journal* made these claims (with my comments placed in brackets):[6]

> It's been six years since the Abacus deals and other mortgage transactions that gave rise to the lore that Goldman plays fast and loose. [Lore? Talk to the city of Cedar Rapids. Read the FCIC report.] If Goldman is so toxic, why is Mr. Smith only leaving now? [Because it takes a while for toxicity to take effect. It takes a while for a culture to change.]

Without any preceding text to this sentence the article states, "But if there's a case for outlawing parties voluntarily engaging in complex financial transactions, then let's hear it." I know of no one who is against anyone engaging in complex financial transactions as long as they do not affect other parties or bring down the economy. If the transactions do affect a nonparticipant, the nonparticipant should at least be able to examine the sword that might put him down. The sword should at least be transparent (visible).

The article concludes with:

> And none of this [Greg Smith] has anything to do with the challenge for public policy, of whether firms as big and powerful as Goldman can exist without effectively being wards of the government. That question [what question?] would be much less of a question, however, if all were as profitable and intelligently self-interested as Goldman has proved to be.

No question, Goldman is a superior company. But its behavior with Abacus, its packaging junk into supposed jewels, and its "performance" before congressional hearings should lead Goldman's most fervent fans to question what has happened to the company; as well as what has happened to Wall Street.

Unnatural Behavior to Naturally Speaking People.[7] Before I provide another example of self-responsibility and a disturbing story of Goldman's loss of it, I wish to say that the other company involved in this story (Dragon Systems) is a (now defunct) enterprise for whom I have had great respect and have held in (technical) awe. My bias will again be on display. After reading this part of the book, I'll wager yours will join mine.

Prior to my leaving the world of computer networks, I came to understand the extraordinary complexities of the human voice; of the difficulty of digitizing it; of the even more difficult task of translating it into a form that would appear was written text on a piece of paper.

Jim and Janet Baker (founders of Dragon Systems), after many years of research, labor, and looking for money, did just that. I came across their NaturallySpeaking software product in the early 2000s and was astounded by its intelligence and ease of use. For example, it could parse, interpret, and correctly place into Microsoft WORD

CHAPTER 26: DEBT AND RESPONSIBILITY

something as subtle as, "Please write a letter right now to Mrs. Wright. Tell her that two is too many to buy."

The Bakers eventually employed Goldman Sachs to help them find a buyer for their immensely successful company. Here is what happened:

- Goldman assigned four people to guide Dragon Systems through this process. They were inexperienced, did not stay long at the bank, and were aloof to many of Dragon's concerns and requests. Testimony reveals they did not have a lot of top-level support or supervision. But then to Goldman, Dragon was a very small account.

- Goldman informed Dragon its first steps would be doing *due diligence* on a L.&H., the potential buyer of Dragon. Due diligence included, "specific areas of concern, including L.&H.'s sources of revenue, its major customers, its license and royalty agreements, its expected growth, its partnerships, and its financial statements." Records substantiate that Goldman was errant in fulfilling many of these requirements and agreements.

- L.&H. proposed buying-out Dragon for $580m; half in cash, half in stock. Later, L.&H. offered solely $580m in stock. The reason? The company had no cash! It was close to being broke. The Bakers assumed Goldman knew about the status of the potential buyer. After all, the bank had been paid $5 million by Dragon to do due diligence. Goldman's testimony, "[the bank] did not form a point of view as to whether an all-stock deal would be risky or advisable for the Bakers." The bank's managers of this account "could not remember" if it had "crossed [their minds] to warn the Bakers about potential issues with an all-stock deal."

- Later, it was revealed that Goldman told the Bakers they should have an accounting firm perform some of the functions that were part of a due diligence process statement.

- The Goldman men did not know that L.&H. had cooked its books. Yet, all Goldman had to do is what *The Wall Street Journal* did. The newspaper called supposed customers and discovered L.&H. had lied about its customers and that its sales figures were pulled out of thin air! (I've taken the liberty of inserting another exclamation point.)

- But Goldman did know about the flakiness of L.&H. Previously, another part of Goldman had considered investing $30m in the company. In this instance, the Chinese Wall held.

In a nutshell, the Bakers placed themselves into the arms of Goldman Sachs. The Bakers were experts in voice recognition, not mergers and acquisitions. Goldman's actions or inactions, take your pick, resulted in these two brilliant and productive people losing their entire company and every penny in it. The $580m came down to $0. They even lost their software to bankruptcy auctions. (I can personally attest that losing the ownership of software, an act of intense mental creation, can be like losing a loved one.)

We all make mistakes. All of us drop the ball on occasion. The best of us can sometimes become the worst of us. If so, if we are true to ourselves, we admit our failings, take the consequences and move on in life. A bit battered, but overall, better for it.

This writer cannot come to any other conclusion but that Goldman Sachs ill-served the Bakers and Dragon Systems. As I learned more about the case, I put on my rose-colored glasses and said to myself, "Goldman, try to give back to the Bakers. Your incompetence led to their being robbed of their dream."

Again, as this book went to hard copy and e-books, here is what has happened:

- The Bakers' attorneys contend Goldman's employees were incompetent and that Goldman considered the Dragon Systems account too small to warrant much attention.

- Goldman contends: (a) It had no obligation to do any financial analysis of L.&H. (b) That under the terms of the agreement, only Dragon Systems had the right to sue. Because Dragon Systems is no longer in existence, no lawsuits can come forth. (c) Therefore, the Bakers should pay Goldman's legal fees. (For all three claims, once again I add: fantastic.)

If these surreal claims are not shocking enough, Goldman also falls back on the notion that the Bakers were not astute enough to ask Goldman to conduct a "fairness opinion," which is an analysis of an acquisition price.

Yet legal complications, such as the fairness opinion, is what led the Bakers to Goldman Sachs in the first place. All the while, Goldman contends it led the Bakers to "a completed transaction." That it did.

Summary Thoughts. Why spend time on a topical article, a one-day newspaper reading? Because like several other ill-founded pieces cited in this book, Mr. Jenkins distorts the facts and sullies honest debates about matters that are crucial to this nation's welfare. Had I read about Greg Smith's lambasting Goldman four years ago, I would have dismissed his statements as sour grape rantings.

After reading the findings of Michael Lewis and Gretchen Morgenson, studying the FCIC report, watching Wall Street continue to construct is own private financial word, hearing Goldman's CEO's testimony before Congress, having dinner with my rafting companion, learning about the evisceration of Goldman's own clients, and comparing my Main Street existence to that of Wall Street, I can only conclude Wall Street's ethical responsibility to each of its clients has taken a back seat to its fixation on revenue and its increasingly fragile reputation.

Union Responsibility

I travel down the middle of the political road. I am also an empathetic person and in favor of helping the helpless. But I look askance at some of the ridiculous programs our government has put into place since the New Deal.

I have also grown weary of the heavy-handedness of many of the labor unions. They may help their members but they often do not help our society with their extreme demands on the citizenry.

To compound matters, in some situations the unions' actions to fleece the taxpayer are abetted by politicians who pass solicitous legislation favoring unions in order to obtain the unions' support. Here is one particularly egregious example.

With the exception of gas-powered trucks instead of horse-driven wagons, Chicago's garbage pickup system is straight out of a Dickens' novel. Because of local gerrymandering, Chicago's political wards (described earlier) are defined to give city officials power over even the most mundane of city services: garbage pickup. Without regard to efficiency, but only to political largesse, garbage trucks for a political ward routinely cross over other wards but are not allowed to stop and pick up garbage.

In many wards the work day is 5.5 hours. One man defended this schedule by declaring that no one works a full day, not even the mayor. He is as delusional as an AIG sales agent. I would wager that mayor Rahm Emanuel's time on his job of hauling around political garbage at least doubles the time of this person spends hauling around human garbage.

If that short workday—on a taxpayer payroll—is not enough to arouse the concern of an average taxpayer, one who likely makes, say, about $40,000 to $50,000 a year, consider this: A Chicago trash collection engineer with an eleventh grade education is making $90,000 a year. Salaries of $60,000 to $70,000 a year are common.

My ire in this book has been directed toward Wall Street and Wall Street regulators. This small section evens, if only a bit, the blame game playing field.

Personal Responsibility

In several reports in Part I, I presented data on the debt American citizens have taken on. I claimed the mortgage meltdown's culprits included millions of clueless or irresponsible home buyers. I wish I had been more emphatic about this idea: Much of the nearly perfect financial storm came about because American citizens became even less responsible in managing their finances.

As well, the herding instinct has encouraged an individual to go deeper into debt, even though taking on this debt is a very poor idea for the citizen's own welfare. *Everyone else is in debt. I'm missing the consumer bandwagon!* With proceeds from their second mortgage, Joe and Josephine citizen head for Best Buy to purchase another wide-screen TV.

During these past three years, I had thought American consumers, sobered by the meltdown, would make efforts to clean up their balance sheets. For several months the statistics I came across appeared to support my prediction (and hope) that the consumer would wise up and straighten out. No such luck. Consumers increased their credit card debt as follows:[8]

Second quarter, 2009: $3.9 billion
Second quarter, 2010: $11.1 billion
Second quarter, 2011: $18.4 billion

An official with a credit counseling agency told the *USA TODAY* that some consumers may have a bailout mentality. If they lose their jobs they are counting on unemployment benefits to come to the rescue. The moral hazard issue once again.

Government Responsibility

If the news about American consumers is unsettling, the news about the precarious financial positions of towns, cities, counties, and states is equally disturbing. Recently, Harrisburg, the state capital of Pennsylvania, filed for bankruptcy.[9] Harrisburg is not alone. Other governments are considering the same route to insolvency. Government bankruptcies are not unheard of. There have been forty-eight filings since 1980. Harrisburg, population 47,000, is one of the largest municipalities to file.

In the previous paragraph, I stated that this news is disturbing. Perhaps I'm off base. A law professor at the University of Pennsylvania said, "To the extent there was a stigma associated with municipal bankruptcy, that is rapidly declining."

Let's jump on board the bankruptcy bandwagon. Let's herd ourselves, as lemmings nearing a cliff, to yet more fiscal failures. According to *The Wall Street Journal*, the city council made a mistake by guaranteeing the debt on $310 million that was tied to a trash-burning incinerator. The incinerator trashed and the city was left holding the debt.

Nonetheless, *all* government employees, including *all* trash managers and *all* city council leaders, will continue to receive their salaries.[10] *All* bond holders will continue to be paid.

Cities are not alone. The state of Rhode Island is free falling from an unattainable goal of keeping its employees' retirement funds from free falling.[11] The unions refuse to compromise to help resolve the problem. As of this writing, it appears some states in the United States will go bankrupt.

Fannie and Freddie Responsibility

Since the United States government took control of Fannie and Freddie, taxpayers have taken on the responsibility for paying legal fees for these institutions to defend their alleged illegal practices.

In yet another touch of irony, Uncle Sam is the prosecutor but on the other side of the courtroom, Uncle Sam is paying for Fannie's defense. The U.S. government is suing itself and defending itself!

The SEC has filed civil suits in New York that state Fannie "intentionally and repeatedly misled investors about the exposure of the companies to risky subprime loans...Between March 23, 2007, and Aug. 6, 2008, the company told investors that the exposure of its single-family guarantee unit to subprime loans was $2 billion to $6 billion, or 0.1 percent to 0.2 percent of its portfolio. But the SEC said the real exposure started at $141 billion at the end of 2006 and rose to about $244 billion by June 30, 2008—14 percent of its portfolio."[12]

Congressman Randy Neugebauer (R-TX) released the following figures representing the costs to taxpayers: "Over $160 million of the taxpayer's money...was spent for securities-related lawsuits and indemnification agreements for Freddie and Fannie executives."[13] The items below provide a summary of Congressman Neugebauer's findings.

- Total Amount of Legal Expenses Post Conservatorship for Freddie and Fannie: $410.7 million.

- Total Legal Fees for Securities related Lawsuits and Indemnification Agreements for Freddie and Fannie: $162.4 million.

- Post-Conservatorship Indemnification Legal Fees Broken Down by Company:
Freddie - $5,792,314 (excludes positions below Executive Vice President)
Fannie - $51,741,767
Total: $57,534,081

- Fannie Legal Advances Post Conservatorship:
Franklin Raines: $7.9 million
Leanne Spencer: $11.8 million
Tim Howard: $4.5 million
Other Executives: $12 million
Non-Executives: $15.3 million
Total: $51.7 million

- Pre-Conservatorship Indemnification Legal Fees Broken Down by Company:
Freddie: $27.8 million
Fannie: $93.1 million
Total: $120.9 million

- Fannie Pre-Conservatorship Indemnification:
Franklin Raines: $29.8 million
Leanne Spencer: $19.5 million
Tim Howard: $13.4 million
Other Executives: $12.4 million
Non-Executives: $17.9 million
Total: $93.1 million"

Responsibility of Nations to Look After Themselves

Several western European countries have put themselves at risk because of their irresponsible behavior. As one example, Greece, the land of mystical, heroic legends, has coddled itself into a nearly helpless state of insolvency. This proud country is considered to be the cradle of Western civilization. It is now in the humiliating position of its "cradle" being rocked not by itself, but by the actions of other countries.

Those who rock a cradle are in control of that cradle. Greece is at the mercy of the affluent and well-managed country of Germany. In years prior to this meltdown, Germany opted for pulling in its belt. It cut unions' payouts, reduced government retirements, and invested (even more) in its technical factories.

Paradoxically, the richer countries such as Germany are divided about using their own wealth to bailout a country that, yes, did fall prey to the worldwide recession, but also fell upon its own swords of welfare indolence, incompetence, and corruption.

The moral hazards issue raises its head again. Germany asks: Why should hard-working Germans, who are weathering the nearly perfect financial storm without too much mildew, pay for an umbrella to shield Greeks from a storm they themselves helped to create?

Sorry, you prudent and wise Germans. Your frugal approach to life does not match with Zorba the Greek's let-it-all-hang-out philosophy. Zorba lived his life on the immediate horizon of pleasure and satiation. It is surely an entertaining way to go through life, one to attract a lot of fun seekers.

The problem with countries like Greece is they do not take on the responsibility of policing themselves, of curtailing their Zorba-inclined immoderations. I write this last sentence hesitantly, as I am not a model for moderation. Still, I practice a semblance of self-imposed abstinence. I often forego when I do not want to forego. Some people and nations do not. Take a look at the data below:[14]

Debt as a Percentage of GDP:
1. Japan (220%)
2. Greece (155%)

3. Italy (130%)
4. Iceland (125%)
5. Ireland (120%)
6. Portugal (115%)
7. United States (98%)
8. Belgium (96%)
9. France (95%)
10. United Kingdom (94%)

America's Responsibility to Look After Itself

This book focus is on America. As such, this chapter returns to America's debt. As of June 10, 2012 the public debt for the United States was $15.744 trillion.[15]

What happened? A few years ago, public debt was in the black. The sudden deficit came about because of: (1) George W. Bush's tax cuts, which reduced revenue by over $2 trillion;[16] (2) the drug prescription plan, courtesy of K Street and Congress; (3) the wars in Afghanistan and Iraq; (4) the continued excesses of ongoing entitlement programs; (5) the taking over of Fannie Mae and Freddie Mac; (6) the waste of state and local governments, some of which is absorbed by the federal government; (7) and the migration to a ideologically gerrymandered and stalemated Congress.

The Congressional Budget Office—as well as Roger C. Altman and Richard N. Hass—describe several types of risk factors related to this debt level, as summarized below.[17]

- A growing portion of savings will go toward purchases of government debt and paying interest of the debt, rather than investments in productive capital goods such as factories, road, and research (the vital cog to America's wealth). Private capital's base will shrink. Severe austerity will be imposed on many citizens and companies.

- There will be lower output and net income than in the past.

- If higher marginal tax rates are used to pay rising interest costs—which seem inevitable—savings will be reduced. Work itself will be discouraged.

- Rising interest costs will force reductions in important government programs, including the sacred cows of defense, Social Security, Medicaid, and Medicare. It will be inconsequential if patriotic zealots and gray panthers protest because the interest on debt owed by the American government will have to be paid. Yet in the near future, the aging U.S. population will increase health care costs and reduce the working tax base. The Congressional Budget Office predicts between 2030 and 2040, mandatory spending on entitlements, interest, and other government programs will *exceed* government revenues. The CBO estimate (from 2007) is optimistic. More recent studies place this time closer to 2020.

- Government policymakers will be severely constrained in how to respond to economic challenges.

- There will be an increased risk of a fiscal crisis in which investors demand higher interest rates for U.S. Treasuries.

The National Commission on Fiscal Responsibility and Reform

In December, 2010 the National Commission on Fiscal Responsibility and Reform issued "The Moment of Truth," a White House sponsored study. This section provides a summary of the commission's assessment of America's economic (fiscal) problems. I have edited the commission's summary slightly for brevity and clarity. Chapter 27 provides more details on the commission's recommendations.

By 2025, federal revenue will be able to finance only interest payments on debt, Medicare, Medicaid, and Social Security. Every other federal government activity, from national defense and homeland security to transportation and energy, will have to be paid with borrowed money. Debt held by the public will outstrip the entire

American economy, growing to as much as 185 percent of GDP by 2035. Interest on the debt could rise to nearly $1 trillion by 2020. These mandatory payments, which buy no goods or services, will squeeze out funding for all other programs.

If the nation does not act soon to reassure the markets, the risk of a crisis will increase, and the options available to avert or remedy the crisis will both narrow and become more stringent. If action is not taken, the Congressional Budget Office projects America's economy could shrink by as much as 2 percent by 2020, and spending cuts and tax increases needed to plug the hole could nearly double what is needed today.

Solutions Exist

As grim as the news in this chapter may be, there are solutions. The solutions require America's citizens and lawmakers to accept self-responsibility and support programs that lead to a situation in which *revenues match spending.*

Given a citizenry accustomed to spending beyond its means, can it be done? It will require an increase in taxes and a decrease in government spending, two issues that a divided partisan Congress cannot come to grips with. It is repellent to hear our leaders shuck real problems by couching them in pseudo philosophical and quasi-religious terms.

Sam Rayburn, the Speaker of the House for seventeen years, offered these thoughts, "I've always wanted responsibility because I want the power responsibility brings."[18]

This sentiment is obsolete. Too many of our business and political leaders offer this opinion. While never stated publicly, both parts of this book offer ample evidence of its reality: "I always want power because I want the money power brings."

Nonetheless, we can solve the problems put forth in this book. Chapter 28 offers blueprints to bring America back into the black. Before we review these ideas, Chapter 27 introduces several social, political, and religious factors that are currently undermining the proposed solutions cited in Chapter 28.

I place these two chapters in this sequence in order to make for a happier ending to this book: Get the bad news out first (Chapter 27). Follow it with good news (Chapter 28). It's the American way.

---

[1] *Time*, August 22, 2011, p. 25.

[2] Elbert Hubbard, *An American Bible*, 1946, p. 219. Secondary source: Frank, p. 724.

[3] Cassidy, "Paging J. P. Morgan: Who Should Pay Korea's Bills?" *The New Yorker*, January 19, 1988.

[4] "Faster, Faster, Faster," *The Economist*, January 28, 2012, p. 65.

[5] Greg Smith, "Why I Am Leaving Goldman Sachs," *The New York Times*, March 14, 2012, p. A25.

[6] Holman W. Jenkins, Jr. "Greg Smith Is Too Sexy for His Cat," *The Wall Street Journal*, March 17-18, 2012, p. A15.

[7] This section, including the quotes, is sourced from Loren Feldman, "The $580 Million Black Hole," *The New York Times*, July 15, 2012, pp. BU1, BU 4-BU5.

[8] Christine Dugas, "Debtors Burying Heads in the Sand," *USA TODAY*, October 13, 2011, p. B1.

[9] Michael Corkery and Kris Maher, "Capital Files for Bankruptcy," *The Wall Street Journal*, October 13, 2011, p. A3. Other facts and quotes in this section are sourced from this article.

[10] I am simplifying this story for purposes of providing examples of tottering municipalities and the moral hazard scepter. In fairness, there is a more complex story to be told about the relationship of this city to the state of Pennsylvania, which is beyond the scope of this book. But my points remain valid.

[11] Mary Williams Walsh, "The Little State with a Big Mess," *The New York Times*, October 23, 2011, p. BU 1.

[12] http://latimesblogs.latimes.com/money_co/2011/12/sec-fannie-mae-freddie-mac-2.html. This information was released to the public January, 2011.

[13] http://randy.house.gov/index.cfm?sectionid=20&itemid=1088.

[14] *Time*, August 22, 2011, p. 25.

[15] United States Department of the Treasury, Bureau of the Public Debt (January 2012). "The Debt to the Penny and Who Holds It". For more recent information, see: http://www.brillig.com/debt_clock/.

[16] The eight years of Bush Jr. witnessed "the largest fiscal erosion in American history." See Roger C. Altman and Richard N. Hass, "American Profligacy and American Power," *Foreign Affairs*, November/December, 2010, p. 26.

[17] Jonathan Huntley, (July 27, 2010). "Federal debt and the risk of a fiscal crisis." Congressional Budget Office: Macroeconomic Analysis Division. Also: Roger C. Altman and Richard N. Hass, "American Profligacy and American Power," *Foreign Affairs*, November/December, 2010, pp. 25-34. Also, my research supports these contentions, some of which is available at Blog.UylessBlack.com.

[18] Robert A. Caro, *The Path to Power: The Years of Lyndon Johnson*. New York: Alfred A. Knopf, 1982. Secondary source: Frank, p. 724.

Chapter 27

A Broken System

⊷

Most Americans realize the United States is in serious trouble with its finances. Unless significant and immediate steps are taken, the country is headed for the perfect financial and social storm, one that will have long-lasting, negative effects on the American society and America's citizens. In Chapter 26, I cited predictions from the Congressional Budget Office, Roger C. Altman, and Richard N. Hass to substantiate my claim.

The next chapter (28) contains three sets of recommendations that focus on repairing America's financial infrastructure. These recommendations address the dire prognostications cited in Chapter 26. In addition to financial matters, several recommendations focus on social issues.

Before we examine these recommendations, let's focus on where many of America's problems lie: America's political process.

Uncle Sam: CEO of America Inc.

In the Preface to this book, I stated:

> An objection several readers expressed about Part I of this book is my taking issue with the federal government using borrowings and taxpayer money to rescue insurance companies, car companies, and banks. They claim Uncle Sam will get this money back. I agree that these companies will likely find ways to gain credit and recapitalize, and I also

agree with these readers who said the bailout—however noxious—was essential. The U.S. government might break even or make a profit from its rescues.

I have made the case that even if we taxpayers are paid back this money, the process constitutes corporate welfare. These bailouts distort the roles government and commerce should play in a free market society. I have argued that many government/business relationships emerging over the past few decades are counterproductive and dangerous to our society.

Some of Uncle Sam's debts have been repaid but others have not:[1]

- The Treasury Department recently made a $25 billion profit by selling mortgage backed securities it had purchased to keep Fannie and Freddie above water.
- The U.S. government TARP investment is expected to lose about $34 billion.
- The Federal Reserve still has "about $850 billion in mortgage debt on its books along with about $1.7 trillion in Treasury debt."
- The Federal Housing Agency projects another $121 to $193 billion loss to the taxpayer for assistance to Fannie and Freddie.

CNN tracks the U.S. government expenditures used to recover from the nearly perfect financial storm. Just over $11 trillion has been committed by *U.S. Inc.* to act as a lender of last resort.[2] The term committed is important. Not all of this money has been spent. CNN reports $3 trillion has been sent to various parties.

What if all this committed money is spent? As of this writing, the U.S. public debt is slightly over $15 trillion. I have taken these data from respected sources: CNN, the Congressional Budget Office, and others. If the data are correct, let us hope Uncle Sam has negotiated contracts with his debtors that are at least on a par to a commercial bank's agreement with its debtors.

The United States government has taken on the patina of a commercial bank. Uncle Sam is the CEO of U.S. Inc. However, unlike the customers of Walmart, the customers of U.S. Inc. do not have to pay their bills. By virtue of being the lender of last resort in the financial food chain, U.S. Inc. is saddled with absorbing losses from the uncollectable bills of the Fannies and AIGs of the world. However, the lender of last resort is not the U.S. government. It is the American citizen.

Congress Prevents a Government Institution from Healing Itself

Here is one (among hundreds) example of the inability of Congress to move beyond selfish political deadlock.[3] The U.S. Postal Service is hemorrhaging money, losing $25 million a day. The Senate voted to give the Postal Service $34 billion, yet passed rules that restrict the organization from implementing several of its self-imposed reforms:

- The Service wants to close half of its mail processing centers and about 3,000 post offices. These postal services would be taken over by the installation of offices in local stores; an effective and simple solution. The Senate bill prevents or delays these actions. Both Democrarts and Republicans do not want the sacred cow local post office to close on their watch; a sure fire way to lose votes.

- The Service wants to renegotiate realistic and practical no-layoff contracts in order to be able to shrink its work force faster. The Senate says no, at least the Democratic side.

These actions would almost put the Postal Service toward the long-term road to solvency. I say *almost*. The Senate bill stipulates the Service is required to fund 80 percent of its employees' health care benefits. You and I—in addition to our purchasing a 42 cent postage stamp—will fund the other 20 percent. (Personally, I support government support of the Postal Service. I lived in rural areas for much of my life. I understand how vital the post office is to the lives of non-urban citizens.)

Meanwhile, we increase the number of our Internet e-mail transmissions and decrease our Postal Service hard copy mailings. Our actions lead to more expensive stamps and the resultant decreased use of the Postal Service, which leads to even more expensive stamps. The Autocatalytic Process in action, with the taxpayer funding part of the spiral downward.

Rubberless Lawmakers and Fixations on Moraligious Issues

Congress has lost its bearings. Many of its members are unable to place the good of the country above their ideological preferences. While Rome burns, Congress fiddles with religious and morality based issues that have nothing to do with the physical welfare and security of the country.

I have coined a term for this politically and financially debilitating malady: *Moraligious*. It deals with radicals who foster their religiously based morals on people who just want to be left alone. These silent citizens simply ask that others' positions on missions and missionary positions be kept out of the political process. The moraligious will have none of that. They are determined to embed their beliefs into every bed in America.

A recent study reveals a fissure that is incapacitating the political process:[4]

> In [a] 2011 survey, 80 percent of respondents said that is not proper for religious leaders to tell people how to vote, and 70 percent said that religion should be "kept out of public debates over social and political issues."
>
> It should thus come as no surprise that many Americans have negative views of the Tea Party...[it] ranked at the bottom of the list of two dozen U.S. religious, political, and racial groups in terms of favorability. (It was even less liked than

Muslims and atheists, two groups that regularly meet with public opprobrium.)

However, the Supreme Court ruling and resultant Super PACs have given minority groups such as the Tea Party (and especially Tea Party silent supporters) significant leverage in the political process. Lawmakers must spend their time kowtowing to minority groups funding Super PACs or they will find themselves outspent and out of office.[5]

Poster Child for the Moraligious

As one example, Rick Santorum, a staunchly religious man, was a leading candidate for the office of president of the United Sates. For a while, he came close to securing the Republican Party nomination. This man, who has ascended into the high ranks of America's political elites, preaches the comingling of church and state. Fantastic. And even more fantastic is the fact that he has a huge segment of America's citizenry behind him.

He tells us, "One of the great blessings I've had in every political campaign is people underestimate me, people underestimate what God can do."[6]

Notice the comma that joins Santorum with God. Stated another way, notice the comma that Santorum joins himself with God. It is a simple yet sobering sentence, especially if you are of a different political ilk.

Separation of church and state is vital to a democracy. Yet Santorum has said:[7]

> "I don't believe in an America where the separation of church and state are absolute," he told 'This Week' host George Stephanopoulos. "The idea that the church can have no influence or no involvement in the operation of the state is absolutely antithetical to the objectives and vision of our country...to say that people of faith have no role in the public square? You bet that makes me want to throw up."

Mr. Santorum stated he "almost threw up" (again) when he came across John Kennedy's 1960 speech on the necessity of keeping church and state separated.

Mr. Santorum, what happens to your agenda if a Unitarian sits in the White House? Or consider another religious group that might someday have control of America's political process, one that does not believe in the separation of church and state: Muslims.

If so, what happens to your Catholic church? The Muslims even kill-off brethren within their own ranks because they are not of the proper religious ilk. It happens every day Mr. Santorum. Just read the news.

Separation of church and state; gay civil unions; prayer in schools; right to life/abortions. What do these issues have to do with America's security and physical well-being? Nothing, because most of these issues have long been written into law. Yet our lawmakers spin their wheels trying to fiddle with them—while America's Rome burns.

Politicizing Nonpartisan Issues with Further Stalemates

The effects of politically based gerrymandering have led to more ideological enthusiasts sitting in the nation's capitol and politicizing what should be nonpartisan issues. These politicians (admittedly not a majority, but a force to be reckoned-with) are consumed by their moral and religious dogmas to the extent they place their doctrines above the long-term physical welfare of their country. If they are not really true believers in what they espouse, they must toe the line of the voters in their districts and the Supreme Court's Super PACs.

This attitude and way of thinking often leads congresspeople (as well as the executive branch) to be intellectually and emotionally incapable of compromise. But the situation is more serious than a politician standing by his/her ideas. If they dare compromise to move the nation forward—to reduce our menacing debt for example—their compromise will likely result in the cut-off of their campaign funds from uncompromising parties.

One Example Among Many. To cite one example of the dangers of politicizing practically every process that comes across the desks of Congress members, consider America's space program, for decades a nonpartisan issue. Both sides of the aisle in Congress were onboard the space shuttle and associated programs, such as the planet fly-bys.

In a speech on April 15, 2010 President Obama put forward a plan for a new space policy. The plan included retiring the space shuttle.

Fear mongers, who also suffer from Obamaphobia, came out of the woodwork.[8] Picket lines formed displaying placards that declared the president was out to destroy NASA. Charles Krauthammer, once again the poster boy for the Ignorant Therefore Doctrinaire Syndrome, "scoffed at Obama's 'abdication' of the United States' leading role in space, labeling the plan 'a call to retreat.' " Texas governor Rick Perry said Obama left "American astronauts with no alternative but to hitchhike into space."

There was one problem with these people's statements. As documented by Neil deGrasse Tyson (see footnotes), Obama was merely reaffirming a set of policies endorsed by Republican George W. Bush. Earlier, I also documented how America's conservatives blamed Obama for the TARP bailout package. TARP was initiated by George W. Bush and his Republican administration.

The disturbing aspect of these two examples is they do not reflect sincere differences of opinions. They reflect deep-seated, unyielding, ideological-based partisanship. Because a Democrat is at the helm of America's ship of state, Krauthammer, Perry and their like automatically oppose his *every* initiative.

The same stonewalling occurs for a sitting Republican president. Democrats will attempt to politicize his every move. The result is political gridlock. The pitiable result of this stalemate that it is one of many examples of Congress and the President unable to resolve—not just the space shuttle issue—but America's major financial problems.

If America's financial ship is not fixed, our nation is in danger of losing its place as leader of space exploration. Simply stated, we will not have the money to go to Mars.

Why is this eventuality a problem? Why worry about building an outer space bridge to Mars when the bridges in America are collapsing? Because advanced projects such as the space program lead to new ideas and innovative research. They keep America's creative engines fired-up.

America's space program has led to improved kidney dialysis and water purification systems, implantable pacemakers, LASIK eye surgery, sensors to test for hazardous gases, fire-resistant fabrics, energy-saving building materials, digital imaging, collision-avoidance systems—to mention a few.[9]

Bush and Obama knew the space shuttle had a few trips left in it. They wisely retired it in order to move on (and keep funds available) to more advanced space projects; ones that will likely spawn more technologies to enhance our lives.

For the ideologues, the plan was acceptable when a conservative president made the decision. It was unacceptable when a liberal president carried it out. In this regard, I am reminded of this idea, "Any fool can criticize, condemn, and complain—and most do."[10] Meanwhile, there are no actions (requiring compromises) from either side to fix a broken system.

Losing More than the Space Race

I use the space program as one example of many of America's creative and aggressive ventures to build a better country. As another, if the U.S. government had not funded ARPAnet the Internet might not have come about. It cost the taxpayer money but the payoffs have been beyond measure.

As stated, if corrective measures are not taken soon, America is danger of not having the resources to do anything but cover entitlements and pay interest on its debt. Funding a mission to Mars? A next generation Internet? Repairing our infrastructure? No, we will not have the money to do anything but keep our heads slightly above water. This decade has witnessed underwater residences. It is quite possible that the next decade will witness an underwater nation.

An old saying fits the profile of too many lawmakers who occupy Capitol Hill today, "People who are wrapped up in themselves make very small packages." In the meantime rudderless America drifts into perilous waters.

Fixing America will require our leaders to compromise. It will require sacrifice and the exercise of will from all of us, leading to these thoughts on this matter.

Will

We can solve our problems. We created them, we can fix them, but only if we have the will to do so. This thought by Abraham Lincoln provides a fitting framework for all us to use in confronting our fiscal and social problems: "Will springs from the two elements of moral sense and self-interest."[11]

Lincoln's concept should cover the bases for the reds, the blues, the Ayn Randians, the Tea Party goers, the Occupy Wall Street occupiers, the media pundits, and the inhabitants of Wall Street, Pennsylvania Avenue, and K Street.

In the long run, the two elements of moral sense and self-interest, when taken together, can take us across any financial or social abyss. They are not only compatible, they jointly reinforce ideas that can lead to a fairer, more humane, and more affluent life for all of us.

The next chapter lays out ideas for fixing things—if we have the will.

---

[1] Annie Lowrey, "U.S. Profits from the Sale of Some Mortgage Securities," *The New York Times*, March 20, 2012, p. B2.

[2] http://money.cnn.com/news/storysupplement/economy/bailouttracker/.

[3] "The Senate's Pony Express," *The Wall Street Journal*, May 2, 2012, p. A14.

[4] David E. Campbell and Robert D. Putman, "God and Caesar in America," *Foreign Affairs*, March/April, 2012, p.40.

CHAPTER 27: A BROKEN SYSTEM 393

[5] I respect the goals of the Tea Party that espouse conservative and libertarian ideas, as well as beliefs that endorse reduced government spending, reduction of the national debt, and a reduced federal budget. I leave the Tea Party camp on its religious issues. My concern with the Tea Party is its fiddling with tea leaves while it inhales religious incense.

[6] http://www.huffingtonpost.com/2012/03/18/rick-santorum-catholics-_n_1357050.html?flv=1

[7] http://www.huffingtonpost.com/2012/02/26/santorum-church-and-state_n_1302246.html, which is also the source for the material in the remainder of this section.

[8] Neil deGrasse Tyson writes about several aspects of the space program budget, from which I have sourced the material in this section of the chapter. See Neil deGrasse Tyson, "The Case for Space," *Foreign Affairs*, March/April, 2012, pp. 23-33.

[9] Ibid,. pp. 27-28.

[10] Frank, p. 285.

[11] From a June 26, 1857 speech at Springfield, Illinois. Frank, p. 926.

Chapter 28

Fixing a Broken System

A nation must spend money to create wealth.
—anon

You know what happens if you don't invest in the future? Nothing.

I have written twenty-seven reports and chapters describing human behavior and how some of our deficiencies led to the nearly perfect financial storm. Shakespeare also skewers our race but with far fewer words and with elegant verse.

One of my friends, a supporter of my work, has informed me I am no Thoreau, to which I agree. But he has also told me that I put out useful thoughts about topical subjects. Thus both humbled and encouraged, this chapter—for want of any elegance of prose—offers three straight-forward sets of ideas to fix America's broken financial and social systems.

Paul Volcker's Recommendations

My former boss at the Federal Reserve Board, Paul Volcker, supports many of the suggestions made in this book about fixing America's broken-down financial system. In a speech to a group of economists ("Three Years Later: Unfinished Business in Financial Reform"), he made the following points:[1]

CHAPTER 28: FIXING A BROKEN SYSTEM   395

- Make capital requirements for banks higher.
- Make the trading of financial instruments (such as credit default swaps) transparent and subject to regulation (which as of this writing, is under review).
- Address the too big to fail problem by either "reducing [banks'] size, curtailing their interconnections, or limiting their activities."
- Eliminate Fannie and Freddie as government-sponsored enterprises.
- Don't do much in the way of guaranteeing mortgages for low income people, at least not through a quasi-private institution, such as Fannie Mae.

Recommendations of The National Commission on Fiscal Responsibility and Reform (NCFRR)[2]

The National Commission on Fiscal Responsibility and Reform (also called Bowles-Simpson or Simpson-Bowles from the names of co-chairs Alan Simpson and Erskine Bowles) was created in 2010 by President Obama to identify America's federal government's fiscal problems and to establish a plan to address them. The commission released a report on December 1, 2010 but the plan failed to be approved. Eleven of eighteen votes were in favor of the plan but fourteen were votes needed to endorse it.

The commission's document is organized around a six-part plan. The commission states the plan will:

- Achieve nearly $4 trillion in deficit reduction through 2020, more than any effort in the nation's history.
- Reduce the deficit to 2.3% of GDP by 2015 (2.4% excluding Social Security reform), exceeding President's goal of primary balance (about 3% of GDP).
- Sharply reduce tax rates and cut backdoor spending in the tax code.
- Cap revenue at 21% of GDP and get spending below 22% and eventually to 21%.

- Ensure lasting Social Security solvency, prevent the projected 22% cuts to come in 2037, reduce elderly poverty, and distribute the burden fairly.
- Stabilize debt by 2014 and reduce debt to 60% of GDP by 2023 and 40% by 2035.

Here is a brief description of the six parts, which are direct quotes from the plan:

1) Discretionary Spending Cuts: Enact tough discretionary spending caps to force budget discipline in Congress. Include enforcement mechanisms to give the limits real teeth. Make significant cuts in both security and non-security spending by cutting low-priority programs and streamlining government operations. Offer over $50 billion in immediate cuts to lead by example, and provide $200 billion in illustrative 2015 savings.

2) Comprehensive Tax Reform: Sharply reduce rates, broaden the base, simplify the tax code, and reduce the deficit by reducing the many "tax expenditures"—another name for spending through the tax code. Reform corporate taxes to make America more competitive, and cap revenue to avoid excessive taxation.

3) Health Care Cost Containment: Replace the phantom savings from scheduled Medicare reimbursement cuts that will never materialize and from a new long-term care program that is unsustainable with real, common-sense reforms to physician payments, cost-sharing, malpractice law, prescription drug costs, government-subsidized medical education, and other sources. Institute additional long-term measures to bring down spending growth.

4) Mandatory Savings: Cut agriculture subsidies and modernize military and civil service retirement systems, while reforming student loan programs and putting the Pension Benefit Guarantee Corporation on a sustainable path.

CHAPTER 28: FIXING A BROKEN SYSTEM

5) Social Security Reforms to Ensure Long-Term Solvency and Reduce Poverty: Ensure sustainable solvency for the next 75 years while reducing poverty among seniors. Reform Social Security for its own sake, and not for deficit reduction.

6) Process Changes: Reform the budget process to ensure the debt remains on a stable path, spending stays under control, inflation is measured accurately, and taxpayer dollars go where they belong.

The Commission claims the plan would lead to the following federal outlays, revenue, deficit, and debt (as a percentage of GDP):

	Outlays	Revenue	Deficit	Debt
2010		23.8%	-8.9%	62%
2015		21.6%	-2.3%	70%
2020		21.8%	-1.2%	65%
2025		21.8%	-0.8%	57%
2030		21.6%	-0.6%	49%
2035		21.0%	0.0%	40%

The commission's plan failed to gain traction because of the inability of ideologically handicapped lawmakers to compromise on (admittedly) contentious issues.

It was criticized by conservatives as being unbalanced and too lenient regarding entitlements. Liberals took offense because the plan would reduce the social safety net. Some liberals call it the cat food provision, claiming that some people would be forced into such extreme poverty they would only be able to afford cat food for their supper. (Apparently, they have not looked at the prices of a can of cat food.)

To gain a sense of the futility of trying to move forward, here are quotes from Wikipedia providing a real-time snapshot of political gridlock.

Keynesian Economist James K. Galbraith submitted a statement to the NCFRR on behalf of Americans for Democratic Action. He argued that the current deficits were caused by the financial crisis; that cuts in Social Security and Medicare would be harmful and would not reduce the deficit; and that the Commission would do best "by advancing no proposals at all."

Dean Baker of the Center for Economic and Policy Research in Washington criticizes the deficit report for omitting a tax on the financial industry, as was recommended by the International Monetary Fund. He also denounces co-chairs Alan K. Simpson and Erskine Bowles for claiming to have looked everywhere on ways to increase revenue, but not including the financial industry. Also, Baker said that a possible conflict of interest exists regarding Erskine Bowles for serving on the board of Morgan Stanley while being on the commission and asks for further investigation into the connection between Bowles' role as a director of Morgan Stanley and the omission of any financial taxes in the report.

President Obama spoke briefly about the commission's work, but took little action. I continue to be puzzled by his aloof behavior. Perhaps he thought it was dead in the water to begin with and did not want to gamble his political chips on a losing cause.

Result? As this book goes to press, nothing. Meanwhile, America's ship is heading for the shoals.

Suggestions from This Writer

I offer ten supportive amendments to the thoughts of Mr. Volcker and the NCFRR. I suggest:

First, return to the practice of self-responsibility this country has exhibited in the past: More reliance on ourselves and less on Uncle Sam.

CHAPTER 28: FIXING A BROKEN SYSTEM 399

Second, dismantle both individual and corporate welfare. Stop capitalizing profits and socializing losses. As part of this idea, forbid financial institutions from attaining a size and an interconnectedness that qualifies them as too big to fail.

Third, condemn leaders who routinely buy-off others, or who are bought-off by others. (Moral indignation was once a great force in America.)

Fourth, question the rationale of corporate executives paying themselves more than four hundred times than the lowest paid employees in their own (!) companies.[3]

Fifth, dismantle the corruptive influences of lobbyists as well as the anti-republican idea of corporate free speech.

Sixth, shame members of Congress into living like the rest of us live:[4] 1. They will have no pension plan funded by taxpayers (they purchase their own). 2. They must participate in Social Security and dismantle their congressional retirement fund. 3. They must place their finances in a blind trust while they are in office (as well as the finances of their senior aides) and may not engage in stock market or other speculations that pertain to their work. 4. Pay raises will not be voted on by members of Congress, but will be apportioned through the consumer price index. 5. They must dismantle their own health care system and join their fellow Americans in the queues at the local clinics. 6. There will be restrictions on how and when former congresspeople can be registered as lobbyists or work for a lobby firm.

I make no mention of imposing term limits. If these ideas were adapted, Congress would initiate their own term limits. They would have no reason to stick around Capitol Hill and K Street. Instead of sticking it to their constituents from Washington DC, they would go home to become part of that constituency.

Seventh, shame ourselves into living within our means, including the curtailment of our obsession with personal debt.

Eighth, accept the simple fact that if we are going to get ourselves out of hock, we are going to experience cuts to entitlements and state/federal government pensions.

Ninth, any charity should be given only with this goal in mind: "Will my act to this party lead the party to become more self-sufficient?" This idea does not pertain only to a ghetto resident, it applies to car companies, insurance companies, banks, and politicians.

Tenth, institute the public funding of political campaigns in order to curtail the excesses of K Street and its contamination of the legislative process.

I mentioned briefly that one of America's biggest problems is an increasingly under-trained workforce. I'll save that subject for later. For now, what are the chances of my ideas coming about? Not likely. They are so unrealistic and idealistic I hesitated placing them in this book. I suspect we will continue doing what we have been doing since the 1960s. We will continue to talk about our problems, as that costs nothing and requires no will power.

---

[1] Gretchen Morgenson, "How Mr. Volcker Would Fix It," *The New York Times*, October 23, 2011, p. BU1. As well as an interview Ms. Morgenson had with Mr. Volcker.

[2] Sources: The National Commission on Fiscal Responsibility and Reform, with edited excerpts from Wikipedia.

[3] Packer, "The Broken Contract," p. 23.

[4] Parts of point six are taken from Warren Buffett's ideas.

Chapter 29

The Invisible Hand and the Visible Mind

Does the invisible hand have a mind of its own?

I began writing these reports and chapters as a neutral and somewhat naïve party. Granted, I had ten years of experience in the banking industry but my work was on the periphery of financial trade: writing software the experts used for their work at the Federal Reserve Board. I owned one-third of a mortgage brokerage firm, but I was mostly a silent partner; occasionally peeking-in to see what was going on. For one year, the Federal Reserve Broad sent me to the Dallas Federal Reserve Bank. As Senior Vice-President of Payments for the Fed's 11th District, I was only able to gain a superficial appreciation of the Fed's more prosaic responsibilities.

Knowing I was entering into a subject in which I was not an authority, I approached each report and chapter in this book with more caution than I ordinarily did when writing about my specialty: data communications networks. I have an intuitive feel for the Internet. I do not have an intuitive feel for the world of finance.

As you amply know by now I left my position of neutrality. I am writing this final part of the book, not of astonishment about the humans in this story who did nothing more than obey the Rules of Life. I am reflecting on what I have learned about the magnitude of the power and influence big money and big business have had (and have) in undermining the underpinnings of America's republican foundations.

After leaving the Fed, my circumstances as a small business owner, plying my trade for twenty years, instilled in me a mistaken belief that all of America's commerce operated by the same laws that established a level playing field for the competitors. I was not so cornpone to be oblivious to the imbalances of gerrymandering, congressional insider trading, the corrupting presence of K Street, and other Darwin in Guccis syndromes. I had chronicled human's nasty dispositions in *The Deadly Trinity*. But the research for this book altered my views about America's so-called free market society.

The Rules of Life are Called Rules for a Reason

I have documented many examples of the state of America's downturn these past few decades, both financially and socially. Were they avoidable? In hindsight, maybe, but the Rules of Life also came into play and dictated the actions of a lot of bad actors.

With hindsight comes a 20-20 view of what could have been done, as well as what should not have been done. It's been said, "Only in hindsight do humans have insight."

The Rules of Life were used in this book as parody but that does not diminish their validity. As we have witnessed, time and again, humans went about practicing these rules to the long-term detriment of everyone but a very few of the practitioners.

I will conclude this rather somber introduction to the final chapter with two quotations I copied into my notebooks in the 1960s and 70s. The sources are not documented in accordance with accepted grammatical conventions. I jotted them down without thinking about rules of sourcing, so forgive my happenstance attributions:

> "Civilization is thus a hopeless race to discover the remedies for the ills it produces." (William Ebenstein, commenting on Rosseau's philosophy.)

"Democracy is like a raft: you never sink, but your feet are always in the water."(Max Ways)

How do we move beyond the first thought? How do we accept and embrace the second one? Let's look at two philosophies in their relationship to these quotes and the nearly perfect financial storm.

Hands On or Hands Off?

As I delved into the subject of these reports and later these chapters, I often came across the opinions of the experts about the role the "invisible hand" might (or might not) have played in the unraveling of this specific financial debacle—and in the world of finance in general.

Invisible, in that natural forces guide the markets along, without human (especially government) manipulation. As I put pen to paper for this book, I was biased toward semi-*laissez-faire* (a semi-invisible hand), toward a business and political environment in which state intervention into transactions between private parties is minimal.[1] By minimal, I mean the state sets the stage for transparent and fair trading and gets out the way to let the contending factions have it out with one another.

I remain a proponent of the free market with government looking over its shoulder; but with caveats. In this book, we have witnessed the frequent slipshod hand of Uncle Sam, of Uncle's lethargy and incompetence, of Sam's diluting competitive markets with inept legislation. Competitive markets, if they are indeed competitive and open, are efficient. They make certain consumers obtain what they want or need, in the right amount, at the best price. We need look no further than the former USSR to see that intrusive government intervention into markets will spell disaster.

During this current crisis, many writers and politicians have used the philosophies of the economists Adam Smith and John Maynard Keynes as principal examples for discussing what went right or wrong. I reintroduced myself to the work of Smith and Keynes in an attempt to equate their ideas with my own experiences as a businessman and consumer.

The Invisible Hand: Government Stays Away

Most advocates of an unregulated free market (Alan Greenspan, Milton Friedman, and other conservative economists) regularly employ Adam Smith's invisible hand to justify having limited (or no) regulatory control over commerce; any commerce. They say:[2]

> The theory of the Invisible Hand states that if each consumer is allowed to choose freely what to buy and each producer is allowed to choose freely what to sell and how to produce it, the market will settle on a product distribution and prices that are beneficial to all the individual members of a community, and hence to the community as a whole. The reason for this is that self-interest drives actors to beneficial behavior. Efficient methods of production are adopted to maximize profits. Low prices are charged to maximize revenue through gain in market share by undercutting competitors. Investors invest in those industries most urgently needed to maximize returns, and withdraw capital from those less efficient in creating value. Students prepare for the most needed (and therefore most remunerative) careers. All these effects take place dynamically and automatically.

I disagree with the notion that self-interest drives actors to beneficial behavior. My take on human behavior is that self-interest often drives actors to behavior that is detrimental to all but the actor doing the behaving, as evidenced in the reports and chapters of this book. But then, I am not an economist—only an observer of human behavior. Still, I was curious about this key aspect of one of the most influential thoughts in economic history.

When in doubt, read the user's manual. Here is what Smith has to say about the invisible hand in *The Wealth of Nations* (italics are my emphasis):[3]

> By preferring the support of *domestic* to that of *foreign* industry, he intends only his own security; and by directing that

industry in such a manner as its produce may be of the greatest value, he intends only his own gain, and he is in this, as in many other cases, led by an *invisible hand* to promote an end which was no part of his intention. Nor is it always the worse for the society that it was not part of it. By pursuing his own interest he frequently promotes that of the society more effectually than when he really intends to promote it.

First, Smith used the term invisible hand *only* in the context of supporting domestic *vis-à-vis* foreign industry. Second, aside from the notion that he would not like NAFTA, his statements are reflective of 1790's England-centrism and associated trade barriers. England's centuries of economic imperialism clearly demonstrated any society that was *not* part of the Englishman's unintended actions was worse off. Third, poorer products often capture the marketplace over rivals, leading to products of lesser value. Often, superior or predatory marketing overcomes superior technology.

Aside from disagreeing or agreeing with the idea of the invisible hand, I was struck by how narrow Smith's use of the idea is: domestic vs. foreign industry. Yet, the idea has been expanded by *laissez-faire* proponents to encompass everything but the kitchen sink.

There seems to be a mystical alchemy at work with the invisible hand. Our visible minds end up producing invisible hands! One critic said something to the effect that the reason the invisible hand was invisible was because it was not there.

Anyway, Smith's theories need not be analyzed in any more detail. We conclude with the notion that Smith and his fans do not favor government intervention in the marketplace.

The Visible Hand: Government Stays

The proponents of John Maynard Keynes favor government intervention. They advocate the use of government fiscal and monetary interventions to mitigate the effects of economic downturns.

Keynes's influence led to highly regulated markets for most of the post WW II period. Then, in the 1970s, Adam Smith and Milton

Friedman came to the fore and government intervention waned. Ronald Reagan and Alan Greenspan abetted this trend.

Thus, during the run-up to the nearly perfect financial storm the invisible hand proponents ruled the day. Glass-Steagall was rescinded. The regulation of most of the huge security derivatives market was abandoned or never taken up in the first place. America's financial sector was as close to Smith's invisible hand has it had been for many decades.

The invisible hand was made into a powerful argument for *laissez-faire* by those who believed in its efficiency, those who benefited from it personally, and those who did not care but were bought off by its benefactors.

However, the nearly perfect financial storm has led to a resurgence in Keynesian economics. Presidents Bush and Obama turned Adam Smith away. The result has been the near take over by the federal government of huge parts of America's so-called capitalistic industries.

The Argument Will Never End

The invisible hand proponents say their philosophy has never had a fair chance to work. They say that the Great Depression came about *because* of government. The Keynesians make the opposite claim.

Today, the causes of America's current "great depression" revolve around the same arguments: Too much government or too little government. Who's correct? Your guess is as good as mine, but I rest my case on the factors cited in Report 4.

Government started the process with the Bush and Clinton administrations pushing for more home ownership to lower and middle classes. Their decrees were reinforced by the laxity and incompetence of government oversight. What followed? The nearly perfect financial storm:

(1) Excess liquidity coupled with (2) a long period of low interest rates for (3) subprime mortgages with (4) adjustable rate interest loans led to (5) massive loan defaults and (6) foreclosures,

which fueled a decline in (7) home prices, leading to the collapse of (8) mortgage backed securities and other Wall Street instruments.

Did the invisible hand shuffle these cards? Did the visible mind deal them? I think it fair to say the hands and minds of both John Maynard Keynes and Adam Smith came into play.

I also say the issue is irrelevant because—regardless of political and financial theory—Wall Street will always look for ways to circumvent Uncle Sam.

So, where does this financial witches brew and its toxic seasonings leave you and me? We must look after ourselves. Uncle Sam is too inept to do it. Wall Street is too selfish to care. Benjamin Franklin gives us the answer: "Distrust and caution are the parents of security."

---

[1] The term *laissez-faire*, in French, means "let do"; that is, just leave it alone.

[2] Wikepedia, key in "Adam Smith."

[3] Wikipedia and from Book IV, chapter II, paragraph IX of *The Wealth of Nations*. Key in "Adam Smith".

READERS' COMMENTS ON PART I

During the time I was writing Part I of this book, I posted the reports to a private list of readers. I have included some of the comments below. I have no feedback on Part II, as I did not post this material.

These e-mails do not have names attached. In some instances, I do not know who the sender is, as my material was later sent to unknown readers who responded only with an e-mail address, or from a less-identifiable blog response.

If I do have names, for privacy purposes, I have deleted the name of the sender. If you would like to know the sender, if I have his/her identification (and I have domain names for most of these e-mails), I will contact the sender and ask for his/her permission. In this way, you can also verify the accuracy (pro and con) of this correspondence.

Unless a person included something personal, I have altered no words (or grammar) in this material that pertain to the subject matter of this book. I have used " **** " in place of profanity or other words that a reader might find offensive. On a few occasions I must substitute a person's name with a noun or pronoun, in which case, I place brackets around my change. Any notes I add are also surrounded by brackets. I have made the text the same font size and type, and changed minor formats. In some cases, an e-mail was several pages. I took the liberty of using only the first part of these e-mails. I did not selectively choose passages for inclusion or exclusion.

I look forward to your thoughts about my book and these readers' ideas as well.

++++

In my view.....granted, from hindsight, but something I believed at the time and still do.....the banks (and I include AIG here) should not have been "bailed out" by the USA (i.e., by you and me and every other taxpayer), but rather a policy of laissez faire should have been followed and let the banks (and GM, etc.) pursue the "normal course" of Chapter 11 or, perhaps, even Chapter 7. As a financial character, I went through quite a few chapter 11's while at [a hedge fund]. While it was painful at the time, the system worked as it was supposed to......those who took the big risks got burned (at least in the near term); others survived and, ultimately, flourished. Yeah, relative to the banks, we were small potatoes...only several hundred million dollars involved....but the processes I encountered and endured demonstrated at least to me the "beauty" of the free enterprise system. P.S., keep writing. Your thoughts are interesting.

++++

I think you would put Judge Judy out of business! It certainly would help to balance the weird behavior called Tush, opps, Rush Limbaugh. I was radio surfing on the way home today and there he was ****. What fun to read your reports!

++++

Perhaps the Tea Party needs to add derivatives to their list to really accomplish something worthwhile. The Main Street public can be easily fooled now since Wall Street has become more difficult to understand. The general public loves things like Clinton and the blue velvet dress, not derivatives. If you showed derivatives to be related to oral sex, it would capture the public's interest.

Keep up the flow of information about this; someone needs to be explaining this to the public so that we can write our Congressional delegates. Thanks, one voice can make a difference~ especially a voice that speaks in terms that are understandable to Main Street.

++++

And here I thought that George Bush was ill equipped to hold his office. Your work in the boardroom [writer: the word was bedroom, but I chose to alter to what I think is the intent of the sender.] during your ten years at the Fed probably helped you form, more than you realize, your opinions on monetary policy and certainly must have been more rewarding.

I do read your work and the only meaningful criticism on this subject I have is that you fail to put enough emphasis on the influence of money on the politicians who then cave into the special interests. After the politicians have been "bought" their "oversight" responsibility turns into a limp ****. Wall Street and money control the levers of power and not the people. I predict that the growing divide between the rich and the poor will someday come back to bite them as it did in the Gilded Age, the depression. Hopefully you and I will be long gone. [I agree and included considerable material on the subject in Part II.]

You have a vast range of points of view that I find unusual and appealing. To move through them with the agility and wit that you do is amazing talent. I love watching your mind work in your various works.

++++

I look forward to reading your essays. I had started a notebook a while back with things that you had written that my sister had forwarded to me.

++++

I hope this email finds you and yours doing well. It was great seeing this email this morning. Thank you so much for your Journalism Report 1. Please keep me posted.

++++

Another fine piece of research and writing. When I die, I told my wife to send you my voting proxy! I will share this with my friends and family.

++++

The voice of reason is like the proverbial "voice crying in the wilderness." You are speaking reason; blame and fear negate reason; it is popular. Thanks for being the voice of reason.

++++

Thanks for the reports. It makes some areas of this mess a bit clearer to me. Good luck with the book, it should sell well in my opinion. Loved the quotes also, Benjamin Franklin's especially.

++++

I appreciated your latest offering which I am sure had to be "too much like work". You hit (pgs 4 and 11) on misguided Barney Frank. I do not agree. He has received a lot of bad press concerning Fannie and Freddie especially a statement in 2008 that there was no problem with these institutions. I have heard Barney a couple of times on the night time Boston talk shows and he presents a different picture blaming the Republicans on the escalation of the subprime game. The Carter Administration started it all with the passage of the "Community Reinvestment Act". He noted that the Republicans over 12 years continued to increase the role of F&F and he fought it (see Wikipedia excerpt below). He stated that in 2004 the Bush Administration told them (House Committee) to raise the subprime percentage offerings to 54% from 42%. He fought it as he believed that there was a large percentage of society that could never handle a mortgage due to their life style and work ethic. He did not become Chairman until January 2007 after the Democratic win in November 2006. He said he immediately pass legislation to rein F&F in and started working on fixing F&F. I have been very impressed with Barney watching him on CNBC and other business channels. You may want to read the Wikipedia file on Barney. Granted it is not totally fact.

++++

Very interesting and well organized report. I already knew most of the material, but this was well organized and I will forward it to a number of people.

I agree that the derivatives must be traded on a public market. Within the past week I have written to our senators strongly on this topic and basically said to get off their asses and get sensible reforms passed. Bob Corker of Tennessee was making progress with Dodd and our own Gregg was working on the derivatives section - and then Shelby got his nose pushed out of joint and the whole effort died. As I told Senator Gregg, it appears to me that the Republicans are trying very hard to grasp defeat from the jaws of victory. Right or wrong, the public is angry and failure to develop a bill - probably an imperfect bill even - well, you'd damn well better not be on the wrong side of that. Thanks for the article.

++++

Thanks for report. Excellent work! Possibly the Glass Stegall Law/Act should be reinstated and under no condition or circumstance should non-banks be granted Bank Holding company authority with FDIC and Federal Reserve membership and privilege.

++++

You hit one of my buttons here. Great report and a great series. Based on the goals you set forth I have a few suggestions about how some of these might be encouraged.

It is highly unlikely that the government will allow the behemoths in the financial world to fail. The result would be too disastrous for everyone. As much as I'd like to see AIG, Goldman, etc. dissolve into dust for what they did; I do not think the satisfaction I and others would experience would be worth the pain to most everyone.

++++

You should think about publishing "The NPS". It's worthy.

++++

Your explanation of the financial weapons of mass destruction is absolutely correct.

++++

Your financial report was excellent.

++++

I love reading your articles because your view is well balanced and documented. I have watched the Tea Party because I'm interested in what is happening in our nation, but I am also interested when I know people who are involved. Quite a few **** ranchers are actively involved in the Tea Party. The things that they say seem simplistic to me in a society so overcome with both corporate greed and big government and political greed and ethical impotence.

I also noted that Karl Rove has established two organizations that are helping to fund efforts of the Tea Party clandestinely.

++++

Great insight. I enjoyed reading it. No surprise - I'm not a dues paying Tea Party member.

++++

You've highlighted some of the issues to be addressed if the TP or any party is to serve the people and not the organized special interests - which never serve the people.

The TP is making a difference is some not so subtle ways. Candidates supported by the TP do much better than if they had not been supported. They tend to support new blood, vs. entrenched good ole boys - although I'm not sure they are the best candidates. They haven't seemed to support a Democrat yet - that I'm aware of. Unless they are a subsidiary of the GOP, they should be supporting the best candidates that reflect their basic goals and they are not always GOP'ers.

Too often the GOP and Dems see regulation in black and white. The GOP wants to dismantle regulations and the DEMs want more and more. Dismantling existing Gordian Knots throughout regulations and rewriting clear, simpler rules that effectively achieve their goals is a thought neither one of them has considered.

++++

I like to think that I have a minimal amount of common sense to say the least, and a pretty good grasp of what is happening to us in this country. Where in heavens name could they have ever pulled out of your excellent writing that you are anti Bill of Rights and anti Constitutional? That is just stretching it more than a bit. We are slowly (?) being nibbled to the bone and that is pretty evident to me and most people I know. Keep writing and jogging people's brain cells so they have to come out of their complacency and use their heads for something other than a hat rack!!

++++

From my perspective and leanings this is the best essay you have written. It is straight forward and has a lot to offer. I guess we are in lock step. I wish that I could express myself as well. I would think that most of your learned readers will score you extremely high on this piece. I will be out voting today to try and get the best Republican to take down our Pelosi Democrats in New Hampshire.

++++

An interesting report (#17). I have a few comments to offer.

I think the idea of the bailouts, fed loans and stimulus all are great ideas at the headline level. However, once you get into the table of contents and the actual details it breaks down terribly. Not surprisingly considering my take on the effectiveness of the government when it comes to regulation and sticking their finger in the eye of the financial system. The things they should do, they don't do. The things they actually do, they do badly. (Not all, but too many.)

As for your definitions, I don't know if you tweaked Webster or someone else, but my definition of capitalism actually describes a system we've never had and probably couldn't tolerate nor should we consider. Pure capitalism is as close to the law of the jungle as an economic system can get. You might start out with a *competitive free market system*, but very shortly the alpha companies will crush the competition and make entry by new competitors impossible.

Even with our "modified" capitalism we see that the largest competitors carve out their niche and the ground around them becomes sterile. They pretty much make it damn near impossible for a competitor to gain market share or even gain entry if they perceive it as encroaching on their turf. The government in these cases is often impotent, incompetent, corrupt or out to lunch. Everyone has an opinion as to which description to use…Regulation is firstly ineffective, watered down and shot full of loopholes by bought off members and then the industry in question joins in the sales pitch knowing they already have half a dozen ways around any anemic rules.

++++

I look forward to the letters to the Tea Party! I had lunch with [a sister in law] today and [she] spent the ENTIRE time whining about Obamacare and planning her attendance at the next Tea Party. For some reason, she thinks [my husband] and I are on her side. I didn't bother to argue - you never change anyone's mind (especially if that person is 78) over lunch.

Please give me good news - I am hungry for it. Is there any? Should Obama start having Fireside Chats? What I see both printed and on screen is so depressing that I may have to turn to you completely for updates that don't make me tired and depressed. You make a lot of sense, U, and I am eternally grateful.

++++

As always, your reports are so "learned" and a much bigger picture than I can view from my neat little world. You make me realize that I see everything in very simple terms. Consequently, I never really know how to discuss with you.

I am grateful to hear your agreement with the tea party. One thing I wish to add that is a priority to me is that the tea party is making getting back to the U.S. Constitution one of its goals. The progressives in charge of this country seem to believe that we have "progressed" way past the Constitution and the Bible. NOT! Both require personal responsibility as well as a sense of honor and responsibility to our fellow citizens of this county and world.

++++

I believe Ulyss's [writer, that would be Uyless's] argument is one of the best and most pertinent to today's issues I have seen. I hope it gets published in a widely read medium.

++++

If you wrote the bill [the financial reform bill], it would clear the so-called bramble bushes that snag the mind trying to extract the solid parts, the worthy parts. You are so correct about the inclusion of women, etc. and the Congo. Grafting to the worthy parts often kills both parts. No wonder the banking business can succeed at being deceptive. As they say in **** "Kill them with BS." This BS certainly created a rancid mess.

Your explanations make the other parts evident. What a fine mind; what clarity you give the verbose plan for regulating the industry.

That reminds me of a joke related to not knowing whether something has been accomplished or not as it seems was the practice of the previous regulators as well as being easily and willingly deceived.

++++

Report # (18) Another good one.

There are many root causes for the growing disparity in income. Among them is a deficit in educational opportunity and a lowering of the quality of the education actually received by too many in the population? If you want a prosperous nation, educate them.

Second we're getting older and the younger ones we have in the population are illegal immigrants with little or no education. These guys do not drag down the dividends and interest income of the top 5%, they merely depress the wages of the lower two quintiles, moving the profits upward. Also the geezer population is slowing down and retiring.

While they may have enough saved for a "comfortable" retirement, many don't need and don't generate the same level of income they did when they were in their prime.

++++

I'm with you 100% on the corporation as illegitimate citizen issue. The Supremes (Citizens United v. Federal Election Commission) bowed to their masters in that one – a reflex genuflect I suspect since they are the ultimate arbiter of the issue; they just forgot...

I could see that ruling in a case brought by a bunch of individuals without corporate money, with contribution limits, but not the *carte blanche* that they issued. The concept that money equates to speech is BS. That makes money king and the everyday American a serf.

++++

I found the report 17 & 18 very informative. It is the kind of report that really interests me. Good work.

++++

Excellent!!!! You are absolutely correct that the Big 9 will continue to control the closed derivatives operations with no oversight or regulation form US Government.

Pile it on Uyless!

++++

Excellent analysis of example of executive and legislative cranial/anal inversion.

++++

The two chapters clearly state the problem. The solution with the "humans' behavior within the institutions" seems impossible as long as our current financial system is not forced to change by the visible hand of financial disaster. And, like war, it is the ones on the battle field who die, not the generals, usually. As you can see, your chapters ignited my thoughts and concerns.

Thanks for your wisdom.

++++

**** my paltry offerings here are, at least in part, a result of your good work at the front end.

I just began to sample "Republic Lost: How Money Corrupts" and I watched a CNN special on how voting in House Congressional elections is often a waste of time. (Gerrymandering rigs the districts so that incumbents are virtually guaranteed reelection.) For instance in 2000 98% of incumbents were reelected and the results for other House Seats (and Senate) are essentially the same. When an incumbent loses an election, it's really big news. Even when they are disclosed as thieves, scoundrels and tax evaders they get reelected.

When you add this to the corruption fertilized by our campaign finance behavior, you begin to see that the "elected" Congress (at least the House and often the Senate) are actually all but 100% insulated from pressure by the people. As long as they keep the people in their pockets somewhat happy (who vote party line 85% of the time) they can ignore the rest of the country.

This leads me to your analysis of the "Nearly Perfect Storm: An American Financial and Social Failure". **** I would favor a title that reflected the near certainty of this result due to biology/evolution/DNA coupled with our inevitable failure to acknowledge the same. Like an addiction, denial of the truth is a major symptom of the problem.

Banking Experience of Uyless Black

Uyless Black has had a diverse career in banking and finance. While working his way through college, Black spent one summer as an employee with Universal CIT Finance at a branch office located in Watts, California. While in Watts, a few years before the riots took place, he was a field collection agent—also known as a bill collector. During this fruitful time of tutelage, he learned several fundamental facts about finance, including how to brow beat and threaten late-paying borrowers; as well as how to hot wire—in the middle of the night—their soon-to-be repossessed cars. He returned to college in one piece, but wise in the ways of low level finance and loan sharking operations.

After joining the U.S. Navy and serving in the Western Pacific, Black was assigned to a Washington, DC billet in the new field of computer programming. There, the Navy contracted with the nearby Jet Propulsion Laboratory facility to use JPL's IBM 360/90, at that time the largest and most powerful computer in existence. Black was assigned to a team to write code simulating navy battles between Communist Chinese submarines and U.S. submarine attack forces. It mattered little if China had almost no submarines and that Black did not know a hill of beans about submarine warfare. "Any port in a storm; any code for a programmer."

While laboring away to save America from a non-existent Chinese threat, Black took on a night time job at Riggs National Bank; his first introduction into high level finance. There he worked in a check clearing house and gained insight into the banking industry by manually entering into a check processing machine the data from thousands of checks. Upon discovery that a check processing clerk was also a programmer, Riggs' managers asked Black to write programs to assist the clearing house analysts in balancing their nightly books.

After several years of U.S. Navy duty, Black became a civilian and was hired as a software programmer by the Federal Reserve Board in Washington, DC. He was taken-on by the nation's central bank because of his "extensive" banking experience at CIT Finance and Riggs; plus his computer-based modeling work on imaginary Chinese submarine stealth attacks.

On his first day at the "Fed" he was assigned to write programs that would simulate the nation's money supply. This model's output was currently being calculated by brilliant MIT, Harvard, and University of Chicago economists using desk-size adding machines.

Black knew little about money because he had little of it. He was selected as the sole programmer to write the first computer-based model of America's money supply because (a) he was "deeply experienced" in computer-based modeling and (b) the money supply economists distrusted and disliked the Board's current Data Processing staff.

After the first meeting with money supply gurus, Black asked his team leader, "Why me?" His leader replied, "No one at the Board knows anything about computer-based modeling and besides, you're fresh meat."

It mattered little that the output of these brilliant economists' calculators was used at the Federal Reserve's Federal Open Market Operations to manage two modest commodities: the nation's money supply and its interest rates. It mattered little that no one had ever attempted to create a computer-based model of America's money supply system. No one else at the Fed had the "deep background" to match that of Black.

Amazingly, Black's simulation software was completed ahead of schedule and actually printed acceptable results. From this serendipitous event, Black was sent to the Stonier Graduate School of Banking at Rutgers University to become knowledgeable in the very subjects for which he had written programs.

To round out his in-depth knowledge of money, finance, and banking, Black was assigned for one year as a Senior Vice President of the Federal Reserve Bank in Dallas. There, he was placed in charge of the Fed's 11th District payments operations—one of twelve people in the nation carrying this responsibility. The position was related to a skill in which he had extensive knowledge because he had fed thousands of checks into a check tabulating machine at Riggs bank. He had nothing to do with the bank's computer systems, about which he was an expert.

At the Dallas Fed, Black delved into the nation's electronic payments systems, such as the Automated Clearing House (ACH). He worked with several commercial banks' clearing houses during this time, and was asked to accept a position as director of a Dallas bank clearing house consortium. He declined the offer because he would have been placed into the untenable position of having to cheer for the Dallas Cowboys.

Thus, Black returned to the Federal Reserve Board and the Washington Redskins.

Black served out his time at the Fed helping to setup the framework for the Federal Reserve's new packet switching network. For two years, he also served as the Fed's ombudsman. This ancillary job became that of a buffer between systemically disgruntled employees and systemically intractable managers.

Upon leaving the Fed after ten years of service, Black received an autographed picture of Chairman Arthur Burns from the Fed's Public Relations Office, a letter of thanks from the lead economist of the Board's money supply operations, and a cloth-bound suitcase from the Data Processing Department. No watch. (One serious note: Black's computer model of the nation's money continued to be used after Black left the Board.)

For the next twenty years, Black formed several companies. Their focus was on computer networks. Their existence depended on a thriving economy, credit, and the ability to raise capital.

During this time, Black also cofounded a mortgage brokerage company with two friends. He was a silent participant; his partners did the work. It succeeded for a while, but succumbed to the Fed's gyrating practice of raising and lowering America's interest rates. Irony in action: Black's company was affected by the very software he wrote several years earlier.

In spite of these varied and spotty experiences with the financial, banking, economic markets—and almost none with Wall Street itself, Black decided to write *The Nearly Perfect Storm: An American Financial and Social Failure*.

Of more importance, and the second serious note in this resume: He wrote the book with enough experience as a citizen and businessman to be troubled by recent trends in America's political process and the vulnerability of the United States to interconnected financial institutions that are deemed too big to fail.

BIBLIOGRAPHY

"After the Stress Tests." *The New York Times*, May 10, 2009, p.7.

Altman, Roger C. "The Great Crash, 2008." *Foreign Affairs*, January/February 2009, p.4.

Altman, and Richard N. Hass. "American Profligacy and American Power." *Foreign Affairs*, November/December, 2010, p. 26.

"Another Great Leap Forward?" *The Economist*, March 13, 2010, p.28.

Armour, Stephanie. "Millions Could Get Help, but Is the Plan Fair?" *USA Today*, February 19, 2009, p. 2A.

Baumgartner, Frank, Jeffery Berry, Marie Hojnacki, David Kimball, and Beth Leech. *Lobbying and Policy Change*, pp. 257-258. Secondary source: Lessig, p. 349, footnote 60.

Belkin, Douglas."Chicago Mayor Trashes Politics of Waste Removal." *The Wall Street Journal*, October 12, 2011, p. A.

Bello, Marisol, and Paul Overberg, "The Fading Middle Class." *USA TODAY*, October 26, 2011, p. A1.

Bialk, Carl. "Sizing Up the Small-Business Jobs Machine." *The Wall Street Journal*, October 15-16, 2011, p. A2.

Black, Uyless, "The Rules of Life." Glossary. *The Deadly Trinity*. Forthcoming revision in late 2012.

Borrus, Amy. "The Credit-Raters: How They Work and How They Might Work Better." *Business Week*, April 8, 2002.

Campbell, David E., and Robert D. Putman. "God and Caesar in America." *Foreign Affairs*, March/April, 2012, p.40.

Caro, Robert A. *The Path to Power: The Years of Lyndon Johnson*. New York: Alfred A. Knopf, 1982. Secondary source: Leonard Roy Frank, p. 724.

Cassidy, John. *How Markets Fail*. p. 320.

———. "Paging J.P. Morgan: Who Should Pay Korea's Bills?" *The New Yorker*, January 19, 1988.

Citizens United vs. Fed. Election Commission, 130 S. Ct. 676, 910. Secondary source, Lessig, p. 363, footnote 51.

Cohan, William D. *Money and Power: How Goldman Sachs Came to Rule the World*. New York: Anchor Books, 2012.

Corkery, Michael, and Kris Maher. "Capital Files for Bankruptcy." *The Wall Street Journal*, October 13, 2011, p. A3.

Dash, Eric. "If it's too big to fail, is it too big to exist?" *The New York Times*, June 21, 2009, p. 3.

Davidson, Paul. "Study: Tax Break Didn't Create Jobs." *USA TODAY*, October 12, 2011, p. B1.

Day, Donald, ed. *The Autobiography of Will Rogers*. Na, 1949.

"The Debt to the Penny and Who Holds It." United States Department of the Treasury, Bureau of the Public Debt (January 2012).

De Soto, Hernando. *The Mystery of Capital*. New York: Basic Books, 2000.

Dugas, Christine. "Debtors Burying Heads in the Sand." *USA TODAY*, October 13, 2011, p. B1.

Duhigg, Charles. "Pressured to Take More Risk, Fannie Reached the Tipping Point." *The New York Times*, October 5, 2008, p. 30.

Eisinger, Jesse. "The Volcker Rule, Made Bloated and Weak." *The New York Times*, February 23, 2012, p. B4.

"Factbox: How Goldman's ABACUS Deal Worked." Reuters, April 18, 2010.

"Faster, Faster, Faster." *The Economist*, January 28, 2012, p. 65.

Feldman, Loren. "The $580 Million Black Hole." *The New York Times*, July 15, 2012, pp. BU1, BU4-BU5.

Fitzpatrick, Dan, Liz Rappaport, and Victoria McGane. "Well, That was Awkward." *The Wall Street Journal*, May 3, 2012, pp. C1 & C3.

"Fixing Finance." *The Economist*, January 27, 2009, p. 22.

Frank, Leonard Roy. *Quotationary*. New York: Random House, 2001.

Frank, Thomas. "How State Lawmakers Pump Up Pensions in Ways You Can't." *USA TODAY*, September 23, 2011, pp. 1A, 8A – 10A.

Gandel, Stephen. "How Goldman Trashed a Town." *Time*, July 5, 2010, pp. 32-33.

———. "How Stressed Is Your Bank?" *Time*, March 2, 2009, p. 29.

———. "Why Your Bank Is Broke." *Time*, February 9, 2009, np.

Goldbacher, Ray. "N.Y. Fed Chair Resigns Abruptly." *USA Today*, May 8, 2009, p. 4B.

Greenspan, Alan. *The Age of Turbulence*. New York: Penguin Press, 2007.

Herzenhorn, David M., and Edward Wyatt. "Banking Bill Negotiations Begin Again." *The New York Times*, April 21, 2010, p. B1.

Hodge, Roger D. "Readings." *Harper's Magazine*, October, 2010, p.14.

"How to Play Chicken and Lose: Finance Suffers from Reverse Natural Selection." *The Economist*, January 24, 2009, p. 17.

Hubbard, Elbert. *An American Bible.*1946, p. 219. Secondary source: Leonard Roy Frank, p. 724.

Huntley, Jonathan. "Federal debt and the risk of a fiscal crisis." Congressional Budget Office: Macroeconomic Analysis Division, July 27, 2010.

Izzo, Phil. "Bleak News for Americans' Income." *The Wall Street Journal*, October 14, 2011, p. A6.

Jenkins, Jr, Holman W. "Greg Smith Is Too Sexy for His Cat." *The Wall Street Journal*, March 17-18, 2012, p. A15.

Johnson, Simon. "The Quiet Coup." *The Atlantic*, May, 2009, p. 49.

Katz, Richard. "The Japan Fallacy." *Foreign Affairs*, March/April, 2009, p. 10.

Kelly, James. *A Complete Collection of Scottish Proverbs*. Secondary source: Leonard Roy Frank, p. 866.

Kopecki, Dawn, and Shannon D. Harrington. July 24, 2009. Go to link: "Banning 'Naked' Default Swaps May Raise Corporate Funding Costs."

Lessig, Lawrence. *Republic Lost*. New York: Hachette, 2011.

"Lessons from the Collapse of Hedge Fund, Long-Term Capital Management." http://riskinstitute.ch/146490.htm.

Lewis, Michael. "Beyond Economics, Beyond Politics, Beyond Accountability." *Worth*, May, 1995.

———. *The Big Short*. New York: W. W. Norton, 2010.

———. *Liar's Poker*. New York: W.W. Norton, 1989.

Lewis, Michael, and David Einhorn. "The End of the Financial Word as We Know It." *The New York Times*, January 4, 2009, p. 9.

Lieberman, David, and Matt Krantz. "Goldman Sachs Concedes Mistake, Settles SEC Suit." *USA TODAY*, July 16, 2010, pp. B1-B2.

Litan, Robert E. "The Derivatives Dealers' Club and Derivatives Markets Reform: A Guide for Policy Makers, Citizens and Other Interested Parties." Brookings Institution, April 7, 2010.

Lizza, Ryan. "The Contrarian." *The New Yorker*, July 6 and 13, 2009, p. 32.

Lowenstein, Roger. *The End of Wall Street*. New York: Penguin Press, 2010.

———. "Cracked Foundation." *The New York Times Magazine*, April 25, 2010, p. 12.

———. "Who Needs Wall Street?" *The New York Times Magazine*, April 21, 2010, p. 16.

Lowrey, Annie. "U.S. Profits from the Sale of Some Mortgage Securities." *The New York Times*, March 20, 2012, p. B2.

Lynch, David J. "U.S. May Face Years of Sluggish Growth." *USA Today*, May 8, 2009, p. 1B.

Martin, Andrew. "Give Him Liberty, but Not a Bailout." *The New York Times*, August 2, 2009, pp. BUY 1 & 6.

Mayer, Jane. "Attack Dog." *The New Yorker*, February 13 and 20, pp. 42-43.

McIntire, Mike, and Michael Luo. "White House Opens Door to Big Donors, and Lobbyists Slip In." *The New York Times*, April 15, 2012, p. 1.

Morgenson, Gretchen. "Count of Sequels to TARP." *The New York Times*, October 3, 2010, p. BU 1.

———. "Give Me Back My Paycheck." *The New York Times*, February 22, 2009, p. 7.

———. "Holding Bankers' Feet to the Fire." *The New York Times*, July 18, 2010, p. BU-1.

———. "How Mr. Volcker Would Fix It." *The New York Times*, October 23, 2011, p. BU1.

———. "Paychecks as Big as Tajikistan." *The New York Times*, June 18, 2011, pp. BU 1 and 3.

———. "So That's Where the Money Went." *The New York Times*, December 5, 2010, p. BU 1, 5.

———. "Some Bankers Never Learn." *The New York Times*, July 31, 2011, p. BU 6.

———. "Too big to fail, or too big to handle?" *The New York Times*, June 21, 2009, p. BU 1.

———. "Was There a Loan It Didn't Like?" *The New York Times*, business section, November 2, 2008, p. 1.

Morgenson, Gretchen, and Joshua Rosner. *Reckless Endangerment*. New York: Henry Holt, 2011.

Nocera, Joe. "Risk Mismanagement." *The New York Times Magazine*, January 4, 2009, p. 27.

———. "Sheila Bair's Bank Shot." *The New York Times Magazine*, nd, circa July, 2011, p. 29.B4.

OpenSecrets.org: http://www.opensecrets.org/news/2008/11/moneywins-white-house-and.html.

"Order in the Jungle." *The Economist*, March 15, 2008, p. 83.

"Over-Regulated America." *The Economist*, February 18, 2012, p. 9.

Packer, George. "The Broken Contract." *Foreign Affairs*, November/December, 2011, p. 29.

———. "The Ponzi State." *The New Yorker*, February 9 & 16, p. 84.

Paulson, Jr., Henry M. *On the Brink*. New York: Hachette, 2010.

Pear, Robert, and Jonathan Weisman. "Bill to Prohibit Insider Trading by Members of Congress Advances in Senate." *The New York Times*, January 31, 2012, p. A1.

BIBLIOGRAPHY 427

Peterson, Scott. "Mr. Buffett Goes to Bat for Goldman, Moody's." *The New York Times*, May 3, 2010, p. C1.

Philips, Mathew. "The Monster That Ate Wall Street." *Newsweek*, October, 2008, p. 46.

Posner, Richard A. *The Crisis of Capitalistic Democracy.* Cambridge: Harvard University Press, 2010.

President Obama Calls for New Restrictions on Size and Scope of Financial Institutions to Rein in Excesses and Protect Taxpayers. http://www.whitehouse.gov/the-press-office/president-obama-calls-new-restrictions-size-and-scopefinancial-institu tions-rein-e, retrieved from http://en.wikipedia.org/wiki/Volcker_Rule.

Pressman, Aaron. http://www.businessweek.com/investing/insights/blog/ archives/2008/09/community_reinv.html, September 29 2008.

Protess, Ben, and Mark Scott. "U.S. is Building Criminal Cases Over Rate-Fixing." *The New York Times*, July 15, 2012, pp. 1 and 4.

Rajan, Ragburam. "The True Lessons of the Recession." *Foreign Affairs*, May/June, 2012, pp. 74-75.

Reilly, David. "Getting Fed Up with the Repro Man's Loans." *The Wall Street Journal*," May 3, 2012, p. C12.

Rose, Charlie. Interview with Roger Altman on PBS, July 9, 2009.

Schiller, Fredrich von Schiller. *The Maid of Orleans.* 3.6, 1801. Secondary source: Leonard Roy Frank, p. 831.

Schouten, Fredreka, and Gregory Korte. "A Few Rich Donors Fuel Super PACs." *USA TODAY*, May 3, 2012, p. 5A.

Seabrook, John. "Suffering Souls." *The New Yorker*, November 10, 2008, pp. 64-73.

"The Senate's Pony Express." *The Wall Street Journal*, May 2, 2012, p.A14.

Serwer, Andy, and Allan Sloan. "The Price of Greed." *Time*, September 29, 2008, pp. 35-36.

Shakespeare, William. *Titus Andronicus.* 4.4.83, 1593. Secondary source: Leonard Roy Frank, p. 295.

Shell, Adam. "Stock Recovery Will Be a Long Haul." *USA Today*, March 9, 2009, p. B1.

Smith, Greg. "Why I Am Leaving Goldman Sachs." *The New York Times*, March 14, 2012, p. A25.

Sommer, Jeff. "No Bitter Aftertaste from This Stock Offering." *The New York Times*, February 19, 2012, p. BU-3.

Story, Louise. "A Secretive Banking Elite Rules Trading in Derivatives." *The New York Times* Web site, December 11, 2010, p. 1.

"Time to Bury Governor Gerry." *The Economist*, October 9, 1010, p. 20.

Turley, Jonathan. "Do Laws Even Matter Today?" *USA TODAY*, June 15, 2010, p. 9A.

Tyson, Neil deGrasse. "The Case for Space." *Foreign Affairs*, March/April, 2012, pp. 23-33.

Wallison, Peter J. "Dodd-Frank and the Myth of 'Interconnectedness.'" *The Wall Street Journal*, February 30, 2012, p. A15.

"Wall Street and the Financial Crisis." U.S. Senate, Permanent Subcommittee on Investigations, April 13, 2011, p. 35.

"Where Angels Fear to Trade." *The Economist*, May 14, 2011, p. 13.

"Wild Animal Spirits: Why is Finance so Unstable?" *The Economist*, January 24, 2009, p.8.

Williams Walsh, Mary. "The Little State with a Big Mess." *The New York Times*, October 23, 2011, p. BU 1.

Zakaria, Fareed. "Worthwhile Canadian Initiative." *Newsweek*, February 16, 2009, p. 31.

———. Program on Education in America, CNN, November 13, 2004.

Zak, Paul J. "The Neurobiology of Trust." *Scientific American*, June, 2008, p. 88.

Ziobrowski, Alan J., PhD, James W. Boyd, PhD, Ping Cheng, PhD, and Briggitte J. Ziobrowski, PhD, "Abnormal Returns from the Common Stock Investments of Members of the U.S. House of Representatives." *Business and Politics*, May 2011.

Ziobrowski, Alan J., PhD, Ping Cheng, PhD, James W. Boyd, PhD, and Briggitte J. Ziobrowski, PhD, "Abnormal Returns from the Common Stock Investments of the U.S. Senate." *Journal of Financial and Quantitative Analysis*, December, 2004.

INDEX

AAA ratings, risk weighting change, 48–49. *See also* credit rating agencies
ABA (American Bankers Association), 289
Abacus 2004-1 case, 144, 244, 247–248. *See also* Goldman Sachs
Abramoff, Jack, 331–332
ACME example, credit default swaps, 131–133
Adelson, Sheldon, 323–325
adjustable rate mortgages (ARMs), 17, 45, 65–68, 84–86, 104, 137
Advanced Warning Council, 259
Affordable Care Act, 193n10
affordable housing policies, role in financial crisis, 17, 24, 61, 91–92, 98–99. *See also* adjustable rate mortgages (ARMs); Fannie Mae/Freddie Mac; subprime loans
The Age of Turbulence (Greenspan), 107
AIG: Bair's comment, 274; compensation levels, 157, 311n6; credit default swap statistics, 134, 160–161; due diligence neglect, 158; federal equity stakes, 272; in financial crisis loop explanation, 87–89; Goldman Sachs benefits, 135, 144, 247, 272–273; interconnectedness problem, 133, 134–135, 147; in lending standard example, 175–176
Allison, John A., 223
Ally Financial Inc., 311n6
Alt-A loans. *See* subprime loans
Altman, Roger C., 379

American Bankers Association (ABA), 289
The American Economic Review, 161–162
A ratings. *See* credit rating agencies
ARMs (adjustable rate mortgages), 17, 45, 65–68, 84–86, 104, 137
ARPAnet development, 180, 391
author's background, 222, 227n3, 419–422
Autocatalytic Process: overview, 22–25, 30, 61–71; Herd Rule relationship, 164–165; postal services, 387; small business credit, 170–171; and Threshold Lowering Syndrome, 27, 97–98. *See also* financial instruments, interlocking relationships; subprime loans
automobile industry, 212, 273
auto repair shop, financial crisis impact, 170

bailout package: distortion argument, 384–386; Dodd-Frank impact, 270; Goldman Sachs statistics, 14; hindsight argument, 303–304; homebuyer argument, 309–310; initiation of, 390; Limbaugh's accusations, 184–187; necessity arguments, 187, 190–191, 199–201, 366–367; opposition arguments, 274; repayment incentives, 202–203, 311n6; restructuring debate, 218–219; statistics, 270, 386; terminology debate, 58n10
Bair, Sheila, 109, 154, 218–219, 274, 277n8
Baker, Dean, 398

429

Baker, Janet, 370–373
Baker, Jim, 370–373
Bancorp, stress test results, 206
bandwagon effect, 70–71
bank holding company, defined, 15
Bank of America, 8, 112, 118n31, 206, 273, 305
bank runs, improbability argument, 304
bankruptcies, household, 37
bankruptcy filings, government, 375–376
Barclay's, LIBOR case, 355
Barr, Michael, 106
Basel Committee of Bank Supervision, 45–47
Baucus, Max, 335
BBB ratings. *See* credit rating agencies
BB&T, 223
Bear Sterns: Bair's comment, 274; compensation levels, 157; in Goldman Sachs short-selling case, 351; interconnectedness problem, 133, 273, 275; in overnight lending market, 159
beauty contest example, Herd Rule, 162–163
Belgium, debt percentage, 379
Berkshire Hathaway report, 136–137, 148–151
bigness problem: as bailout justification, 187, 190–191, 199–201, 366–367; and creative destruction concept, 224–225; Dodd-Frank bill, 256; and interconnectedness problem, 133–135, 225–227; persistence of, 32–33, 35n10, 290; proposed change, 395, 399; restructuring approach, 214–215, 219–220
black swan metaphor, 78–79, 83n9, 160
Blankfein, Lloyd, 248, 350, 352
blindness problem, summarized, 18–19, 104
board members, 207–211, 255–256, 325
boat dock company, regulation obstacles, 360
Boehner, John, 334
Bond, Christopher, 98

bond, defined, 7
Bond Market Association, 69–70
Boston Beer Company, IPO strategy, 353
Boston Federal Reserve study, redlining, 92–94
Bowles-Simpson plan, 380–381, 395–398
brain research, 162, 178–179, 181
Brandeis, Louis, 216
Buffett, Warren, 104, 249–250, 352
building industry problem, Florida, 171–172
Burns, Arthur, 112
Bush, G. H. W., 91, 186
Bush, George W., 40, 186–187, 189–190, 379, 383n16, 390, 391
Butler, Samuel, 346
buy back contracts, 50

Call Report, 109
campaign finance, 268n1, 309, 314–325, 332, 341–342, 400, 417
Canada, 198–199, 306
capital assets, investment patterns, 204–205
capital gains, taxes, 188
capitalism: creative destruction concept, 223–225; dysfunctional nature of, 306–308; invisible hand argument, 58n10, 78, 115, 154–156, 403–407; Limbaugh's accusations, 183–187, 188–189; myth about, 17, 25, 100, 270–272, 276–277, 414–415; regulation's role, 7, 107; role of property rights law, 348–349
Capitalism, Socialism and Democracy (Schumpter), 224
capital reserves: Canada, 198; credit default swaps, 160; Dodd-Frank bill, 256; proposed increase, 395; regulatory changes, 9, 40–41, 45–46; and risk weighting changes, 47–49. *See also* leverage/leverage ratios
Capito, Shelley, 335
carried interest, 193n5

INDEX 431

Cassidy, John, 162, 167*n*13, 273
cattle rancher story, financial crisis impact, 176–177
Cayne, James, 157
CBO (Congressional Budget Office), 379–381
CBS News, 335–336
CBS television story, 173–174
CD marketplace, for loan financing, 38–39
CDOs (collateralized debt obligations), 49, 120*f*, 124–129, 151*n*4
CDS. *See* credit default swaps (CDSs)
Cedar Rapids, 86, 245, 246, 248
Chicago Mercantile Exchange, 263, 343
China, 349–350
Chinese Wall myth, 16–17
Christensen, Robert L., 273
Chrysler, 273
Citibank, 43, 50, 112
Citigroup: bandwagon problem, 95; buyback contracts, 43, 50; CDOs market, 126; compensation levels, 157; congressional stock trades, 335; federal equity stakes, 273; financial condition, 111, 118*n*31; in lending standard example, 175–176; LIBOR case, 355; stress test results, 206; structured investment vehicle, 138
Citizens United case, 314–315
clearinghouses, 228–229, 263, 281–282
Clinton, Bill, 91, 186
Cohan, William, 351
collateralized debt obligations (CDOs), 49, 120*f*, 124–129, 151*n*4
commercial banks, 38, 41–42
Commodity Futures Modernization Act (2000), 108
commodity speculation, 233
Community Reinvestment Act (CRA), 105–106
compensation levels: in bailout package, 202–203, 311*n*6; CEO examples, 27, 97–98, 99, 156–158, 205–206; change proposals, 211–212, 307, 399; comparison with U.S. average, 187, 205–206; Dodd-Frank bill, 255; and good old boy network, 208–213; increase pattern, 290–291; and taxation, 193*n*5
complexity problem, 6–7, 9–10, 17–18, 105. *See also* financial instruments, interlocking relationships
computer modeling: confidence effects, 77–78, 160; correlation approach, 75–78, 79–80; human judgment role, 74–75, 76, 82; omissions problem, 10, 68, 69, 78–82; purposes, 73–74
Conard, Edward, 322–323
Congo Conflict Minerals, 266, 332, 359
Congress: derivatives monitoring legislation, 108; Fannie Mae relationship, 95, 98–101; lending standards legislation, 107; Postal Service, 386–387; proposed change, 399; savings and loans crisis, 122. *See also* Dodd-Frank Wall Street Reform... Act
Congressional Budget Office (CBO), 379–381
Connecticut, mileage reimbursements, 339
consultant role, credit rating agencies, 103, 114–115
Consumer Financial Protection Bureau, 261
Cooper, Keysha, 175
Corker, Bob, 412
corn subsidies, 341
corporate bond, defined, 7
Corrigan, E. Gerald, 113
corruption patterns: overview, 330–331; insider trading, 333–337, 344*n*12; proposed fix, 399; staff job offers, 331–333; state legislator pensions, 337–339
Cota, Sean, 233
Countrywide Financial, 46, 157
Cox, Christopher, 115
CRA (Community Reinvestment Act), 105–106
creative destruction concept, 223–225
credit card debt, 375

credit card legislation, 333–334
credit crunch, 170–171, 269
credit default swaps (CDSs): Dodd-Frank bill, 256, 265–266; in financial crisis loop explanation, 86–89; in financial instrument relationship, 49–50, 120, 129–136; purpose of, 19–20, 280; regulatory failure, 105, 115; shady mortgage comparison, 279–280; and structured investment vehicles, 138; in synthetic CDOs, 140–145. *See also* AIG
credit rating agencies: and adjustable rate mortgages, 104; CDO instruments, 124–129, 139, 245; conflict of interest problem, 102–103, 104, 114–115, 128–129, 180; in credit default swap example, 131–132; FICO scoring, 103–105; in financial crisis loop explanation, 86–89; in Graveyard Shift Law, 31–32; as meltdown factor, 18; and MSB beginnings, 121–122, 123, 158–159; traditional role, 31

Dalio, Ray, 167*n*13
Danielle, Chiesi, 344*n*12
databases: in Dodd-Frank bill, 262, 263; mortgage loan tracking, 169–170
dead applicant story, 173–174
death panel accusation, 193*n*10
debt, federal, 308, 365, 379–381, 395–398
debt, personal, 37, 374–375. *See also* refinancing practices; subprime loans
debt-to-capital ratios, 42, 108. *See also* capital reserves; leverage/leverage ratios
defaults/default rates: adjustable interest loans, 68–69; in financial crisis loop explanation, 85–86, 87; homeowner decision-making, 54, 172–173; and MBS packaging assumptions, 9–10, 104; in redlining study, 93–94; USAA's difference, 71*n*4
deficit spending, Limbaugh's accusations, 186–187, 189–190. *See also* debt, federal
democracy, threats to, 308–309, 312–317, 325–327. *See also* rule of law, inequities summarized
dependence corruption, 341
derivatives: Buffett's observations, 148–151; market value, 204, 230–231, 280, 283*n*3; purpose of, 53–54, 108, 280; regulatory exemption, 342; transparency problem, 280–283. *See also* credit default swaps (CDSs)
De Soto, Hernando, 348–349, 357–358
Deutsche Bank, 13, 105, 125
Dimon, Jamie, 30. *See also* JPMorgan
discount window, 234–235
Disproportionate Ratio Effect, 29–30, 197, 204–205, 234–236
distribution curves, computer modeling, 77
Dodd-Frank Wall Street Reform... Act: agency creations, 258–266; clearinghouse authority, 282–283; effectiveness probability factors, 254–257; lending standards, 288–289; as regulatory inefficiency, 358–360; transparency requirements, 270, 288
Dole, Bob, 322
downgrade of ratings, obstacles, 103, 104
Dragon Systems, 370–373
Duhigg, Charles, 232
Dukakis, Michael, 318

Ebenstein, William, 402
education system, 326–327, 342, 416
Eisinger, Jesse, 357
Enron, 102, 342
entitlement accusation, Limbaugh's, 187–188
Epicurus, 166

ethical problems, summaries, 130–131, 145–146, 239–244, 273. *See also* corruption patterns; Goldman Sachs
expansion problem. *See* bigness problem

Facebook IPO, 163
fairness ideal. *See* democracy, threats to; Disproportionate Ratio Effect; rule of law, inequities summarized
Fannie Mae/Freddie Mac: CEO compensation, 27, 96–98, 99; computer modeling problem, 82; elimination proposal, 395; funding statistics, 272, 385; historic lending standards, 94; as hybridized capitalism, 271–272, 276; leverage ratio, 159; oversight changes, 98–99; Paulson's perspective, 210; political pressure patterns, 91–92; portfolio holdings, 20, 24, 94–95; SEC suits, 376; securities risk weightings, 47; subprime loan purchase pressures, 95–96
Fannie Neighbors program, 91–92
farm subsidies, 341
Federal Home Loan Bank, 38–39, 57*n*6
Federal Housing Enterprise Oversight, Office of, 98
Federal Housing Finance Agency, 268*n*2, 305, 385
Federal Insurance Office, 265
Federal Reserve of New York, 210, 275, 354
Federal Reserve System: capital reserve regulation, 46; discount window, 234; in Dodd-Frank bill, 262–263; formation incentives, 149; hedge fund rescue, 150; lending processes, 15, 234; as recovery obstacle, 196–197; regulatory failures, 107–113
fee incentives: bond market churning, 11–12; credit rating agencies, 128, 139, 180; high-frequency trading, 232; loan closures, 175; mortgage guarantees, 180–181; short selling, 14; synthetic CDOs, 142, 244–246; with transparency, 283

FICO scores, 103–104
financial crisis, causes, overviews, 17–19, 60–62, 84–89, 191. *See also specific topics, e.g.*, Autocatalytic Process; computer modeling; interest rates; regulatory process
"The Financial Crisis Inquiry Report," 106–107
financial industry. *See specific topics, e.g.*, financial instruments, interlocking relationships; Goldman Sachs; mortgage backed securities (MBSs)
financial instruments, interlocking relationships: overview, 119–120; collateralized debt obligations, 123–129; credit default swaps, 129–136; derivatives, 148–151; mortgage backed securities, 120–123; structured investment vehicles, 138; synthetic CDOs, 139–145
financial instruments, overview of types, 119–120
Financial Literacy, Office of, 261–262
Financial Research, Office of, 260–261
Financial Services Regulatory Relief Act (2006), 40–41
Financial Stability Oversight Council, 260
Finland, 306, 342
Fitch, 128
flat tire story, 170
Fleishman, James, 344*n*12
Florida, building industry problem, 171–173
fluctuating interest rates, introduction, 10–12, 20*n*3, 122
foreclosure rates, 4, 69, 287. *See also* defaults/default rates
foreign profits, legislation, 292–293
Fornaro, Robert, 233
France, debt percentage, 379
Frank, Barney, 100–102, 411. *See also* Dodd-Frank Wall Street Reform... Act
Frank, Thomas, 338–339
fraud problems, 7, 56, 273, 305, 346, 354–357. *See also* corruption

patterns; ethical problems, summaries
Freddie Mac. *See* Fannie Mae/Freddie Mac
free market illusion. *See* capitalism
free speech claim, corporations, 268n1, 305, 309, 314–317, 356, 399
Friedman, Stephen, 210
Fuld, Richard, 157, 163–164, 229
Fuller, Thomas, 166

Galbraith, James K., 398
Galbraith, John Kenneth, 269
garbage service, gerrymandering effects, 339–340, 374
Gauss, Carl, 77
Geithner, Timothy, 211, 217
General Motors, 273, 311n6
Georgia, Fannie Mae presence, 98
Germany, 378
gerrymandering, 309, 339–341, 389, 418
Gingrich, Newt, 98, 323
Gladwell, Malcolm, 178
Glass-Steagall Act, 41–42, 108
GM, 273, 311n6
GMAC, stress test results, 206
going long, defined, 14. *See also* short selling
Goldman Sachs: and AIG bailout, 135, 247, 272–273; bank holding status benefits, 15, 234; CDOs market, 125, 139, 142, 144, 244–247; compensation levels, 157, 273; computer model response, 76, 83n3; Dragon Systems case, 370–373; in financial crisis loop explanation, 86–89; revolving-door network, 209, 210, 215n8; short selling practices, 15, 144, 239–241, 247–251, 350–352
"good old boy" network, 179–180, 207–211. *See also* revolving-door networking
government bond, defined, 7
government-sponsored enterprises (GSEs). *See* Fannie Mae/Freddie Mac

Gramm, Phil, 108
Gramm, Wendy, 342
Graveyard Shift Law, 30–32
Greece, 300, 365, 378
greed problem, summaries, 7, 19, 154–158, 166. *See also* fee incentives
Greenspan, Alan: on computer modeling, 73; on credit rating agencies, 105; on greed, 154–155; interest rate policy, 62; regulatory philosophy, 106–110, 112–113; in revolving door network, 209
Gregg, Judd, 334, 412
growth philosophy, 32–33
GSEs (government-sponsored enterprises). *See* Fannie Mae/Freddie Mac

Harrisburg, Pennsylvania, 375
Hass, Richard N., 379
Hastert, Dennis, 334
health care: Canada, 199; federal cost problem, 380, 396; insider trading, 334, 335; in main street stories, 176–178; political misrepresentations, 193n10
heating oil example, derivatives, 281
hedge funds: at Bear Sterns, 351; Federal Reserve rescue, 150; leverage practices, 229–230; political intelligence industry, 334; purpose, 193n4; regulatory proposals, 357, 359; taxation rate, 188, 193n5; transparency problem, 256, 282
Herd Rule, 161–165
high-frequency trading, 231–233
high fructose corn syrup, 341
homebuyers, bailout argument, 309–310
Home Ownership and Equity Protection Act, 107
home ownership incentives, role in financial crisis, 17, 24, 61, 91–92, 98–99. *See also* adjustable rate mortgages (ARMs); Fannie Mae/Freddie Mac; subprime loans
hotline creation, Dodd-Frank bill, 262

Housing and Community Development
    Act (1992), 91
Housing and Urban Development,
    91–92, 98–99, 264–265
Housing Counseling, Office of,
    264–265
Howard, Tim, 377
Hubbard, Elbert, 365

Iceland, 365, 379
Idaho, stimulus funds, 185
ignorance problem, 6–7, 17–18, 34
Ignorant Therefore Doctrinaire
    Syndrome, 192
IKB Deutsch Industriebank, 246–247,
    248
Immediacy Syndrome, 39, 65–66
income inequality, 287, 308, 312–314,
    325–326
India, 349
insider trading, 333–337, 344*n*12
insurance. *See* AIG; credit default swaps
    (CDSs)
interconnectedness problem: as bailout
    justification, 187, 190–191,
    199–201, 272–273, 366–367; and
    bigness problem, 133–135,
    225–227; myth argument, 300–301;
    proposed changes, 360–361, 395,
    399. *See also* financial instruments,
    interlocking relationships
interest-only loans, 24, 137
interest-only pools, mortgage backed
    securities, 169
interest rates: in bailout package, 270;
    and credit ratings, 104; discount
    window, 234–235;
    Disproportionate Ratio law,
    234–236; in financial crisis loop
    explanation, 84–86; fixed-to-
    fluctuating change, 10–12, 20*n*3,
    122; LIBOR case, 354–357; as
    meltdown factor, 18, 61, 63; as
    recovery obstacle, 196–197. *See also*
    adjustable rate mortgages (ARMs)
interlocking gridlock problem. *See*
    interconnectedness problem
Investment Advisory Committee, 266

investment banks: capital reserves rules,
    41; Chinese Wall myth, 16–17;
    functions of, 13–14, 41–42,
    237–238. *See also* financial
    instruments, interlocking
    relationships; Goldman Sachs
invisible hand argument, 58*n*10, 78,
    115, 154–156, 403–407
IPOs, 163, 352–354
Ireland, 300, 365, 379
Italy, 300, 365, 379

Japan, debt percentage, 378
Jesus, 366
Jobs, Steve, 326
Johnson, James A., 90–92, 99
The Journal of Biological Psychiatry, 162
JPMorgan: credit default swaps, 129,
    134; financial condition, 30, 111,
    118*n*31; LIBOR case, 355; takeover
    of Bear Sterns, 273, 275–276
Juglar, C., 194, 195

Katzenberg, Jeffrey, 323
Kennedy, Anthony, 314, 319, 322
Kennedy, Ted, 98
Kerry, John, 335
Kerry, Teresa Heinz, 335
KeyCorp, stress test results, 206
Keynes, John Maynard, 162–163,
    164–165, 405–406
Killinger, Kerry K., 157, 175
Koch, Jim, 353
Krauthammer, Charles, 192, 390
K Street lobbyists, 319–321, 331–332,
    342

labor unions, 373–374
laissez-faire capitalism, 107, 222
Law of the Instrument, 74–75, 147. *See
    also* computer modeling
Law of Unintended Exponential
    Consequences, 28–29, 30, 46, 114,
    122
Lea County, 240, 244–245
Lefevre, Edwin, 221

Lehman Brothers: Bair's comment, 274; compensation levels, 157; hedge fund impact, 163–164, 229; leveraged position, 42, 52, 110, 147; SEC failure, 115
lending standards: Dodd-Frank bill, 256, 288–289; Federal Reserve failure, 107; government-led changes, 91, 93; lowering of, 26–27, 174–176, 273; traditional commercial bank approach, 38
Lessig, Lawrence, 330, 341
leverage/leverage ratios, 49–50, 58n11, 109–111, 198, 229–230. *See also* financial instruments, interlocking relationships; mortgage backed securities (MBSs)
Levin, Carl, 350–351
Levitt, Arthur, 115
Lewis, Kenneth, 118n31
Lewis, Michael, 45, 52–53, 67, 89n1, 139, 145
L.&H., due diligence problem, 371–372
Li, David X., 75–76, 79–80
Liar's Poker (Lewis), 52–53
LIBOR case, 354–357
Limbaugh, Rush, 183–189
liquidity excess, problem of, 28–29, 61–63
loan financing, changes, 38–40, 57n6. *See also* lending standards; mortgage backed securities (MBSs)
Long Beach Mortgage Loan Trust 2006-A, 242
Long-Term Capital Management, 150

Macey, Jonathan, 359
Madoff, Bernard, 76, 115, 179, 181–182
Main Street. *See* small business *entries*
margin calls, 110–111
marking errors, derivatives, 148–149
Markopolos, Harry, 76, 179
Massachusetts, Fannie Mae presence, 98
"Mastering the Machine (Cassidy), 167n13
mathematical models. *See* computer modeling
MBIA, credit rating problem, 103

MBS. *See* mortgage backed securities (MBSs)
McCarthy, Larry, 318
McCormick, Dave, 164
media misrepresentations, 183–189, 191–192
meltdown causes, overviews, 17–19, 60–62, 84–89, 191. *See also specific topics, e.g.*, Autocatalytic Process; computer modeling; interest rates; regulatory process
Merrill Lynch, 42–43, 125, 157
MERS (Mortgage Electronic Registration System), 169
mezzanine tranches, 123, 139, 144
mileage reimbursements, Connecticut, 339
Minority and Women Inclusion, Office of, 264
Missouri, Fannie Mae presence, 98
money supply model, Federal Reserve Board, 73–74, 75
Monks Do Not Dissolve Monasteries, 32–33
monthly payment changes, ARMs, 66
Moody's, 128, 250
moral hazard concept, 44
Moraligious malady, 387–389
Morgan Stanley, stress test results, 206
mortgage backed securities (MBSs): basics of, 19–20, 120–122; credit rating approaches, 104; Federal Housing agency investigation, 268n2, 305; in financial crisis loop explanation, 86–88; as leverage problem, 49; market value, 69–70; repackaging complexities, 105, 123, 169. *See also* Fannie Mae/Freddie Mac; financial instruments, interlocking relationships
Mortgage Bankers Association, 289
mortgage bonds, overview, 7–12
mortgage brokers, role of, 12–13
Mortgage Electronic Registration System (MERS), 169
Mozilo, Angelo, 157
Mudd, Daniel H., 90, 97

INDEX 437

Munger, Charlie, 250, 253*n*12
The Mystery of Capital (De Soto), 348–349

naked CDS market. *See* credit default swaps (CDSs)
NASA, 390–391
National Commission on Fiscal Responsibility and Reform, 380–381, 395–398
National Partners in Homeownership, 91–92
negative amortization loans, 137–138
negative equity, statistics, 69
Neugebauer, Randy, 376–377
Nevada, campaign contributions, 323, 324–325
Newsweek, 235–236
New York, Federal Reserve of, 210, 275, 354
New York, legislator salary, 338
The New Yorker, 167*n*13
New York Stock Exchange, 343
New York Times, 336
"no house" loan, 175
North Carolina, campaign finance, 318
notional value, derivatives, 283*n*3

Obama, Barack, 186–187, 189–190, 193*n*10, 323–324, 336, 398
Office of Credit Ratings, 265
Office of Federal Housing Enterprise Oversight, 98
Office of Financial Literacy, 261–262
Office of Financial Research, 260–261
Office of Minority and Women Inclusion, 264
Office of Thrift Supervision, 258
Office of Vice Chairman for Supervision, 262–263
off-loading loans, 44–45
O'Neal, E. Stanley, 157
On the Brink (Paulson), 210
O'Reilly, Bill, 101
originate and sell practice, 44
Other People's Money—How Banks Use It (Brandeis), 216
Outliers (Gladwell), 178

overnight lending market, 159
oxytocin, 179

Palin, Sarah, 193*n*10
partisanship problem, 387–389, 397–398
Partnership Offices (POs), Fannie Mae, 98–99
Paulson, Henry, 133, 163–164, 209–210, 215*n*8
Paulson, John, 244–247
Pelosi, Nancy, 333–334
pensions, state, 337–339
performance-compensation statistics, 157
Perry, Rick, 390
personal accountability: banking culture, 51–53, 368–374; consumers/homeowners, 54–56, 374–375; and corporate free speech, 317; Dodd-Frank bill, 255; as financial solution, 398–399; in Goldman Sachs case, 247–249, 352; importance, 250–252, 365–366
Peru, regulation study, 358
physician story, 4
PNC Bank, stress test results, 206
Polis, Jared, 335
political intelligence industry, 334
political paralysis problem, 387–389, 397–398. *See also* campaign finance
Pope, Art, 318
Portugal, 365, 379
POs (Partnership Offices), Fannie Mae, 98–99
Postal Service, 386–387
prices, home, 69, 85
Prince, Chuck, 95
principal only pools, mortgage backed securities, 169
probability modeling, 76–78
profit booking approach, loan assumptions, 45
profits, financial industry, 203–204
property rights law, 348–349
proprietary trading, 13–15, 256, 357

rafting companion's story, 368–369

Raines, Franklin, 377
Rajaratnam, Raj, 344*n*12
rancher story, financial crisis impact, 176–177
Rand, Ayn, 107, 223, 224–225
Ranieri, Lew, 52–53
Rayburn, Sam, 330, 333, 342–343, 381
Reagan, Ronald, 186
recovery prospects, overview, 196–197
redlining, 92–94, 106
re-election campaigns, 340–341, 418
refinancing practices: appeal of, 37, 55–56; dead man story, 173–174; in financial crisis loop explanation, 85; home price problem, 69; USAA's difference, 72*n*12
Regions Bank, stress test results, 206
regulatory process: hedge fund exemptions, 230; improvement debate, 217–220; inefficiencies, 357–358, 361–362; recommended changes, 197–198, 360–361, 394–395, 398–400; role in financial crisis, 61–62, 116–117, 165–166. *See also* Dodd-Frank Wall Street Reform... Act; Federal Reserve System; Securities and Exchange Commission (SEC)
relationship banking, demise of, 9
religious groups, political impact, 387–389
repayment assumption, in book for profit accounting, 45
revolving-door networking, 115, 209, 212–213, 256, 289–290, 331–332. *See also* "good old boy" network
Rhode Island, pension funding, 376
risk weightings, change consequences, 46–49. *See also* capital reserves; leverage/leverage ratios
robosigners, 273
Romney, Mitt, 322–323
Rose, Charlie, 167*n*13, 212–213, 248
Rosen, Leo, 237
Rove, Karl, 412
Royal Bank of Scotland, 248
Rubin, Robert, 209
rule of law, inequities summarized, 107, 347–350, 352–354, 362–363. *See also* democracy, threats to

salaries/wages. *See* compensation levels
Salomon Brothers, 8, 52
Santa Fe Railroad Company, 343
Santorum, Rick, 388
Savings and Loan crisis, 122–123
Schumpter, Joseph, 223–224
SEC. *See* Securities and Exchange Commission (SEC)
second mortgage market. *See* refinancing practices
Securities and Exchange Commission (SEC): credit rating delegation, 102, 114–115, 122; failure summarized, 115; Fannie Mae suits, 376; Goldman Sachs case, 239–240, 247–248; Madoff case, 115, 179, 181–182; monitoring/enforcement obstacles, 113–114, 179–180, 209; VaR requirements, 81
securitization, defined, 7
security, defined, 7–8
self-regulation argument, 58*n*10, 78, 115, 154–156, 403–407
self-responsibility. *See* personal accountability
settlement process, clearinghouses, 228–229
shareholders: capital reserves reduction, 41; Dodd-Frank bill, 255; as lending pressure, 39; and leverage accountability, 51–52
short selling: credit default swaps, 130–136; defined, 14; as ethical problem, 239–244; hedge funds, 229–230; synthetic CDOs, 143–144, 152*n*28, 244–245. *See also* Goldman Sachs
short-term speculation, 231–233
Simpson-Bowles plan, 380–381, 395–398
Singer, Dan, 281
SIVs (structured investment vehicles), 138

60 Minutes, 173–174, 331–332, 333–334
small business, financial crisis impact: overview, 3–4, 16, 194–196, 302–303; auto repair shop, 170; barber shop, 177–178; cattle rancher, 176–177; construction firm, 36; credit restrictions, 170–171; mortgage title firm, 293–294; persistence, 299–300, 304; physician story, 4; store front vacancies, 4–5, 195, 285–286; truck-washing firm, 4. *See also* democracy, threats to
small business, job statistics, 302
Smith, Adam, 404–405
Smith, Greg, 369, 373
socialism, 183–187, 188–189, 270–271
social issues, political impact, 387–389
sociopaths, 181
software. *See* computer modeling
Sommer, Jeff, 354
Sorkin, Andrew Ross, 210
S&P, 128
space program, 390–391
Spencer, Herbert, 310–311
Spencer, Leanne, 377
spending caps, Bowles-Simpson plan, 395–396
spread, in credit default swaps, 129, 130
Stahl, Leslie, 331–332
Stalinism, 188–189
Standard and Poor's, 158–159
state legislator pensions, 337–339
Steger, Thurmond, and Rayburn, 343
Stephanopoulos, George, 388
Stevens, David, 289
Stewart, Martha, 352
Stiglitz, Joseph, 218–219
store fronts, empty, 4–5, 195, 285–286
Story, Louise, 280–281
strawberry picker story, 27
stress tests, results, 206
structured investment vehicles (SIVs), 138
Stumpf, John, 118n32
stupidity problem, summarized, 17–19, 87–89, 135–136, 158–161

subprime loans: in Autocatalytic Process, 23–24, 30; defined, 21n10; in financial crisis loop explanation, 84–86; role in meltdown, 61, 63–64; statistics, 64, 67. *See also* adjustable rate mortgages (ARMs); Fannie Mae/Freddie Mac; lending standards; mortgage backed securities (MBSs)
suicide bomber comparison, 291
suicide rates, 300
Sullivan, Martin, 157
Sun Trust, stress test results, 206
Super PACs, 322–325
Supreme Court, 314–316, 322
Swathmore College study, 161–162
Swenson, Michael, 242
synthetic CDOs, 139–145, 152n28, 244–246

Taleb, Nassim Nichloas, 73, 83n9
TARP. *See* bailout package
taxes: capital gains, 188; and federal debt, 380, 381, 396; foreign profits legislation, 292–293; mortgage interest, 198; reduction consequences, 308
Taylor, Bill, 112
Tea Party, 387–388, 393n5, 412, 415
Tedisco, James, 338
Threshold Lowering Syndrome, 26–28, 30, 97–98. *See also* lending standards
Thrift Supervision, Office of, 258
Tier 1 bank capital, 45–46
tiger comparison, 250, 253n12
Time, 244–245
Too Big to Fail (Sorkin), 210
Toronto-Dominion Bank, 198
total-return swaps, 150
Towns, Betty, 173–174
tranches, 123, 124–125
Transparency International, 331
transparency problem: collateral debt obligations, 146; credit default swaps, 134–135; derivatives market, 268n3, 279–281; Dodd-Frank bill,

256; proposed changes, 197–198, 395; reform resistance, 288; structured investment vehicles, 138; synthetic CDOs, 146; wealth/income distribution, 349–350
triggers, security values, 87–88
truck-washer story, financial crisis impact, 4
Trump, Donald, 146
trust, role of, 179, 347–348
trust preferred securities (TRUPS), 46
Tyson, Neil deGrasse, 390

UBS Americas Inc., 125, 305
underwriting, 241–247
unemployment, 299, 304
unethical practices. *See* ethical problems, summaries
Unintended Exponential Consequences, Law of, 28–29, 30, 46
unions, 373–374, 376
United Kingdom, debt percentage, 379
unqualified buyers, examples, 27, 173–174
unsecured debt, defined, 50
USAA, 30, 71
USA TODAY, 337
USB, LIBOR case, 355

Value at Risk (VaR) model, 75–76, 80–82. *See also* computer modeling

Visa, 333–334
Volcker, Paul, 10, 112, 122, 218–219, 394–395
Volcker rule, 357

wages/salaries. *See* compensation levels
Wallison, Peter J., 300–301
Wall Street firms. *See specific topics,* e.g., financial instruments, interlocking relationships; Goldman Sachs; mortgage backed securities (MBSs)
Wall Street Journal, 230–231, 300–301, 369, 372, 376
Wall Street Reform bill. *See* Dodd-Frank Wall Street Reform... Act
Washington Mutual, 157, 174–175
Ways, Max, 403
wealth gap, 287, 308, 312–314, 325–326, 349–350
The Wealth of Civilizations (Smith), 404–405
Wells Fargo, 112, 118n32, 206
WestLB, 235–236
Wilmott, Paul, 80
Wired magazine, 115
World Savings, 173–174

zombie banks, in bailout hindsight argument, 235, 304

Essays available at Blog.UylessBlack.com

America's Capital: Author's experiences in Washington, DC

America's Cities: Journeys and encounters in USA's towns and cities

America's Finances: A series on issues such as Medicare, Social Security, and debt

Computers and Networks: Essays on Internet net neutrality, copyright issues, and software complexity

Creatures and Computers: Drawing analogies to wildlife and Internet organisms

Customs and Cultures: A look at America and Americana

Eating and Drinking: Surveys of food fairs, cafes, and restaurants

Food Effects and Drug Defects: Reports on toxic foods and drugs' side effects

Foreign Affairs: America's relations with other countries

Foreign Places: Taking roads, ships, and trains through parts of the world

Immigration and Emigration: America's immigration practices and related problems

Politics in America: With several reports on National Press Club speakers

Presidential Places: Presidential homes, museums, and grave sites

Sports and Games: Essays on competition and the beauty of sport

The Deadly Trinity Trilogies: Two sets of essays to compliment *The Deadly Trinity* book

    The Cepee Dialogues (available 2013 as a book)

    Coming to You Live, from the Dead (available 2013 as a book)

Traveling America: Taking roads through America and America's cultures

War Zones: Essays on cold, warm, and hot wars

These books, written earlier in Black's career, offer useful background information for historians and researchers. For current use, some of the technical information is no longer topical. Yet, these books are still offered online. He asks you not to purchase these books, other than for assembling a history of data communications in the latter part of the 20th century.

IEEE Computer Society
Physical Layer Interfaces
X.25 and Packet Switching Networks

McGraw-Hill
The V-Series Recommendations
The X-Series Recommendations
TCP/IP and Related Protocols
Network Management
Frame Relay Networks

Prentice Hall
Data Communications and Distributed Networks
Computer Networks: Protocols, Standards, and Interfaces
Data Networks: Concepts, Theory, and Practice
The OSI Model
Data Link Protocols
Emerging Communications Technologies
Asynchronous Transfer Mode (ATM) Networks, Volume I
Wireless and Mobile Networks
SONET and T1
ISDN and SS7
Asynchronous Transfer Mode (ATM) Networks, Volume II
Second Generation Mobile and Wireless Networks
Asynchronous Transfer Mode (ATM) Networks, Volume IIII
Advanced Features of the Internet
Residential Broadband
Advanced Intelligent Networks
Voice over IP
The Point-to-Point Protocol (PPP)
IP Routing Protocols
Internet Security Protocols
MPLS and Label Switching Networks
Internet Telephony
Quality of Service in Computer Networks
Internet Architecture
Networking 101
Optical Networks
Multiprotocol Label Switching (MPLS) Networks

CPSIA information can be obtained at www.ICGtesting.com
Printed in the USA
LVOW08s1542051213

364044LV00004B/1067/P